From *Brown* to *Bakke*

From *Brown* to *Bakke*

The Supreme Court
and School Integration: 1954–1978

J. HARVIE WILKINSON III

New York · Oxford
OXFORD UNIVERSITY PRESS
1979

Library of Congress Cataloging in Publication Data
Wilkinson, J Harvie, 1944–
   From Brown to Bakke.
   Includes index.
   1. School integration—United States—History.
2. Segregation in education—Law and legislation—
United States—History. I. Title.
KF4155.W54   344′.73′0798   78-20860   ISBN 0-19-502567-9

The chart on page 176 is reprinted with permission.
Copyright © 1976, The Louisville *Courier-Journal*.

Gitanjali #1 from *Collected Poems and Plays*, by Rabindranath Tagore,
reprinted with permission of Macmillan Publishing Company, Inc.

To My Mother

Acknowledgments

I am indebted to my student assistants at the University of Virginia for work far beyond the call of duty or recompense. Jack Costello, Bob Littleton, and Bob Wason helped greatly with the early research. Mike Chapman, Jeff Lankford, and Jack Ross were cheerful and resourceful in the face of many trying requests. Tim O'Donnell and Brad Pigott ably assisted in the final stages of manuscript preparation. Space prevents me from detailing the contribution of many others. I wish only to say that without their efforts, ideas, encouragement, and good company, I would not have completed this book.

Chapters 4 and 5 first appeared in slightly altered form in the May 1978 issue of the *Virginia Law Review* and are published here with its permission. Ken Ayres, Peter Byrne, Dan Rowley, and Jon Sallet all made many useful suggestions and improvements in the editorial process.

My special thanks go to Diane Moss and her staff for capably typing the illegible and to the staff of the Law Library for such prompt and courteous service.

My colleagues here were, as always, most generous. Professors A. E. Dick Howard and G. Edward White read the entire manuscript with their usual care and discernment. Henry Abraham, Staige Blackford, and William Harbaugh each gave me valuable counsel. And no one could have asked for a more supportive Dean than Emerson Spies.

Oxford University Press has been a most helpful and cooperative publisher. The editing hand of Susan Rabiner has made this a better book.

The many newsmen who shared with me their thoughts, articles, and editorials on school desegregation rendered great assistance. Frank Batten and Bob Mason of Landmark Communications, Inc. have my lasting appreciation for their understanding and indulgence during the writing of this book.

My deepest debt goes to Lossie, my wife, who kept me on course.

Charlottesville, 1978   J.H.W. III

Contents

From *Brown* to *Bakke*

Introduction

One quite remarkable aspect of the Civil Rights struggle of the mid-twentieth century is the protective role played by the United States Supreme Court. The Court sired the movement,[1] succored it through the early years,[2] encouraged its first taking wing,[3] comforted and defended it in times of loneliness and despair,[4] and finally—some would say—abandoned it.[5] But to depict the Court as protector is not to denigrate the protected—the individual Americans, many white but mainly black, whose unrecorded sacrifices for human dignity made all the difference. It is simply to say that very little could have been accomplished in mid-century America without the Supreme Court.

In a sense the Court was an unlikely patron. Its members have traditionally been detached from most ordinary happenings, certainly from those in the clapboard shacks and rundown schoolrooms of the rural mid-century South. The Supreme Court building itself seems as much a place of privilege as a temple of justice; a place where, in earlier times, kings and noblemen might have gathered among its marbled columns, there to rule the affairs of other men. Much in the history of this forbidding institution has reflected an aloof indifference to the tides of social change, the protection of property and privilege having been its more abiding concern. Throughout the late-nineteenth century,[6] into the Progressive era,[7] and on through the New Deal,[8] the Court discouraged government efforts to relieve human distress. Even the Great Depression failed to shake Justice George Sutherland's stern sense of constitutional principle:

> The present exigency is nothing new. From the beginning of our existence as a nation, periods of depression, of industrial failure, of financial distress, of unpaid and unpayable indebtedness, have alternated with years of plenty. . . . If the provisions of the Constitution be not upheld when they pinch as well as when they comfort, they may as well be abandoned.[9]

Throughout our history, the Supreme Court may well have seemed to black Americans the epitome of the white man's world and institutions. The character of the Court's personnel undoubtedly fostered this impression. One student of its membership noted that the first 100 Supreme Court justices were overwhelmingly white, native-born, Anglo-Saxon Protestant males of "upper middle to high social status; reared in an urban environment; members of civic minded, politically active, economically comfortable families"; with law degrees from prestigious institutions; and so forth. Nor is the profile likely to change dramatically in the coming years, despite more representative contemporary trends and the appointment of Thurgood Marshall in 1967 as the first black justice.[10]

But the image of a white man's Court runs deeper than the nature of its personnel or even the course of its decisions, many of which, until recently, added heavily to the black man's burden. For, simply, the Court stands as the ultimate symbol of America: of its power, its learning, its values, its prestige. Whatever it is that white America means to blacks finds larger than life extension in the Supreme Court. The feeling surfaces in offhand ways: in Thurgood Marshall's jocular observation on the Court in an NAACP skull session shortly before reargument in *Brown:* "White bosses, you can do *any*thing you want, 'cause you got de power!"[11] Fifteen years and many progressive decisions later, the Court still felt the sting of an article in the *New York Times Magazine* cleverly titled "Nine Men in Black Who Think White."[12]

This portrait, of course, can be overdrawn. Much in the Court's traditions by the time of *Brown* counseled support of the Negro's aspirations. But it was hardly an inevitable partnership—that between the justices and the black man—or one that could be taken for granted. Indeed, its very lack of inevitability—the striking incongruity of it—lent *Brown* and events thereafter their magical and almost unprecedented power.

It is a power one longs to recapture. Martin Luther King once told of a "chill morning in the autumn of 1956" when "an elderly, toil-worn Negro woman in Montgomery, Alabama began her slow, painful four-mile walk to her job." It was then the tenth month of the boycott by Montgomery blacks staged to protest Jim Crow seating on the city's buses. "The old woman's difficult progress led a passer-by to inquire sympathetically if her feet were tired. Her simple answer," noted King, "became the boycotters' watchword. 'Yes, friend, my feet is real tired, but my soul is rested.' "[13]

The old woman's journey ended on November 13, 1956, when the Supreme Court released a brief decision holding Montgomery's bus segregation unconstitutional.[14] "The law and human expression of discontent," wrote Anthony Lewis, "had worked together to produce peaceful change."[15] What *Brown* had begot was a union of the mightiest and lowliest in America, a mystical, passionate union bound by the pained depths of the black man's cry for justice and the moral authority, unique to the Court, to see that justice realized. "I have a dream, . . ." King would say to the multitudes spread before him one August afternoon of 1963 on the Washington mall, "that one day on the red hills of Georgia, the sons of former slaves and the sons of former slave-owners will be able to sit together at the table of brotherhood."[16] Nine years earlier, in *Brown*, Chief Justice Earl Warren had voiced a similar hope: Separation of schoolchildren "solely because of their race generates a feeling of inferiority . . . that may affect their hearts and minds in a way unlikely ever to be undone."[17] Together the song of the street and the calmer evangelism on the Court woke a slumbering spirit in America and accomplished in unison what each alone dare not try.

What follows is a history of the Supreme Court's role in public school integration in the quarter century since *Brown* v. *Board of Education*. The tale begins with *Brown* itself, its place in the history of the Court, its value as a judicial opinion, its perspectives on education and race. It then turns to the Court's attempts over the next decade and a half to implement *Brown* in the South. As the rural South began to integrate, the Court's focus shifted to urban areas and from the South to the nation as a whole. Thus, the third section of this book addresses court-ordered busing, the chief device used to desegregate the American metropolis. Finally, with the *Bakke* decision, the setting shifts—or rather returns—to college and graduate schools, the focus of many Supreme Court cases in the pre-*Brown* era.[18]

In assessing the Supreme Court's role in school integration, attention to its opinions is essential. Yet the broader perspective is just as important. One must look beyond the walls of doctrine to the halls of Congress and statehouses, to the chambers of district judges, to the desks of editors, historians, and sociologists, and, most important, to high school corridors, civic auditoriums, country stores, suburban ranchhouses, and city streetcorners. For it is there, after many years, that the verdict on the Court is delivered. It is there that the American people form a jury on the judge.

The Supreme Court's story, like any other human and institutional history, merits criticism and approbation alike. My own reservations do not diminish my respect for all *Brown* accomplished or for the core principle of human oneness for which it stood. It might be well, before proceeding, to ponder for one moment the abiding meaning of *Brown* itself.

Brown may be the most important political, social, and legal event in America's twentieth-century history. Its greatness lay in the enormity of injustice it condemned, in the entrenched sentiment it challenged, in the immensity of law it both created and overthrew. It is rich in national insight, a beginning point of American introspection. It was a crossroads, not just for an outcast race, but for an outcast region, a testing ground for liberal values and theory, a challenge for the rule of the law and the authority of the Court. The story of *Brown* is the story of revolution: of a thousand tales of human suffering and sacrifice subsumed in the winning of a principle. So also was the triumph in *Brown* the triumph of revolution, a witness both to the end of an old order and the advent of an uncertain, perceptibly better, though unmistakably imperfect new.

Now is yet too soon to render an accounting of all the achievements and failures of the modern Civil Rights movement, known to many as the Second Reconstruction. Centuries hence, some true accounting may be had. Perhaps to that future historian, our America will not prove so terribly complex. Surely a nation that developed the steamboat and railroad, the cotton gin and combine, the telegraph and telephone, the automobile and airplane, electricity, television, and the computer reckons large in the annals of civilized achievement. And this same nation launched unheard of experiments in self-governance, all the while preserving individual liberty and privacy, not just from the tyrant, but from the hands of officials the citizenry had duly elected. Yet a darker side stained the nation's brightest achievements. Was America too consumed in the race for wealth and goods, too confident of its inventions, too enchanted with its own unfolding boundaries and skyward buildings to comprehend the tragedy that had befallen the minority in its midst? And were the guaranties of equal treatment and personal liberty—sworn to in our national charter, honored on every public occasion, recited alike by statesman and schoolboy—were those to be denied forever in their substance to the black?

For a time it seemed so. Yet beginning in the mid-twentieth century, profound and sobering developments took place. Slowly the growth of the Soviet superpower, the seeming endlessness first of Korea and then of Vietnam, the gathering energy shortage, the chemical hazards to our health and electronic hazards to our privacy made clear that national inventiveness, for all its bounty, had limitations, and, indeed, the awesome potential to do us in. But along with a recognition that American power had limits came new hope for the fulfillment of American ideals. To say that humility somehow brought humanity would be, historically, sheer folly. And yet, as with Lear, what was lost in material or military dominance might be regained in the nation's spirit and soul.

Was not *Brown*, then, a gift to the country? Would it come to be more a gift than, say, Henry Ford's assembly line? Depending on our spirit of acceptance, it may prove to be. *Brown* determined that the Negro would be dealt with as a man, not as the currency of the white world's compromise. Compromise had largely been the byword since the original Constitution declared that three-fifths of the slaves, discreetly called "all other Persons" to distinguish them from "free Persons," should count in apportioning representatives to the states.[19] The nineteenth century was the century of national compromise over the Negro: the Missouri Compromise, the Compromise of 1850, the Compromise of 1877, and, of course, when compromise broke down, the Civil War. Nor did compromise end with the 1800s. Most American presidents of the present century—

the two Roosevelts, Wilson, Eisenhower, and Nixon among them—saw each wave of zeal for racial justice compromised against the need for day to day southern political support.[20]

But the problem outlasted the attempts to negotiate it. "When we say there is a Negro *problem* in America," Gunnar Myrdal wrote in 1944, "what we mean is that the Americans are worried about it. It is on their minds and on their consciences."[21] So it has been, from the coming of the first slave in 1619 to the present day. We leave it for a season, but it returns. It always will. Race *is* the perpetual American dilemma. On its fair resolution, much of the verdict on our history hangs.

PART I
Brown

1

The Court Redeemed

Everyone understands that *Brown* v. *Board of Education* helped deliver the Negro from over three centuries of legal bondage. But *Brown* acted to emancipate the white South and the Supreme Court as well. Not that the South immediately recognized *Brown* as a deliverance from economic stagnation, moral debility, and sectional isolation, a deliverance that would end with the installment of one of its own in the White House by 1977. And the Court only barely acknowledged in *Brown* the full weight of history from which it was itself redeemed. Indeed, the true story of the Court's own past attitude toward the black man remains one of the deafening silences of the *Brown* opinion. For half a century after the Civil War, the Supreme Court had, in effect, told the Negro to seek solace not in the law of the land but, like Stephen Foster's Old Black Joe, in cotton fields, mournful song, darkey friends, and the hereafter.

It was President Lincoln who issued the Emancipation Proclamation and Congress that moved to secure Negro rights in the South with no fewer than three Constitutional amendments and four Civil Rights acts shortly after the Civil War. Throughout this period, the Court was eyed distrustfully. The Radical Republicans were "aware of the power the Court could exercise. They were for the most part bitterly aware of it, having long fought such decisions as the *Dred Scott* case." Radicals such as Congressman Thaddeus Stevens of Pennsylvania probably "had little hope that the Court would play a role in furthering their long range objectives."[1] What hopes they did have centered on those sections of the post–Civil War amendments permitting Congress to act through "appropriate legislation."[2]

In 1865 the Radicals sensed a long-awaited opportunity. Many a proud southern planter was left to his ashes and rubble, to scorched earth and wistful dreams. "The Old South," wrote one observer in 1870, "has gone 'down among the dead men'. . . . For that vanished form of society there can be no resurrection. . . ."[3] In the wake of Appomattox, "citizens of the victorious Union believed that the future of the Republic . . . would depend heavily on the extent to which the South could adjust, or be made to adjust, to the national viewpoint."[4] Adjustment meant, among other things, a new day and a new way for the southern Negro. For the Radical Republicans, the time for that new day had arrived.

Their motives, of course, were not all noble. The Radicals were accused, with some truth, of elevating southern Negroes to humiliate southern whites, of enfranchising the Negro to entrench the Republican party in the South, and of using blacks to forestall seating southern delegations in Congress hostile to northern business interests.[5] Yet "a genuine desire to do justice to the Negro," Professor Kenneth Stampp has written, was also "one of the mainsprings of radicalism." Some Radicals "refused to believe that the Negroes were innately inferior. . . . [They] had little empirical evidence and no scientific evidence to support their belief—nothing, in fact, but faith. Their faith was derived mostly from their religion: all men, they said, are the sons of Adam and equal in the sight of God."[6]

The Radical Republicans not only abolished slavery.[7] Their new Civil Rights laws aimed to welcome the Negro to full American citizenship. His vote was to be protected.[8] He was to have the same right as white persons to make contracts and hold property.[9] Harassment of the Negro in his goings and comings was prohibited,[10] and "equal enjoyment of the . . . facilities and privileges of inns, public conveyances on land or water, theatres, and other places of public amusement" was not to be denied on account of race.[11] Civil and criminal penalties for mistreatment of the Negro were provided against private persons and public officials alike. In short, the Negro, at last, was to receive the privileges and immunities of American citizenship.[12]

Or so the Radicals hoped before the Court stepped in. The Court's counter assault was unrelenting. Every kink and flaw in legislative draftsmanship was exploited, every narrowing construction employed, every benefit of doubt resolved against the spirit of the new legislation. By century's end, the fullness of Radical purpose lay victim to the Court's myopic keenness, its countervalues, and, of course, the judge's penchant for having the last say.

It is not true that every decision during this period rebuffed the Negro's rights. The Supreme Court does not move in unqualified fashion; even its clearest trends are muddied by cases that refuse to fit. Thus, because judges find race prejudice in courtrooms particularly noxious or noticeable, the Supreme Court nullified in 1879 a West Virginia statute that restricted jury service to whites.[13] Even in the "jury cases," what the Court gave, it felt free to retake. Negroes, it proclaimed, were not entitled to racially mixed juries, only to nondiscriminatory pools from which jurors were drawn. Then, of course, it fell to the Negro to prove (in state court without the aid of counsel) willful discrimination in his particular case.[14] In the end, the Court's meekness proved no match for the South. Not just racially charged crimes, such as lynching and rape, but every phase of civil and criminal life would be tried before an all-white cast.

If the jury cases did not improve the Negro's lot, they at least contributed rhetoric later useful to the cause of Civil Rights.[15] They are not, however, the decisions by which the Supreme Court will be remembered. History's eyesight, like that of the rest of us, dims with passing years. It sees at the distance of a century only that which is large and prominent; the rest gradually blurs away. And the judicial landmarks of this era were three cases, each harsher than its predecessor, that all but nullified the Negro's Reconstruction gains. The Court had noted in *Strauder* (the West Virginia jury case) that the training of the colored race "had left them mere children, and as such they needed the protection which a wise government extends to those who are unable to protect themselves. They especially needed protection against unfriendly action in the States where they were resident."[16] Yet the effect of the Court's handiwork—especially its three watershed cases—was precisely the opposite: to remove the "children" from the protection of their newfound federal benefactor and remand them to the control of their former masters in the South.

Of the three decisions, the *Slaughterhouse Cases* in 1873 were the

least directly diabolical. Curiously, their facts did not involve race
at all. Louisiana had granted one particular company a twenty-five
year monopoly to maintain slaughterhouses and stockyards in the
New Orleans area. The Court, by a vote of five to four, rejected
the claims of excluded butchers that this monopoly violated their
Thirteenth- and Fourteenth-amendment rights. The purpose of the
three Civil War amendments, held the Court, was to protect
blacks, not the rights of butchers to their calling. Examination of
the Thirteenth, Fourteenth and Fifteenth amendments, wrote Mr.
Justice Miller, revealed ". . . one pervading purpose found in them
all, lying at the foundation of each, and without which none of
them would have been even suggested; we mean the freedom of the
slave race, the security and firm establishment of that freedom, and
the protection of the newly-made freeman and citizen from the
oppressions of those who had formerly exercised unlimited dominion over him."[17]

There is an ambiguity to the *Slaughterhouse Cases*. They are still
invoked as evidence of the Constitution's special concern for the
Negro race.[18] They are likewise cited for an absence of Fourteenth-
amendment protection for anything else.[19] But to the Negro, the
Slaughterhouse Cases were anything but ambiguous. They remained,
at best, sweet music to the ear. After trumpeting the grand purpose
of the Civil War amendments as the "firm establishment" of "the
freedom of the slave race," the Court proceeded promptly to dis-
member that purpose. The first section of the Fourteenth Amendment declares in part that "No state shall make or enforce any law
which shall abridge the privileges or immunities of citizens of the
United States. . . ." It was on these last words, "citizens of the
United States," that the Court fastened. The privileges of United
States citizenship, which the Fourteenth amendment protected,
were few and limited; those of *state* citizenship, the Court declared,
were ample and fundamental.

Lest anyone conclude—as Justice Field did in dissent—that the
privileges and immunities clause was simply being done away
with,[20] the Court listed some privileges and immunities of United
States citizenship: the right to come to the seat of government, to
use the navigable waters of the United States, to petition in habeas
corpus, and to seek the protection of the federal government when
abroad or "on the high seas."[21] But to the black South Carolina
sharecropper of 1873, bowed by debt and bound to the sod, protec-

tion when abroad or "on the high seas" was not exactly the most precious gift.

To this day, the privileges and immunities clause has not recovered from the enervating interpretation of the *Slaughterhouse Cases*[22] and their progeny.[23] And in the *Civil Rights Cases* one decade later,[24] the Court dealt Radical Reconstruction an even more serious setback. The basic issue was whether Congress could protect the black man from private as well as public abuse. Private violence against the Negro scarred the South through the late-nineteenth century and thereafter. While "the 'southern outrage' story was a standard feature of the Republican press, and congressional investigations for partisan purposes often exaggerated the amount of violence in the South,"[25] violence recurred disconcertingly around election time. For example, "the Louisiana election of 1878 cost between thirty and forty lives and after the election of 1884 sixteen bodies were found along the Bayou Teche."[26]

The cutting edge of southern violence was, of course, the lynch mob. Lynching was justified, some editors argued, to save the South from black atrocities. In 1877, a Charleston editor found lynching hardly surprising when a "black villain might burn his employer's barn or his dwelling-house, or waylay and murder him, with but slight chance of ever being caught. If caught, it was next to impossible to convict him, and if convicted, there was nothing for him to fear but a few months, or at most a few years, in the Penitentiary, where he lived better than he did at home, and where he would be contented to remain for the rest of his days were it not for his ineffable laziness, which made the work there, light as it was, something of a punishment."[27]

Law in those years of Yankee occupation had disintegrated. Thus the time had come "for the people to save themselves. In this last and crowning outrage, at least, summary vengeance—justice!—was the only course left us."[28] The sequence of summary vengeance was all-too familiar: a mob of masked men broke into jail, carried a Negro prisoner a mile or so from town, strung him to a tree, and let fire.

Congress addressed this problem in the Civil Rights Acts of 1870 and 1871,[29] the latter known as the Ku Klux Klan Act. Both statutes sought to protect the Negro's vote and his person from private as well as public intimidation. Section 6 of the 1870 Act, for example, made it a felony "if two or more persons shall band or

conspire together, or go in disguise upon the public highway . . .
to prevent or hinder [any citizen's] free exercise and enjoyment of
any right or privilege granted or secured to him by the Constitution
or laws of the United States. . . ." But such provisions did not
constitutionally apply to most lynchings and beatings, which were,
the Court implied, mere private affairs betwixt a man and his
neighbor, and thus beyond the reach of federal law.[30]

Such reasoning bode ill for the Civil Rights Act of 1875. That act
surpassed even earlier legislation by protecting the black against as-
saults on his dignity as well as his person. It was both the gemstone
and the death rattle of Radical Reconstruction, an act once called
"Charles Sumner's last testament to the American people" after the
Massachusetts Senator who served as the nation's "most un-
compromising political advocate of the Negro's complete equality
before the law."[31] It was a law ahead of its time, a forerunner in
concept to the public accommodations section of the 1964 Civil
Rights Act. Section 1 of the 1875 Act provided simply that blacks
should have equal access with whites to inns, theatres, and modes
of public transportation.

But the Court also found this law unconstitutional.[32] Discrimination by owners of theatres, hotels and the like was a private matter, held the Court, and not at all the business of the Fourteenth
amendment.[33] That amendment declared only that *no state* shall
deny citizens their constitutional rights; Congress and the Court
were equally disabled from regulating the affairs of *private* individuals. In light of the lynching cases, the Court's rationale was not
surprising. But the tone of its new ruling certainly was. No longer
were blacks "children" to be looked after;[34] no longer were their
rights what the Civil War amendments were all about.[35] Paternal-
ism, and with it all pretense of federal protection, was suddenly
abandoned. It was high time, the Court now announced, for the
Negro to make his own way: "When a man has emerged from slavery, and by the aid of beneficent legislation has shaken off the in-
separable concomitants of that state, there must be some stage in
the progress of his elevation when he takes the rank of a mere citizen, and ceases to be the special favorite of the laws . . ."[36]

As often happens, the Court was most scathingly criticized by
one of its own. Justice John Marshall Harlan was a reformed Kentucky slaveholder, a supremely confident jurist who "allegedly
went to sleep with one hand upon the Constitution and the other

on the Bible, and thus secured the untroubled sleep of the just and the righteous."[37] The most eloquent dissenters are often the most indignant, though indignation came strangely to Justice Harlan in the *Civil Rights Cases*. While he was at church one Sunday, Mrs. Harlan dusted off a forgotten keepsake—the inkstand Chief Justice Roger Taney used to write all his decisions, including the infamous *Dred Scott* opinion. The effect on her husband was electric. "The memory of the historic part that Taney's inkstand had played in the *Dred Scott* decision, in temporarily tightening the shackles of slavery upon the Negro race in antebellum days, seemed, that morning, to act like magic in clarifying my husband's thoughts in regard to the law. . . . His pen fairly flew on that day and, with the running start he then got, he soon finished his dissent."[38]

Harlan's chief contention—that railroads, inns, and theaters are, in essence, public, not private—was not to find favor for another sixty years;[39] indeed, only one other justice ever entirely accepted it.[40] More memorable by far was his emotional ending plea:

> . . . It is, I submit, scarcely just to say that the colored race has been the special favorite of the laws. . . . To-day, it is the colored race which is denied, by corporations and individuals wielding public authority, rights fundamental in their freedom and citizenship. At some future time, it may be that some other race will fall under the ban of race discrimination. If the constitutional amendments be enforced, according to the intent with which, as I conceive, they were adopted, there cannot be, in this republic, any class of human beings in practical subjection to another class, with power in the latter to dole out to the former just such privileges as they may choose to grant. . . .[41]

Finally, of course, there was *Plessy* v. *Ferguson*.[42] If Harlan's dissent in the *Civil Rights Cases* made him a presidential possibility with some Republican leaders and editors in the North,[43] the South was equally attuned to the Court majority. Left to pursue its own way with the Negro, the South, beginning in 1887, enacted rigid laws establishing racial separation "in the courts, schools, and libraries, in parks, theatres, hotels and residential districts, in hospitals, insane asylums—everywhere, including on sidewalks and in cemeteries."[44] One early such law—a Louisiana statute of 1890 requiring "equal but separate accommodations" for black and white railway passengers—was at issue in *Plessy*.

The facts of the case had a ludicrous quality. Homer Plessy, the man removed from the white railroad car, was himself an octoroon, the offspring of a white and a quadroon (only one of Plessy's eight great-grandparents, then, had been a Negro). For some, that was one great-grandparent too many. "One drop of Negro blood makes a Negro," a character in a best-selling novel of the day exclaimed. "It kinks the hair, flattens the nose, thickens the lips, puts out the light of intellect and lights the fires of brutal passion . . ."[45] At least it was open to the Court to consider the law only as applied to Plessy and inform the nation exactly who was white and who a Negro. But the Court declined that invitation. Resoundingly, it upheld the Louisiana law against whomever the state authorities might decide to apply it.

Subsequent applications were almost comic in their cruelty. North Carolina and Virginia, it was noted, "found it wise to pass laws that forbade all fraternal organizations that permitted members of different races to address each other as 'brother.' Alabama saw fit to adopt a law prohibiting white female nurses from attending black male patients. A New Orleans ordinance segregated white and colored prostitutes in separate districts. A Birmingham ordinance made it unlawful for a black person and a white person to play together . . . at dominoes or checkers. Oklahoma banned any companionship between the races while boating or fishing."[46] The regime *Plessy* sanctioned became meticulous and complete.

In law, as in every other way, *Plessy* pushed beyond the *Civil Rights Cases*. Those cases held only that private discrimination was not for federal law to cure. *Plessy* now held it legal not only for a *state* itself to discriminate but for it to order its citizens to do likewise. Few Court opinions have been more dishonored. Justice Harlan, again in lone dissent, predicted that "the judgment this day rendered will, in time, prove to be quite as pernicious as the decision made by this tribunal in the *Dred Scott* case."[47] If the Court's appeal lies in its timeless principles—those verities that transcend the day's fashion—then *Plessy* is rightly disfavored as a period piece, "redolent with sociological speculation, permeated with theories of social Darwinism, and carrying overtones of white racial supremacy as scientific truth,"[48] a ready receptacle for the racism flourishing in America at century's turn.

Yet *Plessy* disturbs because it is not one day's or even one era's aberration, but a warehouse of segregationist "truths" that echo through our history. *Plessy* insisted that state legislatures acting with reference to local "usages, customs and traditions" should best handle the race problem;[49] that public peace and comfort were best prompted thereby; that a law requiring racial separation did not imply inferiority (unless, of course, "the colored race chooses to put that construction upon it");[50] that the "commingling" of races in trains, theatres, and schools amounted to social equality, implicitly unattainable; and, most emphatically, that law "is powerless to eradicate racial instincts or to abolish distinctions based upon physical differences . . ."[51]

Segregationists in the 1950s and 1960s did not copy entirely from *Plessy*'s book. There were variations on *Plessy*—namely, that integration was "a radical, pro-Communist political movement,"—adopted to suit more modern times.[52] But, for the most part, the arguments of *Brown*'s opponents were wearisome and *déjà vu*. [53] For the Court had said it all in *Plessy* long, long ago.

Plessy sustained a law requiring *equal* facilities as well as separate ones and equality among railway coaches would not seem impossible to achieve. But the nation would learn soon enough that the Court was less interested in equality than in washing its hands of the Negro.[54] In time equal became a ghost word, a balm for the nation's conscience, a token of the law's hollow symmetry and logic, but quite irrelevant in so far as the Negro was concerned. Signs of inequality sprouted everywhere. In the park was the separate water fountain that happened not to work; at the back of the restaurant was the black carry-out line; in the theatre was the Jim Crow balcony, unmaintained, because 'they'd trash it up anyhow.'[55] Nor was there a separate-but-equal election to which blacks might be consigned when excluded from the white one.

In schools, especially, inequalities were manifest. Forty-years experience, noted Governor James K. Vardaman of Mississippi in 1904, had proved the Negro unsuited for the kind of education the white man received. Literate Negroes were criminally inclined, explained Vardaman, and it was folly for the whites to tax themselves to create criminals.[56] And so it went. "Racial discrimination in the apportionment of school facilities in the South is as spectacular as it is well known," wrote Gunnar Myrdal in 1944. The South as a whole spent almost three times as much per white pupil as per black one; Georgia and Mississippi five times as much.[57] It was hardly surprising. Would the South, the nation's most impover-

ished region, spend its sparse resources on a race whose capability
for learning it suspected? Thus was the way of the word *equal*. Not
until fifty years after *Plessy*, when equal facilities seemed the last alternative to mixed ones, did equality come to be taken seriously.[58]

All this the Court might have foreseen. Yet the Court's failing in
Plessy was not finally a failure of prophesy. It simply missed the
point, made as well as it ever would be by Plessy's own counsel:

> *[I]t is not of the smallest consequence that the car or compartment set apart for*
> *the Colored is "equal" in those incidents which affect physical comfort to that*
> *set apart for the white. These might even be superior*, without such conse-
> quences! . . . The White man's *wooden* railway benches, if the case
> were such, would be preferred to any *velvet cushions* in the Colored
> car. If Mr. Plessy be Colored, and has *tasted* of the advantages of free
> American citizenship, and has responded to its inspirations, he ab-
> horred the equal accommodations of the car to which he was compul-
> sorily assigned![59]

How, one asks, had it happened? How did the Court come to
sanction a wrong so apparent? Sin is nowhere so evident as in for-
bears, a fact that imposes on history special burdens of caution. Explanations do exist, short of malice, for the Court's behavior toward
the Negro in the late-nineteenth century.

Charles Warren, in his multi-volume history of the Supreme
Court, argued that, far from being pernicious, the Court's decisions
of the period were "most fortunate. They largely eliminated from
national politics the Negro question which had so long embittered
congressional debates; . . . and they served to restore confidence in
the national court in the Southern States."[60] The decisions, thus
viewed, captured the spirit of the Compromise of 1877. The Compromise, arising from the hotly disputed 1876 presidential election
between Samuel J. Tilden and Rutherford B. Hayes, is too subtle
and complex for full explication here.[61] Its essence, however, was a
pledge of southern Democratic support for seating Republican
President Hayes in return for the withdrawal of federal troops from
the South.

The Supreme Court, for all its eminence, cannot disdain political
moods. If the public profoundly disagrees with a judgment of the
Court, that judgment will not stand.[62] The late-nineteenth century
Court perceived nothing quite so well as the temper of its time.
Nothing, it sensed, would prove more difficult than a crusade for
which the country had lost appetite. And by 1877, America had

wearied of the Negro and his problems. The *Nation* predicted bluntly the effect of the new Compromise: "The Negro will disappear from the field of national politics. Henceforth, the nation, as a nation, will have nothing more to do with him."[63]

The heady spirit of industrial nationalism would shortly eclipse all concern for Civil Rights. But it also seemed in 1877 that Radical Republicanism had misgauged the Negro's own capacity for citizenship. The *New York Tribune* declared that "after ample opportunity to develop their own latent capacities," Negroes had proved only that "as a race they are idle, ignorant, and vicious,"[64] a sentiment that later surfaced in the Court's impatience with the Negro as a "special favorite" of the laws.[65] Given the Negro's oppressed background, only an insistent national effort backed by federal funds and force might have aided him. But, notes a student of the period, "after 1877 any willingness to sustain such force totally disappeared in the North. Instead it wanted reunion; the Hayes-Tilden election crisis provided the excuse for the desired accommodation—an accommodation which had as one of its essential elements the remission of the Negro's destiny to the states. The Supreme Court saw to it that the bargain was not violated."[66]

Was the late-nineteenth century Court thus to be excused or even commended for aptly reading the nation's desires? Ultimately, I think not. The Supreme Court is the one branch of government for which it is never quite a sufficient apology to say simply that it followed, by design or from sixth sense, the temper of its time. The Court, in fact, is where minorities must seek refuge when the time itself becomes too heated, too cruel, too extravagant. And the Constitution fairly commands resistance to majority moods, something the late-nineteenth century Court at least fleetingly recognized.[67] Finally, the temper-of-the-times argument quite overlooks the Court's co-equal obligation to the temper of the framers of the Civil War amendments, something it surely understood and just as certainly emasculated.

The temper-of-the-times argument may actually be reflecting a dread of the Supreme Court's making idle law—law that like a parental admonition is nodded at, assented to, and promptly disregarded. A Court befriending the Negro in late-nineteenth century America, the argument implies, would have been shouting to the winds. For prosecutors would have refused to prosecute and juries refused to convict violators of Civil Rights laws. Legislatures would have evaded Supreme Court rulings with new and ever more ingenious statutes. Jury commissioners, local registrars, and county sheriffs would have continued to practice a law all their own. And in the case of notorious violations of Court decisions, a governor or even the president might embarrass, nay, humiliate the Court by looking the other way.

This fear of idle law is a real one, which preys heavily on every Supreme Court. But carried sufficiently far, it saps the Court of courage and renders constitutional principle a nullity. A Court more committed to the Negro's welfare might have had some effect. Although it may not have been capable of dissipating the gathering mood, perhaps it might have rendered it slightly less stifling and pervasive.

That mood was not always monolithic. By voiding the Civil Rights Act of 1875, for example, the Court hurt Negroes outside the South—in Kansas, California, Missouri, and New York— where four of the five actions in the *Civil Rights Cases* originated. After the federal law fell, thirteen northern states adopted similar statutes, though most were indifferently enforced.[68] But even in the South of the 1880s, rigid segregation had not altogether settled in. One historian saw in it a period of "experiment, testing, and uncertainty" in race relations, where the extent of contact between white and black varied greatly "from one place to another," a decade "quite different from the time of repression and rigid uniformity that was to come toward the end of the century."[69] Not until the 1890s did Jim Crow begin to gather momentum. It captured the South for many reasons, not least of which was the collapse of northern liberal opinion, including that on the Supreme Court.[70] The temper-of-the-times argument must always be one that runs both ways. Not only are the times those to which the Court succumbed, but those to which it contributed.

Lynching was perhaps the Court's great missed opportunity. In its racial hatred and mob fury, lynching violated not just the spirit of the Fourteenth Amendment but the whole concept of the rule of law. On this issue, at least, the Court might have stood ground. For the Supreme Court to hold man's most heinous and racist act not rightly the business of a federal statute—but a matter for reluctant states—was the saddest of its errors.[71] Thus did the justices of that era upset the judgment of an all-white jury[72] but affirm the verdict of the mob. Violence, of course, as much as segregation, was in the spirit of those times. But the Court, more than any other man or institution, owed a duty to something more than the worst the temper of the times might condone.

The irony was that the Supreme Court proved willing enough to resist popular moods when something other than black rights were at stake. Under the guise of defending freedom of contract, the Court protected in the early-twentieth century the freedom of employers to drive a tough bargain. The popular urge to limit employer prerogative through a rising tide of social legislation met disfavor at the Court.[73] And the Fourteenth amendment—originally the freedman's amendment[74]—became for a time the opposite: the favorite of those who would resist venturous public action on behalf of the disadvantaged of whatever race.

In the end, reading the actions of the late-nineteenth century Court from the most pragmatic perspective misses the dimension of tragedy. Suppose that the Court's decisions had not always been minded. It could and would have survived some idle law,[75] a danger—but not the gravest danger—to the Court's reputation. Betraying its charter and blessing gross injustice will eventually bring upon the Court the disrespect of the very public to whose vices it attempts to play. Moments come when the Court must seize hold of principle: if it goes, for a time, unenforced, so be it. For this Court in one of justice's dark hours serves to remind us that those who do not contribute to the solution of the problem can soon become part of it.

High among its achievements, *Brown* lifted from the Court the burden of its history. Yet it must not be supposed that redemption came like a thunderclap in 1954. It began in the late 1930s and 1940s with cases admitting Negroes to white law schools,[76] outlawing the white primary,[77] and voiding racially restrictive convenants in the sale of housing.[78] But such nibblings at the edges of race prejudice would not alone have undone the past. Something as dramatic as *Brown* was necessary.

Of the three landmark decisions of the past, the *Slaughterhouse Cases* were cited only once and favorably;[79] *Plessy* was discussed, briefly and unfavorably; and the *Civil Rights Cases* were ignored. A quiet burial was probably best. Reliving the unpleasantness of the preceding century would have been for the Court in *Brown* a pointless exercise. Yet that history endures. Only through it can the significance of *Brown* be understood.

Brown marked, to begin with, a reversal of position toward the

46683

Negro of our three branches of national government. If the late-nineteenth century saw the Court unravel what Congress had enacted, then the mid-twentieth saw Congress and the Executive unwilling to aid the Court. Earl Warren's memoirs betray disappointment close to bitterness at President Eisenhower's lack of support. If the President had but thrown his broad popularity behind *Brown*, Warren lamented, "we would have been relieved, in my opinion, of many of the racial problems which have continued to plague us." Instead, said Warren, Eisenhower "resented" the *Brown* decision and once told him that southerners after all "are not bad people. All they are concerned about is to see that their sweet little girls are not required to sit in school alongside some big overgrown Negroes."[80]

Thus, the Court waited alone for most of a decade until in 1963 the bombings in Birmingham provoked Jack Kennedy, and Kennedy's ghost, in turn, sped passage of the 1964 Civil Rights Act. If the isolation of the Court proved deeply unfortunate for the nation and the Negro, it assisted, ironically, in the Court's redemption. A century before, the Court's desertion of the black man looked all the worse for Lincoln's and Congress's earlier attempts to befriend him. So now, the Court's restoration was to be magnified by others' reluctance.

The South of the 1950s, like the South of the 1890s, had its face deeply fixed against progress for the Negro. To abolish segregation was to court sectional animosity. On the Court, the justices feared idle law if the South dug in. "Nothing could be worse from my point of view," Felix Frankfurter worried aloud at one oral argument, "than for this Court to make an abstract declaration that segregation is bad and then have it evaded by tricks."[81] The Wallace cry for "segregation now, segregation tomorrow, segregation forever!" would say it all. Segregation as a way of life was implanted and entrenched, perhaps as much as it was in the late-nineteenth century. Nor was the Deep South the only home of diehards; defiance would extend even to the Court's back door in Virginia. Whether opinion in the North would support a bold change remained, at the time of *Brown*, to be seen. At least, mused Justice Robert Jackson, the nation "must wonder how it is that a supposedly stable organic law of our nation this morning forbids what for three quarters of a century it has allowed."[82]

The Court in *Brown* had a route of escape, one in keeping with the sentiment of its day. It might have put flesh on *Plessy*'s bones and insisted that racially separate schools be truly equal. Its recent precedents permitted such a ruling, although they had addressed only the unique setting of graduate education, the level where segregated equality was hardest to achieve. But even those precedents had carefully refrained from upsetting *Plessy*.[83] The lower courts in *Brown* had not gone further; the most adventuresome opinion, that of Judge Collins Seitz in the Delaware case, held only that where "separate but equal" had been palpably violated, the appropriate remedy was admission of black plaintiffs to white schools.[84] Separate but *genuinely* equal was what John W. Davis, speaking for the state of South Carolina, was urging on the Court. And there had long been disagreement—even within the NAACP high command—about whether to argue an "equalization" strategy within the confines of *Plessy* or to take the bolder and riskier course of asking the Court to overrule separate but equal altogether.[85]

Thus was the way paved to please the South without turning away the Negro empty-handed. Yet to its everlasting credit, the Supreme Court in *Brown* rejected that course. Had it not, a century of petty law might have begun to build over the issue of what was equal and what was not. Yet through all the din over quantities of mortar, size of playgrounds and salaries of teachers, the hurt and degradation would have persisted. "Take your new school," the Court would have said and "be still. What more, now, can you want?"

The Court, in *Brown*, for all its bravado, knew only too well the mood of its day. And that mood was not ignored. With the segregation cases, the Court moved in its own sweet time. It called for reargument. It sought unanimity. It spoke in a tone both bland and conciliatory. It postponed in the original *Brown* decision any plan for implementation. When a plan was announced, it refrained from fixing deadlines or uniform conditions. All it asked was the elimination of racial discrimination in public schools "with all deliberate speed."[86] But the temper of the time—for all its influence—stopped short of subverting the principle. That segregated schools were inherently unequal and hence unconstitutional remained clear and intact. Unlike its ancestor, the Supreme Court in *Brown* found a way to be both politic and principled. And therein lay all the difference.

2

The Opinion

To know that *Brown* was a great occasion, one need only think back on the advocates. The old order crumbled, but not without eloquence. Indeed, at the oral arguments in *Brown*, John W. Davis may have mounted segregation's last memorable defense.

He was eighty-years old at the time *Brown* was last argued, and his voice and memory had begun to fade. "Some of his friends," reported *Time*, "were sorry to hear him, at twilight, singing segregation's old unsweet song."[1] Yet he remained the Supreme Court's great advocate, not only of his day but, perhaps, of all time. Like a rock he stood for segregation:

> "If it [integration] is done on the mathematical basis [in Clarendon County, South Carolina], . . . you would have 27 Negroes and 3 whites in one schoolroom. Would that make the children any happier? Would they learn any more quickly? Would their lives be more serene?
> . . . Would the terrible psychological disaster being wrought, according to some of these witnesses, to the colored child be removed if he has three white children sitting somewhere in the same schoolroom?"

Like Robert E. Lee, Davis went the path of ennobling defeat, a testament to the South's ability to recruit men of character and principle to its most woeful cause:

"Let me say this for the State of South Carolina. It did not come here, as Thad Stevens would have wished, in sackcloth and ashes. . . . It is convinced that the happiness, the progress, and the welfare of these children is best promoted in segregated schools."

And he summoned the wisdom of the ages to his side:

"Somewhere, sometime, to every principle comes a moment of repose when it has been so often announced, so confidently relied upon, so long continued, that it passes the limits of judicial discretion and disturbance.[2]"

As it had to Lee, the struggle and the defeat ultimately exhausted Davis. He "was so shattered," writes his biographer, "by what he considered to be the sociological cast of the *Brown* opinion that one of his partners was later to say that the decision had killed him."[3]

What Thurgood Marshall, Davis's chief opponent, represented was equally dramatic. For Marshall, the NAACP's chief lawyer since 1938, *Brown* climaxed years of back roads, spare lodgings, and rough argument in the hot, high-ceilinged trial courts of the border states and South. Those had been years of legal trial and error: which state and court to bring suit in, what type of school to desegregate, which plaintiff to choose, what remedy to pursue.[4] If Marshall's argument in *Brown* was less emotional than Davis's,[5] his presence was yet more symbolic. His color itself signified that blacks in their own destiny would henceforth have a say. And he sought that day for his people neither human sympathy nor a government handout, but opportunity in the schools. He spoke not for revolution but for law, recalling America's traditions and values as the Constitution proclaimed them. But most of all, his presence before the Supreme Court symbolized the courage the Negro would need in what he was about to attempt.

Integration, to many Americans, was something blacks wanted and whites resisted. But it was not that simple. The experience was as traumatic for those who knocked as for those who would be forced to open their school doors. It was not just the jeers and taunts of white classmates and parents who did not hesitate to let black children know they were not welcome. Or the officials who proclaimed them inferior and incapable of participating in any academic attempt. Separation, for all the indignity and suffering it inflicted upon its victims, provided, as well, its own psychic security. Integration was far riskier; black teachers might lose their jobs,[6] black students would be judged not by their own but by the standards of the wider and different white world. The pain of the journey—and the cultural shock it threatened—caused blacks before and after *Brown* not to mistake in integration an answer to all their prayers. "A black child in a predominantly black school," a separatist black professor wrote years later, "may realize that she doesn't look like the pictures in the books, magazines and TV advertisements, but at least she looks like her schoolmates and neighbors. The black child in a predominantly white school and neighborhood lacks even this basis for identification."[7]

Even before *Brown*, there had been omens of the difficulty ahead. When the University of Oklahoma was ordered to accept a Negro, George McLaurin, to its graduate school of Education, the state legislature responded promptly. Instruction, it said, was to be given McLaurin and other Negroes only "upon a segregated basis." McLaurin, in other words, was to be made an untouchable. A rail surrounded the section of the classroom where he sat. Lest the significance of the rail be mistaken, a sign—Reserved for Colored—was attached. To avert contamination of books or food, McLaurin was confined to the mezzanine of the library and seated separately at the cafeteria. Many of McLaurin's fellow students protested such treatment and the Supreme Court eventually held it unconstitutional. But the resistance unwanted arrivals might receive was clear.[8]

Thus, what Thurgood Marshall won in *Brown* was no easy day. That the black man strove so hard for integration is a paean to man's universal longing for dignity and opportunity for his children. *Brown* was, in a true sense, an invitation to the challenge of equality. And with the price to be paid came self-respect. "Blacks," reflected the lawyer who had argued *McLaurin*, "were no longer supplicants seeking, pleading, begging to be treated as full-fledged members of the human race; no longer were they appealing to morality, to conscience, to white America's better instincts. They were entitled [after *Brown*] to equal treatment as a right under the law; when such treatment was denied, they were being deprived—in fact robbed—of what was legally theirs."[9]

Brown, by any measure, was a momentous decision. Why then did the Supreme Court mark so great an occasion with so brief an opinion? Of Earl Warren's landmark opinions, *Miranda* v. *Arizona* was sixty pages,[10] *Reynolds* v. *Sims* (imposing a one-man, one-vote system on state legislatures) fifty-one,[11] and *Brown*, the most important of them all, only eleven.

What really mattered was not length. *Brown* noted the end—or rather the beginning of the end—of racial segregation in a matter-of-fact manner. With the exception of one single sentence, now quoted often in desperation or by default,[12] the Court refused to lift the nation to the magnificence of the principle it had that day redeemed. It even refused to borrow eloquence, for example, from Justice John Marshall Harlan's earlier dissents. In short, the opinion failed to rouse or inspire; it simply existed. A schoolboy of the twenty-first century reading back and expecting to find a Declaration of Independence or Gettysburg Address will likely be deflated. The Court left so little to posterity—or to its own day—with which to honor the occasion.

Of course, there are explanations for the way *Brown* was composed. For a Court venturing into the unknown, discretion was best. In 1954 it was impossible to foresee where *Brown* would lead the Court. It was only a first step. "Not even a court can in a day change a deplorable situation into the ideal," Justice Frankfurter wrote. "It does its duty if it effectively gets under way the righting of a wrong."[13] Loquaciousness seemed inappropriate to this maiden voyage. The Court best kept options open for the long haul by staying taciturn at the start.

Brown thus gave little guidance to future racial debate. Its brevity was a mask for ambiguity. If segregated schools were not constitutional, what kinds of schools were? Was the evil segregation itself or merely the state's imposition of it? Was a color-blind society or the betterment of an oppressed race the Court's chief objective? On these and other questions, *Brown* (and later *Brown II*) gave no clear answers. It left future problems to the future, content to take one memorable step.

Brown neither anticipated the future nor dwelt in the past. A brief opinion, simple and unencumbered, might best suggest to a nation beleaguered by problems of race that it might now begin anew. Thus the Court downplayed the Fourteenth amendment's history, noting it had little to say on public education. The justices asked what the amendment meant in 1954, not in 1868 or 1896. "Never," wrote one approving commentator, "was Thomas Jefferson more clearly vindicated in his insistence that the Constitution belongs to the living generation of Americans."[14]

It is worth noting that the two modern justices with most political experience—Earl Warren and Hugo Black—felt a need as jurists to remain comprehensible to common men. Though most laymen can resist reading Supreme Court opinions, there is virtue in whatever contributes to clear communication from the bench. Justice Black revered clarity and simplicity; his style, notes a recent biographer, "resembled nothing quite so much as the tough, springy, splintery pine of his native Alabama hills."[15] Earl Warren was similarly possessed in *Brown*. He wrote "every blessed word," he said,[16] and "purposely wrote a short opinion so that any layman interested in the problem could read the entire opinion [instead of getting just] a little piece here and a little piece there. . . . I think most of the newspapers printed the entire decision."[17] Yet the desire for brevity and simplicity does not explain the drab tone of *Brown*. For short, simple opinions can also be stirring, as Justice Black himself has shown.[18]

There are better reasons for the blandness of *Brown*, among them the need for a single, unanimous opinion. Often the Court is unanimous, but seldom on so divisive an issue. Unanimity here appeared to breach the Court's most hallowed tradition: that of open and spirited dissent. Yet it was precisely this break with tradition—the unusualness of unanimity—that made it so effective. To speak with one voice was to speak with force and finality; to speak otherwise was but to lend comfort to an enemy already in prey.

That Warren achieved unanimity was remarkable, given the Court's personnel. Justices Robert Jackson and Felix Frankfurter were restless, complicated intellects, quick to find fault and prone to personal expostulation. Jackson, in particular, flirted with writing a concurring opinion. The Court, as a whole, was disputatious and splintered. On one hand was the activism of Black and Douglas; on the other Jackson's and particularly Frankfurter's, canons of constitutional restraint. The Court's gifted intellects were prima donnas, often at odds with one another and quietly contemptuous of the lesser lights. Richard Kluger, in his epic narrative of the *Brown* decision, describes it thusly:

> . . . . Jackson, convinced that Black had intervened with Harry Truman to prevent his succeeding Stone as Chief Justice in 1946, had flown at the Alabaman in open rage that was slow to die. Frankfurter viewed much of Douglas' writing and thinking as slipshod. . . . Douglas found many of Frankfurter's anti-libertarian opinions to be tortured apologias. . . . The tension lines ran every which way. Min-

ton found Jackson pompous and Black prone to demagoguery.
Douglas remained aloof from nearly everybody save Black. Black and
Frankfurter thought Reed often lacked the courage of his convictions.
. . . Burton, a strait-laced teetotaler who never smoked or cursed,
found his neighbor on the bench [Minton] somewhat on the uncouth
side and did not enjoy having his robe sprayed when the tobacco-
chewing Hoosier missed the spittoon provided for him behind the
bench. And so it went.[19]

On such a Court, the less said the better. Each new sentence,
every added word, risked creating offense, engendering suspicion,
and triggering a self-generating chain of separate and debilitating
opinions. If the price of unanimity was a lack of language to anthol-
ogize, then that price, sensed Warren, would have to be paid.

There was one final reason for *Brown*'s subdued approach: the
South. Southern power in the mid-fifties did not stop at Congress;
it sat on the Court. Justices as different as Hugo Black, the Alabaman, Tom Clark, the Texan, and Stanley Reed, the Kentuckian,
would have resisted any opinion that pointed a finger back home.
Beyond that, a prolonged exegesis on the virtues of integration or
the evils of its opposite might, the justices feared, bring forth once
more the drums and bugles of the old Confederacy. Temperance
and tact were the order of the day. Why inflame that region whose
acceptance, above all, would have to be won? The Court understood its opposition: "It was wise to present as small a target as possible to marksmen on the outside."[20]

As it happened, the South erupted anyhow, in part, over a footnote. Ironically, footnote eleven of this tactfully expressed decision
may be the most inflammatory English ever in fine print. On its
face the footnote seems innocuous: a string citation of seven works
of various social scientists. When one learns the reason they are
cited, however, the resultant controversy becomes predictable.
That segregation intangibly harms Negro school children was,
wrote Chief Justice Warren, "amply supported by modern authority."

The modern Supreme Court is peculiarly tempted to employ
social science. Unquestionably, social sciences illumine issues that
are ever more technical and ever more involved in social policy. Citation of empirical studies spreads a blanket of authenticity over the
judge's naked views and evinces that breadth of learning and
sophistication any man would be proud to display. To use the

social sciences is to relate the branches of human knowledge; not to do so is to leave law in an unedifying vacuum.

But applying social science to active controversies is also playing with fire. Most justices lack strong backgrounds in economics, psychology, or sociology; they are not familiar with the current state of the art; they can but poorly distinguish what is reputable methodology from what is sham. For every study that appears to support a justice's conclusions, another might be found to contradict or seriously qualify them. The force of the Court's views may be blunted, as in *Brown*, by a collateral debate on the veracity of its sources.[21] And the social sciences lend to constitutional law a mushy bottom; if the cited authorities are later discredited, should not the opinion that cited them be also? All this is not to say that social sciences have no place in constitutional law—they do—but that for the untutored, caution is advisable.

Brown, however, cast caution aside. It appeared to lean on social science for its central thesis—otherwise unexplained—that segregation damaged the personal and mental development of Negro school children. The first study cited in footnote eleven for this proposition dealt with dolls.[22] Professor Kenneth Clark had shown drawings of otherwise identical black and white dolls to segregated Negro school children between the ages of six and nine. When asked to select the "nice" doll, more children than not chose the white doll, supposedly evidence that school segregation implanted in blacks a negative image of their own race at a tender age.[23]

Almost immediately, questions emerged about Clark's study, even from friendly critics. Wasn't the sample of children too small or improperly screened? Professor Edmond Cahn wanted to know. Why were drawings and not real dolls used? Did the conclusions even follow from the evidence? ("Habituations with *dolls* . . . should be allowed for. . . . Many white children of certain generations were taught to prefer 'Topsy' or other colored dolls; some children would say there is no really 'nice' doll but a teddy-bear.") What, finally, did tests of six-to-nine-year olds show about school segregation specifically, as opposed to other childhood experiences? "Considering the ages of the children, we may conjecture they had not been long at school," said Cahn.[24] Another critic remained "disturbed about the disrepute his [Clark's] 'evidence' could not fail to bring to social science if it were taken seriously. And it seems to be."[25]

To Cahn and others, the social scientists must not seem crucial to *Brown*. It should have been obvious all along that segregation harms; proving this was like proving "that fire burns," or "that a cold causes snuffles." As for the footnote citation of Clark, it was simply "the kind of gesture a magnanimous judge would feel impelled to make" in view of Clark's devoted work in the case.[26] But the question persisted: was *Brown* a matter of social science or a common sense application of equal protection under the law? To Cahn, seeking to give the opinion a stature and permanence beyond brown and white paper dolls, *Brown* expressed civilized truth. But those who wished to see it as a brand of sociology were now given, *gratis* in footnote eleven, an excuse for doing so. The "marksmen on the outside" had their target, and a tempting target it was.

Even less extreme southerners charged the Court with turning "over the making of law to social science opinion and the writers of books on psychology."[27] And the more extreme took a different tack, one that emphasized not so much what was said but who had said it. Here the tactics of McCarthyism gave the forces of racism a special lift. That footnote eleven was a communist front was especially evident to South Carolina Governor and former Supreme Court Justice James F. Byrnes and Mississippi Senator James O. Eastland. Theodore Brameld, one of those cited, was, said Eastland, "a member of no less than 10 organizations declared to be communistic, communistic front, or communist dominated."[28] Worse yet was the treatment given E. Franklin Frazier, another cited in *Brown*'s famous footnote. "The files of the Committee on Un-American Activities of the United States House of Representatives," reported Eastland, "contain 18 citations of Frazier's connection with Communist causes in the United States."[29]

But last-cited Gunnar Myrdal, the Swedish economist whose *An American Dilemma* was the premier work on race relations in America, most stirred xenophobia in the South. "A contributor to his work," charged the Georgia attorney general, "was Negro educator W.E.B. DuBois, who sent a message of condolence upon the death of Joseph Stalin."[30] "Foreign sociologists" such as Myrdal would not do, wrote one prominent Montgomery lawyer. "Over the years we have had sociologists of our own and we prefer the voices of our own students of men and manners and morals—the voices of the Knoxes, the Almons, the Carmichaels, the Cobbs, the Colemans, the De Graffenreids, the Howzes, the Jones, the Merrills, the Oates, the O'Neals, the Rogers, the Spraggins, the Weakleys, the Weatherbys, and the Whites (to name a few amongst the many), who wrote the Educational Provisions of our Alabama Constitution."[31]

Those promoting an idea can do no better than hire intemperate opponents. And the vindication of *Brown* owes much to them. *Brown*'s serenity simply outlasted hysterical critics and their time. But *Brown* also elicited criticism from those whose only axe to grind was a legal one. One of the strongest criticisms came not from the Mississippi Delta but from the Columbia School of Law, from a man who remembered that: "In the days when I was joined with Charles H. Houston [Thurgood Marshall's predecessor as chief counsel for the NAACP] in a litigation in the Supreme Court, before the present building was constructed, he [Houston] did not suffer more than I in knowing that we had to go to Union Station to lunch together during the recess."[32]

Herbert Wechsler, whose article on *Brown*, "Toward Neutral Principles of Constitutional Law," is now a classic, had not only been consulted by NAACP strategists on *Brown* but had helped them long before. Though the implications of the article travel far beyond *Brown*, the school segregation cases provided the setting. What bothered others about *Brown* did not so much concern Wechsler. It was defensible for the Court to depart from precedent, to disturb the "settled patterns" of life in the South, to give the Fourteenth Amendment a contemporary construction, and not to wait for Congress to ban segregation. Such steps were necessary, on occasion, if the Court were properly to discharge its function of judicial review. What was indefensible was the Court's bare, unreasoned conclusion that separate schools were "inherently unequal" and hence unconstitutional. How did the Court reach that point? Wechsler wanted to know. By examining the motives of legislatures that enacted segregation statutes? Or the views of those affected by segregation? And how were other pieces of separatist legislation—such as sex discrimination and anti-miscegenation laws—to be judged? None of this had the Court explained. In fact, Wechsler thought the real constitutional dilemma in *Brown* to be between segregation's forced denial of free association and integration's forced imposition of it.[33]

Thus did a high priest of academia accuse the Court in *Brown* of original sin. The justices, implied Wechsler, ignored their paramount obligation to neutral reasoning in their longing for a desired result. And Wechsler's fellow academics have been trying to defend *Brown* ever since.[34] Their problem was that *Brown* never explained—indeed, never tried to explain—its crucial conclusion that segregated schools, however equal their facilities, still intangibly harmed black children. True, *Brown* kept repeating this conclusion, at least five separate times.[35] But the Court essentially asked the country to take it on faith: that because nine justices thought segregation wrong, it must be so.

For *Brown*'s more eager adherents, this was more than enough. What did the opinion matter, so long as the Court's judgment was "right?" Why apologize for the Court, asked Professor Edward Beiser, "when desirable results are achieved? . . . *Brown* was decided properly because racial segregation was a grievous evil. Were this not so, the Supreme Court's decision would have been unjustified. Peckham's majority was wrong [in a 1905 case voiding a New York maximum hours law]; Warren's was right."[36] That *Brown* was not "tightly reasoned," agreed Professor Paul Bender, was beside the point. We all know, he said, that the opinion was "right. . . . If the Court had waited to strike down segregation until an airtight opinion could be written (I still couldn't write one), it would have sadly failed the country and the Constitution."[37]

Why, *Brown*'s defenders ask, should the Court be required to demonstrate the obvious? "Does anyone doubt today," Bender asked, "(did anyone really doubt in 1954) that legally enforced racial segregation in Southern public schools hurt blacks more than it did whites?"[38] Professor Black was not a doubter. If asked whether segregation offends against equality, "I think," he said, "we ought to exercise one of the sovereign prerogatives of philosophers—that of laughter. The only question remaining (after we get our laughter under control) is whether the segregation system [in the South] answers to this description. Here I must confess a tendency to start laughing all over again."[39]

Sometimes, however, obviousness takes saying. This is especially so when what is obvious to some is not obvious to others. In 1954, there were—as there are today—Southerners who believed their traditional way with the Negro more beneficent: more kindly, more intimate, more caring, and altogether more humane.

To many white Southerners, the Negro was forever that curiosity of a child's brain implanted in an adult's body. He had a "childlike love of pageantry, of finery, and of frills and furbelows. . . . His automobile . . . is marked by shiny accessories, fox-tails, and other unnecessary but gaudy appurtenances. . . . He may sleep three or four in a bed, but chances are that the bed will be covered with a colorful chenille bedspread."[40] As a child, the South argued, the black was naturally wayward and mischievous. "Boss," a Negro farmhand is quoted as saying, "if you could be a nigger for 'jes one Sattidy night, you'd never want to be a white man ag'in!"[41] As a child, the Negro had to be disciplined, sometimes harshly. But he had to be loved and cared for too: the doctor summoned to his ailing bedside, a turkey sent over for Thanksgiving and at Christmastime. As a child, he was to gurgle at what mindless pleasures came his way; agitators, such as the Supreme Court and the NAACP, were only vexing nature's contented. Finally, as a perpetual child, the Negro had a limited capability for learning. He would be given what education he could handle, as much as was needed to get along.

Such notions merit more that the sound of enlightened laughter. For they made up the self-fulfilling prophesy transfigured into gospel for generations in the South. Segregationists, said Senator Sam Ervin of North Carolina, believe that "man finds his greatest happiness when he is among people of similar cultural, historical, and social background." But segregation did not prevent Southerners from "forming warm and mutually helpful friendships with members of the other race. Interracial friendships of this character are, in fact, commonplace in the South."[42] For Ervin, as for many Southerners, the cruelty of it all had simply been shut out, the paternal and benevolent only, noticed and remembered.[43] It was a gross but not uncommon deception. To that region whose way of life it condemned, whose daily goings and comings it uprooted, did the Court not owe at least some reasoned explanation? To the Southerner's question—"Why is my way wrong?"—the Court simply declined to answer.

This has nothing to do with the rightness or wrongness of the Court's judgment, only with a willingness to explain its action to those most affected. And, of course, there were explanations in abundance for why segregation, both in principle and as practiced in the South, was constitutionally intolerable. For principle, I rely again on Professor Cahn:

> The moral factors involved in racial segregation are not new . . .
> but exceedingly ancient. What, after all, is the most elementary and
> conspicuous fact about a primitive community if not the physical
> proximity of human beings mingling together? When the members of
> a community decide to exclude one of their number from the group
> life without killing him outright, what else can they do but force him
> to remove himself physically (as in the case of Cain), ostracize him for
> what they consider the general welfare (as the Athenians did), banish
> him from the cluster of community dwellings (as in outbreaks of lep-
> rosy or other plague), assign him a fixed area or ghetto to occupy (as
> with the Jews in medieval times), or lock him in a penitentiary (as we
> do with convicted criminals)? . . . Segregation does involve stigma;
> the community knows it does.[44]

Segregation, as practiced in the South, fit well enough this ancient pattern. The stigma of it permeated all manners and mores of
the people. "If the Negro is a shunned topic in formal intercourse
among whites in the South, he enters all informal life to a disproportionate extent," wrote Myrdal. "He creeps up as soon as the
white Southerner is at ease and not restraining himself. He is the
standard joke," told by whites to prove "the inferiority of the
Negro"[45] through some knee-slapping tale of bumbling ineptitude.

But there were serious references also. When a white Southerner
spoke of putting "them in their place," the listener was hardly to
infer a status of elevation. Negroes, so the saying went, were not to
get "uppity." Up-down, front-back (as in bus) were intuitively used
to give relations between the races "proper" order and perspective.
There were even put-down words and devices, one of which later
reached the Supreme Court. Mary Hamilton, a Negro, appeared in
Alabama court as her own witness in a habeas corpus hearing.
Though the state's attorney had addressed white witnesses as "Mr."
or "Mrs.," the following colloquy took place:

> Q: What is your name, please?
> A: Miss Mary Hamilton.
> Q: Mary, I believe you were arrested—who were you arrested by?
> A: My name is Miss Hamilton. Please address me correctly.
> Q: Who were you arrested by, Mary?

She refused to answer; the trial judge held her in contempt; the
Supreme Court of Alabama affirmed; and the Supreme Court of
the United States reversed summarily.[46]

Not just in its minutiae but in its grand functioning did segregation work to harm the Negro. It was imposed on him; his consent was neither invited nor required. Separate facilities almost never meant equal ones. Opportunity in all areas—schooling, housing, employment, and politics—was denied. Capability meant nothing; race everything. Evidence was everywhere—literally everywhere—of a legally enforced destiny of inferiority for the black. And in law, the evidence was clearest of all. Calling a white man a Negro was for many years actionable defamation in the South. Even "a small portion of Negro 'blood,' " Professor Black observed, "put one in the inferior race for segregation purposes: this is the way in which one deals with a taint, such as a carcinogen in cranberries."[47]

In a sense the ubiquity of the evidence posed the problem. If signs of segregation's harm indeed were everywhere, was the Court in *Brown* not obliged to take note? Why wait for commentators—whose words are belated and little read—to turn its bare conclusion into documented fact? The standard answer is again the political one. Explanations would alienate, not convince or convert. To upbraid segregation, however gingerly, was to divide the Court and offend the South. Yet one is stimulated, reading *Brown*, to wonder anew whether the Court's political and intellectual missions were meant to co-exist and, indeed, which was paramount.

How finally does the Supreme Court rule, if not through reason? Reason is not an aesthetic requirement that Justices—like ballerinas—perform for the pleasure of those who watch the Court. It is the citizen's hedge against the Court's perennial potential for arbitrariness. It is neither our sole hedge nor a complete one, only an expectation that the branch of government least politically accountable will remain most intellectually so. Reason permits, indeed requires, value choices, but only those logically deduced and candidly explained. "Like others who have spoken on this subject," wrote Professor Louis Henkin, "I believe that the Court owes an obligation . . . to articulate the bases for its decisions—what ingredients have gone into the judgment, in what weights, absolute and comparative. The writing of an opinion will help assure that the decision is based on principle, and will help make clear what the principle is."[48] There is no more basic axiom in all constitutional law.[49]

To imply that *Brown* was sui generis, that it was enough for the Court on this one grand occasion to draw on its "oracular authority,"[50] to trade on its reputation and prestige, is to suggest that the Court may forsake its principle of being on the occasions—whichever they are—that matter most. It is not a pretty argument. "Is it *Brown*'s legacy," one may ask, "that the Supreme Court can impose its will more abruptly than before, with smaller or sloppier explanation? It is a disturbing thought, no matter what one's urgent political goals. . . . For many people, including many judges, *Brown* may have forced the insight that the technical and structural abstractions that make laws into a legal system need not be paramount; . . . the Court in *Brown* struggled greatly to prove to itself that the case was unique and transcendent. In the next case, the effort is smaller, and in the next and the next."[51]

Brown raises a cluster of uncomfortable questions. Do noble ends permit questionable means? What price in process for agreeable results? Do the well-meaning deserve ample latitude? How, properly, may we excuse untoward methods in our friends? May we properly, as Victor Lasky reminds almost *ad nauseam*, forgive a Kennedy his transgressions but not a Nixon?[52] Do we simultaneously excoriate the muddled reasoning of a *Plessy* while overlooking the fact that *Brown* never attempted to reason much at all? *Brown* is probably the hardest test for equal application of standards to friend and foe alike. If the departure from appropriate process was so evident in *Brown*, never was the temptation greater to look the other way.

Perhaps the more one thinks of *Brown*, the more in danger he is of missing the point. It is important, after this passage of years, to place the opinion in perspective. It was humane, among the most humane moments in all our history. It was, with the pardonable exception of a footnote, a great political achievement, both in its uniting of the Court and in the steady way it addressed the nation. But if *Brown* spoke without rancor, it also spoke without eloquence, racial equality's solemn celebration. That it was an intellectual *tour de force*—or even an intellectual credit to the Court—is a claim few would propose. How much, finally, does that matter? Was *Brown* good or bad? Right or wrong? Is that not judgment day? Will history care but for result? Is all else nit? That we might see *Brown* whole. Then do we grieve for what might have been? Better we be thankful for what was.

3

As *Brown* Saw the Problem

There is always a nostalgia for simple times past, times when the knight on a white horse rode forth to save the beautiful princess from the bad guys. Never mind that the princess had no defensible right to her riches, that the bad guys had more than sufficient cause for redress of their grievances, or that the knight was more interested in the protection of privilege than of virtue. So it was that when the South rode forth to save segregation it understood itself to be defending the memory of the ante-bellum South—not the ugliness of slavery but all the beauty that had long been gone with the wind.

But *Brown* v. *Board of Education* attacked one simplistic view with another. Surely segregated schools were wrong; no number of Old South choruses could change that. But, on the other side, ghetto riots, school-busing controversies, and charges of reverse discrimination had not yet appeared to cloud the nation's vision. For the most part, *Brown* was a time of innocence, when men of new dreams attacked the old dreams that had held back the nation's rendezvous with racial justice.

Simplicity of analysis is the father of moral reform. Unfortunately, it can also sire deep trouble. Some of *Brown*'s assumptions about race seem naive today, quite sadly so. In this naiveté, the Court was not alone; it merely reflected the thinking on race elsewhere in the land. But the naive assumptions on which *Brown* was based were, in time, to bring Americans not only hope and progress in their race relations but also shock, disappointment, and eventually renewed despair.

The Supreme Court first sanctioned "separate but equal" in public transportation.[1] Its demise, on the other hand, came in public education. The setting was important. For *Brown*'s faith in the power of education was touching in its simplicity:

> Today, education is perhaps the most important function of state and local governments. Compulsory school attendance laws and the great expenditures for education both demonstrate our recognition of the importance of education to our democratic society. It is required in the performance of our most basic public responsibilities, even service in the armed forces. It is the very foundation of good citizenship. Today it is a principal instrument in awakening the child to cultural values, in preparing him for later professional training, and in helping him to adjust normally to his environment. In these days, it is doubtful that any child may reasonably be expected to succeed in life if he is denied the opportunity of an education. Such an opportunity, where the state has undertaken to provide it, is a right which must be made available to all on equal terms.[2]

Schools were then the great hope. To Felix Frankfurter the public school was nothing less than "the symbol of our democracy and the most pervasive means for promoting our common destiny."[3] Our schools, "the red brick PS on the city street and the red schoolhouse on the village green," had welcomed Europe's immigrants—the Irish, the Italians, the Poles, Greeks, and Swedes—"made room for the frightened children with broken accents, peculiar religions, undernourished lunch boxes, and lice in their hair; contained the cruel curiosity of earlier settlers; taught the lessons of democracy and saw that they were put into practice."[4] Now the same opportunity awaited the Negro.

Not surprisingly, *Brown* spoke only of the promise of public education, nothing at all of its problems. And in the 1950s that promise fairly gleamed. If integration were only allowed to happen, the kids themselves could make it work. "I have seen them do it," Thurgood Marshall told the Court in *Brown*. "They play in the streets together, they play on their farms together, they go down the road together, they separate to go to school, they come out of school and play ball together. They have to be separated in school."[5]

An article appearing in the *New York Times Magazine* the same month as *Brown* seemed to bear Marshall out. Integration would work, the author noted, if it were taken "out of the hands of the parents and teachers and turned . . . over to the children themselves." The author had seen it for himself in the small community of Jeffersonville, Indiana, "as Southern in its culture and outlook as Louisville or Richmond." Before the first year of integration was out, the kids "found themselves romping together on the playgrounds, playing together on the same basketball and baseball teams, serving together on the high school student council, belonging to the same scholastic clubs and societies and even attending the same school parties in a free and easy spirit of harmony."[6]

There was more to it, of course, than camaraderie on the playground. Integrated education promised a new generation of Americans, free at last of the yoke of race prejudice. The bitter-enders in the South might for a while "line the narrow streets" with "hate-contorted faces" shouting "Niggers . . . coons . . . go back to Africa! You'll never stay in that school!"[7] But their sons and daughters would come to see blacks as classmates, as peers, and as friends. And blacks, in turn, would learn not to bow the head and doff the hat, but to compete on terms of equality and respect. That at least was the hope of *Brown*. Education might create generation gaps in both races: the bigger, in this case, the better.

Racism in *Brown*'s day was vicious all right, but it was also thought to be eradicable. Color, it was believed, was not cultural but only skin deep, an irrelevant outer layer to be peeled off or looked through. "We're all the same inside," the saying went. And as Rodgers and Hammerstein reminded, "you've got to be taught to hate and fear." The children, we swore, would be taught something else: the human oneness within us all.

That was education's social, or to use Professor Bickel's term, "assimilationist" mission.[8] The black, at last, was to be Americanized: the cultural and psychic isolation, imposed by generations of segregation, would be dispelled. The Court and the nation also believed that with *Brown*, education would break for the black the old, oppressive cycle of ignorance and poverty. Education's promise was the thrilling one of upward mobility. Integration improved one's chances for college, which, in turn, improved one's shot at a job. If, as *Brown* observed, success was doubtful without an education, it was achievable with one. Education was, as Horace Mann had once declared, truly "the great equalizer of the conditions of men."[9]

Thus ran the cherubic view of public education. Social isolation would vanish, educational handicaps disappear, and public schools were the place to begin the job. It would begin quickly too. School segregation in America would be stamped out in no more than five years, Thurgood Marshall predicted the day after *Brown*.[10] The idealism was exhilarating; the alternative simply a surrender to ancient wrongs. Yet in the world of reality, the cherubic view shortly began to wear thin.

For one thing, the white South resented it. For many southern whites, the Negro was uneducable, with "a place in the biological hierarchy somewhere between the white man and the anthropoids."[11] Integrated schooling would help blacks little and it would definitely hold whites back. Socially it presented a graver threat, whose expression is best left to a true believer:

> "Amongst young folks of opposite sex propinquity brings about marriage. . . . [W]ith mixed schools, mixed transportation, mixed churches, this final step is inevitable. I hope the common sense of native Alabamians will repel it. But there is no reason to enhance the risk of mixed marriages by the compulsory maintenance of mixed schools."[12]

It was not just the attitudes of the elders that dimmed *Brown*'s hopes for public education. Student life itself posed problems. Some frictions seemed amenable to adjustment. When black students finally entered Strom Thurmond High School in Edgefield, South Carolina, for example, they learned that "the school newspaper would be called the *Dixiecrat*, that the band would step to the strains of 'Dixie,' that the Old Rebel would be the mascot for athletic teams, [and] that the Confederate Battle Flag would appear on class rings, graduation announcements and would be carried onto the football field at home games."[13]

Such symbols and trappings could, in time, be changed. But the problem ran deeper. Children themselves were not always color-blind. Self-segregation was frequently the rule; students continued to eat, study, and fraternize at school as they did outside school—with members of their own race. At Norfolk Virginia's Lake Taylor High, wrote one reporter in 1978, "blacks hold sway over the south cafeteria, the front of the building, the front patio, foyer, and entrance hall. Whites dominate the north cafeteria, back parking lot

and patio."[14] Disciplinary problems proved more common to integrated schools than to segregated ones.[15] Blacks generally were
two- or three-times more likely to face suspensions than whites.
Blacks felt these suspensions to be racially motivated: the acts of
white school officials who "see black and think trouble." But to
whites, especially in the older grades, blacks *were* the trouble, at
worse a source of bodily danger, at best a distraction from
classroom instruction.[16] By 1975, the New York *Times*, the Washington *Post*, and a Senate subcommittee reached identical conclusions: that "crime and violence, in varying degrees, have become
the norm in schools throughout the country."[17] Far more than
racial tensions caused that crisis; but one suspected also that racial brotherhood among the young had not universally taken hold.

One must not overgeneralize. In many places, under auspicious
conditions, blacks and whites made integration work.[18] And integration was itself an education. As Willie Morris wrote of his
boyhood home in Mississippi: "This generation of children, white
and black, in Yazoo will not, I sense, be so isolated as mine, for
they will be confronted quite early with the things it took me years
to learn, or that I have not learned at all."[19] Yet the most hopeful
truths—the *Brown* truths—about public education suddenly seemed
vulnerable. How had the children, in whom we once placed such
faith, learned their racism, and at how tender an age? Was it fantasy to expect that the first generation, the children of people who
had known only segregation, could so readily cast off the values of
their parents? Was race, more visible than ethnicity, less eradicable
too? And, most chillingly, did propinquity intensify race-hatred
among the young, rather than relieve it? "Unfortunately," wrote
Harvard educator Christopher Jencks, "we have no good evidence
as to whether attending school with blacks makes whites less prejudiced as adults. Most people assume this is the case, but one could
also argue the opposite view."[20]

Doubt was cast not just on integration's social mission but on its
educational one as well. There had been progress.[21] But integration
was not proving the great eradicator of inequality based on race that
many had hoped it would become. Reasons were not hard to
fathom. Schools alone were not capable of a mission of massive
racial uplift. They were but one element in the total matrix of
American life, every phase of which had conspired for generations
to oppress the black and prejudice the white. Studies suggested that

with changed community attitudes and supportive teachers, black academic performance might improve in integrated classrooms.[22] But there were limits to which any school could "offset the malignant effects of growing up in the ghetto"[23] or for that matter in tarpaper shacks of the rural South. Home life and background mattered more perhaps than what transpired at school.[24] By the time black children entered school, they performed far less well than whites on standardized tests. And twelve years later, "after the schools had done their best and their worst," the black's relative position had not much changed, while his absolute handicap had grown enormously.[25] Florida's experience was instructive. Many Florida school districts have been thoroughly desegregated since 1970. In 1978 the State Department of Education administered to high school juniors a basic literacy test, a prerequisite for a high school diploma. Among white students, 24 percent failed math, 3 percent communications. The failure rate for blacks was 77 percent in math, 26 percent in communications.[26] All the predictable allegations of culturally biased tests[27] do little to explain such disheartening disparities.

How wise, one wonders, was *Brown*'s exclusive emphasis on public education? Of course *Brown* had to start somewhere. It never thought to resolve the enormity of racial disadvantage at a single stroke. Thus it began, logically enough, with public schools. Therein lay hope. But because *Brown* spoke to public education, schools would henceforth be the yardstick by which racial progress would be judged. Yet they were always the hardest going. Parents were most protective when it came to offspring. The very hope of the schools—the new day in the offing—caused old sentiments, north and south, to harden fast. There were always alternatives of personal avoidance: private schooling and movement to the suburbs. Cynics, in fact, came to define "integration" as "the period between the time the first Negroes move in and the last whites move out."[28] And there were the strategies of subterfuge—school closings, fund cut-offs, pupil-placement boards, tuition grants, freedom-of-choice plans, altered attendance zones and school-district boundaries, after which courts had chased, one by one, in impatient perpetuity. Even where integration was achieved, there were all manner and means of tracking and curriculum placements by which it might be undone.

Thus, inevitably, there was periodic lamentation over horizons never reached. In the South, by 1970 the most integrated region of the country,[29] the principle of school segregation had been broken. But "in large urban areas of the country, North and South . . . ," noted Harvard Law Professor Derrick Bell in 1975, "public schools today are more racially segregated than they were in 1954, and . . . the barriers to desegregation, for all practical purposes, are virtually insurmountable."[30] How much, he asked, "of the unfinished burden may realistically be apportioned to a judicial precedent [*Brown*] grown old before its time in the service of a worthy but still unfulfilled cause."[31] There were those who insisted, despite all the obstacles, that the old cause plug on. "We have suffered too many heartaches and shed too much blood in fighting the evil of racial segregation," said Roy Wilkins, "to return . . . to the lonely and dispiriting confines of its demeaning prison."[32] The talk at the table, as they say, was sad. Was not the whole irony of *Brown*'s dream now apparent? Schools, "the great equalizers of the conditions of men," would prove the most difficult egalitarian conquest of them all.

In following the NAACP's own lawyers and social scientists, the Court in *Brown* dealt blacks an unwitting slight. Even if school facilities were equal, *Brown* had held, blacks were still being deprived.[33] Separate, *Brown* emphasized, was *inherently* unequal. If this holding on the surface buoyed black morale, its undercurrents, in time, just as certainly depressed it. For *Brown* implied first, that black schools, whatever their physical endowments, could not equal white ones; second, that integration was a matter of a white benefactor and a black beneficiary. Events in the aftermath of *Brown* were even more insensitive. Progress was measured in HEW statistics by how many blacks entered the promised land of white classrooms. "In 1964," Secretary Caspar Weinberger announced, "about two percent of the black students in the 11-state South were in school with white students. Today [1974], more than 90% of the black students are in school with whites."[34] The whole gamut of integrationist ideals—from *Brown* to busing to affirmative action—would incorporate this same condescending assumption: that contact with whites was necessary for black students to improve.

Brown need not have been interpreted in that way. It may have intended only that in a land of white majorities, minority schools are not likely to be treated equally. Or that state-imposed, not self-imposed, separation was the evil. Or that integration would permit each child to find his own individual level of achievement regardless of race. But patronizing overtones undeniably existed. By the mid-1960s, blacks predictably reacted. Black Africa, not white America, became the referent. 'Black Power' replaced the old slogan, "We Shall Overcome." Traditional black leaders would have none of it. Kenneth Clark labeled the new black power, or separatism, "an imitation of white racism,"[35] while Bayard Rustin saw in it a threat "to ravage the entire civil rights movement."[36] Though it never enlisted mass support, black power was broadly felt, a menace to whites in its cresting wave of violence, but a salve to black identity and pride.

Black Power resisted comprehension. Its leaders—Stokely Carmichael, H. Rap Brown, Huey Newton, Bobby Seale, Eldridge Cleaver—were fed by the media, and pampered by the fashionably guilty in the North. At the same time, Black Power's threatened violence and proclaimed separatism neatly assisted Richard Nixon's southern strategy.[37] Its cutting edge was boastfully black, its fringes genocidally anti-white: "Young black men," it warned, "are learning [in Vietnam] the most modern techniques for killing —techniques which may be used against *any* enemy. . . . The issue finally rests with the black masses. When the servile men and women stand up, we had all better duck."[38]

Militant separatists demanded a black "Republic of New Africa," carved out of five southern states, and the flying of the black, red, and green flag over "liberated" black schools. Others sought black control of inner-city politics, education, health and welfare programs, and the establishment of black studies in higher education.[39] Black clothing, hairstyles, speech, and handshakes became the vogue, wherein "black people will set their own standards of beauty, conduct, and accomplishment."[40]

School integration remained the separatists' *bête blanche*. Full integration meant "full assimilation . . . [E]ven if it [integration] should somehow be achieved, its price might be the total absorption and disappearance of the [black] race—a sort of painless genocide."[41] Whether it was frustration in achieving integration or the cultural engulfment it threatened was not the point. There had developed among blacks a countercurrent to *Brown*, a challenge to integrationist policies of traditional Negro leaders, a rebuke of sorts to those black student pioneers who less than a decade earlier had risked white wrath to seek *Brown*'s promise in the public schools. In the late 1950s there had been only segregationists to fight. By the late 1960s the progeny of *Brown* had been assailed at both ends: by white and black in mutual anger and frustration.

Today, some dust has settled. Black rage may have ebbed, but not before leaving its mark. Blacks are not all determined to seek integration at all costs. They are hardly of one mind on the whole subject of the schools; indeed, they never had been. "There are some blacks—although a minority—," wrote Derrick Bell, "who reject school integration as worthless educationally and dangerous politically. Others, including many civil rights leaders, believe that *Brown* intended school integration, and no other remedy is conceivable. A majority, however, probably . . . [favor] continuing to work for school integration, but [recognize] the barrier to this goal posed by white flight." In the future, Bell believed, "flexibility of approach" would be crucial in achieving equal educational opportunity. "The principles of *Plessy* v. *Ferguson* as well as *Brown* v. *Board of Education* can be used effectively. No approach should be discarded, and few should be universally embraced."[42] Thus the past not only refused to die, but oddly gained new life. *Plessy*—once the scourge of blacks in America—might now be summoned to service, to ensure black schools their rightful share of public funds.

A quarter century after *Brown*, the school problem is far—very far—from being settled. We are yet too close to *Brown* and too little versed in the new phenomenon of school integration to understand it properly. Are present problems a symptom of a time of transition or an ominous expression of some more permanent malaise? From today's perspective, there is little to do but guess and hope.

However beneficial integrated schooling proves to be in time, it has not been the "quick fix" for America's racial problem. The strands of inequality, we do know, are so complex, so interwoven, so ingrained, that they may be with us forever, or stricken only in the long, long haul. While we are close to *Brown*, we are also distant enough to make its simple homilies on public education amusingly obsolete, were it not for the sadness of good hope lost. Sadder still when that hope had been three hundred years in gestation.

Brown's emphasis on public schools obscured much of its own true significance. To look only at schools is to see, in part, the evidence of failure. Much of *Brown*'s meaning lay outside schools, in the groundwork it laid for a massive attack upon Jim Crow itself. Before *Brown*, "enforced separation of Negroes and whites, the

American precursor of South African apartheid, was common."[43] After *Brown*, public beaches and buses, golf courses and parks, courtrooms and prison cell-blocks began to open to black and white alike.[44] *Brown* was the catalyst that shook up Congress and culminated in the two major Civil Rights acts of the century, one opening restaurants, hotels, and job opportunities to blacks, the other making black voters a new southern and national political force.[45] Finally, there was in *Brown* the spirit that altered daily dealings of the races so profoundly, that displaced the indignities of caste with new respect. "A whole generation," reported the Washington *Post* in 1974, "has been born, grown up, and gone to college without having seen a restroom door marked 'white' and 'colored.' "[46] All this, and more, might pass unnoticed amidst the unresolved fate of integrated public education.

It may seem unfair to criticize *Brown* for false hopes and flawed perceptions. Here, one might contend, is a decision that should be forgiven its shortcomings. Yet it was *Brown*, after all, that shaped the nation's outlook on race through the Second Reconstruction. Because it was not just the first event, but also the most memorable, *Brown* defined the race issue and became, for a time, the nation's spectacles. Because *Brown* focused upon public schools, America would also. And because *Brown* viewed racism as it existed primarily in the South, race would henceforth be, until events incontestably proved otherwise, a southern problem.

Of the four appeals consolidated in *Brown* v. *Board of Education*, two were from states outside the South, Delaware and Kansas.[47] The companion case to *Brown*, *Bolling* v. *Sharpe*,[48] was from the District of Columbia. But no one doubted where *Brown* was targeted. The segregation condemned was that as practiced in the South; of the seventeen states with laws permitting or requiring segregated schools at the time of *Brown*, eleven were from the old Confederacy. *Brown* and its progeny long indulged the fiction that the only condemnable racism was that which existed openly, in law. Many years later, the Court would still pretend concern only with those states that "deliberately operated . . . a governmental policy to separate pupils in schools solely on the basis of race. That was what *Brown* v. *Board of Education* was all about."[49]

"The Supreme Court had set the stage," wrote Carl Rowan in 1957. "The Nation and the world could wait to see whether Herman Talmadge [the racially conservative governor of Georgia] or Jonathan Daniels [the moderate editor of the Raleigh *News and Observer*] spoke for the American South. . . ."[50] For "in a very fundamental sense, . . ." wrote one *New York Times* reporter, "the historic [*Brown*] decision on school integration is a blow at the heart of the Southern way of life. The whole social, economic, and political structure of the region has been cemented with the mortar of the Negro's subordinate status. . . . Political dynasties have been built upon it. . . . Even churches and community social arrangements have been geared to the central fact of the Negro's fixed position. For many Southerners the emotional stake is all-important. Sanctioning an inferior status for the Negro guarantees ego fulfillment for every white person, however lowly otherwise."[51]

Racism, then, was the South's burden. Books abounded whose titles—*Go South to Sorrow, The Deep South Says Never*—bespoke their content. Northern writers relished the repulsively quotable leaders of the White Citizens' Councils: "If we submit to this unconstitutional, judge-made integration law, the malignant powers of atheism, communism and mongrelization will surely follow, not only in our Southland but throughout our nation. . . . Mississippi is considered a poor state in cash values. Yet we have only one known Communist, the best record of any state in the Union. . . . We are certainly not ashamed of our traditions, our conservative beliefs, nor our segregated way of life."[52] And the self-flagellation of southern moderates was duly recorded by northern visitors: "We are a sick people, we Southerners," a young white newspaperman is quoted as saying. "We are in America, but not of it. We can see justice and recognize it at a distance, but we cannot embrace it."[53] Even the reply volleys—*The Southern Case for School Segregation* and *The Case For The South*—only reinforced the view that racism was the Southerner's sin.[54]

It is worthwhile to ask why the Court and the country were certain this was so. For one thing, there was history, which seemed, on the surface, to be repeating itself. "Students of Negro life in America have enjoyed some rare opportunities over the last dozen or so years," wrote C. Vann Woodward in 1967. "As if adopting the techniques of cinema, history has obligingly thrown in a succession of flashbacks or replays of hauntingly familiar lines, encounters, whole episodes from the past."[55] The chief flashback, of course, was that of the First Reconstruction, when the South had been lectured on its treatment of the Negro. But the lesson had too soon been forgotten. Now *Brown* signaled a resumption of historical roles. Changes wrought North and South in the intervening century were conveniently brushed aside. It was high time, thought many Americans, for school to begin anew.

But more than just history underlay the southern assumption. In 1950 the South was still the region where Negroes were most concentrated. Mississippi, "the most racist state," had the highest percentage of Negroes (almost 50 percent); the South generally had a 22.5 percent black population, compared to a 10 percent black population in the nation as a whole.[56] And the South discriminated most visibly, in state statutes and constitutions. The South, moreover, held segregation a matter of high principle. Thus, it posed the issue in the most absolute and unabashed way: no Negro, however gifted, in any white school. And the nation responded gullibly by believing racism a simple matter of dusting off southern statute books. Indeed, the notions that racism was a southern problem and that it could be easily eliminated went hand-in-hand. "Segregation," noted one observer, "was seen as a simple denial of access to be eliminated, rather than as an intricate negative process for which an affirmative process, no less intricate, needed to be substituted. If only the South could be stopped from carrying out actions that were impermissible in the rest of the nation—so the reasoning went—the basic problem would be solved."[57]

The bare-fisted nature of the South's opposition further confirmed this national view. Some Southerners, led by a gritty band of newspaper editors,[58] recognized segregation's immorality and sought its demise. But theirs were not generally the voices the nation heard. For the South beat a chant of defiance, not just in the rantings of its demagogues but in the maneuverings of its statesmen, whose interpositionist bent survived from the days of John C. Calhoun. Yet resistance to *Brown* might have been tolerated, were it not for a mean streak in the South's opposition. "There was an unforgettable scene . . ." wrote Alexander Bickel, "in one CBS newscast from New Orleans, of a white mother fairly foaming at the mouth with the effort to rivet her distracted little boy's attention and teach him how to hate. And repeatedly, the ugly, spitting curse, NIGGER! The effect, achieved on an unprecedented number of people with unprecedented speed, must have been something like what used to happen to individuals . . . at the sight of an actual slave auction. . . ."[59]

But there was something beyond history and demography, beyond the commitment to complete segregation, that comforted Americans of 1954 in the southern assumption. That was the knowledge that the South was unique, as different from the rest of America as some exotic tropical land. In fact, Southerners themselves believed this. "Now and then, . . ." wrote W. J. Cash in *The Mind of the South*, "there have arisen people, usually journalists or professors, to tell us that it is all a figment of the imagination, that the South really . . . is distinguishable from New England or the Middle West only by such matters as the greater heat and the presence of a larger body of Negroes. Nobody, however, has ever taken them seriously. And rightly."[60]

Because the South was, by consensus, not wholly nationalized, Southerners were presumed capable of behavior from which right-thinking Americans would shrink. Wrote Howard Zinn in *The Southern Mystique:* "There is considered to be . . . something special about the quality of the white Southerner's prejudice. The Yankee is rather businesslike in his matter-of-fact exclusion of the Negro from certain spheres of ordinary living. The British imperialist was haughty and sure of himself. But the violence, the passion, the murderous quality of the white Southerner's feeling against the Negro has become a canon of American thought that is deep in our consciousness and our literature. . . ."[61]

The notion of southern distinctiveness indeed flourished in academic and literary communities before and shortly after *Brown*. Writers as diverse as William Faulkner, the novelist,[62] John Dollard, the sociologist,[63] Gunnar Myrdal, the social economist,[64] and Charles Black, the lawyer,[65] all found relations between the races the core element of the separate South. "The race issue, . . ." V. O. Key, Jr. concluded in his classic study, *Southern Politics*, "must be considered as the number one problem on the southern agenda. Lacking a solution for it, all else fails."[66] But for many Southerners segregation was the solution, a comforting, perpetual, identifying landmark. Resolution of that issue, on others' terms, threatened the regional identity they cherished most. "The threat of becoming 'indistinguishable,' of being submerged under a national steamroller," wrote Professor Woodward, "has haunted the mind of the South for a long time."[67] More than drawled speech or downed bourbon, more than one-party politics or one-crop agriculture, segregation appeared to define the southern way.

The premise of *Brown* was the South's distinctive moral deficiency. *Brown*, and many successor opinions,[68] proceeded unquestioningly from this premise. *Brown*, it is true, accused no one. It hardly needed to, to make its point. All America knew where enforced separation was the norm, and thus where culpability lay. Yet when suddenly the South began to look less unique, the nation was ill-prepared for what now seem, with the help of hindsight, rather commonplace revelations.

So embedded was southern imagery in the nation's mind that when the race problem moved north early in the 1960s, it still had to be explained in southern terms. Thus the titles of articles in the *New York Times Magazine* such as " 'The South' in the North"[69] or " 'Mason-Dixon Line' in Queens."[70] Recognition of a national racial problem struck northern intellectuals in different ways. "In a sense," wrote Anthony Lewis in 1964, "it should not be disturbing that all the country is now engaged in the race problem. The pretense that the problem existed only in the South was just that, a pretense, and it is better to have the truth out, however painful it is."[71] In others, the thought was less charitably conceived. "What we are beginning to perceive," Yale Law Professor Louis Pollak explained, "is that, although the Deep South has had longer and more extensive training in bigotry than the rest of the nation, no region lacks an aptitude for bigotry."[72]

It took the first long hot summer of 1964, with riots in Paterson, Elizabeth, and Jersey City, New Jersey; Chicago, Philadelphia, Rochester, and New York to bring full public awareness that race tensions ran nationwide. The riots, of course, resulted from the biggest racial change since the First Reconstruction: namely, the great migration of rural southern Negroes to the cities of the North.[73] In 1900, more than half of all American Negroes lived in the rural South; by 1960 almost three out of four blacks lived in urban areas, many in the West and North.[74] But the new national awareness, in the wake of the riots, did not create new national unity on matters of race. Many in the North cursed the South that year for having created the problem in the first place; many Southerners delighted at the sudden discomfort up North. And in between was the Negro, still the outsider.

Black Americans had journeyed north since the century's beginnings—chased first by the boll weevil and later by the mechanization of agriculture—to work in northern cities, especially in times of industrial prosperity or of war.[75] But theirs had also been a voyage of hope: to the land of Lincoln that might welcome them, provide them with a decent-paying job, and homes in the cities, where a black didn't have to stand aside for white folks, and the sheriff wouldn't shove him if he so much as looked suspicious. To the Negro in the Mississippi Delta, the North was simply the place "up there where it's better."[76] In eastern North Carolina, that state's black belt, Negroes boarded a northbound train called the "Chickenbone Special," because many young travelers, freshly out of high school, carried picnic lunches of fried chicken with them.[77] Ahead for those young blacks stretched a land of deliverance and opportunity, thankfully "far from the old folks at home."

But matters did not work out as hoped. The North was no sanctuary either. Even the meager solace of the land left behind was lost. "I never see a tree or hear a chicken or see a bird," lamented one black woman who had migrated to Boston from the South. "The other day I woke up dreaming there were some chickens running through my house, and of course it was the old place, down there." Gradually, blacks who stayed south felt less left out. "Now my brother [in Chicago] says *I'm* the one who is lucky," one Alabama black remarked in 1967. "I live poorer down here, but up there they don't live at all. They have more money than we can get down here, but they're packed tight into the buildings and they can't do anything, not even dream of going North, the way I do when it gets rough. It's bad, real bad; and they hate it."[78]

Black discontent made itself known. And Northerners began to discover in themselves an attitudinal racism that might exist with or without legal sanction. In one sense, attitudinal racism was not as openly degrading as apartheid in the South. In another sense it was much worse, because it was not easily remedied by law or even ascertainable. But it was pervasive: parents, teachers, employers, landlords, officials practiced it, to the staggering cumulative detriment of the northern black. Often it was even practiced unawares. For example, the old expression, "We're all the same inside"—a symbol of enlightened thought in the fifties—was seen by the mid-sixties as subtly racist because being "the same inside" implied something different—and wrong—about blacks on the outside.[79]

In other respects northern and southern racism proved different. "There is a current folk-saying," observed one article in the *New York Times Magazine*, "that in the South white people don't mind how close a Negro gets to them as long as he doesn't rise too high (economically or socially), while in the North white people don't mind how high a Negro rises as long as he doesn't get too close."[80] The folk-saying, of course, flatters the Southerner's boast of inter-racial amity. But in some respects the races in the South were closer than in the North after the Negro's great migration. Greater intimacy owed to longer experience of each race with the other and to the South's more rural character.[81] Farm life might mean shared chores and shared adversity. Even residential segregation was imperfect in the southern countryside; on the dirt road leading to the "main house" one often passed black tenant shacks along the way. Though small towns of the South also had their neglected "colored sections,"[82] they and white areas were often not so very distant. Finally, there was the intimate tradition of domestic service—from the "house slave" to the "maid"—on which Negroes in the South had a virtual monopoly.[83] Yet, alas, intimacy had its limits. Segregation, in fact, was devised to relieve the hazards of excessive propinquity, to enforce distance artificially, in case naturally there might appear none.

The North had its own way of distancing the Negro, all without segregation statutes. In the North, the barrier was housing, potentially the most effective of all. For if the races lived apart, then separation in other phases of life (schools, for instance) could be expected to follow. Housing was a spectacle of never-ending flight, expressed by one Chicago suburban housewife: "We moved to Deerfield from Glencoe—some call it Glencohen now, you know—to get away from the Jews, and now here we are with the Negro problem in our lap."[84]

What accounts for white flight in metropolitan America? What explains the large number of upper- and middle-income blacks still excluded from the suburbs?[85] Many whites saw the problem merely as one of economics. When blacks arrived, property values would be expected to plummet, and, of course, whites had to leave before the bottom fell out. Thus suburbs mobilized against black intrusion. Zoning laws directing minimum lot and yard requirements, street frontage and setback distances, and restrictions on apartments were all erected. And where the zoning ordinances left off, felt the black, the rental agent, the real estate broker, or the credit agency was around to take over.[86] Later, whites resisted public housing projects, those great transporters of the ghetto to the suburb. "Nearly everyone's against anything that smacks of a project," a resident of Bedford in New York's Westchester County explained. "A project is a project is a project."[87]

The result was that the northern black remained mostly where he first arrived: in the inner-city ghetto. And the story of Negro distress in our century will be told in the schools of the South and the tenements of the North. Not that they were the whole problem, only its symbols: the one-room frame schoolhouse of the rural mid-century South with its dirt floor, splintered benches, small pot-bellied stove, and underpaid black teacher imploring underclad black children of all ages with their eyes off yonder and their notebooks, of necessity, in their laps; and the Boston slum apartment "in a building," wrote Robert Coles, "that has been condemned again and again for its rats, its faulty plumbing and heating systems, its poorly lighted halls, its garbage-strewn yard that takes up the slack when two—exactly two—cans become filled with the refuse of 10 families."[88] Of the two, housing would prove the more stubborn. A chief irony of *Brown* was that the northern (or, more accurately, urban) ill of residential segregation would come to vex the Supreme Court more than racism in its pristine form, as practiced by the rural South.

The discovery of race prejudice in the North had one further bizarre effect. "The other America," Michael Harrington had written in 1962, "the America of poverty, is hidden today in a way that it never was before. Its millions are socially invisible to the rest of us."[89] When suddenly and violently in the mid-sixties, those millions became visible, northern reaction was sharply paradoxical. For some, the ghetto eruptions brought only a stiffening resolve not to associate with the Negro in any way. To that extent, the white Southerner's desire to avoid integrated contacts achieved perverse empathy.

Yet many a northern liberal became so distraught at the blight of the ghetto that the South, on which all America once kept watch, was suddenly overlooked. "[T]he southern black is out of fashion," complained Yale Law Professor Charles Black in 1970. "It is the unspoken assumption, at least in the circles wherein I move, that all human wrong is in the northern urban centers. The very word 'concerned' is a term of art, meaning 'concerned with northern urban racial problems.' To talk about the South is to be a bore."[90] "Who gives a damn about the South any more? . . ." regretted Willie Morris, that moving chronicler of Mississippi travail and triumph. "Back in the days of the Movement, that lost, lyrical time of innocence when the better part of the nation saw integration as the goal and fulfillment of our deepest impulses as a people, the South had once again been the symbol of our ills, the terrain on which to fight our noblest battles."[91] By 1970 for whatever reason—the greater urgency of the ghetto, fresh doubts about integration on the part of both races, the new Nixon administration's accommodating southern strategy, or just plain old fatigue—the South, like some distant planet in rotation, passed quietly, once again, from the nation's eye.

What *Brown* initiated, then, was a view of American race relations that from the outset was sectional in character. Like a serpent threading its course through our national body, racism was first southern, then northern, but never sufficiently an American dilemma that the different regions might together work to overcome. After *Brown* race was seldom approached by Americans as one national problem, but rather through regional hypocrisy and recrimination. It was hardly a courageous or forthright way to address a nation's most persistent moral ill. And yet, perhaps the sectionalism was oddly necessary. Northern opinion and the federal government might never have responded, save in the self-delusion that it was dealing with a southern problem. A sectionalist outlook was necessary to make the Freedom Rides and Mississippi summers the glorious crusades that, to many, they were.

For all its universality, *Brown* v. *Board of Education* was very much a period piece. It both borrowed from and lent to the narrow national perspectives of its time. The Court, in *Brown* and sequel cases, failed in important respects to broaden the nation's vision or to alert the country to the pitfalls of continuing in those assumptions in which it was once upon a time so comfortably engaged. Eventually the nation learned—on its own—that public schools were not the panacea and that the problem existed beyond the South. But it learned at the high cost of dashed hopes and dreams, a cost we are paying still.

PART II
Southern School Desegregation, 1955–1970

4

"All Deliberate Speed"

A Negro child—let us call her Mary Jones—entering first grade that fall of 1954 probably had her thoughts elsewhere than on *Brown* v. *Board of Education*. Whatever she might have heard about *Brown* was less absorbing than her new teacher and schoolmates and the novel environment of the school-yard. And it was just as well. This noisy crowd of children would be together for years to come, adding and subtracting, reading and writing, studying maps and pictures of faraway lands. Twelve years later, at graduation, some of Mary Jones's first grade friends would still be standing beside her. Chances were, however, there would be no white faces among them. And chances were, too, that the best jobs or colleges did not await them. But they would scatter all the same, many for whatever labor the northern metropolises might hold. Because as Mary Jones and her friends would begin to sense more fully with each passing year, *Brown* v. *Board of Education* had scarcely mattered. A generation of black schoolchildren in the South—Mary Jones's generation—had grown up and graduated after *Brown* in segregated schools.

Where during this time, one might ask, was the United States Supreme Court? And the answer, not much exaggerated, is that from 1955 to 1968, the Court abandoned the field of public school desegregation. Its pronouncements were few,[1] given the proportions of the problem. And its leadership was almost nonexistent. The question of history is whether the Court's low profile can ever be adequately justified.

The next two chapters discuss the Supreme Court's approach to southern school integration in the years after *Brown*. It is not a conventional discussion, in part because the school cases were not conventional decisions. There did, of course, develop over time a set of constitutional principles concerning school desegregation. But the principles themselves were often creations of events beyond the courtroom: the South reacted to Court rulings, the Court, in turn, responded to the South. No set of cases, in fact, better illustrates the non-jurisprudential side of the Supreme Court's job. In one sense, the school cases are moral statements. No single decision has had more moral force than *Brown;* few struggles have been morally more significant than the one for the racial integration of American life. Yet school desegregation also may be the most political item on the Court's agenda. The outcome has affected the lives of many millions of Americans; success for the Court's position has depended mightily on the balance of political support; the management of public schools has traditionally been a local political prerogative; and the nature of desegregation remedies was perforce discretionary and hence political.

There were, in fact, two *Brown* decisions: the 1954 case declaring segregation unconstitutional and a 1955 case addressing how that declaration would be implemented. Interestingly, both *Brown* decisions eschewed legal reasoning for their ultimate authority: *Brown I* expressed itself as a short moral statement, *Brown II* as a yet briefer pragmatic reality growing out of *Brown I*. Thus, examining the wisdom of the Court's approach to race and education in the South must require more than legal analysis alone.

The 1954 *Brown* decision, in most unusual fashion, refrained from setting forth a remedy or issuing a remand. Instead, because of the "wide applicability" and "considerable complexity" of the school cases, the question of how desegregation was to be accomplished was postponed until the following term.[2] Because of the death of Justice Robert Jackson and grumblings of southern Senators over the appointment of John Harlan as his replacement, oral argument on *Brown II* did not begin until April 11, 1955. Integration, the NAACP's lawyers insisted, must begin at once in the affected localities, preferably in September 1955 but in no event later than September 1956. What the Court had declared, Negro children must exercise—not tomorrow or the next day, but now. "They are graduating every day," as Thurgood Marshall put it. Then " 'gradual' has no place in your thinking as far as the decree is concerned?" asked Mr. Justice Reed. That's correct, Marshall in effect replied.[3]

But the South sought a gradualism with infinity as the deadline. Representatives of six former Confederate states were heard by the Court, an exercise not without redundancy. The South's object was to frighten the Court into caution. Immediate integration, Attorney General J. Lindsay Almond of Virginia warned darkly, would be "provocative of unending chaos, engendering of racial bitterness, strife and possible circumstances more dire."[4] A similar message was less delicately delivered by Archibald Robertson, a tough, veteran litigator from a leading Virginia law firm. "Negroes constitute 22 percent of the population of Virginia," Robertson informed the Court, "but 78 percent of all cases of syphilis and 83 percent of all cases of gonorrhea occur among the Negroes. . . . Of course the incidence of disease and illegitimacy is just a drop in the bucket compared to the promiscuity[;] . . . the white parents at this time will not appropriate the money to put their children among other children with that sort of a background."[5]

On May 31, 1955, a full fifty-four weeks after the initial *Brown* decision, the Court spoke to its implementation. *Brown II*[6] demonstrated, if demonstration were ever needed, the vast political potential of American courts of law. A unanimous Court, speaking briefly almost soothingly, through its Chief Justice in language laymen could understand, sought to cajole the South, not to overrun it. The function of law was to persuade and mediate, not to dictate or demand. And acquiescence need not be immediate; *Brown II* set no definite date for desegregation to occur. There was only that final, capping phrase: black plaintiffs must be admitted to public schools on a racially nondiscriminatory basis "with all deliberate speed."[7] In the grand tradition of politics, there was in that phrase something for everyone. "Speed" was promised the long-denied Negro. And the South was permitted to "deliberate," to move, as was its wont, in the fullness of time.

The real political feat of *Brown II* came in saying one thing and meaning another. Desegregation might not be accomplished right away, the Court announced, because of "problems related to administration," such as the physical conditions of the schools, the school transportation system, personnel problems, and the revision of school district boundaries and local laws.[8] Yet this greatly exaggerated the logistics of conversion, which, by themselves, posed no insurmountable problem. All that had to be done in most of the South was to divide the existing school population into geographic rather than racial groupings.[9] Though geographic zoning invites the gerrymander and would not achieve much integration in areas segregated residentially, it certainly would have put pupil assignments on a nonracial basis and thus in compliance with the original *Brown* decision. Indeed, this was precisely the course of action the Court suggested, at least for rural areas, thirteen years later.[10] *Brown II*'s deference to administrative difficulties thus seems all the more curious; where constitutional rights hang in the balance, the Court has often dismissed administrative convenience as an insufficient state concern.[11]

There had to be, then, some other reason for the patient tenor of the *Brown II* opinion. And that was, as even the least artful soul might guess, the continued prospect of southern obstruction. Yet the Court in *Brown II* insisted otherwise. "[I]t should go without saying," observed Chief Justice Warren, "that the vitality of these constitutional principles cannot be allowed to yield simply because of disagreement with them."[12] But that was precisely why they were yielding, because to whites in a large section of the country, those principles were not acceptable.

Not surprisingly, the South was audibly relieved by *Brown II*, a victory of sorts snatched from the total defeat of only a year ago. It was, as the New Orleans *Times-Picayune* noted, "pretty much what the Southern attorneys in general had asked for."[13] The Tampa *Tribune* was moved to lurid compliment: "The Court's wisdom, we think, will dissipate the thunderhead of turmoil and violence which had been gathering in Southern skies since the Court held school segregation unconstitutional a year ago. . . ."[14] *Brown II*'s sole discernable shortcoming in southern eyes lay in its not having repealed *Brown I*.

But in all other particulars, the opinion did humor the South. Despite its disclaimer, *Brown II* implied that local resistance might, indeed, delay desegregation. For the Court thrice suggested that varied local problems and obstacles might require a varied pace of school desegregation,[15] an encouragement to volatile racial feelings in rural, black belt communities in every southern state. But it was the identity of those to whom the Court now handed over the problem that most delighted the South. Local school authorities would bear primary responsibility for dismantling segregation, subject to supervision by local federal district judges. "We couldn't ask for anything better," exulted attorney Tom J. Tubb of West Point, Mississippi, "than to have our local, native Mississippi federal district judges consider [the integration problem]. . . . Our local judges know the local situation and it may be 100 years before it's feasible."[16] Better still, the "hometown" boys were left virtually without guidance. All they were told was to go forward in the spirit of equity, which "has been characterized," said the Court, "by a practical flexibility in shaping its remedies and by a facility for adjusting and reconciling public and private needs."[17]

The paradox of *Brown II* was that its words summoned forth the South's nobler instincts, even as its implications indulged its darker, more violent side. If Southerners—school boards and local judges—bore responsibility for desegregation, so the hope went, the South would meet the challenge on its own, just as the border states had in the preceding year. How that hope miscarried is one of the saddest stories in American history. Sad for the Court, sad for the South, saddest of all for the schoolchildren affected.

For the segregationist South held out even longer than its Civil War predecessor. As late as 1962, not a single Negro attended white schools or colleges in Mississippi, Alabama, or South Carolina.[18] By 1964—one decade after *Brown*—a scant 2.3 percent of southern blacks were enrolled in desegregated schools.[19] That was hardly what the Court had wished or anticipated. "*Brown* never contemplated," wrote Justice Arthur Goldberg in 1963, "that the concept of 'deliberate speed' would countenance indefinite delay in elimination of racial barriers in schools. . . ."[20] Even Southerners on the Court had lost patience. "There has been entirely too much deliberation and not enough speed" in complying with *Brown*, Justice Black wrote for the Court in 1964.[21] Indeed, the adjective of *Brown II*'s famous phrase had become more operative than the noun.

The mounting impatience of the Court's rhetoric served only to unmask its own prior miscalculations. Many insisted that the Court had only itself to blame for southern foot-dragging. "I cannot ac-

quit the Court of having made a terrible mistake in its 1955 'all deliberate speed' formula," Professor Charles Black observed. "There
was just exactly no reason, in 1955, for thinking it would work better than an order to desegregate at once."[22] "In deciding to oversee
the pace of desegregation," agreed Robert Carter, "which was what
Brown II entailed, the Warren Court took upon itself an unnecessary responsibility for the South's failure to respond."[23]

To Loren Miller, a former NAACP vice-president, "[t]he harsh
truth [was] that the first *Brown* decision was a great decision; the
second *Brown* decision was a great mistake. . . . [C]hange," contended Miller, "would have been gradual in any event. Negroes
habituated to segregation would have moved slowly. As the chosen
instrument of Negroes seeking change, the NAACP lacked financial resources and manpower to proceed in any other than a gradual
manner, district by district. . . . [I]t could not have wrought a
revolution."[24] Delay would have been present anyway, Professor
Black agreed, "for many specious evasive schemes—'pupil assignment,' fictionally 'private' schools, 'freedom of choice,' 'tracking,'
'gerrymandering,' and so on—had to go through litigation."[25]

Had the Court been determined, however, it might have shortened both the litigation and the desegregation process: by setting a
fixed date for integration to take place,[26] by approving only those
plans that resulted in substantial integration, by requiring that desegregation proceed in certain ways (for example, through pairing
of schools or geographical zoning), by excusing black plaintiffs from
state administrative remedies, by permitting the joinder of state defendants (because southern segregation statutes at the time of *Brown*
were of statewide effect), by consolidating appeals, and by summarily reversing laggard district judges and generously supporting active ones. Indeed, from 1968 to 1970, the Court took just such a
forward course, with stunning effect.[27] As it was, the Court in
1955 seemed content to let litigation act both as a time of catharsis
and a period of adjustment in which the inevitability of at least
some integration would slowly sink in.

For its caution, some have argued, the Court paid a terrible
price. Normally, constitutional rights may be exercised at once.
Yet *Brown II*, insisted Professor Black, "asked of the laity an understanding of which lawyers are scarcely capable—an understanding
that something could be unlawful, while it was nevertheless lawful
to continue it for an indefinite time."[28] For the Court, argued

Black, to declare a constitutional right and then in this one instance to so postpone its enjoyment was to do more than mistreat the black man; it was to undermine in the eyes of all Americans respect for fundamental law. Yet respect for law is equally undermined when it overshoots human capacities to adjust. For the Court to have issued decrees the public thought abrupt and disruptive, that the political branches were reluctant to support, and that the South might successfully evade, defy, and, in the end, ignore would visibly have diminished the authority of law and the standing of the Court.

But, perhaps it was *Brown II* that invited "white dissent and obstruction,"[29] a theme Dr. Kenneth Clark had sounded only shortly before. "In practice," Clark contended, "[*Brown II*] seems to have led to more rather than to less disruption. . . . [P]rompt, decisive action on the part of recognized authorities usually results in less anxiety and less resistance [than] a more hesitant and gradual procedure. It is similar to the effect of quickly pulling off adhesive tape—the pain is sharper but briefer and hence more tolerable."[30]

The most apoplectic indictment of *Brown II* came in 1968 from one Lewis M. Steel, an associate counsel of the NAACP. In fact, Steel's charges were so controversial that he was promptly fired from the NAACP's legal staff, which thereupon resigned en masse.[31] Praise for the Warren Court as a liberal institution, Steel insisted, was sadly mistaken. The Court had made clear in *Brown II* that "it was a white court which would protect the interests of white America in the maintenance of stable institutions." *Brown II*, Steel charged, was even "more shameful than the Court's 19th century monuments to apartheid." For by the mid-twentieth century, there was no longer any way segregation could be justified. Nazi Germany had only just been defeated and scientific racism discredited. "[Crimes] against humanity had been defined and punished at Nuremberg. American justices had shown themselves to be capable of harshness when judging another people guilty of ghettoizing and destroying an ethnic group. Their failure to take an equally strong position when reviewing the sins of their own countrymen . . . will long remain a blot on the record of American jurisprudence."[32]

Putting that last to one side, one would like to believe the critics of the second *Brown* decision. The alternative to "deliberate speed," they thought, was a quicker, more moral, and possibly more peaceful way to end segregation and subdue the South. If only the Court had proceeded promptly, the nation might have been spared its ordeal and the Court its dishonor. Whether they were right, of course, will never be known, for theirs was not the road taken. But would it have proved to be the road of wisdom or just another of the pat solutions that overlooked both the complexity of racism and the psychology of the American South?

Arguments can be made that the Court's gradualist judgment in *Brown II* was correct. That while the Court might have been firmer and more definite in laying down guidelines, any head-on challenge of the segregated South in 1955 would have produced civil strife sufficient to make Little Rock and Birmingham seem gatherings of good will. Was it not better to have given the South time to adjust to the inevitable, to understand that closed schools did not attract new industry or prepare children for future citizenship? Better to have set in motion a course of steadily mounting federal pressure, which allowed the South its filibusters and fulminations, but all the while forced private reckonings that Southerners were, after all, a part of the nation and that segregation was not the hallowed good it had been proclaimed to be.

Even the tiniest tear in the fabric of segregation was certain to alarm. The presence of a single black in white southern schools was for some shock treatment. After centuries of caste contact, the offspring of planter and sharecropper were to meet on equal terms and learn to see one another with a different eye. Gradualism, by its nature, set an educative course. The races would first learn to live together in the least stressful, most agreeable circumstances and ease into more intimate, extensive contacts later on. But for integration on a broad scale to succeed, the shoots and buds of the experience had to please. Substantial forced contact at the beginning might generate mutual withdrawal and hostility, hardly the atmosphere for human explorations to begin. Robert Penn Warren put the idea best in a self-interview a year after *Brown II*.

Q: Are you a gradualist on the matter of segregation?

A: If by gradualist you mean a person who would create delay for the sake of delay, then no. If by gradualist you mean a person who thinks it will take time, not time as such, but time for an educational process, preferably a calculated one, then yes. I mean a process of mutual education for whites and blacks. And part of this education should be the actual beginning of the process of desegregation. It's a silly question, anyway, to ask if somebody is a gradualist. Gradualism is all you'll get. History, like nature, knows no jumps. Except the jump backward, maybe.[33]

Professor Bickel advanced a related argument for gradualism, not touched upon by the *Brown II* Court. "[S]ince Negro schools had seldom been fully equal to white ones," he contended, "and since many Negro pupils came from economically and culturally depressed families, differences in educational background and aptitudes would be found between Negro and white children, and allowance might have to be made for these in the process of integration."[34] That proposition presents several difficulties, however, including that of permitting past wrongs against the Negro to excuse present and future delays. Moreover, differences in aptitude would be present whenever blacks first entered white schools, whether in one, five, or twenty years. What reason was there not to face the problem now? "All deliberate speed" may have contemplated that only blacks academically and socially prepared for white schools could enter. But in light of the large numbers of culturally depressed whites already there, that notion also is suspect.

The real argument for "deliberate speed" supposes that the South in 1955 was prepared to resist aggressive judicial action at almost any cost. Some rhetoric, of course, created that impression, just as the predictions of southern attorneys general before the Court in *Brown II* had done. There were also those unable to resist political advantage. "On May 17, 1954," Senator James O. Eastland told constituents at Senatobia, Mississippi, "the Constitution of the United States was destroyed because the Supreme Court disregarded the law and decided integration was right. . . . You are not required to obey any court which passes out such a ruling. In fact, you are obligated to defy it."[35] Such talk, so heavy in the southern air the decade after *Brown*, could hardly be allowed to dictate terms to any court. Its purpose, in part, was to bluff the "federals" to back off. Yet the Court still had to take silent cognizance of the southern mood. Not to have done so would have been foolish. What the Court had to evaluate in the mid-1950s was the extent to which the South's bark presaged its bite.

The experience of the border states was often offered as evidence of integration's achievability in the South. In the year after the first *Brown* decision, the border states had voluntarily taken large strides toward desegregation. "When schools opened in September 1956," wrote Benjamin Muse, "desegregation was far advanced in Missouri and Oklahoma, and in West Virginia public schools remained segregated in only two small counties on the Virginia border. In Delaware, Maryland and Kentucky desegregation was proceeding more slowly, though on a scale which would have looked revolutionary in any of the states farther south. . . . The desegregation accomplishments of Wilmington, Baltimore, Washington, Kansas City, St. Louis, and Louisville demonstrated that peaceful elimination of school segregation in large cities of substantial Negro population was possible. They were hailed as illuminating pilot operations for Southern cities."[36]

Yet the South, most assuredly, was not the border states. There was one overriding difference: the percentage of Negroes in the population. At the time of *Brown*, border state black populations ranged from 6 percent in West Virginia to 17 percent in Maryland. Every southern state, save Texas (13 percent) had a considerably larger percentage of black inhabitants, from Virginia with 22 percent to Mississippi with 45.[37]

But the total number of Negroes in a southern state mattered less than their distribution. The more blacks there were within a given jurisdiction, the more stubborn and resistant were white racial attitudes. In the South, the contiguous bands of coastal or river delta counties with heaviest Negro concentration were known as black belts,[38] partly for their majority black populations and partly for the dark, rich soil that once supported the plantation aristocracy and its slaves. Generally, whites in the black belt possessed political power quite out of proportion to their actual numbers.

Whites in Southside, Virginia, for example—that state's black belt—formed, both in votes and leadership, the backbone of the Byrd machine.[39] In Alabama, one 1957 study reported, "16 Black Belt counties with 13.5 per cent of the state's total population have 27.3 per cent of the House representation and 28.5 per cent of the Senate seats."[40] Similar malapportionment existed in the legislatures of most southern states.[41] Whether black belt influence owed more to the single-mindedness of its convictions, the luxuriant courtliness of its leaders' style, the political status attached to large landholdings, or historical habits of agrarian rule is unclear. But it had forever been clear that the fullest force of black belt influence was reserved for matters of race.[42]

Perhaps this was so because the power of black belt leaders was most directly threatened by the mass of mute Negroes within their own constituencies. "[I]n the southern black belts," V. O. Key noted, "the problem of governance is . . . one of the control by a small, white minority of a huge, retarded colored population."[43] Most dreaded was the prospect of Negro domination in all its forms: political, economic, social, and sexual. If the Negro ever voted his numbers, he might control local office, soak whites with high taxes and assessments, fill white schools with black teachers and principals, form a black police force, and call whites to answer before the law. Thus poll taxes and literacy tests, white primaries, and grandfather clauses had been widely adopted at the turn of the century to make certain the black man never would tell the white man what to do.[44]

But schooling, even more than voting, raised the specter of black rule. The literate Negro was a demanding Negro, asking and getting who knows what. Education did not produce good domestics or farmhands, but only grumblings with one's economic lot. Yet the driving fear was the least rational, and it was social, not economic. The Southerner, wrote *Look* editor William Attwood in 1956, "will tell you that, sooner or later, some Negro boy will be walking his daughter home from school, staying for supper, taking her to the movies . . . and then your Southern friend asks you the inevitable, clinching question: 'Would *you* want your daughter to marry a Nigra? . . .' [S]exual neurosis makes many whites impervious to logic. They are obsessed by the notion that Negroes, given a chance, will take over their women as well as their golf clubs and legislatures."[45]

The whites of the black belt well knew that the burdens of compliance with *Brown* were uneven. Integration, for example, would be least traumatic for the upcountry and mountain counties of the South where Negroes were few. Adjustment would be most difficult where blacks were in the majority. What the black belt feared most was a policy of "rolling surrender," beginning in those areas of slight black population, spreading slowly across the state, and at last leaving the black belt isolated in opposition. Thus opposition to integration had, of necessity, to be rigid and absolute; even gradualism held its special terrors. "[I]ntegration, however slight, anywhere in Virginia, would be a cancer eating at the very life blood of our public school system," insisted Mills Godwin, a state senator from the heart of Virginia's black belt. "The [*Brown*] decision is either right or wrong. If we think it is right, we should accept it without circumvention or evasion. If it is wrong, we should never accept it at all. Men of conscience and principle do not compromise with either right or wrong."[46]

So what, one might ask, if black belt neuroses were obstinately held? How was it that this most extreme faction even of southern opinion came to exert such leverage on national racial policy and force even the Supreme Court to counsels of caution? The answer plumbs further the folkways of southern politics. When a black belt senator rose to address his colleagues, it was often a case of the defiant talking to the only slightly less defiant. Blacks did not have to be the majority in a locality to pose a threat. Even where they lacked the numbers to install black local government, they still might "rule" white politics by playing whites off against one another to win black votes.[47] Literate Negroes, in the black belt or outside it, would want jobs and rights heretofore exclusively white. As for social and sexual contact, well, that took only two. Thus across the post-*Brown* South, apprehension rose. Nowhere in the region did black rights make good white politics. Seldom in the Upper South and almost nowhere in the Deep South did the black man have an open white friend. The most moderate governors, such as Luther Hodges of North Carolina, Frank Clement of Tennessee, LeRoy Collins of Florida, hardly favored integration. Political courage in the late 1950s meant standing for open schools, refusing to sign the Southern Manifesto, or admitting that *Brown*, however hateful, still was the law.[48]

Thus with the black belt purposeful and determined, and opposition meek or nonexistent, one might guess who carried the day. The South after *Brown* closed ranks and turned inward. Tolerance and humanity succumbed to "the cause." "Here, on the surface at least," wrote Harry Ashmore, the editor of the Arkansas *Gazette* in 1959, "the South's oneness shows again. Despite our growing diversity we stand together on this issue, segregation, or pretend to. This is the inner shrine, where the mildest dissent is treason, the one place where that vaunted individuality that is so much a part of the Southern style is denied. No one can know whether the dedicated keepers of the shrine are a majority or in fact a small minority; what we do know is that they exploit a tradition so deep-rooted, and exercise a social sanction so powerful, they have largely silenced, or driven out, all those Southerners . . . who have dared to suggest that the rigid racial status quo would have to yield. . . ."[49]

Rabid segregationists sought, after *Brown*, to hammer "southern opinion into an embattled, unified state of feeling which will brook no compromise."[50] One hypocrisy of massive resistance was that Virginia, which claimed the right to go its own way on segregation, refused to allow its more moderate urban localities to do likewise. "We cannot allow Arlington or Norfolk to integrate," insisted Congressman William Tuck, from the heart of Virginia's black belt and a member of the innermost circle of the Byrd machine. "There is no middle ground, no compromise. We're either for integration or against it and I'm against it. . . . If they won't stand with us then I say make 'em."[51] So together they stood, until massive resistance collapsed under court edicts in the winter of 1959.

Blacks paid a high price in the post-*Brown* South for stepping forward as plaintiffs in school desegregation suits. Sometimes the sanctions were economic, as in Orangeburg, South Carolina: "those Negro plaintiffs . . . who worked for white employers were fired. Those who rented from white landlords were evicted. Those who bought from white merchants and suppliers were denied further credit and asked to settle outstanding accounts at once. Some were no longer able to buy in some places, even for cash."[52] But the sanctions were not all monetary. On occasion, newspapers listed names and addresses of all Negro plaintiffs, an open invitation for shameless elements in the community to work their will.[53]

But the spleen of the South was saved for the white moderate, the ultimate betrayer of his region and his race. The upstart Negro was understood to have been brainwashed by northern agitators and the NAACP; the deviant white could not be so easily explained. As Roy Harris, president of the Citizens' Councils of America, put it to one Florida audience: "We are engaged in the greatest struggle and the greatest crusade in the history of mankind. If you're a white man, then it's time to stand up with us, or black your face and get on the other side."[54] Governor Herman Talmadge of Georgia warned: "Anyone who sells the South down the river, don't let him eat at your table, don't let him trade at your filling station and don't let him trade at your store."[55] The moderate Southerner, noted one observer, "became first an isolated figure, then more and more the subject of comprehensive efforts to silence him. . . . Those who spoke out in opposition were pasted with the labels of 'traitor' and 'nestfouler,' 'Red' and 'nigger lover' and coveter of 'Yankee dollars.' The device was greatly effective."[56] Dissenting books as well as voices were hounded and pursued. *Time, Life,* and *Look* were banned from high school libraries in several Louisiana parishes. The South Carolina legislature adopted a resolution requesting the State Library Board to remove from circulation "certain books such as *The Swimming Hole* . . . that are inimical to the traditions and customs of our state."[57] The sin of the *The Swimming Hole* lay in illustrations of white and black boys swimming together. "The First Amendment," noted Hodding Carter with some accuracy, "is probably in more danger in the South today than are either our white or Negro children."[58]

With its ranks thus forcibly locked and its loins girded, the South, most especially the Deep South, prepared to do battle. The hopelessness of the struggle only made it the more necessary. "The Southerner's trouble," wrote Harry Ashmore, "in the middle of this disturbed twentieth century may be that too many generations have passed since the South won a victory—that we have rationalized defeat to the point where the hallmark of Southern success is a magnificent failure."[59] For the failure to be magnificent, it must also be proud, principled, protracted, and violent; in the true tradition of "the Southern spirit—that stubborn, defiant, outrageous cussedness that may lead a man into error but never prompts him to prudently count the odds. I think often these days [Ashmore concluded] of Douglas Southall Freeman's story of the ragged, wounded, starving Confederate soldier left on the field for dead after the last fighting before Appomattox. A spruce federal soldier came upon him in a henhouse, where he crouched holding a scrawny chicken by the neck. The Yankee leveled his musket and cried, 'I've got you.' The battered Rebel could still grin through his whiskers and drawl, 'Yes, and what a hell of a git you got.' "[60]

I mention southern stubbornness because it is the only reply possible to critics of "all deliberate speed," who advocated a markedly more aggressive judicial course. It was not hesitancy on the part of the Supreme Court that amplified the volume of southern protest in the years after *Brown*. The impulse of obstruction was too indigenous, too deeply embedded politically, historically, socially, psychologically, economically, sexually, and in every other way. Defiance, and with it some violence, was to any realistic observer a price to be paid for moral progress. The exorcism of so rooted an evil as school segregation would not come free of pain.

The question facing the Supreme Court was how to contain and minimize what was certain to come. There was one way not to contain it. The Court could not march south preaching "integration forthwith" and have the crisis over in one brief but agonizing gasp. The South was accustomed to not winning all right, but not to tame or easy defeat. Thus the Court had to outwit subtly the black belt and its allies. "All deliberate speed" in the hands of southern federal judges meant that tokenism, in one form or another, would provide the alternative to massive resistance for a few years to come. That, the Court sensed, was the safest way to breach the principle. Over time it turned the diehard into an empty and ludicrous posturer, not just in the eyes of his less crazed fellow Southerner but in the eyes of the nation on whom the Court would have to depend for southern compliance. Were school closings and fund cutoffs, standing in the schoolhouse door and drawing lines in the dust, cursings, bombings, and all the warped paraphernalia of diehard histrionics really worth denying a single Negro or tiny clutch of black children admission to white schools? Put that way, the question would come to answer itself. And "all deliberate speed" meant that was the way in which the question would be put. Like the black philosophy of passive nonviolence in the spring days of the Civil Rights movement, "all deliberate speed" outsmarted the South, because "right" in the larger court of public opinion came to be seen increasingly on one side. What the South won, of course, from "all deliberate speed" was time, considerably more than was needed or deserved. Yet had the alternative to massive resistance been massive integration, what sorts of pitched struggles might have ensued?

But suppose that "all deliberate speed" was the least disruptive and most persuasive way of beating the segregated South. The question still remains why courts should subordinate racial justice to sectional peace. "We rationalize this travesty of delay," charged Carl Rowan, "by saying that we want 'peaceful change' and by convincing ourselves that to comply with the court's decision would cause 'trouble.' And, of course, everybody's against trouble. But does any American know of any great social advance in the history of mankind that was not accompanied by 'trouble'? When we Americans reach the point of soft indifference where we hate trouble more than injustice, we shall have reached the dawning of our era of greatest troubles."[61]

Perhaps the Court would have risked violence and righteously stormed the barricades had it possessed something with which to storm them. But for so major an undertaking as the transformation of southern society, the Court needed help. Constitutional principle was a rallying point, but what if the nation refused to rally? To induce widespread compliance, or to weather a crisis, the judiciary needed executive leadership and support. Yet the initial *Brown* decision somewhat offended President Eisenhower, who cherished the rights of states and who did not believe "you can change the hearts of men with laws or decisions."[62] From the moment *Brown I* was announced, the president stood aloof; aloof, that is, when he was not sympathizing with the "great emotional strains" white Southerners suffered from the decision.[63] The amicus brief of the government in *Brown II* reflected the president's coolness: the government, in essence, agreed with the South that compliance must come through a process of localized gradualism.[64] Nor was Congress, with its senior southern contingent, ready to move forward, as the timorous Civil Rights Act of 1957[65] indicated.

For a Court bent on great social reform, such considerations mattered. "[T]he Court," Alexander Bickel wrote, "was entitled to consider that those institutions [Congress and the Presidency] are uncomfortable in the presence of hard and fast principles calling for universal and sudden execution. They respond naturally to demands for compromise. . . . [They] can most readily be expected to exert themselves when some leeway to expediency has been left open. Therefore, time and an opportunity for accommodation were required . . . to form part of the invitation that the Court might be extending to the political institutions to join with it in what amounted to a major enterprise of social reform."[66] Hence, it is argued, "all deliberate speed."

Even for a Court certain of presidential backing, the phrase "deliberate speed" would still have made sense. The thing to be avoided was a test of wills, regardless of who won. The Supreme Court in the mid-fifties dealt with two distrustful peoples: black and white Southerners. Ending segregation would help restore each to fuller participation in the nation's life. Yet how it ended was important. Too protracted a process would disillusion the Negro and echo the infamous abandonment of 1877, when the promise of equality was all but repudiated.[67] Too precipitous a process would realienate a part of the country whose sectional estrangement was only just beginning to heal. Federal force, the Court knew, would recall the Civil War and Reconstruction like nothing else. "Deliberate speed" thus tried to balance the historical realities, to redeem the injustices of history without reopening its wounds. The Court later erred tragically in implementing and monitoring that famous phrase, but not in formulating it.

Ironically, *Brown II* came in the midst of an era of blind national pride and prowess, when little seemed beyond American ingenuity and reach. Yet the Court managed to see that absolute justice was not immediate, that "the law proposes but, for a time at least, the facts of life dispose."[68] It was only fitting that the American South occasioned the lesson. "For Southern history, unlike American," wrote Professor Woodward, "includes large components of frustration, failure, and defeat. It includes not only an overwhelming military defeat but long decades of defeat in the provinces of economic, social and political life. Such a heritage affords the Southern people no basis for the delusion that there is nothing whatever that is beyond their power to accomplish."[69] Human nature, the Southerner believed, was like a roadside mule that could be prodded, cajoled, sweet-talked, and downright cussed but not pushed infinitely against his will. "All deliberate speed" accepted, a bit too completely, this southern view. The mule came too close to lying down in the road. Thus, *Brown II* can be justified, but just barely. Deliberate speed was better at first for the nation than full speed ahead. Yet the Court's true-to-life politics imposed terrible moral costs. Those who bore the costs of prudence were those who pay the toll for much political compromise—the poor and powerless. In the South of the recent past, this meant those black schoolchildren who, like Mary Jones, began their education in that fall of 1954.

5

Desegregating the South, 1955–1970

Southern school desegregation after *Brown* progressed through four successive stages. The first might be termed *absolute defiance*, lasting from 1955 until the collapse of Virginia's massive resistance in 1959. The second was *token compliance*, stretching from 1959 until passage of the 1964 Civil Rights Act. With that act, a third phase of *modest integration* began with the efforts of southern school officials to avoid fund cutoffs by the Department of Health, Education, and Welfare. The 1968 Supreme Court decision of *Green* v. *County School Board*[1] commenced a fourth phase of *massive integration* during which the South became the most integrated section of the country. Yet even as the fourth phase developed, a fifth—that of *resegregation*—was emerging in some southern localities.

Breaks in history, of course, are never so neat as their chroniclers might wish. During the defiant stage, for example, North Carolina, Tennessee, Texas, and Florida practiced token compliance.[2] And during much of the token compliance stage, Mississippi, Alabama, and South Carolina practiced total defiance. The different phases thus express only regional momentum as a whole and not the progress, or lack thereof, of a particular state. Even as a gauge of regional momentum, moreover, these phases are imperfect, given wide differences in temperament between the Deep and Upper South. These differences, particularly at first, were important. "In terms of immediate progress toward desegregation in the South," noted Numan Bartley, "there was precious little to choose between the complex machinations of upper South states and the bellicose interposition of Virginia and the Deep South. But in terms of the future of the *Brown* decision, the difference was considerable. States of the upper South, with the exception of Virginia, accepted the validity of the Supreme Court decree and aimed to evade its consequences; Deep South states refused to accede any legitimacy to the decision." Prior to the Kennedy presidency, this division "helped to keep alive the principle of *Brown* v. *Board of Education* in the South."[3]

From 1955 to 1968 the Supreme Court remained largely inactive in school desegregation. It would not be fair to say the Court did nothing significant in race relations during this time. In a series of per curiam orders, the Court struck down segregation in public facilities other than schools.[4] It broadened the concept of the public facility subject to constitutional restrictions.[5] It protected the NAACP against demands of southern officials for disclosure of its membership lists, because "on past occasions revelation of the identity of its rank-and-file members has exposed these members to economic reprisal, loss of employment, threat of physical coercion, and other manifestations of public hostility."[6] The justices also reversed trespass and breach of peace convictions of black sit-in protesters[7] and mass demonstrators.[8] And in 1967 the Court even invalidated state statutes prohibiting interracial marriage,[9] though by this time fears of "mongrelization" had receded, and the decision "was so unsurprising that it was given only passing attention in the nation's newspapers."[10]

Yet these pronouncements, important as they were, failed to touch the real problem, which was understood all along to be school desegregation. On this question, the Court ducked a leading role by refusing even to review most rulings of the lower federal courts.[11] The Court spoke mainly when it absolutely had to: at the point of crisis when obstruction was so apparent,[12] delay so prolonged,[13] or violation of constitutional principle so manifest[14] that quiet was no longer feasible. But for the most part, silence prevailed.

1. The Collapse of Defiance; the Coming of Tokenism

The job of desegregation after *Brown II*, then, fell to the lower federal courts, principally the forty-eight district judges in the eleven southern states and their immediate superiors, mainly on the Fourth and Fifth Circuit Courts of Appeal.[15] Handing the lower federal courts this task without telling them how to accomplish it had several crucial consequences. First, it ensured a lack of uniformity among localities in the pace of desegregation. Only the Supreme Court could have promoted uniformity with frequent and specific rulings, which it steadfastly declined to do. As it was, the district judge possessed virtually limitless options: dismissing the complaint, remitting black plaintiffs to administrative remedies, admonishing school boards to take "positive" action at some future time, requiring school authorities to submit a desegregation plan to the court, or actually ordering school boards to admit a certain number of Negro pupils to specified white schools by a particular date.[16] Thus the governing factor at trial became, not surprisingly, the personal leanings of the federal district judge. These varied markedly, all the way from Judge J. Skelly Wright who, in the face of at least thirty-six motions for delay, ordered the New Orleans School Board in the fall of 1960 to implement "his personally devised desegregation plan"[17] to Judge T. Whitfield Davidson who declared at the end of a suit to desegregate the schools of Dallas, Texas: "I received my first nourishment from a Negro woman's breast. There is no animosity, no hatred of any kind in my heart. The southern white gentleman does not feel unkindly toward the Negro." But Negroes must understand "the white man has a right to maintain his racial integrity and it can't be done so easily in integrated schools. . . . We will not name any date or issue any order. . . . The School Board should further study this question and perhaps take further action, maybe an election."[18]

If an uneven pace of school desegregation was the first consequence of *Brown II*, a more or less cautious pace was the second. *Brown II* left federal district judges much too exposed. The nebulous nature of the Court's decision stripped from them much of the majesty of the cloak of law and the collective authority of legal institutions. Very often a district judge, who finds himself making an unpopular ruling, can point upward, confess personal displeasure at the decision, but regret that appellate rulings leave him no choice.

Community vengeance is thereby deflected somewhat from the district judge to the more faceless and numerous judges of the courts of appeals or the Supreme Court. Some limited shifting of responsibility was attempted in the wake of *Brown*. As Judge Hobart Grooms explained his order to admit the first black student to the University of Alabama: "There are some people who believe this court should carve out a province, man the battlements and defy the U.S. Supreme Court. This court does not have that prerogative."[19]

But *Brown II* gave trial judges little to hide behind. The enormous discretion of the trial judge in interpreting such language as "prompt and reasonable start"[20] and "all deliberate speed" made his personal role painfully obvious. If the judge did more than the bare minimum, he would be held unpleasantly accountable. Bold movement meant community opprobrium. Segregationists were always able to point to more indulgent judges elsewhere. *Brown II* thus resembled nothing more than an order for the infantry to assault segregation without prospect of air or artillery support. That some of the infantry lacked enthusiasm for the cause only made matters worse. District Judge E. Gordon West of Louisiana, for example, regarded "the now-famous *Brown* case as one of the truly regrettable decisions of all times. . . . As far as I can determine, its only real accomplishment to date has been to bring discontent and chaos to many previously peaceful communities, without bringing any real attendant benefits to anyone."[21] Given the vague and sparse character of *Brown II* and the Court's low profile thereafter, stagnation was inevitable.

Judge John J. Parker of North Carolina most influenced school desegregation in the years following *Brown*. Parker had been nominated in 1930 to the Supreme Court by Herbert Hoover but was rejected for being "unfriendly" to labor and for the statement, made in the heat of a race for governor, that "the participation of the Negro in politics is a source of evil and danger to both races and is not desired by the wise men in either race or by the Republican Party of North Carolina."[22] But Parker proceeded to become a respected and moderate jurist who issued several racially progressive rulings from his position on the Fourth Circuit Court of Appeals.[23] His interpretation of *Brown*, however, could not be so categorized. That decision, Parker declared in July 1955, had "not decided that the states must mix persons of different races in the schools. . . . What it has decided . . . is that a state may not deny any person on account of race the right to attend any school that it maintains. . . . The Constitution, in other words, does not require integration. . . . It merely forbids the use of governmental power to enforce segregation."[24]

The distinction between Thou Shalt Integrate and Thou Shalt Not Segregate is all-important. If *Brown* were read to require integration, southern school boards would be under an immediate duty to submit plans for substantial racial mixing. If, as Parker contended, *Brown* merely prohibited segregation, then the question became what evidence courts would accept that school boards were no longer doing so. At first, very little evidence sufficed. For at least five or six years after *Brown*, "tokenism was allowed where the local authorities were prepared to symbolize their acceptance of the principle of desegregation by the actual physical introduction of Negro pupils into white schools."[25] Certainly there was "no requirement that the school population be generally reshuffled."[26] Anything other than outright defiance stood a decent chance of judicial approval. Many federal judges sought only to move the South from the first, impermissible stage of absolute defiance to the second stage of token compliance. The aim was for a breach of the principle, a beachhead, however narrow, that might widen over time. In the late 1950s that was seen as no mean task.

Southern legal resistance to *Brown* was of two kinds. Most extreme were school closing and fund-cutoff laws, adopted by many southern states but most spectacularly put into practice by Virginia. In Virginia, the Governor was required by law to seize and close any school threatened with racial integration. If, by some chance, a school dared or was ordered to reopen on an integrated basis, state funds promptly would be terminated to all schools of that class within the district. Funds then would be made available to localities as tuition grants for pupils attending private (and segregated) schools.[27]

What, one asks, were such enactments to accomplish? For a state to deprive itself of public education seems only masochistic. Some commentators suggested that Virginia segregationists "hoped that the governor could persuade Negro students to withdraw voluntarily" their applications once schools were shut down.[28] More likely, school closings and fund cutoffs were designed by state officials to convince both their own constituencies and the rest of the nation how far they would go to maintain segregation, even to the point of abandoning public schools. Finally, the Virginia plan owed much to Senator Harry F. Byrd, determined in his last years to reap the drama and glory of another Lost Cause. "Let Virginia surrender to this illegal demand" said Senator Byrd to a gathering of the faithful at his apple orchards at Berryville, "and you'll find the ranks of the South broken. . . . If Virginia surrenders, the rest of the South will go down too."[29]

But the school closing experiment was reckless and foredoomed. In the first place, improvised private education proved an inadequate substitute for a public school system, especially in larger jurisdictions. In Norfolk, Virginia, where six white high schools closed in the fall of 1958, one private class "used a vacant store. Others met in basements, attics, or living rooms of private homes. The majority met in the twenty-seven churches and synagogues that had made rooms available. Many classes had been organized simply by groups of mothers who would bring together a dozen or two dozen children, then find a classroom and a teacher for them. . . . Between 2,500 and 3,000 [of the 10,000 displaced Norfolk children] were receiving no education or tutoring of any kind."[30]

Secondly, school shutdowns generated strong public opposition to the bitter-enders, primarily from parents and businessmen for whom public education and appeal to new industry proved more important even than segregation.[31] Finally, such schemes, enacted in open contempt of *Brown*, stood little chance of court approval. And on January 19, 1959, a three-judge federal district court pronounced Virginia's selective school closings unconstitutional. "[T]he Commonwealth of Virginia," held the court, "having accepted and assumed the responsibility of maintaining and operating public schools, cannot . . . close one or more public schools in the state solely by reason of the assignment to . . . that public school of children of different races or colors, and, at the same time, keep other public schools throughout the state open on a segregated basis."[32] To do so was to deny citizens and taxpayers of that school district the equal protection of the laws.

More popular, more ingenious, and more successful by far than the school closing laws were pupil placement statutes, which ten southern states enacted shortly after *Brown*.[33] In complexity and length they varied considerably, from less than a page in Louisiana to over seven in Tennessee.[34] The placement laws were supposed to help southern states make a gradual adjustment to *Brown*. In theory at least, they comported with *Brown*. Students were to be assigned by local authorities to public schools on non-racial criteria "to provide for the orderly and efficient administration of such public schools, the effective instruction of the pupils therein enrolled, and the health, safety, and general welfare of such pupils."[35]

In practice, pupil-placement laws suited segregationist aims quite nicely. They were an ideal delaying device, a maze of administrative hearings and appeals through which Negroes on an individual basis had to wind before reaching federal court. And the loose, multiple criteria in the statutes allowed officials to hold to an absolute minimum the number of blacks setting foot in white schools. "In short," wrote one commentator, "the statutes, functioning as intended, make mass integration almost impossible, place the burden of altering the status quo upon individual Negro pupils and their parents, establish a procedure that is difficult and time-consuming to complete, and prescribe standards so varied and vague that it is extremely difficult to establish that any individual denial is attributable to racial considerations."[36]

Where the statutes were transparent devices to maintain rigid segregation, as in Louisiana and Virginia, federal courts struck them down.[37] But where they promised even the slightest forward movement, some courts were anxious to bestow a carrot of approval. In the leading 1956 case of *Carson* v. *Warlick*,[38] Judge Parker pronounced North Carolina's pupil-placement statute—in both its criteria and procedures—constitutional on its face. "Somebody," noted Parker, "must enroll the pupils in schools. They cannot enroll themselves; and we can think of no one better qualified to undertake the task than the officials of the schools and the school boards having the schools in charge. It is to be presumed that these will obey the law, observe the standards prescribed by the legislature, and avoid the discrimination on account of race which the Constitution forbids. Not until they have been applied to and have failed to give relief should the courts be asked to interfere in school administration."[39] The Supreme Court declined to review Judge Parker's ruling.[40]

With North Carolina thus blessed and sent on its way, observers waited to see what would happen. To some limited extent, Judge Parker's confidence proved justified. North Carolina was often regarded as the model of an enlightened southern response to the

Brown decision. Real differences existed between that state and Virginia. Governor Luther Hodges stood for open schools, and shapers of public opinion, headed by former Governor and Senator Frank Graham, literary celebrities Harry Golden and Paul Green, and most of the North Carolina press, counseled orderly adjustment to the *Brown* ruling.[41] Local option (rather than statewide resistance as in Virginia) allowed three North Carolina cities—Charlotte, Winston-Salem, and Greensboro—to enroll Negroes for the first time in the fall of 1957.

Yet it soon became obvious that North Carolina was going nowhere fast. Charlotte, for example, had three blacks in white schools in 1957–1958, four in 1958–1959, and exactly one in 1959–1960.[42] Durham kept Negro entry to white schools at a trickle until in 1963 the local federal judge was "finally persuaded that the 'pupil assignment' plan was intended to discriminate against Negroes rather than to further sound educational programs. . . ."[43] And the rural areas of the state lagged behind the Piedmont cities. As a rule, however, adjustment was less traumatic in North Carolina than in Virginia and the Deep South. Token compliance often "succeeded" where total defiance fell flat.

But the North Carolina way was not gratefully received by the nation's Negroes. "[I]n the tradition of the old guards," wrote Martin Luther King in 1962, "who would die rather than surrender, a new and hastily constructed roadblock has appeared in the form of planned and institutionalized tokenism. Many areas of the South are retreating to a position where they will permit a handful of Negroes to attend all-white schools or allow the employment in lily-white factories of one Negro to a thousand whites. Thus, we have advanced in some places from all-out, unrestrained resistance to a sophisticated form of delaying tactics, embodied in tokenism. In a sense, this is one of the most difficult problems that the integration movement confronts."[44]

What hurt most was that tokenism won the tacit approval of the black's supposed friend: the United States Supreme Court. "For eight years after its implementation decision," regretted Robert Carter, "the Court refused to review any case in which questions were raised concerning the validity of pupil placement regulations or the appropriateness of applying the doctrine of exhaustion of administrative remedies to frustrate [desegregation] suits."[45] One-grade-a-year desegregation plans also were left standing.[46]

One can argue that Virginia's massive resistance, North Carolina's passive resistance, and the cautious course of federal judges closest to the problem all confirmed the need for a period of southern adjustment and thus justified tokenism. The token blacks that whites first encountered would be elite members of the race, carefully selected by white pupil-placement boards from those blacks courageous and determined enough to apply to white schools in the first place. Thus, favorable first impressions would be formed; integration would brightly begin. That rationale, of course, was insulting. Integration, it implied, was a one-way process of black supplication and white approval. Yet in the South of the late 1950s, that was exactly how it was seen.

But the Court's prolonged patience with tokenism was its greatest mistake. "To describe [tokenism] as gradualism," wrote Walter Gellhorn in 1964, "is to overlook its true nature. It is in fact sheer obstructionism, using the public treasury to protract the processes of adjudication rather than using adjudication to determine genuinely uncertain questions of law."[47] For the Supreme Court to allow the legal process to be used solely to frustrate its own lawful mandates seemed anomalous at best. The Court's great error lay not in the formulation of "all deliberate speed," but in not monitoring "deliberate speed" after *Brown* to ensure that some genuine progress actually took place.

Of tokenism, as with all previous racial policies, blacks bore the brunt. In many ways the tokenism of 1960 was no better than total segregation prior to 1954. In some ways it was worse. It was certainly just as profitless; the mass of black schoolchildren still lacked an equal education. And because tokenism was more sophisticated, it was more likely to be condoned. But tokenism was roughest of all on the token. There he sat, a conspicuously black face in a classroom of forty or an auditorium of one thousand. Sitting there was insulting and uncomfortable. "We'll accept one or two of you if we must," the message of tokenism went, "but not too many." And that, in fact, was tokenism's calculated effect: to make entry into white schools so unpleasant and disagreeable that few blacks would want to apply. "I have had many a Negro parent tell me now that the Negro has won his fight in the courts, they would prefer that their children go to all Negro schools if they are improved to the point of near-equality with the white schools," wrote Hodding Carter. "Much of white South is banking on this understandable reaction. . . ."[48]

The poignant story of one Negro token, Dorothy Counts, tells much. In the fall of 1957 she was the one black student to enter previously all-white Harding High School in Charlotte, North Carolina. Charlotte's first day of "integration" took place without incident, except, that is, for Miss Counts. Walking home after classes, "she was pursued by a rowdy crowd of juveniles—evidently indoctrinated by adult racists—jeering, spitting, and throwing pebbles, sticks, and paper balls. A white girl, who spat in [her] face, and a white boy, who threw a stick, were arrested." Throughout the ordeal, Miss Counts kept her poise. "A comely young lady of unmistakable gentleness and breeding, in a neat plaid dress," wrote Benjamin Muse, "she walked in front of the bawling mob with a quiet dignity that made theories of Negro inferiority seem grotesque." Yet there were limits to what she might endure. After one week, apparently "seeing no hope of enjoying tolerable relations with her white schoolmates," Dorothy Counts left Harding High for a biracial school in suburban Philadelphia.[49]

White hostility, however, was the lesser of tokenism's burdens. The first black entrants into white classrooms represented not only themselves but the entire black race. Theirs was, indeed, the burden of racial worth. Their performance would determine whether Negroes generally were intelligent; their personalities whether Negroes were worth befriending; their adaptability whether Negroes could "fit in." The token was expected to prove himself the equal that courts were now proclaiming him. Though for some black students, this posed a welcome challenge, it placed others under intolerable pressure and strain. The tragedy was that the Court's commitment to gradualism overlooked the cruelties of tokenism. The role of Jackie Robinson was too steep a price for the exercise of basic constitutional rights.

Thus, tokenism could never be permitted to become the accepted state of racial affairs. Black leaders, in the face of growing restlessness and anger, still tried in the early 1960s to project optimism and hope. "I am confident," wrote Martin Luther King, Jr., "that this stratagem [of tokenism] will prove as fruitless as the earlier attempt to mobilize massive resistance to even a scintilla of change. . . . Many of the problems today are due to a futile attempt by the white South to maintain a system of human values that came into being under a feudalistic plantation system and that cannot survive in a democratic age."[50]

2. Little Rock

Although the Supreme Court avoided the routine of school desegregation for thirteen years after *Brown II*, it could not escape its melodrama. The Court's involvement in these years will largely be remembered through two crises: Little Rock and Prince Edward. In both, the Court reaffirmed, with near unanimity and a flourish, its commitment to the principles of *Brown* v. *Board of Education*.[51] Yet its lustrous pronouncements on southern trouble spots, divorced from precise and meticulous desegregation guidelines, were of limited effect, much like a president coming into office with a stirring inaugural, but no program.

The Little Rock school-crisis was largely the doing of Arkansas Governor Orval Faubus, a shrewd and not untalented man of hardscrabble origins who "spoke often of hard work on the farm, of following the harvests as a berrypicker, of the ring of his axe as it bit into the trees of the Pacific Northwest in his days as a lumberjack."[52] It was Faubus who demonstrated the rich political profit in racial theatrics. Of all the southern notables to "strut and fret their hour upon the stage" after *Brown*, Orval Faubus seems about the least forgivable. But for his opportunism, the battle of Little Rock would never have been fought.

Orval Faubus was no visceral racist. Racism was more a political gambit than something loose in his veins. Faubus hailed from the Ozarks town of Greasy Creek in the northwest section of Arkansas, where race had always been less an obsession than in the old plantation lands along the Mississippi. His earlier career and gubernatorial victories of 1954 and 1956 had been free of race baiting. In 1956, he easily withstood a raw racist challenge from former state Senator Jim Johnson.[53] One observer claimed that Faubus even used to boast that "during his [first] administration all transportation systems had been integrated . . . that he was the first Democratic governor in the South to put Negroes on a Democratic state committee . . . that he had recommended to the Democratic state convention that the white primary be abolished . . . that Negroes had been appointed to boards and commissions where no Negro had ever sat before . . . and that his son was attending an integrated state-supported school."[54]

Arkansas, though opposed to integration, was not the Deep South. Even before the *Brown* decisions, several Negroes had attended the University of Arkansas. By the end of 1955, ten Arkansas school districts had announced plans for gradual desegregation. That same year, Negroes enrolled in five of the six state-supported white colleges, all without intervention from Governor Faubus.[55] And Little Rock, especially, did not seem the place for racial politics to prosper. It was, wrote Anthony Lewis, "a city of the New South, a middle-class, moderate town with an enlightened mayor (Woodrow Wilson Mann), congressman (Brooks Hays), and newspaper (The Arkansas *Gazette*, edited by Harry Ashmore)."[56] Thus, when the school board proceeded under a court-approved plan to admit nine Negroes to Little Rock Central High School in the fall of 1957, nobody expected unusual trouble.

But none had reckoned on Governor Faubus, in need, so he thought, of a lively issue in his quest for an unusual third term. Several friends begged him to resist the race issue. "I reasoned with him, argued with him, almost pled with him," not to intervene in the Little Rock affair, recalled Winthrop Rockefeller, then on good terms with the Governor as head of Arkansas' industrial development effort. Rockefeller reports (and Faubus denies) that Faubus told him: "I'm sorry, but I'm already committed. I'm going to run for a third term, and if I don't do this, Jim Johnson and Bruce Bennet [two hard segregationists] will tear me to shreds."[57] Former Governor Sid McMath remembers that Faubus "made no bones about it. He said he had to have an emotional issue. . . . He knew he was making a choice between entrenching his machine, or pushing the state ahead."[58]

Race, of course, had been used cynically in southern politics before Orval Faubus. Like war, the issue had the wondrous ability to divert attention from other pressing problems. It was the great welder of white solidarity. At the turn of the century, white supremacy was the cry used to submerge differences between upcountry populist and lowland planter.[59] And after *Brown*, race would revive the fortunes of men and political machines otherwise facing obsolescence and decline.[60] But though the issue had often been turned to local political profit, seldom was it employed at such great national cost as at Little Rock Central High.

On the night of September 2, 1957, with schools set to open the next day, Orval Faubus told his fellow Arkansans that it would "not be possible to restore or to maintain order if forcible integration is carried out tomorrow" at Little Rock.[61] But the predicted difficulty in maintaining order proved scarcely more than a pretext. On September 3, "Little Rock arose to gaze upon the incredible spectacle of an empty high school surrounded by National Guard troops called out by Governor Faubus to protect life and property against a mob that never materialized."[62] That same day, the federal district court ordered the school board to proceed with desegregation, despite the Guard's presence. But when, on September 4, the black students attempted to walk through a now assembled mob and enter Central High, guardsmen "stood shoulder to shoulder at the school grounds and thereby forcibly prevented the nine Negro students . . . from entering, as they continued to do every school day during the following three weeks."[63]

Not until September 20, when federal district Judge Ronald Davies enjoined Faubus from preventing the attendance of Negro children at Central High, did Faubus remove the troops. And on Monday, September 23, 1957, the nine Negros entered Central High, to the distress of the assemblage outside. "I tried to see a friendly face," recalled Elizabeth Eckford, one of the nine. "I looked into the face of an old woman and it seemed friendly, but when I looked at her again she spat on me."[64] "They've gone in," a white man shouted. "Oh God," shrieked a woman, "the niggers are in school." A mother threatened to enter Central High and bodily remove the blacks. With the mob demanding that white students leave and with parents withdrawing their children to the cheers of the multitude, the police announced shortly after noon that the Negroes had been withdrawn. Little Rock had experienced roughly three hours and fifteen minutes of racial integration.[65]

The rest is well known. President Eisenhower, hoping that Little Rock would "return to its normal habits of peace and order and [that] a blot upon the fair name and high honor of our nation in the world will be removed,"[66] promptly dispatched troops to that city to assist the execution of federal law. By nightfall of September 24, "twenty-six vehicles, including trucks, half trucks, and jeeps—filled with troops dressed in battle fatigues—drove up to Central High School."[67] The following day, under the eye of one thousand paratroopers and a federalized National Guard, the nine Negro children re-entered the school.

But the ensuing year at Little Rock Central High was not a happy one. In many ways, the school became an intense and hellish microcosm of the South at large. Gangs of segregationist toughs en-

forced conformity and made sure that new black students received
no kindly glances from "aberrant" whites. They patrolled the halls
and cafeteria loudly warning "anyone approaching the Negroes,
lunching alone, to 'stop that if you don't want to get beaten up.' "
To reporter Gertrude Samuels, the segregationists bore "an as-
tonishing resemblance to the tough-gang appearance of New York's
problem children, a sort of southern counterpart, down to their
blue jeans, leather jackets, duck-tail haircuts, large buckled belts,
and cigarettes." Against the small contingent of Negro students,
the segregationists practiced a steady harassment, "kicking the colored children, banging them against their lockers, spitting on them,
tripping them in halls, pushing them downstairs, stepping on their
heels, sticking nails on their seats, and pouring soup over one of
them." Only the guardsmen patrolling the school appeared to protect them from serious harm.[68]

Against this background, in February of 1958, the Little Rock
school board returned to district court asking that the Negro students be withdrawn from Central High and reassigned to segregated schools, and that its desegregation program be postponed
for two and one-half years. The district judge, citing conditions of
"chaos, bedlam and turmoil," "repeated incidents of more or less
serious violence directed against the Negro students and their property," a deterioration in the "education of the students," and the
need for continued "military assistance or its equivalent" for Central High to operate, agreed to the postponement.[69] The Court of
Appeals for the Eighth Circuit reversed,[70] but stayed its mandate
so the school board might petition the Supreme Court.

The stage thus was set for a test of wills. The basic question,
which could not be evaded, was whether the ploy of a demagogue
might delay a desegregation plan approved in federal court in fur-
therance of *Brown*. The Supreme Court answered, as it absolutely
had to: No. To do otherwise was to concede the fate of *Brown* to
extremists in the South. The Court might tacitly accommodate the
South with "all deliberate speed" and denials of certiorari on challenges to pupil-placement laws. But Faubus left the justices no
graceful avenue of retreat. True, the Governor himself was not
party to the proceedings before the Supreme Court and had been
careful not to disobey the lower court injunction forbidding him
from blocking black attendance at Central High. Yet Faubus's show
of force had disrupted a plan of integration theretofore proceeding

smoothly, and Faubus, by the school board's own admission, was responsible for the poisonous climate existing at the high school.[71]

The Court sensed keenly the challenge to its authority. Little Rock commanded its immediate attention; lawyers were given but two weeks notice to submit their briefs.[72] The Court convened in special session to hear oral argument. Judgment was announced on September 12, 1958, just in time for the scheduled opening of school. Seventeen days later, on September 29, the full opinion was released in *Cooper* v. *Aaron*,[73] signed, in an unprecedented show of solidarity, by each of the nine justices. John Marshall's famous sentence from *Marbury* v. *Madison* was quoted (as the Court likes to do when stakes are high and its authority is questioned): "It is emphatically the province and duty of the judicial department to say what the law is."[74]

Little Rock's plea for postponement was resoundingly denied. "The constitutional rights of respondents," the Court announced, "are not to be sacrificed or yielded to the violence and disorder which have followed upon the actions of the Governor and Legislature."[75] Justice Frankfurter's concurrence put it best: The school board's request for postponement meant essentially that "law should bow to force. To yield to such a claim would be to enthrone official lawlessness, and lawlessness if not checked is the precursor of anarchy. On the few tragic occasions in the history of the Nation, North and South, when law was forcibly resisted or systematically evaded, it has signalled the breakdown of constitutional processes of government on which ultimately rest the liberties of all."[76]

On the facts of the case—that no state official may forcibly frustrate the execution of a federal court order—the Supreme Court was unquestionably correct. The performance of Orval Faubus could in no way be condoned. But in the drama of the occasion, the Court went somewhat overboard, with a sweeping and unprecedented assertion of its own authority and place.[77] The Constitution, said the Court, was "the supreme law of the Land"; it was the duty of the Court to interpret that supreme law. "Every state legislator and executive" was bound by this interpretation and sworn to uphold it.[78]

Taken literally (and not merely as a rhetorical flourish), that statement implies that all state officials, whether or not party to a case, are obliged to immediately support, in word and in deed, whatever the Court has said. That view is both unrealistic and un-desirable. It is unrealistic because elected officials do not rush into line behind unpopular decisions on such matters, for example, as abortion and school prayer. It is undesirable because the edicts of our least democratic branch of government must enjoy some period of testing before they become, in the most pervasive sense, the law of the land. At a minimum, verbal dissent to Court decisions is to be welcomed. But should there not also be what Professor Bickel once termed "the dissenter's option to wait for litigation. He waits to see how intensely others are concerned to have the rule enforced; the speed and extent of litigation will reveal that, . . . [h]e waits to assess the reaction, in the interstitial area left them to react in, of the Supreme Court's first constituency—the lower federal and state judges. And he waits to allow time for the agitation of public opin-ion, since he knows that if he turns out to be in the majority, or to feel intensely where all others are merely indifferently acquiescent, he can change the law, or make it a dead letter, without recourse to the extremely cumbersome process of constitutional amendment. . . . [The dissenter] . . . ought . . . to be brought around in time; and it gives rise to no contradiction, merely to some untidiness, to hold also that in the meantime, while the issue is in doubt and sub-ject to settlement by political means, coercion does also take place, as litigation proceeds and produces specific decrees."[79]

That, of course, is how it happens, whatever the Court may wish. Democracy is trained to move by consensus or not at all. The indispensable ingredient of that consensus must be, as Faubus re-fused to recognize, obedience to law as embodied in a specific court decree. But we are likewise too independent a people not to haggle and dispute that with which we disagree. Our Constitution blesses our contumaciousness, individually through the First amendment, collectively through our system of federalism and the rights of the states. It is the duty of the Supreme Court to prick consciences, to ruffle settled modes of practice and behavior, to rally allies, and to win converts to its cause. But that, on the gravest matters, is the challenge of a generation, not the work of a day.

The wonder is that *Cooper* v. *Aaron* did not provide momentum for a renewed assault on segregation in the South. The country had been aroused over Little Rock, the president had acted, the Court's own role had been reaffirmed, and southern intransigence had been laid shameless and bare. Yet after *Cooper,* the Court rehibernated;

five long years would pass before another major school case.[80] Why the Court did not seize the initiative after *Cooper* is, of course, a speculative matter. It always is easier, moreover, to speculate on why the Court did act than on why it did not. Possibly the Court felt more secure confronting direct, rather than subtle, challenges to its authority such as those embodied in tokenism and pupil-placement statutes. Only official lawlessness, the justices may have sensed, would generate sufficient public backing of the Court's position. The very turmoil of Little Rock may, ironically, have persuaded the Court that gradualism was the wisest course, that insistence on more integration would only make Faubusism more commonplace.

Further explanation may lie with Justice Felix Frankfurter, a dominant influence on the Court of the 1940s and 1950s.[81] For Justice Frankfurter, *Brown* created a difficult dilemma. Declaring segregation unconstitutional was morally congenial; implementing that declaration was something else again. Aggressive judicial action risked the Court's enforcement capabilities and, perhaps worse, abridged the rights of states and localities to manage their own schools.[82] Two of Justice Frankfurter's favorite opinions, *Wolf* v. *Colorado*[83] and *Colegrove* v. *Green*,[84] had helped establish that state systems of criminal justice and legislative redistricting were not normally the concern of federal courts or the Constitution. During the 1960s, states' rights would become rather a quaint concern; in the late 1950s, they mattered still. It is often thought that *Brown* and the school cases that followed it loosened the Court's inhibitions in such areas as reapportionment and criminal justice.[85] But the process also worked in reverse; the vitality of federalism in those areas influenced the pace of school desegregation as well. Not until Justice Frankfurter's last years on the Court and his replacement in 1962 by Arthur Goldberg did states' rights barriers begin to weaken.[86] In the 1950s, it still took a governor's blatant defiance to lower them. Thus, in school desegregation, *Cooper* dawned no new day. It stands as that occasional constitutional case with a larger-than-life script and limited immediate impact.[87]

A postscript exists to the crisis of Little Rock. Arkansas did not bow gracefully to the Court's decision. By order of Governor Faubus, all Little Rock high schools were closed during the 1958–1959 school year, to be reopened only in September, 1959 after a federal court declared the school closing unconstitutional.[88] And Faubus himself was handsomely reelected in 1958, 1960, 1962, and 1964, due in great part to his "heroics" at Little Rock. Only on his retirement in 1966 did the governorship change hands.[89] But a longer perspective is a happier one. A visitor to Central High in 1972 found "one of the most successful ventures in school integration anywhere in America. One looks at Central High, a decade and a half after 1957, and sees a still handsome school, set in a wooded residential area, Negro and white children talking and playing sports and associating freely together. . . . [S]tudent leaders of both races and the school administration (now also thoroughly integrated with a black principal at Central High) have worked hard to correct [racial] antagonisms."[90] Old ways did change: Faubus himself, in a 1970 comeback try, finally met defeat.

3. The Court Becomes Restive: Prince Edward

By the early 1960s, the attitudes of lower federal courts toward southern evasion became perceptibly less indulgent. Blacks were permitted to maintain more frequent class actions and were increasingly relieved from jumping the administrative hurdles in the pupil-placement statutes. Even the placement acts themselves began to be recognized for what they were: the barest tokenism superimposed on still segregated school systems.[91] And there were clues, albeit faint ones, that the Supreme Court was beginning to bestir itself.

The Court's first significant pronouncement of the decade, *Goss* v. *Board of Education*,[92] concerned "minority to majority" transfer provisions in the desegregation plan of Knoxville, Tennessee. By the standards of 1963, Knoxville's plan was not a regressive one. It went well beyond the pupil-placement stage and had won cautious approval both from the local district court and the Sixth Circuit Court of Appeals.[93] Residential zoning, not race, was the basis for public school attendance. But to mollify those whites zoned into heavily black areas, the local school board permitted a pupil to transfer from a school where his race was in the minority back to a school where his race would be in the majority. Because this transfer provision turned explicitly on race and because it could only encourage significant resegregation, the Supreme Court, having taken the case, had no choice but to strike it down. Yet curiously the Court re-entered school desegregation by disapproving a relatively "moderate" plan after years of sanctioning more obstructionist ones. Moreover, the Court's ruling doubtless discouraged other localities from adopting residential zoning by removing the "sweetener" to skeptical whites.

In *McNeese* v. *Board of Education*,[94] delivered the same day as *Goss*, the Court held that black plaintiffs challenging school segregation under a federal Civil Rights Act[95] need not exhaust unpromising state administrative remedies before bringing suit in federal court. *McNeese* was significant because it came not from the South but from Illinois, because the black plaintiffs charged segregated treatment *within* the school walls, and because the no-exhaustion doctrine the Court announced that day would later be wrenched far beyond its original school context.[96] But why the Court waited until 1963 in a northern setting to address the chief dilemma of southern blacks challenging the pupil-placement statutes remains unclear.[97]

Two years later, in *Bradley* v. *Richmond School Board*,[98] the Court gingerly broached racial bias in teacher assignments. In some ways, teacher assignments were the least visible and most flammable part of the entire school picture.[99] Many white parents found it difficult enough to accept black classmates for their children, let alone a black teacher. Was a black to be permitted to discipline their offspring and teach them "nigra talk"? Many white teachers, moreover, had their prejudices about teaching black schoolchildren. Some left teaching altogether at the onset of integration, and others went to private schools. "Everyone worries about the children," said one small town Georgia teacher, "but I think desegregation is harder on us than anyone. . . . I almost had to pinch myself that first day when they came down the hall."[100] For those who remained, an Atlanta teacher perhaps best expressed the anxiety: "I just didn't believe it would work. I've known nigras all my life, and I didn't think they would adjust to our schools. I have nothing against them. I just thought their minds weren't like ours. And I *still* think many of them have a long way to go. . . . Yes, I'm ready now to let those who can do it come to our schools. . . . That's where I have changed. . . ."[101]

Black teachers, too, faced problems. For them, more than anyone else, integration's blessings were most mixed. In the segregated system, noted Helen Nicholson of Hattiesburg, Mississippi, "Black teachers had to provide their own teaching supplies and, for the most part, knew nothing at all about departmental budgets. . . .

There was a time when Black students who were either sisters or brothers or friends who lived near each other had to share one textbook."[102] Integration might at least mean a schoolbook for each black schoolchild and better resources with which to teach. But it held many uncertainties. Black teachers sensed that in a desegregated school system, their jobs would be the least secure.[103] And they wondered too, after years with all-black charges, how well they would teach in integrated schools and whether white students and parents would accord them proper respect.

Faced with so delicate a problem, many school boards focused solely on student placements and left the teacher problem for later, much later. By 1965, for example, none of the 36,500 Negro teachers in Alabama, Louisiana, or Mississippi taught with any of the 65,400 whites.[104] But in *Bradley*, the Court forbade further procrastination. District courts, the Court held, must not approve desegregation plans without addressing claims of racial bias in faculty assignments.[105] In a companion case, the Court warned that racial segregation of teachers would invalidate an otherwise constitutional pupil desegregation plan.[106] But exactly how teachers must be assigned, the Court declined to say. That, in the tradition of *Brown II*, would be left to the lower federal courts.[107]

The Court doubtless recognized that to be effective, faculty and student desegregation must occur simultaneously. White students would not attend schools with all-black faculties, and few white teachers cared to teach only black students. For a school to be identifiably black in any way—by the composition of its student body, faculty, or staff, even by its school name or traditions—was the surest way to stiffen white resistance to attending it. Yet the Court's adoption of simultaneous faculty-student integration was of limited practical effect. So long as the justices continued to indulge only token student integration, faculty integration would likewise be frustrated.

The Court's most notable decision of the mid-sixties involved "rural, remote, and resolute" Prince Edward County, Virginia,[108] on the upper tier of the state's black belt, known as the Southside. The Southside is Virginia's brush with the Deep South, "Dixie below the James," one writer has called it.[109] In Southside, the eternities of the land—sun-lit tobacco fields, forests of scrub pine, sleepy river rolls—lay side-by-side with such man-made eternities as segregated schools. Here in the Civil War were the South's last strongholds at Petersburg and Appomattox. Here too, exactly one century later, lay the last stalwart hopes of segregation, in "America's most stubborn county," as one detractor called Prince Edward.[110]

Though Prince Edward was the defendant in one of the companion cases to *Brown*,[111] the axe did not fall at once. But in June of 1959, the Fourth Circuit Court of Appeals ordered the county to desegregate immediately.[112] Faced with such an order Prince Edward chose to close its public school system completely. The county could not afford, its leaders contended, to maintain both a public and a private school system.[113] For five long years—all after Virginia's massive resistance had collapsed and statewide school closing laws had been declared unconstitutional—Prince Edward went its own way. The little county would set the course, show the South and, indeed, the world how *Brown* might yet be thwarted. "The spotlight will be on you and your accomplishments," residents were told. "If we have a successful year, the hopes of hundreds of thousands will be kindled."[114]

For the nearly 1,400 white students of Prince Edward, the school closing crusade was no disaster. The leaders of the private school experiment were shrewd and determined. The churches, the Jaycees, and PTA's all aided the effort, to the flattery and encouragement of the local press. "News of the Prince Edward experiment traveled far and swiftly. . . . Donations of all imaginable kinds turned up. A Silver Springs, Florida man sent along 250 pounds of chalk. . . . Editor [James J.] Kilpatrick in Richmond donated some eighty books" to the private school's library.[115] White students met in churches and unrented stores under many of their former school teachers.[116] And though few judged the private school effort an unqualified success, neither was it a sham. Within five months of opening, Prince Edward's private schools had received state accreditation.[117] Most important of all, private schools cost parents very little. After the first year, students attending them received public tuition grants: $125 to $150 from the state of Virginia and an additional $100 from the county. Finally, there was a property tax credit of up to twenty-five percent for any contribution made by Prince Edward taxpayers to "nonprofit nonsectarian private schools" in the county.[118]

For Prince Edward's 1,700 black children, it was a sorrier story. Negroes rejected an offer of private schools, preferring to continue their battle for public school desegregation.[119] From 1959 to 1963, most Prince Edward blacks went without formal education. A handful were educated across the border in North Carolina, a few more sent north to integrated schools at the expense of the American Friends Service Committee. An estimated 200 received "bootleg" education, living as "make-believe" members of families outside Prince Edward so they might attend public schools without paying nonresident charges. But the great mass of them—about 1,400—remained in Prince Edward. About one-third attended makeshift training centers, set up "more for morale than for learning." And 800 or so were lost, "completely and perhaps permanently to any known attempt at education."[120] One visitor, Irv Goodman of the *Saturday Evening Post*, watched Negro children "on the streets at noon, walking or sitting on the steps of the post office or standing on a corner or throwing rocks in what was once a public-school playground." Goodman spotted "a Negro boy, eight years old, sitting in his yard, scratching in the dirt with a stick—not letters or numbers or lines of a pattern, but marks without meaning. After a while, he scuffed out the marks with his shoe and scratched again. The little boy had never been to school."[121]

In time, the lonely vigil of Prince Edward became a national outrage. The Kennedy administration felt something had to be done.[122] By the fall of 1963, federal, state, and local authorities cooperated with a private organization known as the Prince Edward Free School Association to set up schools for Negroes in anticipation that public schools might reopen the following year. But returning to school after so many years would not be easy. Neil Sullivan, superintendent of schools for the Free School Association, found that "living apart from an organized society, without a newspaper, magazine or library (some with illiterate parents), the [Negro] children had learned to communicate by use of gestures and avoided using the spoken word."[123] Attendance was down until it was learned that many of the children "shared clothing and took turns coming to school. Once we were able to clothe them properly, attendance did not prove to be quite as difficult a problem." Field trips were used to acquaint students with the world beyond the farm. On one such trip, the children visited "the Chambers of the Supreme Court [on March 30, 1964], when the Prince Edward case was heard for the third time."[124]

Though there were no mobs and no National Guard, Prince

Edward County affronted the Court as much as Little Rock. Here was a party to the original *Brown* decision, back in Court a decade later, with its private schools segregated and public schools shut down. Here was a county willing to forsake altogether democracy's noble experiment—universal public education—to defy the *Brown* decision. Here were Negro schoolchildren not better off after *Brown* but much worse. And there was the Supreme Court, indeed the entire federal judiciary, seemingly unable after ten long years to help.

Thus the justices, as in Little Rock, had to end the obstruction as swiftly as possible. And in *Griffin* v. *County School Board*,[125] the Court did just that. It curtly rejected four procedural grounds offered by Prince Edward to delay or dismiss the suit. On the merits, the Court was equally blunt. Black schoolchildren in Prince Edward, it held, had been denied equal protection of the law under either of two theories. The first was Virginia's permitting public schools to close in Prince Edward while those elsewhere in the state remained open. The second was the maintenance of private schools with public funds, at least where public schools were closed.[126]

The Court was most emphatic as to remedy. Not only was the district court empowered to enjoin tuition grants and tax credits to supporters of private schools;[127] it was further authorized to order Prince Edward officials to reopen and fund a racially non-discriminatory public school system. For Justices Clark and Harlan, this last proved too much,[128] though the sensitivity of the occasion prevented them from pushing the point. One remedy only the Court did not refer to: that of integrating "private" institutions.[129] The South was left the costly option of private academies, but not of closed public schools.

The object of *Griffin*, as it virtually had to be, was to get Prince Edward in line, never mind how. As in *Cooper*, impatience produced abruptness. "The case," wrote Professor Philip Kurland, "represents one of the many factual situations that compels the Court to resort to unbecoming and unfortunate methods for assuring that its will is done."[130] On school segregation, so it seemed, decisions were to be judged more for moral outcome than for legal content. Cleansing the nation of disgrace did little to assure the orderly development of law.

Prince Edward, more than Little Rock, demonstrates how southern obstruction and the Court's changing expectations shaped the course of school desegregation. Counties like Prince Edward caused the Court, in desperation, to vest district judges with sweeping remedial power. Determination to do whatever was necessary began to take hold of the Court from deep frustration. In Prince Edward, in 1964, that meant reopening public schools. In New Kent County, in 1968, it meant promptly converting, by whatever means, to substantially integrated schools.[131] In Charlotte-Mecklenburg, in 1971, it meant, among other things, massive compulsory transportation of schoolchildren.[132]

Justice Tom Clark, in an interview shortly before his death, recalled that federal remedial power grew in small individual steps, "like Topsy," with no grand design. The Court, Clark explained, had tried in *Brown II* to give localities a chance to change on their own. When confronted with case after case of obvious obstruction, it had no choice but to broaden federal judicial oversight over local schools, and finally to order student busing.[133] Surely the justice had in mind the story of Prince Edward.

In one sense, the cases bear Justice Clark out. The opinions of the mid-sixties—*Goss* (Knoxville), *Bradley* (the faculty assignment case), and *Griffin* (Prince Edward)—are, above all, expressions of exasperation. In *Goss*, the Court noted that "eight years after this decree [of all deliberate speed] was rendered and over nine years after the first *Brown* decision, the context in which we must interpret and apply this language to plans for desegregation has been significantly altered."[134] One year later, in *Griffin*, the temperature rose. "[T]he issues here," said Justice Black, "imperatively call for decision now. The case has been delayed since 1951 by resistance at the state and county level, by legislation, and by lawsuits. The original plaintiffs have doubtless all passed high school age. . . . The time for mere 'deliberate speed' has run out. . . ."[135] By 1965, in *Bradley*, the Court fumed that "more than a decade has passed since we directed desegregation of public school facilities 'with all deliberate speed.' Delays in desegregating school systems are no longer tolerable."[136]

But it is wrong to blame solely southern foot dragging for integration's slow pace. Rather, the Court itself must bear some measure of responsibility. Its decrees, even in the mid-sixties, were couched in the negative. Minority-to-majority transfer provisions, public school closings, public funding of private, segregated schools, racially biased faculty assignments all were impermissible.

What exactly was permissible the Court never said. It simply policed the bare minimum, and that, rather belatedly.

The school cases of the mid-sixties stand in contrast to *Reynolds* v. *Sims*[137] and *Miranda* v. *Arizona*,[138] where more specific constitutional guidelines were promulgated. Even under specific decrees, of course, subsidiary questions inevitably arise.[139] The question is not, however, whether the Court can anticipate all subsequent problems, but whether it will lead in resolving the major ones. This the Court did not do. If school desegregation was a more complex and intractable problem than legislative apportionment or police interrogation, this was only more reason for assisting lower courts in resolving it. In failing to do so, the Court forfeited initiative and leadership on the most significant issue of its day. Like presidents, justices cannot rule effectively by veto alone.

4. *The 1964 Civil Rights Act and the HEW Guidelines*

Brown's tenth anniversary was no time to celebrate racial equality. The Court had raised expectations that had gone unmet. Little Rock and Prince Edward had been more glamor cases than anything else. The Court's intervention in those crises was, to be sure, welcome and symbolic. But those decisions did not so much advance the cause of desegregation as avert a fatal collapse. In fact, all the effort expended after *Brown* had resulted in a mere handful of Negroes in white southern schools: 2.3 percent, to be exact.[140] Some felt the courts had failed to push desegregation; certain local trial judges, complained Walter Gellhorn, "continue to be content with the pace of an extraordinarily arthritic snail."[141] Others thought courts never could work wonders without political support. For whatever reason, faith in law and the legal process—the hallmarks of the early days of the Civil Rights movement—had begun to ebb. Younger blacks in the South "departed the courtroom in favor of the sidewalk" and lunch counter.[142] In the North, where the race problem had rarely been conceived in legal terms, violence prevailed and cities were set aflame.

Yet 1964—that year of failing faith in law—was also the year in which the power of the law was reasserted. "Indeed," wrote Harry Ashmore, "it is being argued in a nervous Congress that the need for civil rights legislation was not to advance the Negro cause, but to control and contain it."[143] On July 2, Congress passed "the most comprehensive piece of civil rights legislation ever proposed":[144] the Civil Rights Act of 1964.[145] Title II forbade discrimination in all public accommodations,[146] defined by the act to include restaurants and lunch counters, motels and hotels, gas stations, theaters, and sports arenas.[147] Public school integration likewise benefitted from this provision. It was difficult, to say the least, for school integration to proceed smoothly in a community with segregated restaurants and rest rooms. Conversely, integration in public accommodations would make future school integration in the South seem a more natural step to take.

After years of defiance or glacial progress, the act presaged for southern school desegregation not a great, but a modest leap forward. To begin with, it made school desegregation more a joint enterprise. Courts no longer had to take the heat alone. With Congress and the executive weighing in on behalf of desegregation, defiance no longer seemed so promising, the national verdict on *Brown* so much in doubt. A sense of inevitability began to descend on the South. Debate on integration progressed from "if ever" to "how much" and "how soon."

The act permitted the Department of Justice to bring suit "for the orderly achievement of desegregation in public education."[148] That in itself boosted and relieved the NAACP, whose lawyers had carried the legal battle since *Brown* almost alone. The NAACP had concentrated on large urban school districts within the South, both because of the greater numbers of schoolchildren there and because of the supposed greater amenability of urban whites to desegregation. By 1966, largely as the result of the earlier efforts of the NAACP, Atlanta, Birmingham, Charleston, Jackson, Little Rock, Miami, Montgomery, Nashville, New Orleans, and Richmond, among others, were operating under court orders to desegregate.[149] But the hope that rural districts might voluntarily desegregate in the wake of court orders in urban areas had not generally borne fruit. Now, with the Department of Justice on board, the resources existed to pursue recalcitrant rural districts also.

But the Department's entry into school desegregation meant much more than legal manpower. Its presence meant integration was not only something blacks were seeking but something the United States government stood behind. Government attorneys helped fortify and strengthen the embattled district judge. Finally, notes Professor Owen Fiss, "[T]he Department's actions in court tended to deepen and solidify the Executive's commitment to equality. In some sense, high Executive officials were educated by and locked into the positions that the Department attorneys—the professionals—took for the United States in civil rights litigation. Those positions could on occasion be abandoned or repudiated, but only with a good explanation."[150]

The Department of Justice was not the only federal agency drawn into school desegregation by the 1964 Civil Rights Act. The Office of Education of the Department of Health, Education, and Welfare drew up guidelines for desegregation in response to the act. The first guidelines,[151] issued in April 1965, were relatively mild. They devoted little attention to faculty desegregation and vaguely accepted both geographic zoning and freedom-of-choice plans as valid tools. The revised guidelines of March, 1966,[152] however, were considerably tougher and offered clearer criteria for integrating schools than had most federal court decrees. "The [1966] guidelines call for school districts with 8 or 9 percent of their Negro pupils in predominently white schools to double this figure next fall," noted the *New York Times*. "Schools with few or no Negro pupils are expected to make a 'substantial' effort to catch up with the leaders. All school districts are expected to integrate their faculties."[153] Though freedom-of-choice plans were still acceptable, "the single most substantial indication as to whether a free-choice plan is actually working to eliminate the dual school structure is the extent to which Negro or other minority group students have in fact transferred from segregated schools."[154] The significance of that last sentence was enormous: racial progress in the South was to be judged not in theory but in fact, not by the paper plans and proclaimed intentions of school boards but by the numbers of whites and blacks together in schools.

The usual expressions of southern outrage were trotted out against HEW and the guidelines, but with several added wrinkles. Federal bureaucrats, Southerners had discovered, were more fiendish than federal judges. "My people," Senator Albert Gore had asserted, "would prefer to submit to a [f]ederal judge whom they know" their plans for desegregation, than be ruled by "some crusader from afar."[155] Editor James J. Kilpatrick of the Richmond *News Leader* denounced the 1966 guidelines as an "arrogant edict" with a "harsh, preemptory, commanding" tone.[156] This time, local school officials led the assault on the guidelines, as opposed to defiant statewide officeholders of earlier years. "I am not going to be a party to assigning teachers and students to any schools—there are other ways to make a living," grumbled Superintendent E. R. Cone of Thomas County at a meeting of angry Georgia school officials.[157] Within a few days, HEW Secretary John Gardner was forced, as the Supreme Court had been in *Brown II*, to reassure the South that nothing precipitous was about to occur. His department was not trying to impose a formula on anybody, insisted Gardner, or the "instantaneous desegregation" of every teaching staff.[158] "A great many [southern] communities last year accepted the notion of having a few Negro children in white schools," admitted David Stanley, assistant commissioner of education. "But the notion that the Negro and white schools will eventually disappear—that we'll just have public schools—is not yet accepted."[159]

Southerners were not in the least pacified by the head of the office issuing those hated guidelines. U.S. Commissioner of Education Harold H. Howe II was a prophet of urgency for whom calmer human moods posed a noxious threat. Gradualists in school integration only reminded Howe "of the prayer that St. Augustine addressed to heaven when he was a young man. 'Oh Lord,' he said, 'make me chaste. But not yet.' " The moral was not slow in coming. "Our words," Howe said, "have urged the nation to desegregate its schools. But our reluctance to act has said even more loudly, 'not yet.' "[160]

Gradualists, Howe contended in a 1966 address, feared "rocking a boat which, no matter how leaky, appears at least to be floating somewhere." But they had failed to sense the apocalypse. "A revolution is brewing under our feet," Howe warned. "[I]t is largely up to the schools to determine whether the energies of that revolution can be converted into a new and vigorous source of American progress, or whether their explosion will rip this nation into two societies. . . . [T]he young Negro must be convinced that the United States is his home, not his prison, and that it is a country worth fighting for, not a cage to be fought out of. It may already be too late to change his mind," though not, Howe reminded, "to provide his younger brothers and sisters with a healthier belief. . . ."[161]

The HEW guidelines promised a novel, more activist approach to segregated schools. Traditionally, school desegregation had been sought through lawsuits. But after *Brown II* lawsuits had proved a protracted, piecemeal, expensive, idiosyncratic, and, for some plaintiffs in the Deep South, very dangerous way of dismantling segregation. School boards cooled their heels and awaited litigation, and litigation, if ever completed, often meant little in the way of integration anyway. Though by the middle 1960s innovations such as statewide lawsuits and more specific court decrees saw occasional use,[162] the courtroom, many felt, was not the final answer to the school problem. "A national effort," noted Judge John Minor Wisdom, "bringing together Congress, the executive, and the judiciary may be able to make meaningful the right of Negro children to equal educational opportunities. *The courts acting alone have failed.*"[163]

But what actual power did HEW have to punish school segregation? To the traditional court injunction, Congress in the 1964 act added the federal fund cutoff.[164] In theory, this sanction was marvelously simple. Offending school districts (i.e., those violating HEW guidelines) would simply have their federal funds terminated. This new weapon, it was hoped, might finally force the progress many believed necessary. It would require school districts affirmatively to justify their behavior to federal officials. And it would strike school officials in the purse—where it hurt the most.

But the fund cutoff or "deferral" was far from foolproof. Like the injunction, it was a piecemeal remedy. Funds could be stopped only to the school system of the offending locality,[165] not to other local programs and certainly not to the state of which the locality was part. As with litigation, there was potential for delay. Funds could not be terminated until there had been a hearing, which included an express finding of noncompliance entered in the record and notice to the affected party of failure to comply, and until attempts at securing voluntary compliance had broken down.[166] As desegregation plans became more complex, facts more numerous and disputable, and school board intentions more obscure, bureaucratic haggles and backlogs would begin to mount.

But the real problem with fund cutoffs was more basic. As Professor Fiss has noted, termination was, in many respects, "like a hydrogen bomb—it is better suited to threats than to actual use."[167] It was a clumsy sanction. Partial or gradual cutoffs, even if permissible, undercut the integrity of the antidiscrimination principle. You either discriminated or you did not: it was hard to admit degrees of prejudice or some other middle ground. In southern communities where public and private schools competed for white

allegiance, fund cuts only disadvantaged public ones, hardly a desired result. Worse still, terminating funds hurt the very persons
the Civil Rights Act intended to benefit: blacks, and, in a broader
sense, innocent public schoolchildren of both races.

Fund cutoffs suffered yet a final weakness in comparison with
court injunctions. The injunction was backed by the power of contempt. No southern official, after the necessary antics had been
performed, chose to risk a contempt of court citation that might
land him in jail. But school districts faced with fund cutoffs had legitimate avenues of escape. They might snub HEW guidelines and
dispense with federal aid, which amounted even after the Elementary and Secondary Education Act of 1965[168] to only 8 percent of
the average school district budget,[169] much less than either the state
or local share. Though the Justice Department, as early as 1965,
promised to bring to court those districts refusing federal aid, that
effort was incomplete. "By August 15, 1967," noted one commentator, "only twenty-five school districts originally subject to final
termination proceedings had come back into compliance as a result
of court orders obtained subsequent to HEW's action. Fifty-five
school districts remain ineligible for federal aid."[170]

This is not to imply that HEW guidelines were exercises in futility. Far from it. Their greatest effect came in being incorporated
into ever more specific court decrees. By the late 1960s, the Fifth
Circuit insisted that "courts in this circuit should give great weight
to future HEW Guidelines. . . ."[171] The reasons for this deference
were not difficult to fathom.[172] To begin with, the Fifth Circuit
contended, "the Guidelines were carefully formulated by educational authorities" while judges lacked "sufficient competence—
they are not educators or school administrators—to know the right
questions, much less the right answers."[173] Undoubtedly, too,
judges did not wish their own decrees to become avenues of escape
from stricter administrative regulations.[174] More fundamentally,
the lower courts looked, after many long years, to share responsibility for the nettlesome school problem, to be freer of the weary
load, so complex and controversial, that *Brown II* had assigned
them. Deference to HEW guidelines promised what *Brown II* had
refused to deliver: a sense of order, uniformity, and specificity to
southern school desegregation.

After the Civil Rights Act of 1964, the South was squeezed in a
tightening vice of new political and judicial determination. That act

represented, as much as anything else, a gathering and coalescence of the national will on the whole question of southern school segregation. Significant progress occurred in the years after 1964. In that year, only 2.3 percent of southern Negroes attended desegregated schools; in 1965 the figure was 7.5 percent, in 1966, 12.5 percent.[175] Only the Supreme Court's continued inactivity kept the percentage from climbing higher. But in 1968 even that would change. The Court, which in the mid-sixties surrendered initiative to Congress and the executive, stood ready to recover it. With *Green* v. *County School Board*,[176] southern school desegregation prepared to enter a new and climactic phase.

5. The Rise and Demise of Freedom of Choice: *Green* v. *County School Board*

Though the South did not win the battle to keep its schools segregated, it did prove adept at orderly retreat. There were endless southern fallback positions in the school controversy, from massive resistance to pupil-placement tokenism to freedom of choice and, lastly, to neighborhood schools. Sometimes federal judges accepted the fallback as an "interim" measure, as if grateful for ground thus far won and anxious to catch a breath before hostilities flared anew. Such was the case with freedom of choice plans in the middle 1960s. The Fifth Circuit remarked in 1966 that "at this stage in the history of desegregation in the deep South a 'freedom of choice' plan is an acceptable method for a school board to use in fulfilling its duty to integrate the school system."[177] The Eighth Circuit noted that freedom of choice "is still only in the experimental stage and it has not yet been demonstrated that such a method will fully implement the decision of *Brown* and subsequent cases. . . ."[178] While the more conservative Fourth Circuit embraced the concept less reservedly,[179] two concurring judges urged waiting to see just how freedom of choice worked in practice.[180] The 1966 HEW guidelines also warily approved freedom of choice, but only if tangible evidence of actual integration were forthcoming.[181]

The South, however, clutched freedom of choice to its breast. It promised only limited integration, all the while winning federal court approval and avoiding loss of federal funds. What was unthinkable five or six years ago suddenly assumed, in light of more threatening alternatives, the status of holy prerogative. The opportunity for a child and his parents to select his own school, one would have thought, was what Thomas Jefferson had meant all along by "unalienable Rights." "One would find," mused an HEW official, "that freedom to choose one's own school was being talked about in the South in the same breath as the freedoms of speech and assembly under the first amendment."[182]

The Supreme Court in 1925 recognized that a parent did have some constitutional interest in the choice of his child's education. In *Pierce* v. *Society of Sisters*,[183] the Court held unconstitutional an Oregon law requiring children to attend only public schools. The law, said the Court, interfered "with the liberty of parents and guardians to direct the upbringing and education of children under their control." The State could not "standardize its children by forcing them to accept instruction from public teachers only. The child is not the mere creature of the State; those who nurture him and direct his destiny have the right, coupled with the high duty, to recognize and prepare him for additional obligations."[184]

Pierce held, in effect, that if parents wished to purchase suitable *private* education for their children, the government could not stop them. That, however, was a very different matter from constitutionally guaranteeing parental control over an offspring's *public* education. For one thing, the guarantee would be impractical. In drafting attendance plans, school boards have always been free to deny parental preference for any one of a hundred reasons, overcrowding being the one most often given. And once a child is in a public school, the parent cannot dictate what teacher he gets, what courses he takes, what grades he receives, or what discipline he meets. Parental views are often welcomed (or tolerated) by school authorities, but parental control over an offspring's education has always been circumscribed. This was nowhere truer than in the South. The region whose system of segregated schools was once the very antithesis of free choice was now arguing the fundamental status of that right.

The problem with freedom of choice was the variance between theory and practice. In theory, each child's school choice was free; in practice, it was often anything but. For one thing, white children did not choose to go to black schools. And doubtless due to ancient southern mores, many Negroes did not select white schools either. "Most Negroes work for white people in the South—and almost everywhere else," Hodding Carter observed early in the sixties. "In a majority of instances a white employer need only mention to his Negro employee that he is certain that both agree that school segregation is the wisest course for everyone concerned."[185]

In the event the employer failed to convey the message, school officials would. To lessen pressures for integration, periods of choice were set few and far between; a child might be stuck throughout high school with his choice upon entering the ninth grade. Choosing a white school proved as troublesome as registering to vote. Sometimes birth and health certificates, personal appearances, and notarized forms were required of Negro pupils. Often Negroes were advised that white schools, "regrettably," were "overcrowded." Or that school buses serving a particular school did not run through "colored" parts of town. Or that blacks entering white schools would not wish or be permitted to "engage in school activities, athletics, the band, clubs, [or] school plays."[186] Thus, opportunity for pressure, covert and overt, was built into every pore of the "free" choice system. In the very communities where blacks were most disadvantaged and illiterate, freedom of choice would be least likely to work.

For blacks, freedom of choice was just another bit of evidence of the lengths whites would go to avoid their presence in school. A report of the Student Non-Violent Coordinating Committee (SNCC), shortly before it turned to black separatism, denounced HEW for condoning free choice schemes. "In most counties where no Negroes have applied for transfer to white schools, *we know that fear of retaliation was the reason. . . .* One of the easiest ways for school boards to comply [with HEW guidelines], . . ." charged SNCC, "is to adopt a so-called 'freedom of choice' plan. The method is simple . . . get a few Negroes to sign up to attend white schools, and then let the local citizens 'encourage' them to withdraw their applications."[187]

The carrot was out as well as the club. Every effort was made to seduce Negro children into remaining at Negro schools. Because "pressure for integration usually speeds equalization,"[188] the South in the mid-sixties hurried to upgrade Negro schools.[189] The white hope was that Negroes would "choose" a decent school of their own—with their own friends and familiar surroundings—to a white environment where they were socially unwanted, academically unprepared, and, in the case of many impoverished Negroes, even unsuitably clothed.[190]

The wonder was that freedom of choice fared with the courts as well as it did. As a means of desegregation, it was transparently similar in concept to the pupil-placement statutes of the late 1950s. Both freedom of choice and pupil-placement schemes were, at best, modest variations on old dual school systems. The rule was that pupils would go where they had gone in the past (i.e., to segregated schools). Interracial transfers were the exception. Like the pupil-placement statutes, freedom of choice made integration depend on Negro initiative, stamina, and fortitude. School officials were absolved from acting affirmatively and permitted to react, in highly discretionary fashion, to Negro requests.

Once again, the South was to pay dearly for its evasion. Judges distrusted freedom of choice primarily because it was so discretionary. And discretion, at this late hour after *Brown*, had to be curtailed and scrutinized. The result: another jump in judicial supervision over community schools.

The man most responsible for this development was Judge John Minor Wisdom of the Fifth Circuit Court of Appeals. It is a measure of the Supreme Court's inconspicuousness that the most influential school opinions from *Brown II* to *Green* v. *County School Board*[191] in 1968 were written by two lower federal judges: Judge Parker of the Fourth Circuit and Judge Wisdom of the Fifth. Judge Wisdom, appointed to the bench by President Eisenhower in July of 1957, had witnessed the long slow course of desegregation. He remembered how "in 1960, six years after *Brown*, the admission of three little Negro girls to one class in one white school in New Orleans was regarded as a great stride forward. I remember when transfers under the fraudulent pupil placement and grade-a-year plans were considered radical. When I see Tulane play the University of Mississippi in a football game with black players on each team, I think of the riots and violence that took place when James Meredith became the first black to attend the University of Mississippi." Nevertheless, Wisdom had the "nagging feeling that it is not how far the blacks have come that is important, but how far they still have to go."[192] Frustrated in the middle 1960s by the lack of real progress, Judge Wisdom determined to make amends.

In three opinions, from 1965 to 1966 (*Singleton* v. *Jackson Municipal Separate School District I*[193] and *II*[194] and *United States* v. *Jefferson County Board of Education*[195]), Wisdom transformed the face of school desegregation law. The foremost student of the Fifth Circuit's history in this area, Professor Frank Read, contends: "Those cases mark the most important doctrinal change" in school integration law since *Brown* itself. "Their importance cannot be overemphasized." Indeed *Jefferson*, Read wrote in 1975, was "one of the four most important school desegregation cases yet decided."[196]

The three Wisdom opinions are best considered as a body. They are laced with phrases of urgency: "The time has come for foot-dragging public school boards to move with celerity toward desegregation."[197] " '[N]o army is stronger than an idea [school integration] whose time has come.' "[198] "The clock has ticked the last tick for tokenism and delay in the name of 'deliberate speed.' "[199] Henceforth, warned Wisdom, school plans must not be "longer on promises than performance"; the overriding question was how well they actually worked.[200] And the crucial indicator of performance was, as we have seen, the HEW guidelines.[201]

Judge Wisdom's critical premise was that school boards had a positive duty to integrate, not merely to stop segregating.[202] A shift from racial to nonracial criteria in student assignment laws was not enough. Nor was the presence of a few blacks in formerly all-white schools. Wisdom saw school desegregation in far grander terms. Its purpose was nothing less than to redress the damage inflicted on the mass of Negroes down through the generations by segregated schools. What the state had done, it must now undo. A wrong had been done the entire race; the remedy must speak in similar terms. Pupil-placement schemes and later freedom-of-choice plans might grant *individual* blacks equal educational opportunity. But, said Wisdom, *"the only adequate redress for a previously overt system-wide policy of segregation directed against Negroes as a collective entity is a system-wide policy of integration."*[203] Remedies now required "liquidation of the state's system of de jure segregation and the organized undoing of the effects of past segregation."[204]

To speak thus is to thrust law to the forefront of social change, to adopt an admirable, if impossible, goal. Relief to the class, as opposed to the individual relief practiced theretofore, initiated the idea of compensatory justice, which later would influence the Supreme Court on such imposing issues as student busing and affirmative action programs. The problem with "undoing the effects of past segregation" is that it lacks a principled termination point; certainly full compensatory justice cannot end with the mere presence of blacks and whites together in schools. Full redress of the wrongs done the Negro is probably beyond the capacity of courts of this century to devise. Compensatory justice, the courts also would learn, was potentially a road of dashed black expectations and white resentments, and, on occasion, of counterproductive results. Judges in the coming decade would have to ask whether the nation's foremost ideal of racial justice was worth the awesome price necessary to achieve it or whether, indeed, it was achievable by the judiciary at all.

The full implications of Judge Wisdom's innovations were, in the mid-sixties, but dimly perceived. Wisdom's ambitious formulations, however, squarely contradicted Judge Parker's venerable dictum of restraint in *Briggs* v. *Elliott*.[205] Parker held that states must simply cease segregating; Wisdom that they had, in effect, a duty to integrate. Parker believed *Brown* to involve only disputes between individual Negro children and the state;[206] Wisdom argued that "Negroes collectively are harmed when the state, by law or custom, operates segregated schools. . . ."[207] Parker's textual justification was the proscriptive phrasing of the equal protection clause ("nor [shall any state] *deny* to any person within its jurisdiction the equal protection of the laws"); Wisdom's the positive grant of citizenship in the first sentence of the Fourteenth amendment[208] and a belief that segregation laws constituted a 'badge of slavery' whose effects, under the Thirteenth amendment, had yet to be undone.[209] It was a measure of the tenacity of the *Briggs* dictum that Judge Wisdom had to thrice attack it before being satisfied of its demise.[210] If Judge Parker's personal prestige had influenced the Supreme Court to accept the dictum, perhaps it took someone of Judge Wisdom's standing to persuade the Supreme Court to bring it down.[211] Wisdom's view, moreover, suited the evangelism of the mid-sixties as Parker's had the greater circumspection of the decade before.

But the most remarkable aspect of *Jefferson* was the remedial decree. Judge Wisdom, again relying largely on HEW guidelines, told local school officials: when the free choice periods must be (March 1 to March 31 of each school year); how public notice of the choice procedure must be given (by newspaper, radio, and television); how the choice form and accompanying explanatory letter must be written; how the choice form might be returned ("by mail, in person, or by messenger to any school in the school system or to the office of the Superintendent"); how students must be assigned (by proximity to the school rather than prior attendance at it); how transportation must be routed ("so as to serve each student choosing any school in the system"); how entering Negro students must be treated ("may not be subject to any disqualification or waiting period for participation in activities and programs"); how school equalization efforts must proceed; where new schools should be constructed (with the object "of eradicating the vestiges of the dual system"); what remedial programs must be conducted (to permit Negroes formerly in segregated schools "to overcome past inadequacies in their education"); and how faculty and staff were to be hired, fired and assigned.[212]

By any measure, the *Jefferson* decree was an extraordinary step. The local approach of *Brown II* was discarded in favor of a model decree to apply throughout the circuit. A piecemeal approach to school desegregation was replaced by a comprehensive view addressing student and faculty assignment, transportation, and curriculum. And the Fifth Circuit introduced, more explicitly than ever before, race as a lodestar for educational decision making. The decree, in fact, left only one major question: if freedom of choice had to be so circumscribed and supervised, why did Judge Wisdom not reject it altogether and require desegregation by other means?

The detail of Judge Wisdom's 1966 *Jefferson* decree finally dashed the Supreme Court's hope in *Brown II* that school authorities would assume "the primary responsibility for elucidating, assessing, and solving"[213] the problems of desegregation. Though Wisdom had hoped reliance on HEW guidelines would help extricate courts from burdensome school controversies,[214] *Jefferson* had precisely the opposite effect. After *Jefferson*, federal courts became bold architects of school desegregation policy. The *Jefferson* decree, in fact, was the fore-runner of the broad equitable discretion exercised by district courts on student busing. Where school board busing plans were insufficient, district judges consulted experts in designing new ones.[215] The lower courts disapproved awkward methods of financing school desegregation as well.[216] And federal judges ordered, with increasing frequency after *Jefferson*, school authorities to offer remedial programs to recently integrated black pupils,[217] to train teachers to deal with integrated classes,[218] and even to alter or suspend testing programs in school systems undergoing desegregation.[219] *Jefferson*, in short, foretold a level of judicial involvement in local education unimaginable at the time of *Brown*.

The final fate of freedom of choice, meanwhile, awaited the Supreme Court. In the spring of 1968, the Court considered challenges to freedom of choice in three southern school systems.[220] The experience of New Kent County, a small, rural locality in eastern Virginia where Negroes comprised fifty-seven percent of the school population, had been rather typical. In many ways New Kent's was a case of classic simplicity. The county had but two schools, New Kent on the east side and Watkins on the west side. New Kent was the white school, Watkins the black one. For a decade after *Brown*, schools in New Kent had remained totally segregated. But in August, 1965, to remain eligible for federal funds, the county adopted freedom of choice. The plan bore modest results. Although no whites chose to attend all-Negro Watkins school, black enrollment in formerly all-white New Kent advanced from 35 in 1965 to 111 in 1966 to 115 in 1967. Such progress notwithstanding, 85 percent of the Negro children in the county still attended the all-black school.[221]

But the county had done all that could be expected, argued Frederick T. Gray to the Supreme Court. To do more would jeopardize public education. Besides, the Negroes wanted their own school to serve as a sort of community center. *Brown*, Gray stressed, had never required compulsory integration; it said only that states must "take down the fence" keeping students apart. Chief Justice Warren was skeptical. "Isn't the net result that while they took down the fence, they put booby traps in the place of it, so there won't be any white children going to a Negro school? . . . Isn't the experience of three years . . . some indication that it was designed for the purpose of having a booby trap there for them, that they didn't dare to go over?" Replied Gray: "If the free choice of an American is a booby trap, then this plan has booby traps."[222]

It was the lawyer for the government, Louis Claiborne, who struck the fatal blow. Claiborne scoffed at the southern contention that free choice was the natural, sent-from-heaven way to run a school system. It was, said he, just the opposite: an artificial, inefficient, and uneconomical device. It made no sense to bus many Negroes all the way across the county to the black school and many whites all the way across the county to the white school when an "old-fashioned, traditional system of neighborhood schools" would do. And why would school officials want to trifle with all the forms they had "to send out, receive, tabulate, [and] count" each year under the free choice system? To Claiborne the answer was obvious. The only reason to endure all that trouble and expense was to preserve some semblance of the old segregation.[223]

The Court saw it that way also. The New Kent case, *Green* v. *County School Board*,[224] traveled far beyond the Court's previous pronouncements on school desegregation. *Brown II*, the Court said, as though it had been clear all along, had charged school boards "with the affirmative duty to take whatever steps might be necessary to convert to a unitary system in which racial discrimination would be eliminated root and branch."[225] But *Brown II* had always been ambiguous. It required only a "prompt and reasonable start"[226] toward some ill-defined end. Many had believed, with Judge Parker in *Briggs* v. *Elliott*,[227] that *Brown II* required only the cessation of segregation, not an affirmative duty to integrate. Though the Court's decisions after *Brown II* tilted increasingly toward the affirmative duty concept, none had done so as explicitly as *Green*. Indeed, the Court might have voided freedom of choice as a continuation of segregation, so great were community pressures and inducements to choose one-race schools. But it went farther—it removed, at long last, from black children the onus of achieving integration and threw it squarely—*affirmatively*—onto the backs of local school boards.

The next question, of course, was what this affirmative duty might entail. "The burden on a school board today," the Court said in *Green*, "is to come forward with a plan that promises realistically to work, and promises realistically to work *now*."[228] Gone forever was mere deliberate speed. And while the Court refused to say that freedom of choice would never work, it made clear that New Kent's plan was not working so long as 85 percent of the black students remained totally segregated. Henceforth, the Court served notice, school plans would be judged not on paper or promise, but on performance.

This open use of a statistic to invalidate a school desegregation plan had limitless implications. Had the Court not condemned the statistical imbalance, integration might have become the prerogative of those few Negro children whose parents had the tenacity and foresight to insist on it. But was this bare statistic of 85 percent significant only when combined with New Kent's history of enforced segregation at the time of *Brown* and its decade of defiance thereafter? Or was racial imbalance in public schooling to be frowned upon, wherever found and whatever the cause? How far beyond the special symbolism of public schools would the Court carry statistical reliance? Might an employer be in violation of the 1964 Civil Rights Act if his work force was 75 percent white? Or a criminal conviction be reversed if the jury was but 8 percent black? Or a zoning ordinance overturned if residents of the community were 95 percent white? Or legislative redistricting invalidated if few blacks were elected? Possibilities were endless. *Green* hardly foreshadowed an enslavement to statistics, a "numerical nightmare," but numbers were definitely encouraged as future evidence of racial discrimination. This thought struck some with especial horror. Statistics were doubtless invaluable in tracing progress toward racial equality. But might they not also chart a course of "reverse discrimination," where both public and private bodies openly favored blacks to win judicial (or executive) approval for their programs?[229] The Constitution was, indeed, becoming color conscious as well as color blind.[230]

Green was novel in yet another sense. The Court actually tendered, albeit in a footnote, some positive suggestions for achieving school desegregation. The Court, for the moment, stopped saying what was not permissible and started suggesting what was. One suggestion was pairing: "[T]he Board could consolidate the two schools, one site (Watkins) serving grades 1–7 and the other (New Kent) serving grades 8–12. . . ."[231] A second suggestion was geographical zoning, which the board could achieve "simply by assigning students living in the eastern half of the county to the New Kent School and those living in the western half of the county to the Watkins School."[232] In this sense, *Green* stands as a traditional "neighborhood school" opinion. But the case must be seen in its setting—in rural New Kent County where there was little residential segregation. In urban areas, where residential segregation did prevail, were neighborhood schools constitutionally sufficient or was some far more drastic remedy required?

Green was a watershed case not because of what was said but because the Supreme Court said it. In its skepticism toward freedom of choice, its reliance on statistical evidence, its insistence on results, and its imposition on school boards of an affirmative duty, *Green* mirrored to a great extent Judge Wisdom's landmark rulings for the Fifth Circuit and the approach of the 1966 HEW guidelines. One wonders, in fact, if the Court would have ruled as it did had not the executive and the Fifth Circuit forced a heady pace. At a minimum, those institutions strengthened the Court's own perception that the time for renewed assault on school segregation in the South now had come.

6. *Toward a Desegregated South: the post-*Green *Decisions*

After *Green*, the Supreme Court quickly warmed to its task. One year later, in *United States* v. *Montgomery County Board of Education*,[233] the Court returned to the problem of faculty assignments. In an opinion by Justice Black, replete with compliments for his fellow Alabaman, District Judge Frank Johnson, the Court affirmed Johnson's order that Montgomery, Alabama must work to achieve racial ratios of faculty at each school that reflected the racial ratio of teachers in the school district as a whole (three whites to two blacks). *Green* clearly had displaced *Brown II* as the governing standard. Judge Johnson's order, the Court emphasized, "was adopted in the spirit of this Court's opinion in *Green* v. *County School Board* in that his plan 'promises realistically to work, and promises realistically to work *now*.' "[234]

Actually, *Montgomery* went well beyond *Green*. *Green* had used racial statistics merely to invalidate a school board's freedom of choice plan. But Judge Johnson, having found that previous plans had not produced integrated faculties, imposed quantitative standards of his own that the school board was expected to meet.[235] Thus in *Montgomery*, for the first time, the Supreme Court sanctioned the inclusion of affirmative numerical goals in a school desegregation remedy.

Montgomery can be commended as an overdue attempt to give lower courts and school boards positive guidance as to what faculty desegregation required. The Court may also have been convinced that only numerical requirements could properly protect black teachers from being dismissed in a newly desegregated school. Yet *Montgomery*, by establishing racial ratios for teacher assignments, restricted the ability of school boards to adopt personnel policies based on competence not race and to assign teachers according to seniority, proximity, and personal preference. Curtailing school board discretion was, of course, the new order of the day. Yet the justices, in effect, had sanctioned minimum racial quotas in the public workplace without any independent discussion of the merits of such a course.

Green influenced even more the Court's insistence in 1969 that southern school systems proceed at once to desegregate. *Green* had alarmed many Southerners who sensed that massive rather than token integration was about to become a reality. By the summer of 1969, thirty last-ditch districts in Mississippi faced imminent desegregation. Help, however, arrived from the newly elected Nixon administration. Reportedly to accommodate Senator John Stennis, who was leading the administration's floor fight for the anti–ballistic missile system,[236] HEW Secretary Robert Finch took the extraordinary step of writing Chief Judge John Brown of the Fifth Circuit, requesting that Mississippi districts be granted a delay in submitting school desegregation plans until at least December 1 to avoid "chaos, confusion, and a catastrophic educational set-back. . . ."[237] On August 25, the Justice Department appeared in court to support the delay,[238] and on August 28, the Fifth Circuit approved it.[239]

But the administration's "southern strategy" provoked revolt and resignation within the ranks of the Justice Department. Lawyers refused to defend the Government's position and, in some cases, passed data to civil rights attorneys opposing it. Attorney General John Mitchell attacked his own staff, and the head of the Civil Rights Division, Jerris Leonard, had to lecture his lawyers on their proper responsibility.[240] On September 3, the NAACP Legal Defense Fund ran a full page advertisement in *The New York Times*, featuring the picture of a young Negro schoolchild. At the top of the page was written: "On August 25, 1969, the United States Government broke its promise to the children of Mississippi." We "cannot let this happen," the ad continued. "We are the chief legal arm of the Civil Rights Movement. Along with many brave people, we are responsible for the Supreme Court Decision of 1954. We defended Martin Luther King in Birmingham and Selma. We were there at the sit-ins and riots. And the Government was with us too. Until last week."[241] For the first time since 1954, Justice Department spokesmen and civil rights lawyers sat across from one another in federal court. For the first time, also, NAACP Legal Defense Fund attorneys broke publicly with the Justice Department and appealed the delay to the Supreme Court.[242]

The Defense Fund prevailed. In *Alexander* v. *Holmes County Board of Education*,[243] the Court abruptly reversed in a one paragraph opinion the Fifth Circuit's three month delay. "[T]he Court of Appeals should have denied all motions for additional time, . . ." the

Supreme Court directed. "Under explicit holdings of this Court the obligation of every school district is to terminate dual school systems at once and to operate now and hereafter only unitary schools."[244]

Alexander was remanded in October 1969 to the Fifth Circuit judges who still "could not believe that the Supreme Court intended for them to issue orders that required the relocation of hundreds of thousands of school children in the middle of an on-going school year."[245] Thus the judges decided, unanimously and en banc,* upon a two-step process. Faculty and staff, transportation, athletics, and other school activities all had to be integrated no later than February 1, 1970. But the merger of student bodies was "difficult to arrange" in the middle of a school year. "Many students," noted the court, "must transfer. Buildings will be put to new use. In some instances it may be necessary to transfer equipment, supplies, or libraries. School bus routes must be reconstituted." Massive student integration, the Fifth Circuit held, could therefore be delayed until next September, 1970.[246]

Again the Fifth Circuit was summarily reversed. In *Carter* v. *West Feliciana Parish School Board*,[247] the Supreme Court scolded it for delaying student desegregation beyond February 1, 1970. Again immediate integration was ordered. Thus, wrote Professor Read, "the Fifth Circuit—which had been the most diligent court in America in desegregating public school facilities—was wrist-slapped for delaying massive student desegregation for a short four month period to avoid disruption in the midst of an on-going school year."[248] This time, Chief Justice Burger and Justice Stewart dissented. The Fifth Circuit, they noted, "is far more familiar than we with the various situations of these several school districts, some large, some small, some rural and some metropolitan, and has exhibited responsibility and fidelity to the objectives of our holdings in school desegregation cases. [Reversal] without argument and without opportunity for exploration of the varying problems of individual school districts, seems unsound to us."[249]

The South now was forced to integrate at once and in earnest. After *Alexander* and *Carter*, integration had to be ordered for all school districts in litigation within the Fifth Circuit. From De-

---

* Normally, circuit judges sit in panels of three. An en banc hearing denotes a case of especial importance where the entire court sits.

cember 2, 1969 to September 24, 1970, the Fifth Circuit issued no less than 166 opinion orders in school cases. Figures showing the actual amount of integration were the determining factors. "Perhaps no court in history," commented Read, "has responded with such alacrity and such monumental effort [as the Fifth Circuit] to a peremptory reversal."[250] The judicial blitz had a stunning impact. By 1971, according to HEW estimates, 44 percent of Negro pupils attended majority white schools in the South as opposed to 28 percent who did so in the North and West.[251] The South, seventeen years after *Brown* (and in the midst of President Richard Nixon's "southern strategy"), became America's most integrated region.

There was, however, a reaction to swift change of this magnitude. *Alexander* provides a singular opportunity to assess the social impact of a broad desegregation order on thirty school districts in the state [Mississippi] with the highest percentage of blacks in the nation. What followed implementation of the order was white exodus from the public schools into segregated private academies on a mass scale. Total white public school enrollment in the *Alexander* counties dropped 25 percent between 1968 and 1970; in those counties with the largest black majorities in the general population, white flight from the public schools reached 90 percent, and even, in one case, 100 percent.[252] The result: "[M]any black children [remained] in schools just as segregated as they had been before *Brown*."[253] Although this extreme reaction was caused by the exceptionally large black populations in many counties,[254] recurrent white flight to private academies etched a somber background to bright hopes for integration.

Against the backdrop of the post-*Brown* era, the Court's boldness in *Alexander* and *Carter* was remarkable. It manifested understandable impatience with unbecoming abruptness. Speed for two years (1968–1970) replaced the deliberateness of the previous thirteen. Summary reversal of a progressive federal tribunal replaced former deference, even to cautious ones. Administrative difficulties, which after *Brown II* excused the delays of a decade, now would not justify waiting for the next school year to begin. The Court that once badly needed executive support now moved in the face of executive opposition.

Thus the Court of the mid-fifties and that of the late-sixties struck a perfect polarity save, perhaps, in one respect. Each court was cryptic. Each made the pace of desegregation clearer than its content. After *Alexander* and *Carter*, desegregation was to proceed at once, though exactly what was to proceed remained obscure. If freedom of choice was not favored, then what was? What if geographical zoning failed to produce the substantial integration *Green* seemed to require? How much integration did *Green* require? How many all-black schools would be tolerated? How far-reaching an effort was required to desegregate them? Did the Court's approval of racial ratios in faculty assignments in *Montgomery* impose a similar requirement for student bodies as well? For the moment, such questions remained to perplex lower federal judges.

In the end, desegregation came to the rural South suddenly but rather peacefully. One vivid exception involved the overturning of two buses bearing black schoolchildren in Lamar, South Carolina. Lamar was an obvious candidate for racial trouble. It was but one-third white. Its token freedom of choice plan had been rejected in favor of neighborhood zoning that sent 520 black students to schools where previously there had been but 19. One hundred and twenty whites also were scheduled to attend the Spaulding elementary and high schools where none had been before. Ordinary whites insisted the school zones were gerrymandered: "Not a single doctor, lawyer, school-board member or anybody prominent got put in nigger schools," protested one.[255] And integration arrived abruptly. On January 19, 1970, five days after *Carter*, Chief Judge Clement Haynsworth announced for the Fourth Circuit that the Court's decisions left him "no discretion" to postpone integration to the following fall. "[T]he disruption which will be occasioned by the immediate reassignment of teachers and pupils in mid-year"[256] was now immaterial. "The proper functioning of our judicial system requires that subordinate courts and public officials faithfully execute the orders and directions of the Supreme Court. Any other course would be fraught with consequences, both disastrous and of great magnitude."[257]

Reporter William McIlwain best described what followed: "It was daylight [March 3, 1970], but barely, and there were one hundred fifty to two hundred men and women in the mob. Some of them, in short sleeves, shivered in the mist and dew of early morning. . . . [T]hey were on the tar-and-gravel road, lining its sides, clotting its middle, spilling over into one of the entrances to Lamar High School." As the school bus neared, the mob closed in front of it, and "men tore at the hood. A woman leaped onto the bus . . .

bent into the engine, tearing furiously at the wires, ripping out parts and throwing them over the heads of the mob into the pecan grove." As another bus came to a halt, "the mob again surged forward, crashing at both buses . . . Ax handles slammed against windows, bricks and bottles hurtled inside the bus, showering glass on the children." Under cover of tear gas fired by patrolmen, the black children were able to escape "just as the mob turned over both buses. If the children had looked back as they reached the school-house door, they would have seen the two buses, their windows shattered, lying together on their sides by the tar and gravel road on the edge of Lamar." Though luckily the blacks had escaped serious injury, the real scars from the incident were more long-lasting. Lamar's schools closed for a week, then opened under close guard. At Lamar Elementary, 5 of every 6 whites were missing, having left for private school, school in nearby counties, or for no school at all. Of the 120 whites scheduled to attend formerly all-black Spaulding Elementary and High School, not one did.[258]

Why had it happened? Many in Lamar blamed the Supreme Court, the distant authority that had tried for years to change "our way of life. If I push you up in that corner and keep pushing you, what're you going to do? You're going to push back. Well, we're pushing back." Mid-year integration was what rankled Lamar, contended the Reverend Ed Duncan of Lake Swamp Baptist Church where the new private school now met. "If the government had waited until summer and done this the following fall, there wouldn't have been anything like as much trouble." One suspected, however, that the timing of integration mattered less than the amount. "The public would permit token integration," said the Reverend Duncan, "but it's when a school isn't a white school anymore that you have a problem." To a person, Lamar's residents denied racist motives for the incident. "It definitely was never a race issue, . . ." swore one of the leaders of the uprising. "It's simply the matter of education, quality of education. I'm not going to get my daughter drug down in her education."[259]

What can the historian learn from such a tragedy? Perhaps, if the Court had intervened so aggressively fifteen years earlier, Lamar would not have been an isolated whimper, but the war cry of the South. If so, then gradualism had its value. The South, in stages, became reconciled to the inevitable, exhausted from battling it, or well versed in escaping it (through private schools). But opposite interpretations are also possible: that southern backwaters would have resisted in 1955, 1970, 1985, in the fall or at mid-year: in short, whenever integration came. If so, what was ever gained by delay?

Lamar is actually an index of both continuity and change. The Louisville *Courier-Journal* saw in the incident only "a montage of racial conflict of 10 years ago."[260] The Cincinnati *Enquirer*, however, found reason to hope. At Little Rock, the *Enquirer* noted, "Gov. Orval Faubus winked at the resistance. . . . This week, Gov. Robert E. McNair recognized his responsibility and sent state troopers to Lamar to restore order."[261] Change seemed confirmed a year later, when an all-white jury in Darlington County, South Carolina (where Lamar is located) convicted three leaders of the rioting. Presiding Judge Wade Weatherford imposed strict sentences, and Governor John West hailed the sentencing, saying "justice is now color blind" in South Carolina.[262]

The Supreme Court's southern and largely rural phase did not end until 1972, four years after *Green*, in *Wright* v. *City Council of Emporia*.[263] If the southern phase began in *Brown* with a show of unanimity, it ended in *Wright* on a note of discord. The justices split five to four, with all four Nixon appointees in dissent.

The issue was whether the city of Emporia could carve out a separate school district from surrounding Greensville County, Virginia. Emporia had been part of the county until 1967 when it became an independent city. Under Virginia law, cities normally provided for the education of their residents. Emporia, however, contracted with Greensville to administer its schools, with Emporia paying a specified part of the school system's total cost. In 1969, however, Emporia sought to form its own school system, whether to better finance quality education, as the city claimed, or to evade a recent desegregation order, as the Supreme Court suspected.

The Court held, citing *Green*, that Emporia's formation of a separate school district would "impede the process of dismantling the existing dual system."[264] Once again, after *Green*, numbers dominated discussion. The combined city-county school district was 66 percent Negro and 34 percent white. A separate Emporia district would have been substantially whiter (48 percent) but left the county system 72 percent black. The Court insisted that raw figures alone had not compelled its holding.[265] Yet other grounds relied upon by the Court either were contradicted by the record[266] or amounted to no more than a variation on the numbers argument.[267] Chief Justice Burger, in dissent, deplored the "obsession with such minor statistical differences," noted that the separate county and city systems would each be nondiscriminatory, and urged the Court not to deny Emporia's demonstrated desire for local control of its schools and better education for its children.[268] Only the majority's longer experience with southern resistance and evasion kept him from prevailing.

After *Wright*, the Court turned north. Its next four major school opinions all involved northern or western cities: Denver, Detroit, Pasadena, California, and Dayton, Ohio.[269] Yet it would be a mistake to view the rural southern and urban northern as distinct and unrelated phases of the school desegregation struggle.[270] There were differences, of course. Emporia's lost battle for a separate school district was won by the Detroit suburbs because, the Court held, they had never joined with the city in supporting segregation.[271] And the South's segregation was always held to be presumptively unlawful, while that in the North had to be laboriously proven so.[272] But generally the seeds of the Court's approach to urban school systems in the North were sewn in the rural South.

Freedom of choice, for example, proved similar to open enrollment, student transfer, and optional attendance zone policies adopted by northern school boards to minimize integration and found by federal courts to be violations of the Fourteenth amendment.[273] Another tactic, routine placement of black faculty in black schools, was judicially condemned both North and South, despite the claim of one northern school board that "black teachers serve as adult role models and inspirational examples to black pupils."[274] *Green*'s insistence on statistical evidence that the duty to desegregate had been accomplished was to become characteristic of urban school litigation, both South and North.[275] And the sweeping judicial decrees issued in the most impatient hours of the southern struggle would characterize school remedies in northern cities as well. Thus, the schools of the rural South, at first isolated sites of a sectional skirmish, over time set the pattern for a larger national war. Indeed, the judicial transfer of rural southern theories to the national urban school scene would become, if anything, too unthinking and complete.

Thus passed the first stage—the southern stage—of school desegregation. School closings, tuition grants, blustering governors and National Guards, pupil-placement laws, and freedom of choice schemes all were transparent southern devices to evade the spirit, and often the letter, of *Brown*. The Court, in time, flushed them out and struck them down. In this respect, *Green* was, as Professor Brest has noted, "the Court's last easy school desegregation case."[276] With *Swann* v. *Charlotte-Mecklenburg Board of Education*[277] and student busing, the school issue became a national one, because busing was meant not to remedy a peculiarly southern obstruction but to overcome the chief problem of the urban metropolis: racially separate patterns of housing.

The southern stage of school desegregation had been the gradualist stage, where token results were humored and tolerated. *Green* marked the end of gradualism and the dawn of something quite new: an attempt at massive integration only dreamed of at the time of *Brown*. The gradualist stage was not without its successes. The principle of segregation had been broken and a national consensus rallied to the core principle of *Brown*. One-by-one, southern tactics of resistance had been exposed and defeated. And though statistical progress in school desegregation was incremental for most of the period, still progress there had been.

Yet those fourteen long years between *Brown* and *Green* do not, in their totality, reflect well on the Supreme Court. "All deliberate speed" was a defensible starting point. Yet the Court neglected to monitor deliberate speed, to insist on more than token progress, or to have done with naked stratagems for evasion and delay. Thanks in part to the Supreme Court, southern school desegregation ran a most uneven course. For a decade after *Brown*, the Court did almost nothing; for two years after *Green*, it acted in unseemly haste. But the real damage ran deeper. By the time the Court awoke to its responsibilities, it already was too late. Blacks had lost hope and faith; many Americans sensed that law, after all, was less moral than manipulable. Much of the meaning of *Brown* had slowly trickled away.

Thus did the Supreme Court fail to provide leadership and direction to the southern school controversy. The Court cannot set in motion so complex and multifaceted a process as school desegregation and fail to give it regular attention. Scores of questions and problems beg for answers. Troops in the field require the high Court's authority and prestige. The Court cannot intervene just at times of crisis; it cannot say what is unconstitutional without suggesting what is; it cannot expect hollow outbursts of displeasure and impatience alone to get things done. The Court, like the rest of us, risks ineffectualness without follow-through. Aloofness, even for our most oracular institution, will not always do. Sadly, in its own mind, the Court became too much *le grand prononceur*. Particulars did not soil its hands; detail was left to other and lesser folk. The failure of the post–*Brown* years is precisely the failure of the Court to sense its full place in a political partnership, not just with black litigants or with district judges, but with all those Americans believing in the new day *Brown* foretold.

PART III

Busing:
Urban School Desegregation
in the 1970s

6

Busing in Southern Cities: Charlotte and Richmond

It was an ugly, worn, but still functional piece of machinery that stopped by the roadside that fall morning to take Robin Smith to high school. Its coming was part of the early morning rhythm for the Smith family, a half-noticed reminder to Robin's father, the town dentist, that it was high time to be off. But following that school bus into town was greatly annoying; it made endless stops, as did the cars piled behind it, all thanks to state law. Yet on other, less hurried days, the bus had a faintly endearing quality, reminding Mr. Smith of his own childhood friends and frolics on the way to school. Back then the old school bus had been quite a necessity; not all families owned cars and the new county high school was quite a ways off.

Neither the Smiths nor the millions of other Americans riding and honking at school buses in 1954—certainly not the justices of the United States Supreme Court—had any idea that this creaky piece of daily routine would become the flash point of domestic politics in the early 1970s, the symbol of America's ceaseless attempt to solve its insoluble race problem. Busing, as all races, ages, and classes understood, rubbed the raw nerve endings of American life. It posed the most vicious questions. Must the children of today atone for yesterday's wrongs? How much must white America compromise its own interests for its mistreated minority? And who should make the compromise: North or South, rural or urban areas, working class neighborhoods or the more affluent suburbs? How much social reform might the judiciary shoulder? To what extent must educational policy be tailored to race? For all such questions, the yellow school bus and its short, hissing derivative— busing—now became the transcendent symbol.

Busing made race seem much more complex. But not to everyone. As one student put it: "Nobody's busing me just so some niggers can get a better deal. I didn't set up the schools. I didn't make 'em like they are. No one I ever knew had anything to do with it. Niggers don't like their schools, let *them* change 'em, but they don't have the right to tell me what to do. Kids don't got any rights anyways. The only right we got is to go to school near where we live."[1]

A parent anxious over a child's well-being, a student angry at leaving a familiar school, a black seeking to escape the ghetto's grimness: all might be pardoned an absence of ambivalence on compulsory bus transportation to reduce racial imbalance. But for students of America's racial prospect, busing has quite a different effect. Student busing, suggested by some as the most promising answer to the racial separateness of the 1970s, was for others so freighted with political, social, and educational costs as to be no answer at all. Indeed, one wonders whether there will ever be any such thing as an answer. In the 1960s, we felt certain that there was. The fear of the 1970s is that there is not, that no solution fair to both races, supported by both races, and advantageous to both races can be humanly devised.

The problem is that we are no longer certain what kind of question public school desegregation really is. Twenty-years ago we were convinced it was a matter of showing southern school segregation to be morally wrong. But with busing, good moral arguments exist on both sides. To the extent that desegregation has become less a moral question, or at least more a moral standoff, is it also less clearly a constitutional requirement the Supreme Court is entitled to impose?

For others the question was not how constitutional school desegregation ought to be, but how empirical. Testing student achievement and attitudes subtly created the impression that law ought to imitate social science in cost-benefiting the need for racial integration. Many social scientists themselves disputed such notions.

"[T]he case for or against desegregation," insisted Christopher Jencks, "should not be argued in terms of academic achievement. If we want a segregated society, we should have segregated schools. If we want a desegregated society, we should have desegregated schools."[2] Yet could courts, in good conscience, avoid asking whether the social and academic benefits actually produced by integration justified the risks and disruptions necessary to achieve it?

The Supreme Court in the 1970s reflected still another view of the school desegregation controversy. Its opinions were neither morally assertive nor empirically grounded. Instead, the Court saw the matter legalistically, as one of "violation and remedy." This framework lent the Court's actions a legal veneer, even as it masked subjective judgments and avoided frank explorations of the issues over which the larger American society was deeply divided. Not surprisingly, the Supreme Court was no more in agreement on the race problems of the 1970s than anyone else. Its vaunted rule of unanimity, which characterized school desegregation cases from 1954 to 1971, was by mid-decade the relic of a more simple past.

For the task of the Court in the 1970s was far more complex than in the two preceding decades. "Nothing in our national experience prior to 1955," admitted Chief Justice Burger, "prepared anyone for dealing with changes and adjustments of the magnitude and complexity encountered since then."[3] In the 1950s the object was simply to enroll a few Negro children in formally all-white schools. By the mid-1970s the Court was asked to transform the face of urban education, to reshape the metropolitan apartheid into which the country had so regrettably lapsed. Not only were the logistics of such an effort more awesome by far than anything in the Court's southern, and largely rural, phase. The Court was now tackling a national, not a regional problem. And popular support for bold action was, to put it mildly, difficult to discern.

Busing, as an issue, has many easy emotional answers, but no pat intellectual or constitutional ones. A rounded picture of so complex and diverse a phenomenon is hard to achieve. Many kinds of snapshots are required. The first is of two southern cities—Charlotte and Richmond—where busing early began. The second is a view from the air, a general look at the arguments for and against compulsory student transportation. The third is taken of two "northern"

cities to which busing quickly spread: Denver, the subject of the
Court's first "northern and western" case, and Boston, the most
publicized of all cities undergoing court-ordered transportation.
The fourth is a metropolitan shot, a glimpse at Detroit and Louisville. It addresses the most volatile issue of all: the inclusion of
suburbia in core city desegregation decrees. The cities selected
for discussion underwent extensive litigation, often before the Supreme Court, and presented a spectrum of demographic conditions and racial outlooks. Throughout this section, attention is
devoted to racially segregated housing, with which student busing
is inextricably linked.

The first of the great school busing cases to reach the Supreme
Court was *Swann* v. *Charlotte-Mecklenburg Board of Education*, in
1970.[4] Yet to term *Swann* a "first" is to slight the traditions of pupil
transportation in this country. For *Swann* involved, in reality, a volatile variation on a long-established practice. In fact, the history of
"busing" antedated even the school bus itself. As early as 1869, Massachusetts authorized public funds to send children to and from
school in horse-drawn wagons and carriages. "A farmer in the
neighborhood was usually contracted to provide the horses and
buggies, and was paid in proportion to the number of students he
hauled."[5] By 1919, public funding for pupil transportation was
lawful in every state.[6]

From the start, student busing was hailed as an educational advance. It was, as the Court noted in *Swann*, "perhaps the single
most important factor in the transition from the one-room schoolhouse to the consolidated school."[7] Though busing began in out-
spread rural areas, it increasingly became a part of the urban educational scene, whether to promote safety in travel, to relieve
overcrowding in the schools of certain neighborhoods, or to carry
handicapped or gifted students to schools with special resources.[8]

Private and parochial schools found busing indispensable. Indeed, the Supreme Court first encountered busing in 1947 when it
allowed New Jersey to reimburse parents of parochial school children for bus transportation costs. The state could conclude, the
Court noted, that all children "can ride in public buses to and from
schools rather than run the risk of traffic and other hazards incident
to walking or 'hitchhiking.' "[9] By 1970, busing had become the
means of daily transportation for over 18 million pupils, almost 40
percent of the nation's schoolchildren. And North Carolina, whose

antibusing law faced the Court that same year,[10] had but two decades before proudly proclaimed itself "the schoolbusingest state in the Union."[11]

This history of busing prior to *Swann* convinced some it was really a spurious issue, that parents objected not to bus rides, but to blacks at the end of the trip. "Let's be candid," said Senator Walter Mondale in 1972, "busing is the way the overwhelming majority of school children outside our central cities get to school."[12] To Mondale the issue was not busing at all, but whether desegregation could be made to work. Yet the busing issue the Supreme Court addressed in *Swann* differed strikingly from the historical concept. Traditionally, busing had been democratically conceived and democratically implemented. Consolidated schools, increased access to special resources, and safer transportation all were educational aims a goodly number of citizens might be expected to support. Control of bus routes by the school board, itself an elected body or a group responsible to such a body, helped assure convenience and economy in the planning of routes. Busing to desegregate, on the other hand, was both involuntary and inconvenient. It generally had to be judicially imposed. Not only was the federal judiciary less attuned to local wishes. Its goal of desegregation presupposed inconvenience: that schools nearer home be bypassed for schools farther away, if racial balance was thereby improved.

There has also been a bleaker side to busing history: one that had nothing to do with efficient education. The school bus was the carrier of the disease of segregation, the indispensable agent of the old dual school system. Busing to segregate was every bit as inefficient as busing to desegregate, as Negroes were carried past white schools to black ones, and vice versa. The buses themselves were, of course, segregated. Sometimes, because busing cost money, Negro children were simply denied the privilege and made to walk.[13] "When I went to a one room elementary school for seven grades," recalled Henry Marsh, a city councilman in Richmond, Virginia, "I used to walk five miles in the morning and five miles in the afternoon. I got out of the way of the bus carrying the white children to a modern well-staffed school."[14]

The southern and border states, where even token integration was forbidden, took the idea to its most hideous lengths. Black students in Selma, Alabama, for example, were bused 50 miles to an all-black trade school in Montgomery, though a white trade school stood nearby.[15] Perhaps the longest reported daily round trip—108 miles—was taken by a Negro in White Sulphur Springs, West Virginia in a "20-year-old bus, warmed by a pot-bellied stove, that somehow managed the twice-a-day journey over the mountains." The boy lived four blocks from a white school.[16] Nor was busing to segregate just a thing of the past. Even as anti-busing fever peaked early in the 1970s, black leader Kenneth Clark reminded that "more pupils are being transported at public expense to racially *segregated* schools—including public schools, private schools, parochial schools and recently organized Protestant Church related 'academies'—than for purposes of school desegregation."[17]

Did whites then get back in court-ordered busing exactly what they had given out? Would years of busing to segregate be avenged by years of busing to integrate? Somehow the Supreme Court refused to use past busing abominations as a basis for the present practice. Perhaps it sensed that Old Testament justice, visited on the white majority, could never command public support; that present racial policies should steer free of recrimination; that the general history of segregation to be remedied was apparent enough without hanging out its most provocative practices.

By 1970 busing veritably begged for Supreme Court review. *Green* had neither defined a racially unitary school system nor the steps necessary to achieve one. Some federal judges in the South interpreted *Green* to mandate the maximum degree of racial integration. In many localities, this meant massive busing. Yet that was an extraordinary step for a federal trial judge to take absent Supreme Court approval. Thus Chief Judge John Brown of the Fifth Circuit, "in the only press release he ha[d] ever issued" announced that the Fifth Circuit would suspend all but the most essential desegregation activity until the Supreme Court had spoken in *Swann*.[18] Until it spoke, busing opponents would expect lower federal judges to be repudiated by a single stroke of the high Court's pen. And community support for busing, dubious under the best of circumstances, seemed all but impossible without the Supreme Court's blessing.

The absence of such approval created great uncertainty in North Carolina and Virginia. "One of the many problems that complicate opening of our schools," wrote the Charlotte *News* in 1970, "is fear that the Supreme Court never will confront and answer great questions of principle it raised in careless fashion [in *Green*]." Would "the 101 schools in Charlotte-Mecklenburg," the editor wished to know, "have to be mixed by the same rule as the two schools in the rural Virginia county? . . . And if simple rules in simple systems were to be applied to complex school systems, resulting in assignment by race or integration-by-the-numbers, what *educational* reason would be offered by the courts or the school board forced to risk destruction of the schools?"[19] In Virginia, four suits involving busing were pending in the summer of 1970 in the state's larger cities: Norfolk, Richmond, Roanoke, and Lynchburg. Conservative state legislators, vigorously supported by the two Richmond newspapers, urged Governor Holton to direct the state to intervene. But Holton refused. "Thousands of Virginians . . . will be dismayed that Holton has decided to walk away from the first truly grave challenge that his administration has faced," lamented the Richmond *Times-Dispatch*. "Since the state itself is primarily responsible for maintaining an efficient public school system, the state has a responsibility to counter the threat of chaos that now hovers over schools in Richmond and the other communities involved in desegregation suits. . . . As the state's chief executive, Holton has special leadership obligations, which he could discharge by seeking postponement of the desegregation suits until the U.S. Supreme Court has ruled on such issues as busing. Is that too much to ask?"[20]

The case before the Supreme Court involved the huge, 550 square mile, Charlotte-Mecklenburg school system, serving more than 84,000 pupils in over 100 schools. Its school population was 29 percent black and heavily concentrated in the northwest quadrant of the city. Handling the school desegregation suit was Federal District Judge James B. McMillan, "a pillar of the community for twenty-two years before he rose to the federal bench in 1968,"[21] and an activist "whose opinions," charged one critic, "show great confidence in his ability to prescribe for social ills and a deep belief that the prescriptions were constitutional commands."[22] Since 1965, Charlotte schools had operated under a court-approved desegregation plan involving geographic zoning with a provision for free transfer. But after *Green*, Judge McMillan bluntly announced that the "rules of the game have changed, and the methods and philosophies which in good faith the School Board has followed are no longer adequate to complete the job which the courts now say must be done 'now.' " Charlotte-Mecklenburg was not in compliance with *Green,* McMillan reasoned, because "approximately 14,000 of the 24,000 Negro students still attend schools that are all black, or very nearly all black, and most of the 24,000 have no white teachers."[23] To disperse such concentrations, the judge, after rejecting school board proposals, adopted the plan of his own expert witness, Dr. John Finger, a professor of education from Rhode Island College. The Finger Plan was to result in schools throughout the system ranging from 9 percent to 38 percent Negro.[24] It would require, by Judge McMillan's estimates, busing an additional 13,300 children, 138 new buses, annual operating expenses of $532,000 and start-up costs of $1,011,200.[25]

Charlotte's reaction at the time seemed feverish, in retrospect almost mild. Julius Chambers, the civil rights attorney in the Charlotte case, had his office firebombed. And white Charlotte made itself heard. Thousands of NO FORCED BUSING bumper stickers blossomed; an antibusing rally in 1970 drew more than 10,000 protesters; a new CPA (Concerned Parents Association) set out to collect 80,000 signatures on antibusing petitions to Congress.[26] "Ministers," wrote one observer, "denounced busing from the pulpit. . . . Sign-carrying crowds gathered at the U.S. post office and courthouse, on the lawn of McMillan's home, and in front of the Charlotte *Observer,* a newspaper which had staunchly supported busing until the economic effect of a drop in circulation caused a tempering of its position." The most memorable statement of resistance came from an ex-soldier: "I served in Korea, I served in Vietnam, and I'll serve in Charlotte if I need to."[27]

Opposition in 1970 was aggravated by the randomness with which busing struck. Absent a Supreme Court mandate, busing depended on the personal activism of the local district judge. Southern cities such as Richmond and Charlotte, hit by busing decrees prior to *Swann,* angrily assumed a Why me? attitude. Charlotte, in particular, held itself to have been unjustly stricken. " 'It is ironic,' " noted the Charlotte *News,* " 'and to some it seems unfair, that one of the three North Carolina school systems that led the South in earlier compliance with court requirements of school desegregation now faces almost incalculable difficulty in complying with the latest. Charlotte, together with Winston-Salem and Greensboro, undertook voluntary desegregation 13 years ago, when most of the political leadership of the South was out on the fool's errand of trying to thwart and defy the nation's courts. . . . A community that has tried to keep abreast of the law is summoned to experiment in very trying ways with its educational system—in behalf of an entire country, no part of which has lived up fully to its ideals. . . .' "[28]

The Supreme Court, as yet, seemed indisposed to listen. Though opposition in affected cities during 1969 and 1970 was intense, the Court had learned to expect that from the South. Busing fever at the time of *Swann* had not yet peaked, either in Congress or around the country. Some justices doubtless saw in Charlotte an extension of Little Rock or Birmingham, the sort of southern resistance they had been dealing with for years. Thus the Court's air was one of business as usual. Its *Swann* opinion routinely deplored the "deliberate resistance" and "dilatory tactics" used by southern school authorities to evade judicial mandates, stated that the nature of these tactics had been "noted frequently by this Court and other courts" and concluded that the problems in implementing *Green* made new guidelines advisable.[29]

But *Swann* did much more than implement *Green*. It established the framework for all future Court decisions involving student busing. At first blush, that framework is disarmingly simple. One first seeks a constitutional violation. If it is found, the focus turns to an appropriate remedy. "[A]bsent a finding of constitutional violation, . . ." the Court emphasized, neither student busing nor any other remedy would "be within the authority of a federal court. As with any equity case, the nature of the violation determines the scope of the remedy."[30] The language of violation-remedy had a comfortable ring. For *Brown I* had itself been a landmark finding of constitutional violation; *Brown II* an attempt at a workable remedy.

Unfortunately, the approach is less simple than it appears. The violation-remedy model is defective for many reasons, not least of which is that it permits the Court to foreclose and manipulate sensitive questions of policy in the guise of establishing some past constitutional offense. How the Court chose to define the constitutional violation, for example, would determine three crucial questions: whether school desegregation was a national or purely a southern obligation; how much effort civil rights attorneys must make in jurisdictions where past school discrimination was less than obvious; and finally what steps would be required of communities to eliminate the massive school segregation still in effect.

To define the violation, the Court had to select which among the many past strands of American racism should become constitutionally operative in school desegregation suits. For the violation-remedy approach requires, above all, a convincing and relevant past racial universe. The Court might have taken a sweeping and interconnected view of American racial history, moving from the early slave auctions to exploitation of slave labor in the plantation economy of the antebellum South, to the Jim Crow laws of the past and present centuries, to the Negro's northern migration and interment in the ghetto.[31] It might have seen school segregation as a product of prejudice in jobs, housing, politics, public facilities, the military, with discrimination and segregation in each part of American life reverberating throughout the whole. This "unity" of the Negro question Gunnar Myrdal had noted long before:

> . . . there is unity and close interrelation between the Negro's political power; his civil rights; his employment opportunities; his standards of housing, nutrition, and clothing; his health, manners, and law observance; his ideals and ideologies. The unity is largely the result of cumulative causation binding them all together in a system and tying them to white discrimination.[32]

But this broad view, which most accurately accounts for present school segregation, is more congenial to historians than to lawyers. History must attempt to digest a problem whole; law seeks a more finite place to begin. Thus large chunks of the Negro's past oppression are discarded as predicates for future legal action. Slavery may be irrelevant because it is remote and was even constitutional until the Thirteenth amendment; private discrimination may not matter because the Fourteenth amendment addresses only state action; employment discrimination may not be considered because its connection with segregated schools is too elusive to identify. And so on and on, until the legal mind whittles the enormity of our own unpardonable past into some narrow and manageable channel. Quite apart from analytical obstacles, the panoramic view offends the law's caution and pragmatism. It suggests that past guilt is indigenous and universal, and that drastic amends must immediately be made.

Laying aside for the moment the grandiose view, important questions still remain. To understand schools one must understand housing. Housing is that part of a community's past history most directly linked with schools, at least in the vast majority of jurisdictions where residential proximity influences pupil assignment. The logical question for the Court was what effect, if any, past housing discrimination ought to have on a school desegregation decree.

The Court's answer largely depends on how it views the whole problem of racially separate housing. Every scholarly study has confirmed what every naked eye can see: that "a high degree of racial residential segregation is universal in American cities. Whether a city is a metropolitan center, or a suburb; whether it is in the North or South; whether the Negro population is large or small—in every case, white and Negro households are highly segregated from each other. Negroes are more segregated residentially than are Orientals, Mexican Americans, Puerto Ricans, or any nationality group. In fact, Negroes are by far the most residentially segregated urban minority group in recent American history."[33]

The extent of housing segregation, however, is clearer than its causes. The popular belief is that the origins of residential segregation are essentially *"private"*: i.e., most blacks cannot afford suburban homes, and both white and black prefer to live among their own race anyway. Justice Stewart later boosted this view by attributing much black ghetto concentration to "unknown and perhaps unknowable factors such as in-migration, birth rates, economic changes, or cumulative acts of private racial fears. . . ."[34] The more private the housing crisis can be made to seem, the more quickly it can be forgotten. Yet *private* may be too facile a label for that to which it is applied. Personal income, for instance, is affected by *public* discrimination, past and present, in education and employment. Even personal racial fears are not wholly private, but influenced by racially stigmatic customs and laws. And generations of public discrimination surely kept blacks from becoming 'the kind of neighbors' whites would want.

Any private view of housing segregation is sharply disputed by many students of the problem. In their seminal study of urban racial concentrations, Karl and Alma Taeuber concluded that "the net effect of economic factors in explaining residential segregation is slight."[35] If, for instance, income differences accounted for segregated housing, one might at least expect poor blacks to live among poor whites and well-to-do blacks to live among similarly well-to-do white families. But that has not been the case. Racially interspersed housing has not generally prevailed in urban areas at any level of income.[36] Affluent whites were frequently closer to poor whites than to affluent blacks.[37] Wealthier blacks, especially, had not penetrated white suburbs. "In Chicago," noted one observer, "only one-sixth of blacks with the necessary income were suburbanites: in Philadelphia, one-third, in Boston, about one-fifth, in Baltimore, about one-tenth."[38] Another argued that opening the suburbs to blacks "is not a problem of opening them to low or middle income families; rather it is very specifically a question of opening them to blacks."[39]

Similarly, recent scholarship has downplayed housing segregation as a matter of black preference. "Nationwide public opinion polls," Professor Taeuber noted recently, "consistently show that most black families express a preference for racially integrated neighborhoods, and one-fifth or less say they prefer to live in all-black neighborhoods."[40] The choice facing blacks, however, was often not between all-black and integrated neighborhoods but between all-black neighborhoods and being the only black face on a white block. Faced with this, many blacks understandably declined to cut contact with their race.

It would be foolish, of course, to discount private explanations altogether. The question, as always, is one of emphasis and degree. But the present housing crisis in the United States is very much the result of longstanding white fears of black-invaded neighborhoods working their way into public law and policy. When Negroes first began arriving in northern cities, whites were more inclined to resist than to flee. "The attempted destruction of homes bought by Negroes in white neighborhoods was becoming frequent, . . ." wrote NAACP pioneer Mary Ovington of the World War I period. "Homes of Negroes who had bought houses in white blocks or nearly white blocks were bombed, dynamited, and occupants were intimidated in many cities."[41] The great Chicago race riot of 1919 was due in large part to friction over housing. The Kenwood and Hyde Park Property Owners Association near the University of Chicago spoke of "bombing out" adventurous black home owners and of singling out a Negro banker living in a "white" block as "the type of man that brings discredit on the honest negroes" by believing "his means justify his living among the whites."[42] The Association, noted Dr. Arthur Waskow, "called for city-wide arrangements to make sure Negroes stayed out of white residential districts."[43] Such official arrangements were common during the early twentieth century, though in 1917 the Supreme Court declared unconstitutional a local ordinance forbidding any "colored person" to move into a house on a block whose majority residents were white.[44]

For most of the first half of this century, housing discrimination was also standard federal policy. During these formative decades of urban development, the federal government did more than its share to establish housing segregation. The Veteran's Administration, for example, generally denied guaranteed mortgages to minority veterans. Worse yet was the mortgage insurance program of the Federal Housing Administration. "By eliminating the risks to lenders of making mortgage loans available," the Civil Rights Commission noted, "the Federal Government was able to induce financial institutions to provide favorable terms, including lower down payments and interest rates and longer periods of repayment, which brought standard housing within reach of many millions of Americans."[45] Yet the FHA's 1936 *Underwriting Manual* instructed appraisers that properties insured by the FHA be protected from "adverse influences," including "the infiltration of business or industrial uses, lower class occupancy, and inharmonious racial groups."[46] Private developers proposing interracial housing projects met obstruction and delay from FHA.[47] As late as 1948, the Assistant FHA Commissioner bragged that the "FHA has never insured a housing project of mixed occupancy."[48]

Private organizations, notably the real estate industry and major lending institutions, took their cue from federal policy. In 1950, the Code of Ethics of the National Association of Real Estate Brokers stated in part:

> A Realtor should never be instrumental in introducing into a neighborhood . . . members of any race or nationality . . . whose presence will clearly be detrimental to property values in the neighborhood.[49]

Although overt federal housing discrimination began to decline in the 1950s, local prejudices often persisted. "Among the various components of the American federal system," notes one recent study, "local governments have had the most direct influence on . . . residential segregation."[50] The most popular device was the racially restrictive covenant whereby a purchaser promised a seller never to sell, rent, or subsequently transfer the property to a

Negro. Whole neighborhoods and subdivisions joined in establishing such convenants, thereby fencing out black residents even where particular white owners might willingly sell. And though the Supreme Court outlawed enforcement of racially restrictive covenants in 1948,[51] their use continued in many communities.[52]

Nor were such covenants the only means of racial exclusion. Local land use controls, the most important of which was zoning, effectively discouraged blacks from better neighborhoods. Single family zoning, minimum lot size and setback distance, strict housing, fire, and health codes, landscaping and service requirements for prospective developers often were passed not only to improve the scenery of the suburbs but to limit "undesirables" as well.

Finally, localities utilized federal housing funds to reinforce existing patterns of separation. Metropolitan Housing Authorities frequently discriminated in site selection and tenant assignment policies for public housing projects, under the knowing aegis of the Department of Housing and Urban Development.[53] One study found that by the mid-sixties, no more than 76 of 250,000 public housing units in the nation's twenty-four largest metropolitan areas were located outside of central cities.[54] Given local powers over public housing in most federal statutes, that trend was likely to continue.[55] Thus, public housing often meant "massive highrise developments occupied almost exclusively by racial minorities and located in black areas of the central city." Such projects—the Pruitt-Igoes of St. Louis and the Robert Taylor Homes of Chicago—had become, in the opinion of the Commission on Civil Rights, "symbols of the failures of policies of racial containment and the resulting pathology and social chaos of ghetto life."[56]

Housing discrimination, therefore, far from being merely personal and private, had been orchestrated at the very highest public levels. Its implications for school desegregation are potentially staggering. It might not be easier to prove than past school discrimination: in both instances discriminatory intent on the part of authorities must be shown.[57] But if discrimination in housing helped establish segregated neighborhoods and thus segregrated schools, the logical way to dismantle those neighborhoods was through widespread, compulsory student transportation. Court decrees, moreover, might include both city and suburbs. For suburban communities with racially restrictive covenants, racially motivated zoning laws, racially primed rejections of public housing, doubtless caused black families to remain or locate within the central city. Remedying the true effects of housing on the schools would almost ineluctably be metropolitan in scope.[58] Finally, if past housing history were held to underlie present school segregation, the problem would, at once, assume national proportions. For housing policy, outside the South, has been indispensable to the maintenance of segregated schools.

Such unnerving prospects may have kept the justices off the housing issue. In *Swann* the Court noted, awkwardly, but with visible relief, that it need not "reach in this case the question whether a showing that school segregation is a consequence of other types of state action, without any discriminatory action by the school authorities, is a constitutional violation requiring remedial action by a school desegregation decree."[59] The Court thus looked to school history only, though housing policy was, if anything, more relevant.[60] In subsequent school cases, also, the Court did not "reach" the housing question; in part because litigants or lower courts chose not to focus on it.[61] Yet the issue will not disappear. Housing, the Court's present reticence notwithstanding, is the time bomb ticking underneath every segregated urban neighborhood school.

Even as to schools, the Court in *Swann* took only a selective backward glance. Race, it was determined, would remain a southern problem a while longer. For the constitutional vice, the Court stated, was a public policy of segregation at the time of *Brown*. Subsequent events had not erased this evil. The fact that federal courts in 1966 approved Charlotte's desegregation plan[62] was of no moment. What was yesterday's compliance was today's subterfuge. The poison of past school history could be extracted only as *Swann* was about to dictate.[63]

Thus, the question turned to remedy, to what dual systems must do to desegregate. Once again, as in *Brown II*, the Court gave school authorities and district judges primary responsibility for school desegregation,[64] though this time with more guidance. The Court's comments in *Swann* merit careful examination for they began the "busing war."

Before tackling busing, the Court delivered a lecture on school construction. School building, it noted, had been used in the past "as a potent weapon for creating or maintaining a state-segregated school system." The Court frowned, for example, on building new schools "specifically intended for Negro or white students."[65] But its advice raised questions. Was a school board not to build a school in the midst of a black community even if that community clearly needed and wanted it? At the time of *Swann*, at least some black leaders preferred black community schools to integrated ones. "The operative word in the Black and Puerto Rican communities of New York," wrote black playwright Ossie Davis, "is no longer 'Please!' but 'Power!' Community power!"[66] Professor Henry Levin of Stanford contended that "the materials, curriculum, and teaching methods" in many integrated schools "were developed for the white middle-class child" and had denied blacks their rightful sense of cultural identity. "In their noble effort to be 'color-blind,' " argued Levin, "the schools have ignored color by demanding that the ghetto child reflect the language patterns, experience, and cultural traits of the white middle class."[67] For some the road to self-discovery lay in black-controlled schools serving black communities. Had the Supreme Court intimated that building black community schools, as opposed to those in racially mixed areas, was constitutionally suspect?

The Court likewise questioned new school construction "in the areas of white suburban expansion farthest from Negro population centers."[68] Was a school board, then, to deny suburbs conveniently located schools because of their distance from a ghetto? Locating schools in integrated neighborhoods was not invariably the answer either. For those were often the neighborhoods in most rapid transition, usually from white to black. Thus the new school might be racially integrated its first year or two, but overwhelmingly black within four or five. Of course, the school board might plan a new school to serve both white neighborhood W and black neighborhood B. But then white parents might leave W, which was zoned to an integrated school, for a neighborhood elsewhere that was not. None of these problems did the Court address. Its homilies on school construction bred mostly confusion.

Not till the end of the *Swann* opinion did the Court broach student busing. Busing, of course, was not the only way to desegregate public schools. Indeed, the Supreme Court encouraged faculty assignments, redrawn school-attendance zones and an optional, publicly funded transfer program for minority students as part of the desegregation process.[69] But beside compulsory busing, these measures were mild. Busing was *Swann*'s feature attraction, the issue that was publicly awaited and advertised.

Unanimity on the Court over busing, guessed one editor, "will take some doing unless unanimity is achieved by ducking."[70] His instinct was true. Though the final *Swann* opinion was unanimous and bore the signature of Chief Justice Burger, everything had not been harmonious on the Supreme Court. Investigation by reporter Nina Totenberg unearthed some most unorthodox inner maneuverings. The first vote cast by the justices in *Swann* was said to have been 6 to 3 *against* busing. But then, wrote Totenberg, "in an unusual move, each Justice went back to his chambers and drafted an opinion. Justice Harlan's was said to have been the toughest pro-busing opinion. Then several Justices had second thoughts and switched their votes. Soon the vote was 6 to 3 for busing, with Burger, Blackmun, and Black dissenting. Eventually, the three capitulated—Black being the last holdout. And Burger, who had envisioned himself writing the opinion against busing, ended up writing the opinion for it and incorporating much of the language from the drafts of the more liberal Justices." According to Totenberg's sources, the chief justice switched for political reasons; perhaps because, as titular head of the Court, he wished to be leading rather than following on so critical an issue. Burger also fretted, according to Totenberg, that a lonely dissent against busing would cause him to be regarded as "an automatic supporter of positions favored by then–President Nixon."[71]

Such glimpses backstage help in explaining the final *Swann* opinion. On the surface *Swann* was a great liberal victory, perhaps the greatest since *Brown*. The Supreme Court had upheld the plan of a progressive southern judge requiring widespread busing to desegregate black city schools. "Desegregation plans," the Court emphasized, "cannot be limited to the walk-in school." Bus transportation was praised as "an integral part of the public education system for years." The Court approved the use of racial ratios for each school not as an "inflexible requirement," but as a "starting point" in shaping busing remedies. It encouraged all manner of alterations in school-attendance zones in the effort to desegregate.[72] It insisted that school officials "achieve the greatest possible degree of actual desegregation" and show the continued existence of any one-race schools to be "genuinely nondiscriminatory." To some, *Swann* seemed the long awaited leap forward to true integration. Its "larger message" for the country, wrote the Los Angeles *Times*, "is that we are definitely going to proceed toward becoming an integrated society. The process is going to be difficult; the problems, multitudinous." Yet *Swann* finally had demonstrated to the nation "what it truly is, and what it must become."[73]

That hopeful a comment was hardly justified. What *Swann* really revealed was a Supreme Court in turmoil, more so than the country at the time ever realized. To preserve a united front, the Court produced an opinion fogged by compromise, compromise that would shatter soon enough in open bitter debate. Some of the compromises, however, comforted conservatives. "As appalling as it was for its approval of busing as a desegregation tool, . . ." wrote the Richmond *Times-Dispatch*, "the United States Supreme Court's latest school decision may not be as harsh and unyielding as a first reading indicated. Here and there, one can find a phrase that lifts the spirits, that kindles hope for a restoration of sanity and stability to the pupil assignment systems of the South's public schools."[74]

The Court had indeed placed limits on court-compelled busing. Not every school need "reflect the racial composition of the school system as a whole"; the presence "of some small number of one-race, or virtually one-race, schools within a district" was not *per se* forbidden. Even student busing might be excessive "when the time or distance of travel is so great as to either risk the health of the children or significantly impinge on the educational process." Younger children, the Court implied, were particularly wearied by long bus rides. And school desegregation need not go on forever. "Neither school authorities nor district courts," said the Court, "are constitutionally required to make year-by-year adjustments of the racial composition of student bodies" once desegregation had taken place.[75] "These, then," concluded the *Times-Dispatch*, "are some of the more hopeful notes in the opinion. They are but weak beacons of hope, to be sure, but any light is welcome to those who are searching for a way out of the darkness of despair."[76]

For all its attempt at specificity, *Swann*'s conflicting signals left discretion where it always had been: with federal district and circuit judges. The *Harvard Law Review* assessed the decision as "only a mixed blessing to blacks seeking judicial aid to overcome racial segregation." Although the Court unanimously approved a "plan involving massive busing," its "broad grant of discretion . . . could easily lead to a less vigorous role for the federal courts in school desegregation."[77] Not only would lower court judges still have to decide how long a bus ride to require and how many one-race schools to let stand. Before them would also be questions the Supreme Court had finessed—whether all white schools were constitutionally more suspect than all black ones, and whether closing black schools and busing blacks to white neighborhoods was a permissible way to integrate.[78]

Sensing *Swann*'s ambiguities, the chief justice pushed lower courts shortly thereafter in a rightward direction with a "punch after the bell." In August 1971, four months after *Swann* and during the Court's summer recess, Burger used a stay application from the Winston-Salem School Board to personally paint on *Swann* a conservative gloss.[79] Whether feeling outmaneuvered by the Court's liberals or having second thoughts about *Swann* himself, Burger chose to highlight the opinion's restrictive language. He pointedly admonished the district judge in the *Winston-Salem* case that *Swann* had not required racial balance throughout the system and that every school need not reflect the racial composition of the system as a whole. And he promised personally to block any court order requiring daily bus travel approaching three hours, if closer school facilities were available.[80] This gratuitous attempt to muddy busing waters further was not well received. The Louisville *Courier-Journal* was incredulous: "The Chief Justice of the United States, after reading what was thought to be a landmark decision authorizing busing in Charlotte . . . then complains that some federal judges who order busing in their districts are misreading the intent of the Supreme Court's decision. Confusion. All is confusion, resulting in almost universal unhappiness, very little progress, very little justice."[81]

Suspicions were further aroused when copies of the chief justice's advice were mailed to federal judges throughout the country, each marked "For the personal attention of the Judge."[82] It was, as Professor Lino Graglia remarked, "surely one of the strangest performances in the history of the Court."[83] Had the emotions of busing caused the chief justice to jettison institutional proprieties in favor of a personal crusade? Now it was increasingly apparent that *Swann*'s was a false calm, and that Burger personally chafed at the opinion bearing his name.

The chief justice's disgruntlement notwithstanding, buses began

rolling in southern cities after *Swann*. Most federal courts agreed
with the Sixth Circuit that *Swann* "requires us to sanction the use
of bus transportation as a tool of desegregation when . . . [it] does
not pose intolerable practical problems."[84] In Memphis, the Sixth
Circuit eventually approved busing 38,000 school children with a
maximum one-way ride of forty-five minutes.[85] In Newport News,
Virginia, the Fourth Circuit affirmed cross-town student bus trips
of forty minutes to one hour, each way.[86] And in Fort Worth,
Texas, the Fifth Circuit directed elimination "of 16 unjustified, virtually all-black, one-race schools,"[87] which the school board fran-
tically predicted would mean daily round-trip rides of seventy
miles and two hours and twenty minutes.[88]

Though the length and number of bus rides must have peeved
the chief justice, parts of his cautionary message did appear to sink
in. In Memphis, a plan for busing elementary students up to two
hours-a-day was rejected, though nineteen elementary schools were
thereby left black. Practical limits placed on busing by *Swann*,
noted the Sixth Circuit, prevented such long trips.[89] Other courts
exempted altogether the youngest children from busing decrees. In
Fort Worth, for instance, kindergarten pupils were permitted to
attend schools nearest home.[90] In Newport News, rides of up to
two and one-half hours-a-day for first and second graders were
found not to be "feasible." The district judge confessed himself
"old-fashioned" enough to want youngsters to begin their schooling
in "happiness and satisfaction," with ears free of parental "griping"
about busing.[91] Yet leaving the young in segregated surroundings
was not universally applauded. For the tender years were crucial
ones both for black children not to fall behind and for interracial
trust and friendship to take seed.[92]

As city after southern city came under court busing orders, resistance built. Anticipation of busing was often the worst. In Raleigh,
North Carolina, before the school board's plan had even been considered by the court, real estate advertisements appeared, indicat-
ing where homes could be bought to avoid busing.[93] Where busing
took effect, "bus-dodging" did also. One white girl in Richmond's
affluent west end, on being "assigned to a Negro ghetto school on
the far side of the city, rent[ed] an apartment in her father's name
in a neighborhood zoned to her old school and liv[ed] at home."
Even more inventive was the Richmond blue collar worker "with
two school-age daughters . . . and a married daughter living in

suburban Chesterfield County, next door to Richmond. Father and daughter simply switched homes and the younger girls attend[ed] schools in Chesterfield, 92 percent white."[94]

Richmond, Virginia exhibited those circumstances under which court-ordered busing was least likely to succeed. The city had a 65 percent black school population when busing began; two over-whelmingly white suburban school systems—Henrico and Chester-field—lay just outside the city limits; many white Richmonders could afford private schools or to leave the city altogether; and the area's attitudes, set by the two daily newspapers, were unabashedly conservative.[95] In upper crust precincts of west end Richmond, busing provoked gestures of earnest futility: petitioning, landslide votes for antibusing candidates, formation of parent associations for neighborhood schools. In August 1970, the editor of the Richmond *News Leader*, Ross Mackenzie, delivered to the Supreme Court 29,122 letters with 37,438 signatures decrying the abolition of free-dom of choice.[96] For others, petitioning was altogether too polite. "It's getting to the point," one attorney told a huge crowd in Ches-terfield, "where federal courts and the federal government will only listen to the mob—so if we have to get a mob, let's get a mob."[97]

From the first, the white suburban schools of Henrico and Ches-terfield feared their forced merger with Richmond in the desegrega-tion decree. The district court so joined them,[98] but the Fourth Circuit reversed, holding that a district judge may not "compel one of the States of the Union to restructure its internal government for the purpose of achieving racial balance in the assignment of pupils to the public schools."[99] At the Supreme Court, the suburbs es-caped consolidation by a narrow stroke of luck. As a former chair-man of the Richmond School Board, Justice Lewis Powell declined to sit in the case. The remaining eight justices split four to four[100] and thus left standing the Fourth Circuit's opinion. The release of the suburbs deflated the most strident resistance. It also left Rich-mond's school system, almost two-thirds black, to desegregate alone.

That proved a failure. To suppose Richmond whites would at-tend black schools with white suburban and private ones close at hand was fatuous. Integration through busing left precious few whites around with which to integrate. In 1970, Richmond's first year of busing, the city's school population was 35 percent white; by 1976, the seventh year of busing, it was less than 20 percent and

heading downward.[101] Unless trends were reversed, white enrollment by 1982 was projected to sink to 10 percent. Not only had
whites fled the system, but many middle class blacks as well.[102] So
severe was the drain that by 1977 Richmond's black school superintendent, Robert Hunter, recommended greater parental free choice
for a few elementary schools. The affected schools promptly registered a slight white enrollment again.[103]

Academic standards plummeted badly after busing in Richmond,
in part, because administrators concluded that white middle-class
standards should not be "yoked on black children from poor families overnight."[104] But in 1978 superintendent Hunter concluded
that eighth grade performance was so poor that his system flunked
34 percent, three times as many as the previous year. Deserted by
the middle class of both races, Richmond schools were fighting
uphill. College preparatory courses were barely holding on; the
outlook for them, in the face of further middle class flight and natural enrollment declines, was not good. A middle-class presence, so
it seemed, helped preserve opportunities for the gifted poor.[105]

"Between the races now, there is a truce," wrote Richmond
Times-Dispatch education reporter Charles Cox in the summer of
1978. "In some schools, some days, it is a fragile truce. Small wars
are fought on occasion. . . . When the last bell of the day rings,
whites and blacks, students and staff, tend to go separate ways to
homes in different parts of town." Everyone agreed, Cox continued, "that Richmond has a 'black' system to which whites are
asked to adjust if they wish to attend."[106] Now whites, not blacks,
had to learn what being in a small minority was like. "It's like living
in a foreign country," said one white at Richmond's Maggie Walker
High, a school of 50 whites and 850 blacks. "I go to school, I go
home, that's it."[107]

White Richmond's headstrong reaction to busing in 1970 had
caused some to opine that "the tone of the late 1950s is back."[108]
But that was too simple a reading of the South in the 1970s. The
region had experienced remarkable change. As Professor William
Havard put it: "Cotton has moved west, cattle has moved east, the
farmer has moved to town, the city resident has moved to the
suburbs, the Negro has moved north, and the Yankee has moved
south." Political change, noted Havard, had been "slower to develop than the conditions would seem to warrant,"[109] but it too
came. Men of moderation occupied many southern statehouses in

the early 1970s: Askew of Florida, Bumpers of Arkansas, Holton of Virginia, West of South Carolina, and Carter of Georgia. Books appeared, heralding *The Changing Politics of the South*[110] and *The Transformation of Southern Politics.*[111]

It was, of course, easy to exaggerate true change in the South, as prophets have been doing since the days of Henry Grady. The South in 1970 remained the nation's most conservative region; racial changes may have owed less to a new spirit of brotherhood than to the rapid increase in the black vote.[112] Yet surely there were deeper currents. The immediate effect of *Brown* v. *Board of Education* had been to give the South's demagogues their day: Eastland, Talmadge, Thurmond, Barnett, Faubus, and Wallace, that long, oppressive verbal heatwave of racial hatred *sans* end. But in the long run, *Brown* helped to convince Southerners that segregation was neither the most moral nor the most practical way to live. "Southern senators like Mr. Eastland were themselves unexpected beneficiaries of the battle they lost in Congress and the courts," noted the Washington *Post.* "They were freed up to think about something other than how every act or proposal that came into their line of vision could be used to bolster the doomed racial dispensation of the South."[113] Whether because of urbanization, black votes, the moral message of *Brown*, (or, indeed, the interaction among them) the early 1970s produced some Southerners committed, as Virginia's Linwood Holton put it, "to an aristocracy of ability, regardless of race, color or creed."[114]

Holton himself performed the single most courageous act in the politics of busing. A moderate Republican from Virginia's southwest hills, Holton determined to erase the racial legacy of the Byrd organization. On the opening day of classes, he personally escorted his thirteen-year-old daughter Tayloe to predominantly black John F. Kennedy High School in Richmond, the school to which she was assigned under the court's busing plan. After shaking hands with teachers and students, the governor was greeted by a Negro honor guard, which led the two of them to Tayloe's ninth grade homeroom. "It's always hard for a child to change schools," explained Holton. "They don't want to leave old friends. But my children go where they are assigned."[115] The governor's wife, meanwhile, was taking two younger Holtons, Ann, 12, and Woody, 11, to Mosby Middle School where they were the only whites in their respective classrooms. "They're going to be all right," the governor commented. "They're going to give this as much leadership as you can expect from 11 to 13-year-olds, which is right much."[116] Holton did not mention that he might have sent the children elsewhere. The governor's mansion was on state, not city, property, and thus technically exempt from any busing decree.[117]

Some Virginians were exultant. Editor Raymond Boone of the Richmond *Afro-American,* confessedly "supercautious about praising most Virginia politicians," felt that "for once the government stood for justice. For once, we felt we were being counted in, not out. For once, we felt we were a part of the whole."[118] And former Governor Colgate Darden called Holton's act "the most significant happening in this commonwealth during my lifetime."[119]

The voters were less rapturous. Holton-backed candidates were clobbered in the next two statewide elections. "Make no mistake," the Richmond *Times-Dispatch* editorialized. "If Mr. Shafran is elected lieutenant-governor of Virginia, the voice that speaks from the Capitol about busing will be the voice of Governor Holton. And what will the voice say? 'Busing is working in Virginia.' Incredible!"[120] The Richmond dailies, countered Holton, "wanted me to stand up on the Capitol, face toward Washington, and shake my fist." His only concern, Holton stated, "was to keep schools open and make sure they survived."[121] Only then could the school-closing heritage of massive resistance truly be overcome. The governor's solitary act of leadership helped do that, but did little to stem Richmond's white enrollment decline.

It is treacherous to generalize about busing from the experience of a single city. Busing has not been a unitary phenomenon; what failed miserably in Richmond might have worked better somewhere else. A more hopeful venture, in fact, was Charlotte, the subject of the *Swann* case. Charlotte, of course, had its problems. Blacks charged that "opposition to integration [has been] led by our school board,"[122] and, indeed, board Vice-Chairman William Booe had predicted that *Swann* would lead to a "complete deterioration of public schools."[123] Community attitudes, thought the Charlotte *Observer*, were to blame for Charlotte's tribulations. "All along," wrote the *Observer*, "the judge showed a willingness—to the degree permitted by law—to make the painful transition as easy as possible for us. But in emotional and often angry tones, people in positions of leadership made him the villain of the piece. This included shameful expediency by elected officials at local, state, and national levels."[124]

In one sense, the *Observer* was correct. Under the direction of Chairman William Poe, the Charlotte school board was willing to adjust attendance zones to increase integration. But it balked at busing because, it insisted, prior to *Swann*, the constitutional mandate was not plain. Thus Judge McMillan was forced to appoint his own expert witness to draft an acceptable plan.[125]

Before reproaching school officials, however, one should understand their position. Service on the board was voluntary, but not always pleasant. The board, as one editor observed, had "to satisfy both the court, in terms of mixing, and the parent and child in terms of teaching."[126] Desegregation was but part of its duty; maintaining public support for public schools the rest. Approbation of busing threatened to erode the board's local standing. Defiance of court orders risked citation for contempt. Many boards, moreover, labored under trying conditions. Often they had to reorganize whole school systems—faculty and students—under tight deadlines (whether imposed by the court or the school calendar). Members were targets for citizen complaints. And busing often required expenditures the school system could ill afford and for which the board itself could not raise funds.[127]

Yet some insist on blaming busing's every woe on an absence of school board or community leadership.[128] Sometimes such condemnation is roundly deserved.[129] One would expect school officials to comply with court orders and not to create an atmosphere that makes desegregation impossible to implement. At some point too, when legal avenues are exhausted and opposition has been aired, personal reservations must be swallowed and support of the prevailing plan urged. Yet school officials clearly are entitled to take public exception to that which courts would impose upon them. To expect them to cheerlead whatever plan a district judge might devise is neither realistic nor desirable. They may be valuable, if exasperating, reminders to judges of community misgivings, as Charlotte's school board doubtless was. "It is all very well to trade on the grand pretense that what went wrong in Charlotte-Mecklenburg was a failure of citizen leadership and that the revival of the same would bring the schools back into sweet harmony," wrote Perry Morgan, editor of the Charlotte *News* and one of busing's unhysterical opponents, in 1971. "The hard fact is that leadership cannot exist among people who have no sense of control or participation left to them."[130]

Elected officials reflect (as well as create) malaise among the public at large. One distressed Charlotte parent living next door to an elementary school grumped at rising before dawn to see her children catch the 7:40 A.M. bus to another elementary school nine miles away.[131] Everyone suspected that they, personally, bore the brunt of the busing. Blacks complained at the closing of black schools and at being bused at younger ages and for more years than whites.[132] Less affluent whites grumbled that Charlotte's plush southeastern section escaped being bused in the fifth and sixth grades by "import[ing] black children without exporting their own children to a formerly all black school."[133] North and westside Charlotte parents thus formed Citizens United For Fairness (CUFF) to insist that busing burdens fall on the southeast as well, where in 1972 six of nine school board members lived.[134] "Constant complaints come from some areas of the county where people contend that their busing burden is greater than in other parts of the county . . . ," explained board chairman Poe. "No one wants any more of the busing burden than anyone else, and everyone is quick to find out what his neighbor's burden really is."[135]

There were other problems also. The Charlotte school board permitted students of the same race to exchange schools, until it found it had created a black market in which some students were offering up to $400 for the privilege.[136] And though elementary schools reported that racial barriers were not a big problem, junior and senior highs experienced tensions almost from the start. Each race often kept to itself in classrooms and cafeterias. Smoldering resentments threatened to erupt, as at Myers Park High School where fighting in the spring of 1971 resulted in twenty-two injured and sixty-eight windows smashed before police stepped in.[137] Some whites fled such turmoil. "Within a year or two [of the busing order]," reported the *New York Times*, "there were more than two dozen [private] 'academies' with a total enrollment pushing toward 10,000 students—one of every six white children in the metropolitan area."[138]

But after several years of busing, Charlotte's problems began to recede. Not that everyone was happy, rather, mainly resigned or fussed out.[139] "I wouldn't care if they bused my children to South

Carolina, I'm so tired of it all," said one mother.[140] Others saw silver linings. A mother of a white fifth-grader bused downtown instead of being allowed to attend the school across the street from her home admitted that busing "hasn't upset my child like I expected, and though I'm surprised to hear myself say this, I think in years to come we'll see that it [integration] is something that had to be done."[141]

In the fall of 1973, civic leaders met "at a series of homey potluck suppers," and agreed that Charlotte needed fairness and stability, whatever the cost.[142] A Citizens Advisory Group emerged to draft new, more equitable desegregation goals. At about the same time, a more moderate school board was elected, and it adopted the group's policies in July, 1974. Judge McMillan likewise approved, noting that "adoption of these new guidelines and policies is understood as a clean break with the essentially 'reluctant' attitude which dominated Board action for many years."[143] The new plan helped equalize busing burdens between black and white and among classes of whites as well. By fall of 1974, there was a tail-off in racial incidents and some slackening in the rate of white flight as well. After a successful first year under the new policies, Judge McMillan decided to close the case, i.e., not to permit repeal of the busing program but to give the school board supervision of it. In an order subtitled *Swann Song*, McMillan wrote: "This order intends to close the file; to leave the constitutional operation of the schools to the Board, which assumed that burden after the latest election; and to express again a deep appreciation to the Board members, community leaders, school administration, teachers and parents who have made it possible to end this litigation."[144]

In communities where the case is "closed," however, school boards were not free to immediately discontinue busing for racial balance. Should they attempt to do so, the matter might quickly return to federal court. How long busing must continue, and under what conditions it can be lifted, remains uncertain. Whether agreement between white and black communities, desegregation of housing patterns, or merely the absence of discriminatory behavior on the part of school officials for some specified number of years will suffice to permit a return to neighborhood school enrollment patterns is a question the Supreme Court has yet to answer.

What, finally, are the lessons of Charlotte's experience? The transcendent problem with busing—that, which until solved, makes all others meaningless—is containing white desertion of the public schools. Some white parents will inevitably seek private schooling; others will move their residence to escape the court order. So the question is never one of preventing an exodus, but of having a trickle instead of a tidal wave.

Here Charlotte-Mecklenburg possessed critical assets. The school system, to begin with, was predominantly white (71 percent). The need to assign or bus whites to majority Negro schools—the death-knell for any busing plan—was avoided. The Court plan, it had been noted in *Swann*, would produce schools from 9 to 38 percent Negro.[145] Charlotte's initial loss of white students thus did not threaten an impending black takeover. And Judge McMillan shifted busing routes to maintain white majorities in schools throughout the system. "[T]he constant shifting added turmoil to the lives of some students," noted the *New York Times*, "but on the other hand it prevented schools from 'tipping,' or becoming 40 percent or more black, a development that generally accelerates white flight."[146]

The second major asset of the Charlotte-Mecklenburg school district was its size. As Professor Finger observed: "North Carolina has a county organization of schools, thus the desegregation plan involved the entire county. Since Mecklenburg County is approximately 40 miles long and 20 miles wide and Charlotte is centrally located within the county, one could not easily work in Charlotte and live outside the school district."[147] Thus white flight was not a problem because there was no place to flee, without leaving the Charlotte metropolitan area altogether. That left disconsolate parents the alternative of private schools which, we have noted, quickly claimed about one of every six whites in the area.

But private academies often turned out to be a lesser threat to successful integration than white public schools in the suburbs. A suburban system presents an established, publicly supported enterprise, compared with the makeshift and financially suspect status of some private academies. The suburban system, unlike the private one, also spares a family tuition. And, for some families at least, attending public school in the suburbs does not impart the stigma of racism that precipitous enrollment in a newly hatched "academy" does.[148] Thus Charlotte's greatest asset, at the time of busing, was the absence of a nearby white suburban system. Charlotte might survive the private school threat; whether it could have outlasted both private and white suburban education is altogether another question. Richmond's white enrollment, at least, wilted under the joint competition.

Busing, finally, was not new to Charlotte-Mecklenburg. The school board had, without regard to integration, previously bused some 23,600 students for an average one-way trip of fifteen miles and one hour.[149] And when expanded compulsory busing first arrived, it still respected white sensibilities. Charlotte whites were not bused into black neighborhoods until the fifth and sixth grades; blacks were often bused to outlying white schools during each of their first four years.[150] As many more schools in Charlotte were located in white than black neighborhoods, blacks, of necessity, bore a heavier busing burden (though not, of necessity, at the youngest years). Though this initial inequality was regrettable, it also had its benefits. For busing young black children minimized the flight of young whites.

Thus aided by demography and constructive civic leadership, Charlotte averted the catastrophe befalling Richmond's public schools. Yet to say that busing "worked" in Charlotte is too easy. The best verdict may still be "that busing is working slightly better than its opponents feared, not quite as well as its backers hoped, and considering the furor of the last three years, probably as smoothly as could be expected."[151] If the decline of racial incidents, the onset of white resignation, and the end of district court surveillance is what is meant by working, then busing in Charlotte worked well. But these are at most superficial indicators of public education's true health. The real question is whether Charlotte's public schools were better after busing. Did white and black learn more? Were the children happier, the parents more satisfied? Was racial understanding fostered? Were black opportunities broadened? Was community support for public schools enhanced? Was civic cooperation among the races aided? These were questions that had meaning. But meaningful answers—or at least complete ones— will not come for years.

Because Charlotte was the subject of a landmark case, the temptation exists to use it as a model, to mark it as a special place whose progress should be watched. The wish is to draw wisdom from how Charlotte feared. Yet differences in America's metropolitan areas—in their racial composition and class structure, in their lifestyle, history, and outlook, in their size and compactness, their form of government and school districting—are so vast as to confound any bold assertion. "Some cities are going to have a terrible time with it," said one Charlotte man, a liberal and a member of the Community Relations Committee. "[B]ecause busing has so many disadvantages to begin with, I just can't see it becoming the uniform policy on desegregation across the country." But, the man admitted, "if [busing] can work anywhere, it can work in Charlotte."[152]

7

To Bus or Not to Bus

The Supreme Court in *Swann* drove the yellow school bus down the road of racial reform. And a bumpy journey it would prove to be. Why, one wonders, did the Court choose busing among all the alternatives available? Why, moreover, was that choice unanimous? Why, lastly, had several justices even swallowed their personal misgivings to join the opinion?

For the Court's commitment to this fateful step, there exist various explanations. One is that the Court never anticipated just how much opposition compulsory busing would provoke. Northern sentiment had not yet been aroused at the time of *Swann;* South Boston was but a speck on the racial horizon. The justices might still have believed opposition to busing just another eruption of the same southern temper that had produced Little Rock, Prince Edward, and the ugly happenings at Lamar. By 1970, moreover, the Court was most impatient with the South[1] and more than a little embarrassed that sixteen years after *Brown* the task of southern integration remained incomplete.[2] Thus *Swann* seemed the final step in the South's subjugation. That busing would soon become the hottest issue of national domestic politics, the justices had not as yet fully foreseen.

There was more to the Court's approval of busing than integrating the South. *Green* had whetted the Court's appetite for numbers.[3] Black-white percentages at last gave the Court a concrete measuring rod, an objective determinant of a school board's good faith.[4] If one's goal for schools was statistical racial balance, busing seemed the most direct way to achieve it. In fact, busing seemed the only way to achieve it in the urban metropolis where the races lived largely apart.

But something more profound motivated the Court's probusing stance in 1971: a mystical force in the catacombs of the Supreme Court known as the spirit of *Brown*. *Brown*'s legacy was a special race consciousness, an understanding among justices that blacks were henceforth to enjoy constitutional priority. *Brown* had been the gateway to the modern era in constitutional law, a catalyst to reform in criminal justice, in the relationship of state to federal courts, and in the law's protection of the poor, all of which were intended, among other things, to benefit blacks.[5] The race cases soon developed their own internal hierarchy. While justices might disagree, for example, over Civil Rights protests or selection of juries,[6] to dissent in a school case was very close to sacrilege. And blacks themselves seldom failed to invoke *Brown*'s memory. "If the court rules against the civil rights movement on this," warned Dr. Kenneth Clark in one major school case, "I would interpret it as a sort of dilution of *Brown*."[7] Never mind that school issues in the 1970s differed from those of 1954. *Brown* had the Court bewitched. For the tenure of the new Burger Court to begin with a setback in school desegregation would have been a dreadful omen for many that the hard-won gains since *Brown* were about to be rolled back.

One can understand, then, why the Court ruled as it did in *Swann*. But understanding a decision and evaluating it are two different tasks. The preceeding and succeeding chapters each focus on the busing experience of particular cities. This chapter assesses from a more general perspective the arguments for and against the student busing approved in *Swann*.

The first justice to openly challenge *Swann* was Lewis F. Powell, Jr., of Richmond, Virginia. Powell was not appointed to the Court until after *Swann*; indeed, in *Swann*, he had submitted an *amicus* brief* on behalf of Virginia in opposition to forced busing.[8] Nine

---

*An *amicus* brief is one submitted by a person or group interested in a case but not a party to it.

months later, in January 1972, Powell arrived on the Court himself. He had long experience in public education. As chairman of the Richmond school board from 1952 to 1961, Powell wrestled with the agonies of transition *Brown* had brought to the South. At the Senate hearings on his confirmation, two quite opposite views emerged on his tenure. The first was that of a man "in a position of complex responsibility during some very turbulent and confused times" whose "primary concern was to keep the schools of Virginia open and to preserve the public education system for all pupils."[9] Possibly "Mr. Powell's outstanding contribution to Virginia," noted the Norfolk *Virginian-Pilot*, "was his leadership in the quiet sabotage by a business-industrial-professional group of Senator Byrd's Massive Resistance."[10] In later articles Powell blamed much of the lawlessness of the 1960s on southern defiance of the *Brown* decision.[11] He was not unsympathetic to the Negro's plight: "It is true," he noted in 1966, "that the Negro has had, until recent years, little reason to respect the law. The entire legal process, from the police and sheriff to the citizens who serve on juries, has too often applied a double standard of justice. Even some of the courts at lower levels have failed to administer equal justice. . . . There were also the discriminatory state and local laws, the denial of voting rights, and the absence of economic and educational opportunity for the Negro. Finally, there was the small and depraved minority which resorted to physical violence and intimidation. These conditions, which have sullied our proud boast of equal justice under law, set the stage for the civil rights movement."[12]

By most measures of opinion in the aftermath of *Brown*, Powell was very much a moderate. That meant he was also a gradualist, a symbol to Negroes of the frustrating pace of progress in the South. By 1961, when Powell left the school board, only 37 Richmond Negroes out of more than 23,000 had enrolled in white schools.[13] Shortly afterward, the Fourth Circuit found in Richmond a system of dual attendance zones and feeder schools[14] designed to keep racial integration to a minimum. "Notwithstanding the fact that the [state] Pupil Placement Board assigns pupils to the various Richmond schools without recommendation of the local officials," observed the Fourth Circuit, "we do not believe that the City School Board can disavow all responsibility for the maintenance of the discriminatory system which has apparently undergone no basic change since its adoption."[15] Simply because Powell "had

sense enough to recognize the futility of the massive resistance program and to go for a more sophisticated scheme of evading the
Brown decision [should] not affect your decision," argued the prominent Richmond black attorney Henry Marsh to the Senate Judiciary Committee. "The Constitution outlaws the ingenious as well
as the obvious scheme, and the fact that Mr. Powell had the knowledge to . . . evade the Constitution more effectively, as he did in
the City of Richmond during the massive resistance era, without
having integration, does not commend him to the Supreme
Court."[16] John Conyers of Michigan, representing the Congressional Black Caucus, was more explicit: "We would conclude . . .
Mr. Powell's own activities on the boards of education, his close association with a variety of corporate giants, . . . his membership in
the largest all-white law firm in Richmond, his support of segregated social clubs, and his defense of the status quo, are inconsis-
tent with the kind of jurist that . . . is desperately needed for the
court in the 1970's and the 1980's."[17]

Once on the Court, Powell was not long in leaving his mark on
school desegregation. Though the occasion was the 1973 Denver
school case, Powell's opinion had little to do with Denver and almost everything to do with *Swann*. "To the extent," wrote Powell,
"that *Swann* may be thought to *require* large-scale or long-distance
transportation in our metropolitan school districts, I record my
profound misgivings. Nothing in our Constitution commands or
encourages any such court-compelled disruption of public education."[18]

The words had not come easily. If few issues concerned Powell
more than busing, on few was he less eager to write. He knew the
solitary statement of a Southerner so soon after appointment would
raise eyebrows. In his freshman term, he refrained from writing in
another school case[19] for just that reason. But in Denver, the time
had come. Powell personally shepherded the opinion through ten
different drafts, seeking firm but unemotive language. He remembered *Dred Scott* and *Plessy* and the dim corners to which history
consigned judicial frustration of black aspirations. And he pondered
the spirit of *Brown*. In the end, he decided to bet that court-ordered
busing was the wrong way to solve America's race problem.[20]

His view of race was a patient one. "It is well to remember," he
cautioned, "that the course we are running is a long one";[21] the racism that persisted for generations would take generations to over-

come. Inequality of opportunity among men was a natural state; courts could go only so far in combatting it. What he could not accept was race as the basis of unequal status. But to believe that a system of accustomed advantages for the children of certain members of the society might suddenly be upturned was folly. Hope for the Negro lay in gradual progress along many fronts: in voting, jobs, housing, and education.[22] But busing was precipitous, calamitous, visionary. It was wrong, he protested, to place on today's schoolchildren the full, crushing burden of historical atonement.[23] To Powell, history alone was not controlling. What practical sense, he began asking, did busing make today?

Had America somehow lost perspective on race? The tingling moments of the Civil Rights struggle, the Montgomery bus boycott, the marches to Washington and from Selma, the Greensboro sit-ins, Meredith and Mississippi, the tiny bands of black students crossing segregated thresholds: all spoke so palpably and eloquently of injustice, a fact few Americans in the quiet of conscience could deny. But were black demands for busing as justly based? And were neighborhood schools quite the evil as lunch-counter and back-of-the-bus segregation? Was *Swann*'s insistence on "the greatest possible degree of actual desegregation"[24] a plea for integration for integration's sake? With *Swann* and busing, had the Civil Rights movement lost its purity and entered a more sterile and mechanical phase, where the form of racial justice had overtaken the substance? Had it come to be that the cart had been put before the horse, and that who was in school together and in what proportions was now more important than what was learned there?

Powell worried that the race issue, in the fractious form of forced busing, might eclipse quality of instruction as the focus of public schools. Busing, he argued, was "likely to divert attention and resources from the foremost goal of any school system: the best quality education for all pupils."[25] To begin with, funds needed to improve instruction might be used to bus. "At a time," wrote Powell, "when public education generally is suffering serious financial malnutrition, the economic burdens of such transportation can be severe, requiring both initial capital outlays and annual operating costs in the millions of dollars."[26]

The costs of busing were often impossible to predict. Participants in school desegregation suits had every reason to distort the figures. School boards resisting busing wished to magnify its hardships: their "wild projections of costs," charged the NAACP, "have been completely misleading."[27] But blacks seeking busing and the district judge about to order it had exactly the opposite bias: each wished to downplay the disruptions, including the additional expense that busing would cause. The result was a wild fluctuation in estimated costs. In Charlotte, for example, the school board predicted that the court's busing plan would require initial outlays of $3,406,700. Judge McMillan, using quite a different method of computation, estimated them at $1,011,200.[28]

It was as difficult to generalize about busing costs as to predict them. The purchase of new buses was, of course, the big initial expenditure. How many had to be purchased chiefly depended on the size of the school district, the amount of busing required, and whether the school board, as Charlotte had but Memphis had not, bused students previously. Annual operating costs for drivers' salaries, fuel, and vehicle maintenance generally represented less than a third of the initial outlay and also varied markedly.

Compulsory busing's operating costs were often but a fraction of the school board's total budget (1 to 2 percent),[29] a fact that led busing advocates to belittle them. The increased annual cost of compulsory busing in Charlotte ($720,000), said one supporter, "is about what we spend on 2 days' operation of our schools. . . . It is worth the cost, I think, of 2 days' operations of the schools not to have a racially divided community."[30] But this, when added to the purchase price of buses, still pinched many a financially strapped school board. Despite Dade County's (Miami) $250 million budget, the chairman of the School Board testified in June of 1971 that start-up costs of $1.5 million and annual busing expenses of $670,000 were still "placing severe demands and burdens" on the school system.[31]

How, then, were local officials to meet the burden? Federal aid seemed the logical place to start. Yet Congress early prohibited federal funds for busing,[32] not only to display its own displeasure, but to make federal judges reluctant to order what hard-pressed localities would be forced to underwrite. Many states had traditionally reimbursed localities for transportation costs. In Florida, for example, 11.2 million of the $23 million in pupil transportation costs for 1970–1971 were bankrolled by the state.[33] Yet states, as well as the federal government, chafed at funding so unpopular a cause. "So far as we can tell," complained the Charlotte school board chairman, "no legislative body anywhere wants to pay for a bus fleet to provide racial balance-type busing. . . . Doubling the size of the largest school bus fleet in the State of North Carolina overnight with no additional funds to pay the bill has been a terribly hard task."[34]

In some instances, impatient federal courts simply ordered states to assume part of the increased busing costs in affected localities.[35] Often, however, localities were left to their own resources and their own sets of unattractive options. Norfolk, Virginia sought to have students and their families foot the bill. Families of the 15,000 children to be bused were to pay sixty-three dollars per student per year for private bus service. It was hard to imagine a more wretched plan. Norfolk's was, in effect, a regressive flat-fee tax, which black families could ill afford. And it salted white wounds, with a forced payment for a detested ride. The levy, moreover, fell unevenly, requiring the bused student to pay for his misfortune, while those left in neighborhood schools got off free. Faced with a scheme that made the busing pill more bitter and the flight of whites more likely, the Fourth Circuit ordered Norfolk to provide free transportation as part of its desegregation plan. Otherwise, said that court, desegregation would amount to a "futile gesture," a "cruel hoax." The $3 million capital outlay for buses and the $600,000 increase in operating costs were, the Fourth Circuit advised, not unreasonable in a district with a "school budget of over 35 million dollars."[36]

That still did not solve the problem. Raising property taxes for busing was not attractive in cities with a declining tax base and restive middle-class population. Even if school boards wanted to raise taxes, many lacked the power and those city councils with the power were loathe to use it so distastefully. That left the alternative of cutting educational programs, which Pontiac, Michigan, and Pasadena, California, among others, did.[37] Busing, designed to help the black and poor, now caused other similarly well-intentioned programs to be dropped.

Finally, there were cost efficiencies made necessary by the operating problems of busing itself. Senator Mondale noted that "[i]n Nashville, Tennessee, because of an inadequate number of school buses, opening times for schools have been staggered so that some children start school as early as 7:00 a.m., and others arrive home after dark."[38] In Charlotte, three high schools began their school day at 7:00 A.M. for the same reasons, with students leaving home before daylight in winter months.[39] Further savings might be brought about by the purchase of used rather than new buses, postponement of repairs, less thorough training or scrutiny of drivers and other corner-cutters, measures that created obvious risks. Not that any public official would deliberately endanger the safety of a schoolchild. But where a budget is tight and a program unpopular, temptations exist. The Charlotte school board chairman admitted pressing "into service 168 old buses retired because of age—around 15 years—by other school systems in North Carolina. . . . Now we are under tremendous pressure to replace these wornout buses, and no [state or federal] money is available. . . . Recently, our county commissioners have grudgingly released enough funds . . . to buy 84 new school buses—half enough to replace the antiques now in service."[40]

Safety was not the only reason to relieve local budgets of busing costs. The success of busing depended on many small conveniences: whether buses ran on time, whether breakdowns were avoided, whether seats were comfortable, whether overcrowding was averted, and whether transportation existed for emergencies and for after-school extracurricular activities.[41] Such amenities, however, were often not forthcoming. Some officials, in fact, wished to prove busing the miserable failure they had forecasted and thus deliberately underfinanced it. A district judge, of course, could always grab the reins and specify the exact number and quality of buses local officials were to buy.[42] But such interference ensnared him ever more deeply in daily school administration, often at some cost in school board cooperation and community compliance.

The real problem of busing finance was not the dollar amounts. More than peanuts, they were still such that most school budgets could absorb in stride. But busing was no more a simple matter of finance than it was a simple matter of transportation. It was a question of who pays for something few persons want. The courts that issued the noxious orders lacked funds to pay for them; when the issue was tossed to politicians, they used their power of the purse to balk, rail, and voice their most electable indignation. Had whites believed busing worthwhile, dollars would have come quickly and amply, as indeed they had through the many decades in the South when buses transported students to segregated schools.

The public purse follows easily programs commanding strong majority support. The financing, on the other hand, of projects forced on the community inevitably sparked frictions far in excess of the actual dollar amounts at stake.

More serious, then, than the drain on public funds was busing's redirection of human energies. To a city beset by busing, nothing else mattered. The year before the commencement of busing and, generally, the two thereafter were ones of strange rumors, passions, anxieties, fears. For the school board and superintendent, the old challenges of education were secondary. Members took calls from irate parents, addressed freshly sprung citizens' groups, submitted, resubmitted, and appealed plans from the district courts, explained new assignments and bus routes, prepared (and prayed) for a smooth transition. Parents rushed to learn their child's new destination, to attend rallies and protests, to investigate private school alternatives, to plan new household routines. Teachers wondered about instruction and discipline among their new charges. And adult tensions did not escape the notice of the children or help fix young minds on matters academic.

Social shake-ups, to be sure, can release human nature from unproductive ruts. To make desegregation work, racial stereotypes would have to be reexamined, new methods of teaching explored, new courses initiated, a new community awareness born.[43] Desegregation was never expected to be easy or painless; but, it was argued, the turmoil it engendered would be transitory. No hysteria lasts forever; after a year or two, that attending busing too would subside. Advocates, in fact, took the first opportunity once busing was in effect to cite relaxed tensions as evidence busing worked; opponents said only that those most opposed had left the public school system, while those who remained were exhausted or resigned. Busing, however, could always reinvigorate the old warriors. Controversy might flare anew when bus routes were redrawn—whether to prevent schools from tipping (i.e., becoming more than 30 or 40 percent black), or to incorporate additional communities, or simply to achieve greater fairness or efficiency.[44] It hardly seemed timely, thought Justice Powell, amidst rising concern and falling indicators[45] of public school performance to turn the attention of communities "from the paramount goal of quality in education to a perennially divisive debate over who is to be transported where."[46]

There was evidence that some blacks shared Powell's priorities, that the frantic quest for racial balance had left both races numb. "At first [blacks] fought to get into white schools to get the same things the whites were getting," remarked Henry Pruitt in 1977, principal of the Englewood Middle School in New Jersey, which had become 80 percent black after fourteen years of desegregation. "[N]ow some of them are saying we can go back to 'separate but equal' as long as we can get quality education. . . . This integration stuff is kind of passé now. All the parents want to know from me is what kind of education are their kids getting."[47]

Both sides in the urban busing dispute appealed to the traditions of rural America. Each claimed to represent in education a simpler, happier time. Busing, some contended, was as American as baseball. "By itself," wrote Herb Kohl, "busing simply means putting kids in buses and moving them around. In rural counties, it's been done for years."[48] Likewise, the rustic red schoolhouse on the bumpers of suburban station wagons evoked pictures of "dear old golden rule days," warning, all the while, that the cozy school environment in which we had grown up was about to expire.

The neighborhood school, which the little red schoolhouse symbolized, was not precisely what its name implied. Many neighborhood schools were indeed in the neighborhood and walk-in schools to boot. Yet in announcing that "desegregation plans cannot be limited to the walk-in school,"[49] the Court in *Swann* implied that neighborhood schools meant only that. It was an unfortunate suggestion. The facilities needed for modern education, especially at the high school level, made schools within walking reach of all a fantasy. Where sidewalks were bad or thoroughfares busy, it made sense to bus, even to neighborhood schools. To those who rally to the banner, "neighborhood schools" meant only a preference for the school closest to home no matter how the student got there. Barring special circumstances, such as overcrowding or special education, one should not be bused past schools nearer home to those farther away. And, indeed, it made great sense that more of a child's time be spent at home or at school and less en route between them.

Others, however, professed to see in bus rides great blessings in disguise. Fast friendships may indeed form and worthwhile reflections occur on school buses. Yet in an article entitled "Billy's Bus Driver," Robert Coles gives the ride too romantic a gloss. Billy's driver was black and "a strong, well-spoken, active man whom the children admire and talk to all the time, and find it a real pleasure to know. I have often thought as I rode with him that he runs a kind of school on that bus of his. He points things out to the children. He asks them questions. They huddle close to his seat and listen to his stories, his jokes, his clever remarks, full of irony and vigorous social satire. They are allowed to move about, change seats, even scrap a little. . . . 'That way,' [notes the driver], 'they get the mischief out of their system here on the bus. That way, they're quieted down and ready for school when we get there. 'Give 'em Hell,' I call to them when they get off. And I believe they listen to me.' "[50]

For every such trip, there were the recollections of L. C. Bowen, a bald, stout bus driver in Richmond, Virginia, whose daughter had just been assigned under court-ordered busing to a heavily black school. She "stayed up all night crying, . . ." said Bowen. "I'm not opposed to her going to school with these here black children, but I'm dead set against her riding the bus every day. It's not safe, and there's lots of filthy indecent language. I should know. I hear it every day, and it's sickening."[51]

Whatever the charisma of its driver or the temperament of its passengers, the school bus, like the subway, is not one of life's garden spots. Exercise is impossible (unless the bus becomes a madhouse), organized activity is not attempted (who would dare?) and studying is difficult (and probably quite unpopular). In the absence of monitors and with no place to which to retreat, the bus may be hazardous for members of the outnumbered race. The school bus is really the child's commuter train, and commutes, by and large, are something to be shortened or avoided. In the adult world at least, there are few known instances of longer routes being chosen where shorter ones were available.

Not that adult commutes are all wasted time: one reads the paper, listens to radio, chats with a friend, or generally collects one's thoughts. But at least with adults, commuting is voluntarily undertaken to achieve such magic combinations as a suburban home and desirable urban job. Court-ordered busing, on the other hand, is a commute involuntarily imposed, against the child's, the parent's, and the community's wishes and often to their considerable inconvenience. The longer the bus ride, the less time for athletics, piano, hobbies and homework, (and, in fairness, too, for sheer idleness and television). For judges to risk tying children's days in uncreative knots seems a curious way to implement constitutional policy.

Neighborhood schooling, Professor Fiss has noted, "enables a parent to control his children's association in the public schools through the choice of residence."[52] Selection of a home, it is said, should carry stable expectations as to schooling as well. Good schooling for one's offspring, the argument runs, is rightly part of that advantaged lifestyle to which people should aspire, a most potent incentive in our free enterprise society.

Neighborhood schools symbolize, above all else, the effort of America's vast middle class to transmit shared values and aspirations to its children. For those who could not afford or did not desire private education, neighborhood schooling was their pride. There, children would meet socially acceptable friends and get sound instruction in the parents' values, all in a safe environment. This hardly was an ignoble impulse—to want the best for one's children in schools and in schoolmates, as in every other way. Providing advantages for one's offspring well may be the first of life's satisfactions. It is an instinct the law has sanctioned: gift and inheritance taxes, graduated though they be, do not forbid transmission of sizable estates. But education, as much as income, was the precious inheritance. The chance to bequeath premier schooling had long existed. To send one's child to a private—and privileged—school or college is a right the Court has protected.[53] By upholding Texas's reliance on local property taxes and the resultant disparities in school district revenues this system of taxation engendered, the Court itself had buttressed the notion that a child's public education may reflect parental income.[54]

Yet the argument that schools, like homes, should reflect parental status is not free from difficulty. Homes tend to symbolize attainment, schools opportunity. A home is purchased on the open market, a school is something to which one is assigned. Homes thus represent free choice, while parental choice as to public schools has always been less than absolute.[55] School boards often defer to parental wishes on school assignment, curriculum, teachers, and the like, but they are hardly obligated to do so.

Quite beyond that, how much of a parent's own advantaged status ought to pass to his child? Middle-class parents already give their children many things: more spacious and comfortable homes and surroundings, better nutrition and health care, greater cultural and intellectual stimulation, higher personal expectations and aspirations, more acceptable diction, dress and manners, greater awareness of life's traps and pitfalls, well positioned friends and acquaintances, and so on and on and on. To such advantages, do we want to add a superior school?

To answer yes is to weight the scales of life ever more formidably against the dispossessed. For blacks, argues Professor Fiss, the choice of good homes and thus good schools is "virtually meaningless." While "some Negroes may prefer the emotional security of living in a ghetto, ghettoization is forced upon most Negroes by racial discrimination in housing, the . . . [white exodus] that occurs when Negroes move into a white neighborhood, and the Negro's present economic disabilities, which to a large measure are inflicted by racial discrimination in employment."[56] To declare schools solely within the province of parental choice and status—when most blacks had neither—might be the final affront.

Neighborhood schooling thus carried contradictory connotations for the races. To many blacks it meant confinement, a slow suffocation in the dankness of the ghetto. The school bus might mean hope, escape, the door to a new life of challenge and opportunity. "The very bus ride," wrote Robert Coles, "gives Negro children vision, a sense of cohesion with one another, and even a feeling of pride. It is *their* bus; it is taking them places they have never seen before, places which, to them, mean a better life in the future."[57] A black schoolchild of eleven in Boston's Roxbury, looking down with hands folded in his lap, put it best: "Busing's just got to be, man. Got to be. We got it coming to us. We got to open up ourselves, spread out. Get into this city, man. Move into all those places we can't go at night, you know. Go to good schools, live in good places like white folks got. . . . That's why they're busing us."[58]

In the end it is hard to defend neighborhood schools as part of a parent's right to pass along class advantage. The historic mission of public education has been to counter, not reinforce, social encrustation.

The grand justification for neighborhood schools is their inculcation of a sense of personal identity. Each life needs its points of anchor and ports of call. These were once found close to us: in our family, our neighborhood, our place of work and worship, and our school. They should, above all, be warm, personal, durable, dependable. Justice Powell, for one, feared they no longer were:

> Today, we are being cut adrift from the type of humanizing authority which in the past shaped the character of our people.
>
> I am thinking, not of governmental authority, but rather the more personal forms we have known in the home, church, school, and community. These personal authorities once gave direction to our lives. They were our reference points, the institutions and relationships which molded our characters.
>
> We respected and grew to maturity with teachers, parents, neighbors, ministers, and employers—each imparting their values to us. These relationships were something larger than ourselves, but never so large as to be remote, impersonal, or indifferent. We gained from them an inner strength, a sense of belonging, as well as of responsibility to others.
>
> This sense of belonging was portrayed nostalgically in the film "Fiddler on the Roof." Those who saw it will remember the village of Anatevka in the last faint traces of sunset on Sabbath eve. There was the picture of Tevye, the father, blessing his family, close around their dining room table. They sang what must have been ancient Hebrew hymns, transmitted from family to family through untold generations. The feeling of individual serenity in the common bond of family life was complete.[59]

The threat to traditional institutions seems clear enough: the increasing divorce rate, the automation replacing artisanship in work, the turn from the church, the retreat of individual home ownership before the high rise. To lament such trends is to be a sentimentalist. Yet Powell viewed them with disquiet, fearful that we, as a people, might be losing our rootedness, our unifying bonds. He recalled earlier days, less vulnerable to technological change and great social reform. For him, the issue of busing was clear: whether students whose friendships and loyalties had arisen out of their experience at certain schools were to be sacrificed to a social experiment of dubious worth:

> Neighborhood school systems, neutrally administered, reflect the deeply felt desire of citizens for a sense of community in their public education. Public schools have been a traditional source of strength to our Nation, and that strength may derive in part from the identification of many schools with the personal features of the surrounding neighborhood. Community support, interest, and dedication to public schools may well run higher with a neighborhood attendance pat-

tern: distance may encourage disinterest. Many citizens sense today a
decline in the intimacy of our institutions—home, church, and
school—which has caused a concomitant decline in the unity and
communal spirit of our people. I pass no judgment on this viewpoint,
but I do believe that this Court should be wary of compelling in the
name of constitutional law what may seem to many a dissolution in
the traditional, more personal fabric of their public schools.[60]

The Court admitted grudgingly in *Swann* that neighborhood
schools made educational sense. "All things being equal, with no
history of discrimination," the Court noted, "it might well be desirable to assign pupils to schools nearest their homes."[61] The advantages, especially in the elementary years, seemed obvious.
Parents, for one thing, were nearby. They could reach school more
quickly in the event of an emergency. They could attend more
PTA meetings and individual teacher conferences, be present at
more concerts, plays, and sporting events, and, in general, demonstrate greater knowledge and interest in school affairs. Closer
friendships might develop where children met both in and out of
school: at history class on Wednesday, the cafeteria on Thursday, a
Friday night party, a Saturday movie or playground basketball
game, and over the summer on the swimming team. With busing,
however, one's best neighborhood friend might attend school across
town.[62] While busing might broaden a student's acquaintanceship,
the sharing of personal experience in neighborhood schools was
likely to be more complete.

All too frequently, busing dampened school spirit. Consider the
example of Louisville, Kentucky. In 1975, the district judge devised a busing plan for the Louisville metropolitan area designed to
insure black elementary enrollments between 12 and 40 percent and
black secondary school enrollments between 12.5 and 35 percent.[63]
But because "the pupil population ratio in at least 28 elementary
schools did not satisfactorily reflect the racial guidelines set forth"
in the 1975 plan,[64] the district judge next summer juggled pupil assignments to achieve better results.

Annual reshufflings, of course, hardly aided the formation of
lasting school ties.[65] But even under the judge's revised plan (see
table 1), problems abounded. The objectives of the plan were to
achieve the desirable racial balance and distribute the busing burden more or less evenly within each racial group.[66] And that
created difficulties. White children, for example, whose last names

began with A, B, F, or Q were to be bused in the eleventh and twelfth grades, thus guaranteeing that their high school years would be split between two schools. Blacks whose last names began with D, E, N, W, or Z were to be bused during grades two and four, but not one and three, thus insuring that no two of their first four elementary years would be spent consecutively at the same school. Thus, a sense of belonging often failed to take root. "The school loyalty problem," noted the Louisville *Courier-Journal*, "seemed sharpest at Shawnee, the inner-city [high] school whose white majority is bused in and changes each year. The turnover was 79 per cent this year; at pep rallies some Shawnee students reportedly boo their own school to show loyalty for the old schools to which they will return next year."[67]

Alienation was not unique to Shawnee. Toward the end of Louisville's second year of busing, many students complained of feeling no "ownership" in schools to which they were transported. Bused students—white and black—were observed to act more belligerently in schools away from their own neighborhoods, as if they had something to prove. Mary Kelly, a white senior at Atherton High School, attributed increased vandalism to the bused student's

How to tell when your child will be bused...unless

If child's last name begins with letters:	White child will be bused in grades:	Black child will be bused in grades:
A, B, F, Q	11, 12	2, 3, 5, 6, 7, 8, 9, 10, 11, 12
G, H, L	2, 7	2, 3, 4, 6, 7, 8, 9, 10, 11, 12
C, P, R, X	3, 8	2, 3, 4, 5, 6, 7, 8
M, O, T, U, V, Y	4, 9	2, 3, 4, 5, 9, 10, 11, 12
D, E, N, W, Z	5, 10	2, 4, 5, 6, 7, 8, 9, 10, 11, 12
I, J, K, S	6	3, 4, 5, 6, 7, 8, 9, 10, 11, 12

Exempted students:

✔ Kindergarten students

✔ First graders

✔ Students in special schools, primarily for the emotionally or or physically handicapped

✔ Students attending schools exempted under the plan

✔ Some students with specific handicaps

Source: Louisville Courier-Journal, June 18, 1976

sense of being on "foreign soil." "I had pride in [Atherton] because my older sister went here," she said. "The kid bused in doesn't care if he breaks a window or something like that. . . . I think I can understand the feeling of the kids bused in, though. If I was sent down to Manual [an inner city school], I'm not sure I would care about how the building looked."

The lack of attachment was not surprising. Teachers and principals in Louisville complained that bus schedules discouraged students from participating in extracurricular activities after school. In fact, busing seemed to make school more like work. "Since busing occurred, there's been a lot more apathy," noted Tony Clayton, senior class president at Doss High School. "Kids just want to get through school and out."[68]

One may argue for bus schedules that permit extracurricular participation and for busing plans that assign elementary or high school students to the same school throughout. The latter, however, entails an unfair busing burden (some children being bused all five elementary years, others remaining in their neighborhoods the entire time). And buses leaving school after the day's extracurriculars might, if rides are long, arrive home too late.[69] But will any plan really overcome the estrangement of those bused in? The perception by the student of his school as a component of his own neighborhood, the proximity of the school to home, the easy access of parents to the faculty, the school as the recreational hub of the surrounding community, may be what creates student loyalties and ties. For judicial edicts to break such communal bonds was a weighty moral step, no matter how lofty the proclaimed constitutional ends.

The most demonstrable adverse consequence of busing involves white flight. Integration is thought to be beneficial only if whites and blacks associate in substantial—not token—numbers and at all levels of the socioeconomic ladder.[70] By removing large numbers of middle-class whites, white flight thus threatens the two ingredients indispensable to integration's success.

Traditionally the phrase "white flight" described neighborhood turnover, whites leaving at the sight of the first black face on the block. Destruction of neighborhood schools, it was predicted, would produce this phenomenon on a city-wide scale. "No one," warned Justice Powell, "can estimate the extent to which dismantling neighborhood education will hasten an exodus to private schools, leaving public school systems the preserve of the disadvantaged of both races. Or guess how much impetus such dismantlement gives the movement from inner city to suburb, and the further geographical separation of the races."[71]

"White flight" is an ugly term. It suggests, not so subtly, that blacks are unacceptable schoolmates or neighbors, that if one cannot keep too many blacks from coming in, the only alternative for whites is to move out.[72] Given white flight's many depressing implications, some reacted by disputing its existence. But what if white flight were a real, if ugly, threat, whose potential devastation to urban schools was incalculable? The dilemma then becomes quite painful. For courts to ignore the reality of white flight is to risk making racial segregation worse through the very plans devised to end it.

In assessing white flight, one must first ask who flees. One answer is that the prejudiced leave, while the tolerant remain. That theory is too simple. True, the bigot may depart public schools first. But his exit may gradually increase black enrollment percentages to levels that change the meaning of integration for even the more tolerant and receptive whites. Rather than being directed to have their children share their good schools with other children less fortunate, these whites now find themselves forced to send their children elsewhere. Each white departing public schools adds pressure on those remaining. At some point even the most reasonable are susceptible to panic.[73] The challenge, of course, is to rally support to the integrated school before white flight becomes irreversible.[74]

An alternate—and plausible—hypothesis is that well-to-do whites escape, while working-class whites want to but cannot. Flight, we do know, takes money. Not everyone can afford to pay both public school taxes and private school tuition. And not everyone can leave his present residence for one in the suburbs. Strong feeling may, in some cases, overcome limited means. The white mother in Pontiac, Michigan, who promised to "go to jail" before submitting to busing,[75] might also moonlight, drop vacation plans, and otherwise bend the budget to seek alternative schooling for her child. But such sacrifice must be rare. In the wake of white flight stand public schools for the poor—white and black—hardly the most hoped-for combination or the least flammable mix.

One must ask not only who flees but where they flee to. Flight to

the suburbs and to private schools have very different consequences. Flight to the suburbs often means the student's presence
and his parent's taxes are lost to city schools for good. Flight to
private academies seems more reversible. Pupils may return to public schools as private tuition begins to weigh, the emotionalism of
initial integration dies down, or disenchantment sets in with private
instruction or facilities. Some rural southern communities have
now begun to experience the first glimmerings of white return. By
1974 even Prince Edward County, whose private academy was
among the South's finest, had 200 whites in public schools. "That
doesn't sound like many whites, but consider that five years ago
there were only 50 in the public system," said Clarence Penn, the
black principal of Prince Edward County High School. "We're
going to win this one," he promised. "Every year we get back several dozen more whites. The academy's tuition has shot up to about
$700 now, and that's got a lot of white daddies hurting and a lot of
white mommies working. And the word is out that blacks and
whites in the public schools are getting along and learning. Just ask
any of our kids."[76]

Though warnings of white flight had long been standard antibusing fare, the issue rocketed to national attention in 1975 with publication of a report by Dr. James S. Coleman, professor of sociology
at the University of Chicago.[77] Normally, public yawns greet the
views of learned men. But Coleman somehow was different. A
thickset, cigar-smoking man of forty-nine, Coleman was much revered by integrationists for findings in 1966 that disadvantaged
children stood to benefit substantially from middle-class (i.e., racially integrated) schools.[78] Coleman himself had even stated that
integration might reduce racial learning gaps by as much as 30 percent—a figure later conceded to be an overestimate.[79] And his 1966
report was widely used to convince courts that greater efforts were
needed to bring about integration, because, it had now been
shown, those efforts would pay off.

But Coleman's latest findings were a different story. He now
concluded that busing did, indeed, chase whites from urban public
schools. True, conceded Coleman, city schools were losing whites
well before busing came along. And true, the rate of loss declined
after the year busing first took effect.[80] True also, the extent of
white flight varied sharply between cities. Miami, Tampa, Nashville, and Charlotte, for example, experienced only modest loss at-

tributable to school desegregation. But where school systems already featured high black percentages, and where white suburban systems were available, the white loss was staggering. In Memphis, Coleman noted, 35 percent of the whites left the public school system in 1973, the first year of busing. In Dallas, the rate of white loss rose from 2 to 9 percent when partial busing began in 1971 and has remained at the higher figure ever since. In Atlanta, the rate of white loss in the years before busing was 7.5 percent, an average of 20 percent for the four years thereafter. And so on and so forth, in Houston, and in northern cities such as San Francisco, Boston, and Indianapolis, though Coleman admitted the northern data to be less conclusive.[81]

More shocking than the figures were some words Coleman had for erstwhile friends, among them leaders of the past decade's Civil Rights movement. Busing leaders such as Dr. Kenneth Clark, charged Coleman, were blind to uncomfortable data and unable to understand where their own advocacy led.[82] What most bothered Coleman about Harvard sociologist Thomas Pettigrew—"one of the most untiring public advocates of court-ordered compulsory busing, sometimes with data, sometimes without"—was "the very lack of social responsibility" Pettigrew's blindness to white flight entailed.[83] Pettigrew, Coleman charged, was racially so confused that if he "saw the fires in the sky during the riots of 1967 [he] would have attributed them to an extraordinary display of the Northern Lights."[84] In their search for racial balance, Coleman argued, busing supporters simply had failed "to take into account people's reactions to their plans." It was they, said Coleman, who must bear ultimate responsibility for a resegregated society, with "a black school system in the central city with black staff and administration, a white school system in the suburbs with white staff and administration—and a set of entrenched interests on both sides that are not going to give up their students for integration."[85]

Coleman's remarks exposed the decreasing number of all-out integrationists in the mid-1970s. Forsaken first by black separatists late in the 1960s, the ranks of integrationists were further thinned by defections of white intellectuals over the issue of busing. Judges themselves had to recognize, Coleman argued, that the "much greater commitment" to school integration during the 1960s had ebbed, that integration is no longer "the first national priority."[86] Perhaps because they sensed the tide turning against them, integrationists assailed Coleman all the more vigorously. Nathaniel Jones, chief legal counsel of the NAACP, recalled that "less than a decade ago, white people were telling black people to get out of the streets, stop public protesting, and go use our constitutional safeguards through the courts. Now that we have followed that advice successfully in American cities, Coleman tells us to stop using the courts for they are an inappropriate source for remedies. Can black people seriously be expected to listen to him?"[87]

Professors Pettigrew and Robert L. Green assaulted Coleman's data and, it must be added, Coleman personally. Coleman, they charged, played sycophant to the media.[88] He well knew, insisted Pettigrew, the distortions the media would serve up, yet he persisted in courting them. And he made public his views before fellow social scientists had properly reviewed them. "To be candid," said Pettigrew, "academicians are often flattered by sudden attention from the media and offer bold views which contrast markedly with the cautious presentations they make to their colleagues. . . . In time, the public might understandably conclude that social scientists have nothing to contribute to policy debates except their own highly politicized opinions."[89]

After attacking Coleman's alleged lust for publicity, Pettigrew turned to his conclusions. Coleman's sample of cities, claimed Pettigrew, focused almost exclusively on the South, "inexplicably" omitted large school districts failing to show white loss, and depended for its "white flight" conclusion on just "two atypical cities in the deep South—Atlanta and Memphis."[90] Other studies, charged Coleman's critics, had failed to link busing and white loss. A study by Professor Christine Rossell, for example, found that of eleven school districts under busing orders outside the South, only two—Pontiac, Michigan and Pasadena, California—showed any significant increase in white flight. "Desegregation under court order does not increase white flight," Rossell concluded, "nor does massive desegregation in large school districts." In fact, "by the third year after desegregation, white flight stabilizes to a rate lower than the predesegregation period in these districts."[91]

Coleman, added his critics, worked only from aggregate data. Not one white schoolchild or parent was ever asked *why* he had left the city. There were reasons other than school integration for whites to seek suburbia. Thus, wrote Professor Gary Orfield, "a family that leaves Detroit when a school integration plan is implemented will also be aware of the city's income tax, its 1967 riot, the extremely high level of violent crime, the cutbacks in the police force, the city's Black mayor, the massive housing abandonment in the city, the recent loss of more than a fifth of the city's job base, its severe current economic crisis, etc."[92] It made little sense, argued Coleman's opponents, to make busing a scapegoat for a demographic phenomenon well in motion since the invention of the automobile.

To such charges Coleman was ready enough with answers, many of them convincing.[93] But obscured in the cross fire was the critical question. Should courts accept as relevant inputs to decision the dangers of triggering white flight? Certainly the Supreme Court could not openly announce that busing was appropriate only where whites were least likely to flee. That would impose, on nothing more than demographic proclivities, gross disparities in the burdens different communities would undergo. Lower judges divided sharply. The issue was best fought by two departed giants of the Fourth Circuit Court of Appeals, Braxton Craven and Simon Sobeloff.[94] Craven was the pragmatist. Judges, said he, "cannot successfully ignore reality. . . . Some degree of moderation in selecting a [desegregation] remedy is more likely to accomplish the desired result . . . than is unyielding fidelity to the arithmetic of race. . . . The threat of flight from the public school system ordinarily should not be allowed to influence the selection of the plan [for desegregation] or its judicial approval. It is relevant here [in Clarendon County, South Carolina] only because the whites constitute such a small minority. . . . A practical approach to the problem would . . . greatly diminish the temptation to flee the system. . . ."[95]

Sobeloff disagreed, and heatedly. The Supreme Court had noted ever since *Brown II* that "courts must not permit community hostility to intrude on the application of constitutional principles." That was the lesson of Little Rock and of the Court's battle with the segregated South. To have yielded to white prejudice would have compromised the courts, lost the South, and held forever hostage the black man's fate to the white man's threat. White "dissidents who threaten to leave the system may not be enticed to stay by the promise of an unconstitutional though palatable plan. . . . The road to integration is served neither by covert capitulation nor by overt compromise." Craven's moderation, regretted Sobeloff, offered only "a premium for community resistance."[96]

In a sense, the whole furor was misdirected. The issue is no longer what causes whites to flee the city but what now can be done to induce them to return or to take up city residence in the first place? What, for example, might persuade a middle-management employee only recently transferred to a metropolitan area to locate within the city rather than in the suburbs? Few dispute the value of middle-class reentry into urban life: the removal of blight, the restoration of a tax base, the return of consumer spending, the rise in employment, the renewal of state political concern, and the reduction of racial separation. Yet larger cities all too often represent in middle-class eyes a place for the very young or very old, for the very rich or very poor, but, above all, a place not to be when Dick and Jane reach school age.

Is there not reason to hope that this unhappy image will one day change: that easier access to work, opportunity for culture, the appeal of old restored homes, the savings of energy, and the unique sense of community possible in traditional urban neighborhoods may again make larger cities appealing places to live? In some cities, this trend is just beginning to show.[97] Yet time, one senses, is not unlimited. As the suburbs build population, the city's one-time advantages—jobs, spectator sports, culture, cinema, restaurants, shopping, all manner of public and private services—flow to them. Mass transit and wider freeways develop to meet commuter convenience. And the suburban lifestyle becomes, perhaps, irreversibly ingrained.

Whether busing is the foremost factor in causing whites to flee urban schools thus may be beside the point. It certainly does not encourage them to stay or to come back once the system is installed. And no one has yet disputed the position that neighborhood schools are more attractive to whites than racially balanced schools achieved by forced busing. All the arguments of Coleman's critics were essentially negative: that busing was not the most important factor in white flight; that whites would not remain in central cities anyway; that flight was not so great three years after busing as one year thereafter; or that smaller or northern or whiter school districts were not so prone to white flight as larger or southern or blacker ones. None of that, however, encourages urban school policies with positive middle-class appeal.

The debate on white flight, while a starting point, is not the gut issue in the busing controversy. Busing made Americans ask something far more serious: whether school integration itself was a genuinely worthwhile goal. That question, previously, had been safe to ignore. *Brown* said only that segregation by law was not right, and around that modest but powerful proposition a national consensus built. Yet the consensus that maintained that enforced segregation was always wrong was something less than one that held that integration was always required or right.

For a time, this latter notion went untested. The years after *Brown* touched mainly the South; for the nation as a whole they were painless ones. Then suddenly, with busing, the entire nation was summoned to sacrifice for integration as well. And the reaction was to wonder whether perhaps all along our faith in integration had been too naive, too complete. If the old southern defenders of segregation—total and eternal—spoke only for a dying viewpoint, opponents of busing represented growing numbers of Americans who questioned whether the search for maximal racial ratios really did anybody any good.

The new mood spread to intellectual circles also. Race had always fascinated the social scientists, particularly psychologists and sociologists. And the Supreme Court, in ruling on integration, had generally looked to see what social science had to say. It was a "chicken and egg" relationship: whether sociologists swayed the courts or vice versa was really impossible to say. But a remarkable telepathy existed. When late nineteenth century sociologists preached the Negro's "animal nature" and uncontrollable immorality,[98] the Court made certain that so "inferior" a species could be constitutionally excluded from American life.

But modern social science had pushed hard for integration. "Few persons, perhaps, know of the role played by the social sciences in helping to sustain the forces behind desegregation," wrote sociologist David Armor in 1972. "It would be an exaggeration to say they [the social sciences] are responsible for the busing dilemmas facing so many communities today, yet without the legitimacy provided by the hundreds of sociological and psychological studies it would be hard to imagine how the changes we are witnessing could have happened so quickly. At every step—from the 1954 Supreme Court ruling, to the Civil Rights Act of 1964, to the federal busing orders of 1970—social science research findings have been inextricably interwoven with policy decisions."[99]

Brown itself climaxed a revival of sociological advocacy for integration. The influential book of the 1950s was Gordon Allport's *The Nature of Prejudice*,[100] which held that interracial contact under proper conditions would reduce racial prejudice. The better one got to know one's fellow man, so "contact" theory posited, the more one would like him. That was the hope of *Brown:* that integration would yield positive gains even as segregation had worked incalculable harm. In the 1960s sociology held more good news for integrationists—the Coleman Report—which trumpeted the capacity of mixed classrooms to reduce racial learning gaps. The studies, of course, were always more complex than the lay understanding of them. Yet they served effectively to authenticate great movements of emotion.

The 1970s, however, saw sociology more skeptical. Integrated schools, proponents had claimed, would boost black aspirations and self-esteem, raise black achievement levels and college-career prospects, and reduce racial prejudice. Blissful results only were forecast, unhappy ones often ignored. But by the 1970s, the unhappy possibilities began to receive more serious attention. Might not integration heat up racial tensions instead of relaxing them? Might black self-confidence not be greater in an all-black school than in an integrated one? And did putting the races under the same school roof or even in front of the very same teacher really boost minority achievement?

To all such questions, sociologist David Armor, in an article entitled "The Evidence on Busing" (1972) gave rather pessimistic answers. Studies of community busing programs in five northern and western cities had shown, said Armor, that integration had little positive effect. Not one study was able to demonstrate "that integration has had an effect on [minority] academic achievement as measured by standardized tests."[101] In fact, one investigation of Ann Arbor, Michigan had shown that after three years "integrated black students were even further behind the white students than before the integration began."[102] The surveys also demonstrated, Armor said, no increases in aspiration levels for bused students; on the contrary, one showed "a significant decline for the bused students, from 74 per cent wanting a college degree in 1968 to 60 per cent by May 1970." In this respect, explained Armor, "some educators have hypothesized that integration has a *positive* effect in lowering [black] aspirations to more realistic levels; of course, others would argue that any lowering of aspirations is undesirable."[103]

What startled Armor most were suggestions that school integration increased racial animosity. This did not square with conventional "contact" theory. The idea that familiarity breeds friendliness, noted Armor, had been "a major feature of liberal thought in the western world, and its applicability to racial prejudice has been supported for at least two decades of social science research." But blacks bused to integrated schools from 1969 to 1970 "reported less friendliness from whites, more free time spent with members of their own race, more incidents of prejudice, and less frequent dating with white students." White students, too, showed negative effects from interracial contacts. Could it be, Armor wondered, that for "black students, initial stereotypes about white students as snobbish, intellectual, and 'straight' may be partially confirmed by [the] actual experience [of integration]; the same may be true for white stereotypes of black students as non-intellectual, hostile, and having different values."[104]

How, asked Armor, could the benevolent assumptions about integration, "supported by years of social science research, be so far off the mark?" Though that question was not easily answered, Armor did not doubt the proper public policy. Voluntary integration through busing and other means should be continued and "positively encouraged by substantial federal and state grants." This was needed, among other reasons, to give social scientists further time to study integration's effects. But mandatory, court-ordered busing was a different matter altogether. "[M]assive mandatory busing," Armor concluded flatly, "for purposes of improving student achievement and interracial harmony is not effective and should not be adopted at this time."[105]

Busing's opponents predictably put Armor to over-eager use, so delighted were they to have a sociologist on their side.[106] But Armor's views on integration were far from definitive. His conclusions on busing were attacked by Pettigrew and others as "a distorted and incomplete review of this politically charged topic."[107] Armor, charged Pettigrew, evaluated busing under an unrealistically high standard and for an unrealistically short time span (one year). Studies reporting positive results from busing were ignored. And those actually used by Armor, claimed Pettigrew, suffered serious methodological flaws, especially in the use of control groups (i.e., those with whom the progress of bused students was compared).[108] But the point really was not whether Armor was right or wrong. That only time would tell. The conventional wisdom of court-ordered integration had been opened to debate. For a social scientist of acknowledged stature had come to doubt whether integration really was worth the prodigious effort courts were making to achieve it.

Doubt was the byword of social science in the 1970s. Professor Nancy St. John concluded in 1975 after reviewing 120 school desegregation studies that "biracial schooling must be judged neither a demonstrated success nor a demonstrated failure." Years of studying its effects both on academic achievement and racial attitudes, she noted, had "netted such inconclusive results."[109] State-imposed segregation, the Court had held in *Brown*, gave Negroes "a feeling of inferiority as to their status in the community that may affect their hearts and minds in a way unlikely ever to be undone."[110] But was it not possible, St. John suggested, that court-imposed desegregation did the very same thing? Planned desegregation, she noted, "focuses attention on racial differences and, unless very carefully managed, makes minority group children the object of curiosity and study, if not hostility. They are further stigmatized if they are singled out for remedial help, if they are tracked into a low-status program, or if they are the only children who arrive and leave by bus."[111]

A self-styled committed integrationist,[112] St. John could not be accused of an antibusing bias. And other observers confirmed that the "present mood [of social scientists toward school integration] is one of less certainty. There is growing doubt that the hopes many have had for the outcomes of school desegregation can be fully achieved. . . . Desegregation does not appear to be the panacea many hoped it would be. . . . If we are to achieve any of the several objectives that school desegregation is meant to achieve, we will have to abandon the simplistic notion—now largely discredited by available evidence—that the mixing of the races *in itself* will invariably have positive educational and social consequences."[113] No one, of course, urged a return to pre-*Brown* days. Yet as leading thinkers of the 1950s helped discredit rigid segregation, integration as an inflexible requirement now likewise has come under heavy intellectual assault.[114]

None of the new skepticism was intended to portray integration as a failure. Only that it was ever so complicated, that it might convey to a black child either hope or discouragement, fulfillment or emptiness, a sense of worth or of worthlessness, a feeling of being wanted or of being merely trouble. And the relevant new question was not whether integration was per se good or bad, but under what conditions it could be made to work.

The answers to this are still far away. For one thing, we have yet to agree on what we, as a society, expect of integration. We have never really spelled it out. To be successful, must school integration profit whites as well as blacks? In what terms must it succeed? Academic or social? Suppose it were shown that the most socially successful integration is the least academically rigorous. That student tracking, for example, was academically worthwhile but racially divisive. And how long do we wait for integration to yield positive returns? One year? Five? Twenty? Or, given segregation's long dominating past, one hundred? Here we have all fallen victim to our own ideals. The hope of *Brown* was for a new day now. When the new day proved elusive, some despaired. Slavery, and then segregation, lasted over three centuries. Does not genuine integration deserve at least a patient try?

Though the magic combination for successful integration has not been found, suggestive questions have certainly been raised. Must integration, to be effective, begin at the earliest grades? Can integration prosper at low income levels or is a middle-class majority necessary? Can it be worthwhile if tracking produces only college-bound whites and vocationally trained blacks?[115] Are grades and competition compatible with racial rapport? How may teachers, staff, and principals best motivate black students? How is any racial minority—white or black—made to feel part of the school? What contributes most to successful integration? Parental involvement? Extracurricular participation? Community attitudes? Stable patterns of enrollment? Course and textbook selection? Individualized instruction? Remedial education? Or do any of these make any difference at all?[116]

Unfortunately, the answers may defy social science. The presence of so many variables makes it difficult to isolate one and point with confidence to its effect. "Researchers [on school integration]" admitted Professor St. John, "have not controlled on such variables as the level of community controversy over desegregation, the friendliness of white parents and students, the flexibility or prejudice of the staff, the content of the curriculum, or the method of teaching."[117] Yet controlling for such variables—that is, designing a test in which the subjects of comparison are alike in all respects save the one to be tested (e.g., age at which desegregation commenced)—will be difficult, indeed, in the diverse conditions of the real world.

Often periods of reaction are also periods of despair. But the countercurrents of the 1970s, though vigorous, were not altogether disillusioning. For some, the faith of the fifties bore marvelous fruit. E. L. Bing, an assistant school superintendent in Tampa, Florida, sensed it every day. "The longer the [black] youngsters have been a part of the integration process, the more articulate they seem to become," said Bing in 1977. "Now I can walk into a school and talk to a group of black kids and they can express their ideas in complete, understandable sentences. They no longer talk in fragments and monosyllables. Believe me, that's a long way from where we were before desegregation."[118]

Experimentation need not await academic approval. In the end, sociology was often corroborative of common sense. No special wisdom was needed to confirm that a teacher with personal interest in students of all races helped make integration a success. Sam Horton, principal of Thomas Jefferson Junior High School in Tampa, watched integrated couples stroll arm-in-arm through his hallways and groups of blacks and whites study together under the campus palms. Horton's formula was straightforward enough. He abolished the course in black history, replacing it with an American history course, designed "to bring in the contributions of all ethnic groups." And he disbanded separate "culture clubs," such as the Black Student Union and Latin American Club. "Initially," he explained, "those kinds of clubs were good for the minorities. They allowed the kids to adapt to a new environment without getting lost or losing their identity. But I found that the longer that kind of thing stays, the more divisive it becomes. I think if you're going to integrate a school, it has to be integrated all the way down the line."[119]

Successful integration demanded all kinds of creativity. Professor Elliot Aronson designed an experiment in "jigsaw learning" to improve racial feeling after massive busing in Austin, Texas was instituted. Aronson feared black and chicano students, because of poorer preparation, would be competitively disadvantaged in newly integrated classrooms. Thus, he and several associates devised learning games that depended on cooperation, not competition, for success. Fifth grade classes were divided into learning groups of six students each. As Aronson explained it:

> . . . We based our technique on the principle of the jigsaw puzzle: each child would have a piece of information and it would take all six group members to put the puzzle together.
>
> For example, in the first classroom we studied, the next lesson happened to be on Joseph Pulitzer. We wrote a six-paragraph biography of the man, such that each paragraph contained a major aspect of Pulitzer's life: how his family came to this country, his childhood, his education and first jobs, etc. Next we cut up the biography into sections and gave each child in the learning group one paragraph. Thus, every learning group had within it the entire life story of Joseph Pulitzer, but each child had no more than one-sixth of the story and was dependent on all of the others to complete the big picture.
>
> We explained to the children that they should master their paragraph and teach it to the others and that we would test them on the life of Pulitzer later on. Each child went off by himself to learn his paragraph, . . .
>
> Then the children rejoined their groups. . . . Thrown on their own resources, they had to learn to teach each other and listen to each other. They would have to realize that none of them could [learn the life of Pulitzer] . . . without the aid of everyone else in the group, and that each member had a unique and essential contribution to make. It's a whole new ball game.[120]

The experiment seemed to bring positive results: "Children in the jigsaw groups liked their peers more at the end of the six weeks than kids in traditional classrooms. This was particularly true for Anglos and blacks."[121] But no one, least of all Aronson, thought this any final solution to the riddle of school desegregation,[122] only an inventive approach.

What impact, finally, would the new intellectual currents have on the Supreme Court? The onset of doubt about the value of integration probably influenced the Court in the middle 1970s to temper its probusing position. Yet social science research, as Judge Wisdom once noted, "appears to have had no effect" on the most important decisions of the decade.[123] Unlike *Brown,* the Court in the school cases of the 1970s assiduously avoided citations of sociologists. Perhaps the Court, once burned in *Brown,* would know to keep future affairs with sociologists more secret. Perhaps it declined to draw on a discipline in turmoil, whose conclusions were now more contradictory than confidently aligned. Perhaps it distrusted a discipline whose leaders had demonstrated an inability to impersonalize their debates. Maybe it felt achieving integrated schooling more a moral or legal matter than an empirical one. Perhaps, too, the Court believed its own mythology: that the remedying of past segregation was the issue, not the value or lack thereof of integrated schools.

Out of the confusion of social science, one conclusion did emerge: merely tossing whites and blacks together in court-contrived ratios might do more harm than good. Yet the Supreme Court retained an obsession with how many black and white bodies were in the same school together, not with how they related, or what transpired in the classroom. Though identical racial balances were not required in all schools, racial ratios reflecting school district populations were the "starting point" and by far the most important point in court-ordered transportation. But this mathematical approach, undeviatingly applied, wrought havoc in some American cities: Atlanta, Memphis, Richmond, Boston, Pasadena, to name but a few.[124] "For too long," noted Professor St. John, "courts, legislatures, schoolmen, and social scientists have been obsessed with questions of quantity rather than quality, with mathematical ratios, quotas, and balance, rather than with the educational process itself. The real task—to translate desegregation into integration—still remains."[125]

What role might courts play in helping integration not just to occur but to succeed? Assisting integration, as opposed to insisting on desegregation, asks of the judiciary two things. The first is to avoid making biracial schooling a self-destructing enterprise. Where substantial flight of whites is likely, or the length of bus rides inordinate, or the quality of racial interaction predictably volatile or unproductive, are not headstrong judicial remedies especially inappropriate? Strategic withdrawal, of course, has its dangers. It is pragmatic and subjective, two things numerical racial ratios are not. Aiming for racial balance, moreover, at least kept pressure on communities, confronted them with the inevitability of desegregation, and challenged them to find ways to make it work. Yet in many jurisdictions maximal mixing offered scant hope. In those cases, is not a modest plan that will succeed preferable to massive integration that will disrupt, embitter, and ultimately resegregate? Indeed, the Court itself once noted that in school desegregation "there is no universal answer to complex problems . . . ; there is obviously no plan that will do the job in every case."[126]

Would the battle for successful integration also require courts to extend—as well as to curtail—school mixing plans? Ought the judiciary to support, or indeed require, local initiatives aimed at making integration work? In June, 1977, the Supreme Court addressed directly for the first time "the question whether federal courts can order remedial education programs as part of a school desegregation decree."[127] The district judge had ordered the Detroit School Board and the state of Michigan to fund, as part of a desegregation plan, teacher sensitivity training, the removal of "racial, ethnic, and cultural bias" from all school tests, a counseling and career guidance system, and a remedial reading and communications program.[128] In upholding the district judge, the Supreme Court at last acknowledged that school integration involved more than a jumble of white and black students. "Pupil assignment alone," the Court admitted, "does not automatically remedy the impact of previous, unlawful educational isolation; the consequences linger and can be dealt with only by independent measures."[129]

Yet the Court explored the new territory most gingerly. It worried that a judge who required remedial programs one day might police their content the next.[130] The Court thus approved the programs only after the school board had itself suggested them and was permitted to control their content. Whether federal judges might order such programs against the will of school boards[131] and how far they might supervise their adequacy was a question left for another day. But the Court in 1977 finally did enter the latest—the qualitative—stage of school integration. District judges, it implied, might now help integration make good. The federal judiciary, it must also be noted, had been too long and too deeply involved in race and education to let go. The impulse to direct others' affairs was not readily curbed or contained. Too much of the Supreme Court's authority had been invested to allow the high hopes of *Brown* to be dashed on the mere stubborn refusal of people to respond as it had been predicted they would.

8

Busing Moves West
and North:
Denver and Boston

Busing students for integration did not please Senator John C. Stennis of Mississippi. "[P]arents," said he, "are not going to permit their children to be boxed up and crated and hauled around the city and the country like common animals." Senators thinking there was public support for busing ought to "get [their] ear a little closer to the ground." To help make his point, Stennis and other southern Senators sought to require that new federal desegregation guidelines be enforced uniformly across the country or dropped altogether. Their strategy was simple: to arouse racial feelings in the North and bring the whole desegregation effort to a screeching halt. "If you have to [integrate] in your area," Stennis informed his northern colleagues, "you will see what it means to us."[1]

On February 18, 1970, the Senate adopted the Stennis amendment, thanks largely to a speech by Abraham Ribicoff of Connecticut charging the North with "monumental hypocrisy" in condemning segregation in the South while tolerating it in its own backyard.[2] Senator Ribicoff, predictably, was denounced for playing into southern hands. But some in the North felt he had "done a rare and useful thing: He has told his colleagues the truth, which is that many of them would rather flay the dying carcass of southern segregation than face the racism in their own bailiwicks."[3]

Swann had flayed that carcass roundly. The case, said the *New*

York Times, reflected "the Court's belief that the school authorities of Charlotte, N.C., and other Southern districts, have openly defied the 1954 Supreme Court ruling that outlawed the maintenance of dual school systems."[4] That, precisely, was *Swann's* viewpoint. The Court noted that it dealt only with school systems having a "long history" of official segregation. It cited the traditional precedents of southern recalcitrance, expressed impatience with the South's "dilatory tactics," and spoke to all the world as if the transcendent issue was how finally to bring the South into compliance with *Brown*.[5] It implied that southern and northern racism were different animals, that the South practiced an evil segregation known as *de jure*, while that of the North was more "natural," *de facto*. That outlook was one thing at the time of *Brown*. Seventeen years later, in *Swann*, it was an unprincipled regional approach to what had become a national problem.

The regional approach brought the Court under fire. So what, it was argued, if mostly southern states had segregation laws on the books when *Brown* was decided? Why should 1954 act as the magical cutoff date, giving the rest of the country immunity from busing? Many northern states too had their laws on segregation, some until quite recently. Indiana, for example, had a statute authorizing segregated schools as late as 1949.[6] Repeal of that statute hardly reversed the cumulative effects of past discrimination. And "if Negro and white parents in Mississippi are required to bus their children to distant schools on the theory that the consequences of past [legal] segregation cannot otherwise be dissipated, should not the same reasoning apply in Gary, Indiana, where no more than five years before *Brown* the same practice existed with presumably the same effects?"[7]

Why should past practice matter anyway, now that southern schools were the most integrated in the country? By 1971 the Department of Health, Education, and Welfare estimated that 57 percent of all Negro pupils in the North and West attended overwhelmingly black schools while only 32 percent in the South still did so.[8] The *New York Times* noted that "the rural South, supposedly the ultimate stronghold of what civil rights workers call the 'redneck seg' . . . is now the national leader in school integration."[9] Bringing up the rear were northern and western cities. In Cleveland and Detroit, Kansas City and St. Louis, Milwaukee and Los Angeles, at least three-quarters of all Negro pupils attended schools more than four-fifths black.[10]

Segregated neighborhoods, not school laws at the time of *Brown*, accounted for urban school segregation, both North and South.[11] These neighborhood patterns, both North and South, resulted partly from official policies of discrimination.[12] Thus, the question arose: if the causes of urban school segregation were the same throughout the country, why was the applicable law not also?

There was yet another reason why racial dispersion for southerners only was, as Alexander Bickel put it, "morally and politically, and therefore ultimately legally, an untenable position. . . ."[13] The Court, quite simply, had dealt unfairly with America's schoolchildren. Why should a student in Atlanta be uprooted from his neighborhood school while the child in Cincinnati remained in his? Constitutional law requires, above all else, uniformity and fairness in application. And what of the Negro in the North? Wasn't it the fact, not the origin, of segregation that counted? Why would the black schoolchild care whether a state did or did not have segregation in 1954 if he remained culturally isolated and educationally forgotten? Was a slum school in New York more bearable than one in Charlotte because courts had decided to call it *de facto?*

During the 1960s, the Supreme Court had given northern cities a reprieve.[14] Urban neighborhood schools across the country, in fact, were left judicially undisturbed. The justices were too preoccupied with the rural South. To launch a nationwide offensive against segregated schools was to risk precisely the backlash Senator Stennis so desired. Yet when, in 1971, *Swann* switched the spotlight from rural to urban schooling, the ills of the North lay exposed. "[Y]ou cannot conclude," wrote the Los Angeles *Times* in unintended understatement, "that Los Angeles and other California and Northern cities are wholly unaffected by the Court's chain of reasoning [in *Swann*]."[15] The effect would be felt sooner than anyone realized. On October 12, 1972—sixteen months after *Swann*— the Supreme Court heard its first "northern and western" case.

The case was *Keyes* v. *School District No. 1*. The setting, Denver, Colorado. At stake was "whether the Court intends to launch a major attack on school segregation in the North."[16] Denver, like Charlotte in the South, was a fortunate test city. The commercial hub of the Rocky Mountain region, its population of half a million was relatively affluent and well educated. Denver's 97,000 pupils (as of 1969) were only slightly more than Charlotte's and not so many as to be unmanageable. Like Charlotte's, Denver's school system still had a white majority: 66 percent Anglo, 14 percent Negro, and 20 percent Hispanic. Unlike Charlotte, however, Denver was bordered by suburban school systems to which disgruntled whites of means might repair.[17]

On the surface Colorado's racial history was exemplary, very unlike the travails of the South. In race relations, the state had come far on its own, without the judicial prod. In 1895, the year before *Plessy* v. *Ferguson*, Colorado forbade racial discrimination in public accommodations. From the beginning, the state constitution prohibited segregated schools. As early as 1927, the Colorado Supreme Court held that Denver's exclusion of blacks from school programs at a junior high and high school violated state law.[18] In 1956, George L. Brown became the first black state senator west of the Mississippi, largely on the strength of white votes. Brown successfully sponsored fair-employment legislation the next year and a fair-housing law two years later (one of the toughest in the nation at the time). In 1970, Brown seemed bullish about Colorado's prospects. Colorado's blacks, he claimed, had higher achievement and income levels than those of any other state and "the best legal front of any state in the country to ban discrimination." A visitor to Denver at the time noted also that the city's "black belt shows few of the signs of decay in the familiar eastern ghetto."[19]

Progressive notions had been easy enough to proclaim in the largely white society of the early Rocky Mountain West. But in the years after World War II, Denver's tiny black population had begun to grow, quadrupling between 1940 and 1960. Settling first in what was known as the core-city area, the city's black population spread steadily northeast into a formerly white neighborhood of attractive elm-lined streets known as Park Hill. Once again, on the surface, Denver responded admirably enough. The school board passed resolutions during the 1960s to overcome the increasingly one-race character of many Park Hill schools. These gestures, however, proved ineffectual and frustrating to Denver blacks.[20] "Community pressure," observed the United States Commission on Civil Rights, "reached a peak following the assassination of Dr. Martin Luther King on April 5, 1968. On the night of April 25, thousands of citizens attended a public school board meeting where Rachel Noel, the first black school board member, introduced a resolution instructing the school superintendent to submit an integration plan by the following September. The Noel resolution was passed by a vote of 5 to 2."[21] In the spring of 1969, the school board adopted three further resolutions to desegregate Park Hill schools: blacks were to be bused from Park Hill to white schools around the city and whites were to be bused in. The program, though modest in scope, offended most Denver whites. New school board elections produced an antibusing majority that rescinded the resolutions and replaced them with a voluntary student transfer program. Race relations worsened; sporadic violence flared.[22] And Denver blacks, again frustrated, took to the courts.

The courts, including finally the Supreme Court in 1973, found the Denver School Board guilty of a subtle racism that would surface repeatedly in northern cities. In the face of Negro eastward expansion from the core-city area across six-lane Colorado Boulevard and into formerly white Park Hill, the school board had attempted to keep Park Hill schools Anglo as long as possible. One by one, schools in the path of the black onrush had been surrendered by the school board, even as it sought to protect those white schools still left. New schools had been constructed to contain black expansion. For example, Barrett Elementary School, noted the Supreme Court, had been built "to a certain size and in a certain location, 'with conscious knowledge that it would be a segregated school'. . . . The [district] court found that by building Barrett Elementary School west of the Boulevard and by establishing the Boulevard as the eastern boundary of the Barrett attendance zone, the Board was able to maintain for a number of years the Anglo character of the Park Hill schools."[23] Barrett, meanwhile, in the fall of 1968 had 410 Negro pupils and exactly 1 white.[24]

Other tricks had also been tried. School-attendance zones had been gerrymandered to preserve at least some white schools for the traditional residents of Park Hill. Optional zones had been created in transition neighborhoods, where students chose between schools they wished to attend, white students opting for the whiter school, black students, it was hoped, for the blacker one. Mobile classrooms had been set up to take up the pupil overflow at black schools rather than reassigning the excess to underutilized white ones. A "feeder" pattern had been employed, whereby mostly black elementary schools fed black junior highs, which, in turn, fed black high schools. And minority teachers and staff were assigned by the Denver school board primarily to minority schools.[25]

None of this, however, marked Denver as especially iniquitous.

Its tactics would prove to be quite commonplace throughout the urban North and West. And many of the commonest northern devices—optional attendance zones, open enrollment and free transfer plans—resembled nothing so much as freedom of choice, the southern device for student "selection" of one-race schools. Other ploys such as juggled attendance zones, feeder plans, segregated school construction, and discriminatory faculty assignment had never known regional boundaries. Northern school litigation thus made the racial tactics of school boards seem more universal. It remained to be seen, however, whether the Supreme Court would adopt a uniform and nationwide school approach.

At the Supreme Court, Denver argued that its past wrongdoing touched only Park Hill and did not affect the school district as a whole. Thus anything so drastic as city-wide busing should not be required. But the Court, per Justice Brennan, rejected this contention. "[R]acially inspired school board actions," it noted, "have an impact beyond the particular schools that are the subject of those actions."[26] A finding of intentional school segregation in a meaningful part of a school district, held the Court, also created a strong presumption that segregated schooling throughout the district had been similarly motivated.[27] Though the case was technically remanded to the district judge for further findings,[28] Denver was out of luck.

Thus the Supreme Court for the first time in *Keyes* all but ordered busing for a city outside the South. It relieved black plaintiffs of the task of proving school board discrimination in each and every school in a northern district before city-wide busing could be imposed. And the Court served notice that when two reasonable alternative courses existed, the board had best choose the one of greater integration. Even subtle promotion of racial segregation would henceforth be a dangerous game for northern school officials to play.

The Court did not, however, place northern and southern districts on an equal footing. Court-compelled desegregation, it insisted, must be tied to intentional past wrongdoing on the part of local school officials. Because of school segregation statutes on the books at the time of *Brown*, the entire South, the Court emphasized, could be presumed to have created segregated schooling wrongfully.[29] Thus litigation in the South turned directly to remedy, i.e., to how much busing would be required. In the North, black plaintiffs still had to exhume school board decisions for the past decade or more to establish intentional segregation in a "meaningful" part of a district. A more tedious, expensive, or protracted effort—involving school board minutes, attendance rosters, old newspapers and city maps—could hardly be imagined. Every school board decision had to be mulled and remulled for possible segregative implications. "Six weeks of trial [producing] more than four thousand pages of testimony and nearly two thousand exhibits" was not uncommon in the search for constitutional violations.[30] As much as seventy pages of small print might be necessary for a district judge to show that some northern city's schools were unconstitutionally maintained.[31]

It was enough to discourage many potential black plaintiffs from going to court at all. Worse still, so high a hurdle seemed unnecessary. If Denver, with its history of progressive race relations, had committed constitutional violations, had not other school districts across the country also? Was not school segregation more than the result of private residential preference?[32] Could not school boards be presumed partly responsible for pervasive segregation in schools over which they had charge? And, finally, why did black plaintiffs rather than school officials bear the burden of explaining to district courts just how segregated schools got to be that way?[33]

Thus, the Denver decision, which appeared on the surface to pressure northern cities, was in actuality more forbearing. It continued a North-South dualism in school desegregation law and consigned black plaintiffs to a laborious process of proof. It ignored the North's point of greatest vulnerability: past public discrimination in housing. In practical terms, *Keyes* meant that many northern cities would be a while yet desegregating and that the burdens of doing so would fluctuate wildly among them. Justice Powell begged the Court to adopt a more uniform approach. "The results of litigation [in northern cities]," he predicted, "often arrived at subjectively by a court endeavoring to ascertain the subjective intent of school authorities with respect to action taken or not taken over many years—will be fortuitous, unpredictable and even capricious."[34]

And uniformity was not to be. Northern cities, like the South since *Brown II*, were now to experience the vagaries of district court discretion. The results of that discretion were never easy to prophesy. For many school board actions, there existed both innocent and illicit motives. Some judges would credit the innocent explanation, others seize upon the illicit one. Had Barrett Elementary in Denver, for example, really been located to contain black expansion, as the district judge found, or had it been so situated for safety reasons, involving a six-lane freeway, as the school board, not illogically, contended.[35] "You couldn't win for losing," complained Denver's school superintendent in 1974. "If you are going to use a building program in minority neighborhoods as evidence of a conspiracy by the board to contain youngsters in that section of town, then I think every city in the United States would be guilty of running a dual school system."[36]

Thus district judges "could treat similar facts very differently."[37] One judge, for example, ruled that optional attendance zones, construction of schools in segregated neighborhoods, and assignment of black teachers to black schools in Grand Rapids, Michigan, all had permissible explanations.[38] Another in nearby Kalamazoo held similar practices unconstitutional.[39] The Sixth Circuit Court of Appeals affirmed both judgments.[40] These results, concluded one commentator, "seem to confirm the concern of Justice Powell that [the Denver decision] will lead to results in litigation that are fortuitous and unpredictable."[41] "Although the courts," noted Professor Orfield, "almost always found school districts guilty of unconstitutional segregation whenever litigation was seriously pursued, there were enough contrary decisions to deeply trouble civil rights lawyers. . . . Usually, when appeals were finished, the guilt of local authorities was established. Even then, however, the implications for a local school system were highly uncertain. Although judges normally ordered plans to end segregation throughout a school system by distributing students proportionately at each school, some signed orders leaving a great deal of segregation untouched."[42]

Denver's own desegregation experience drew mixed reviews. The *New York Times* noted in the fall of 1974 that busing in Denver had "caused some complaints and tension but no violence or overt displays of racial hatred. Many pupils and parents here say thay do not like busing and many have moved to the suburbs to avoid it, but there is pride . . . that when legal avenues of opposition were exhausted, residents obeyed court edicts and are thus far giving desegregation a chance."[43] A school boycott, led by the Citizens' Association for Neighborhood Schools, fizzled in the face of low participation and restraining orders by the local judge, William Doyle.

Community leadership sided prominently with desegregation. A council of 40 leading citizens headed by the chancellor of the University of Denver was appointed by Judge Doyle to advise him on the most workable decree. A coalition of forty-nine civic organizations called PLUS (People Let's Unite For Schools), was formed in April, 1974, to promote excellence in Denver public schools. The clergy's support for integration, Methodist Bishop Melvin Wheatly announced, was "unequivocal . . . part of the design that we interpret as God's will." After a few weeks of tension, one high school senior noted, "everybody adjusted and settled down. It's been a positive experience for me and . . . for people who stuck it out and really tried to make something of the school. . . . Integration puts a lot of people through a lot of personal, family and individual changes, but with the proper preparation and positive attitude . . . it can be a very worthwhile experience." [44]

How well busing works depends, in part, on how well it is designed. And the plan for Denver at least was ingenious. About 20,000 students were to be bused under court order, 6,000 more than previously. But many elementary students would spend half a day in a segregated neighborhood school and the other half in an integrated one, either their own or the one to which they were bused. [45] "Thus," explained Professor John Finger, the plan's chief architect, "every child attended and was a member of two schools, had two teachers and two sets of classmates, one integrated, one not." The idea was to combine both the security of neighborhood schools with the outreach of integrated ones. Finger contended that "the part-time feature probably lessened some of the apprehensions about desegregation, and this may well have been one of the features that resulted in Denver's success." [46] Even after this part-time provision was ruled unconstitutional on appeal, [47] useful points remained. These included walk-in schools in integrated neighborhoods (designed to attract new residents to them), and neighborhood elementary schools for those parts of the city most prone to white flight. [48] Though minority elementary students underwent long bus rides from the core city to the far south of Denver, the Court of Appeals noted that the Finger Plan tried "to ease the hardships" by requiring "provision of extra buses" for stragglers, for special emergencies, and "for parents wishing to attend PTA and other activities at school."[49]

Some worried, nonetheless, about Denver's busing prospect. As of December, 1974, an Associated Press report noted, "white enrollment in Denver had decreased nearly 30 percent since 1970."[50] "We lose over 4,000 students every year, most of them Anglo, because parents have made up their minds in the last four or five years that [the courts were] finally going to order what they didn't want," complained Frank Southworth, Denver School Board president and a staunch busing foe.[51] Suburbia beckoned Denver's disgruntled whites. South of the city lay Arapahoe and Jefferson counties, expanding, white, middle-to-upper income, Republican: "a clear example," thought one observer, "of the suburban psychosis, modern U.S.A.: keep the cities, the turmoil, all the problems away from us."[52] In November, 1974, they did just that. Colorado adopted a constitutional amendment removing Denver's power to annex suburban land. Busing, plus the loss of annexation, could, Denver's planning director fretted, "turn the tide and make Denver a ghettoized city."[53]

But Denver's problems paled beside those of sister cities. By the middle 1970s, while southern courtrooms were quieting, school suits erupted across the North. City after northern city was hauled to federal court: Baltimore, Detroit, Indianapolis, Kansas City (Kans.), Louisville, Milwaukee, Omaha, St. Louis, Wilmington (Del.), and in hard-hit Ohio, Akron, Cincinnati, Cleveland, Columbus, Dayton, and Youngstown.[54] Opposition mounted as busing spread. On August 30, 1971, arsonists firebombed ten school buses in Pontiac, Michigan. The following May, Alabama Governor George Wallace swept 51 percent of the vote in the Michigan Democratic primary. On September 8, 1973, the Gallup Poll reported that while a large majority of the nation favored integration, only 5 percent favored busing to achieve it. And 63 percent of white northern parents voiced objections to sending their children to predominantly black schools.[55]

Partly because of such attitudes, city school systems became increasingly segregated. The Civil Rights Commission reported that in 1972, 83.5 percent of New York City blacks attended schools more than half black. In Los Angeles, the nation's second largest school district, the figure was 91.9 percent; in Chicago 98.3 percent; in Philadelphia 93.3 percent; and Detroit 92.8 percent.[56] At least southerners, thought Dr. Kenneth Clark, were "honest and direct" in their resistance to integration. Their northern counterparts had "made one policy statement after another" supporting integration in the course of creating "an unmitigated disaster. . . ."[57]

   The sorriest chapter of the whole northern story was that of Boston, Massachusetts. Jack Greenberg of the NAACP Legal Defense Fund regarded Denver and Boston as opposite poles of the northern experience: Denver, a "very successful integration story," Boston a failure due to "an absence of effective leadership."[58] The sixteen hundred police and federal marshalls patrolling Boston's troubled schools made Little Rock seem close again, racial progress more remote. Boston was not easily dismissed, like Birmingham, as a regional aberration. Indeed, Boston and Massachusetts were the pride of American liberalism: the political and literary pacesetter for the new nation, the home of one of the world's foremost universities, the only state to have resisted the Nixon landslide of 1972. Under the leadership of Horace Mann, Boston in the 1830s had become the first city to adopt "the ideal of the free, universal, and inclusive public school."[59] Over a century later, in 1965, Massachusetts enacted the Racial Imbalance Act, requiring school districts to desegregate any school more than 50 percent black.[60] One year later, the foundation-supported METCO program was launched to bus designated black students from inner Boston to the suburbs. But busing by court order humbled and embarrassed Boston, a fact that gave some in the South a sick satisfaction. "[B]ecause there has been progress in the South," wrote the Dallas *Times Herald*, "Southerners should not gloat over the violence in Boston. It is sad. It is tragic. Southerners have learned from experience just how much so."[61] As indeed it was. That racial violence should so possess this historic city on the Charles was a national tragedy of the first rank.
   In the early 1970s, Boston was as segregated as it was cosmopolitan. Blacks comprised only 17 percent of Boston's total population, but 34 percent of its public school enrollment (primarily because of the younger age of the black population and the large numbers of whites in parochial schools). By 1973, the Racial Imbalance Act notwithstanding, fully 85 percent of Boston blacks were in schools with a black majority, over half in schools 90 percent black.[62] All

but a smattering lived in the Roxbury ghetto. And segregation in Boston was more than just racial. "If you know what section of Boston someone lived in," remarked a long-time observer, "you can generally tell what their ethnic background is, what religion they are, approximately their annual income and occupational level, know something about their educational background, and know whether they are likely to be first, second, or third-generation American."[63]

As "one of the oldest cities in the country," Boston retained "much of its colonial layout, particularly in the downtown area. Bays and rivers and the street layout of the city have . . . isolated some sections."[64] The busing mayhem would occur in two such sections: Irish Catholic, working class neighborhoods of South Boston and Charlestown.

History had paid each a memorable visit. Charlestown High School fronted Bunker Hill Monument, and from atop Dorchester Heights in South Boston, George Washington surveyed the British retreat from Boston harbor. The present, however, was not a time of distant vision. Sporting row upon row of trim wooden houses, each community kept wholly unto itself. Charlestown, an enclave of some 17,000 persons, appeared physically most cut off from the outside world by a network of rivers, highways, and railroad tracks.[65] And though South Boston had "less of a restriction on [physical] access," it remained, in all other respects, "distinct."[66]

By most measures, life in the ethnic villages was both dreary and hard. "Those who have made it in any way," wrote one observer, "have moved out of 'Southie' to other sections of the city like West Roxbury or Roslindale. Unemployment is high in South Boston, the neighborhood is deteriorating, delinquency rates are high, there are lots of kids hanging out on the street with nothing to do, and the schools are poor."[67]

Schools, however, were their pride. Their function, though, was less to open young minds to the world beyond than to bolt the door against it.[68] "In Boston's closed, parochial white ethnic neighborhoods," it was noted, "the schools are often seen not as a way to a different life, but as a socializing force, inculcating the values of family and neighborhood in the face of a changing and threatening outside world. . . . Few of the students in South Boston, East Boston or Charlestown go on to college. It is a different set of values and expectations."[69] The ethnic enclaves did not seek out one another. About the only time of year the Irish in South Boston and Italians from East Boston really mingled, one South Boston native wrote, was "on opposite sides of the field at the annual 'Southie-Eastie' football game, where 40- and 50-year olds still wear their high school letter sweaters, so great has been the identification between school and community." This native wondered whether the allegiance had not been misplaced: "South Boston High and Charlestown High may have suddenly become edifices for local pride recently, but to any outside observer they seem grimy, shabby, uninviting places for the transaction of anything, let alone the important business of education."[70] In the meticulous, stiff symmetry of its ancient windows and columns, sunk deep in a high brick facade, South Boston High looked forbidding to any outsider, let alone black ones bused in.

Quite apart from student busing, blacks had long been unwelcome on Irish turf. Historian C. Vann Woodward wrote that "whites in South Boston boasted in 1847 that 'not a single colored family' lived among them. Boston had her 'Nigger Hill' and 'New Guinea.' "[71] Over a century and a quarter later, 800 police were summoned to keep peace when blacks "invaded" South Boston's Carson Beach for a picnic one August Sunday. Then too, the 75,000 annual visitors to Charlestown's Bunker Hill battleground numbered very few blacks, a fact not wholly explainable by black lack of interest in white heroics during the Revolutionary War. Asked if blacks feared to venture into Charlestown, National Park Service Ranger Frank Montford replied: "That's probably a good surmise." When a group of black students from Pine Forge, Pennsylvania did visit Bunker Hill in 1977, they were beset by five modern-day "patriots" carrying golf clubs and hockey sticks.[72]

Blacks threatened Boston's ethnics and not just economically. Ethnic neighborhoods prized institutional loyalties centered, in South Boston, around the patriarchal family, trade unions, local shopkeepers, the local Democratic party, the schools, and the Catholic Church. Black society was seen as disintegrative: higher crime and drugs and idleness, with female-headed families and vagrant, uncertain masculine roles.[73] Black-ethnic differences extended to talk and walk and hair and dress. The ethnic resented the "slouchy, jazzier life style which he fears blacks will bring to infest his neighborhood,"[74] the cult of "superlubricity," to coin a term from Professor Woodward.[75]

Stir now into this flammable mix W. Arthur Garrity, Harvard law graduate, resident of the fashionable town of Wellesley, and, since 1966, federal district judge. On June 21, 1974, Garrity, in a meticulous seventy-page opinion, found that the Irish-dominated Boston School Committee had "knowingly carried out a systematic program of segregation affecting all of the city's students, teachers and school facilities."[76] It had maintained feeder patterns, as well as open enrollment and student transfer policies encouraging whites to leave black schools. It had transported students and juggled attendance zones to perpetuate segregation and had assigned black faculty and staff to predominantly black schools. In addition, Garrity concluded, the School Committee had "built new schools for a decade with sizes and locations designed to promote segregation; . . . and expanded the capacity of approximately 40 schools by means of portables and additions when students could have been assigned to other schools [thereby reducing] racial imbalance. How many students were intentionally separated on a racial basis cannot be stated with any degree of precision; but the annual totals were certainly in the thousands. . . ."[77] Segregated black schools, moreover, remained "the most crowded, the oldest, the least well maintained, and the most poorly staffed that the school committee could offer."[78]

Judge Garrity also did not overlook certain remarks by a former member and chairman of the School Committee. "I think the facts of the matter are," this member announced at one meeting in June of 1971, "that the Negro immigrants from the South are disinclined to put their effort into our northern type of education. . . ." And earlier: "The Southern Negro pupil is not as spry usually in his eagerness to learn as other children, and therefore the more lively children, the lively Negro children and the lively white children, start to move out. . . ."[79]

Against this backdrop of segregative acts and utterances,[80] Judge Garrity had little choice but to order busing. Boston's acts were of a type condemned by the Supreme Court in Denver, only much worse. "[T]he court does not favor forced busing," Garrity would later note. But given "the racial concentrations of its population, Boston is simply not a city that can provide its black schoolchildren with a desegregated education absent considerable mandatory transportation."[81]

Phase I of desegregation would commence in the fall of 1974 and require the busing of some 17,000 pupils. Phase II was to begin the following fall, with mandatory busing affecting approximately 21,000 students, 12,000 of them in grades one through five. Because of Boston's compact layout, the bus trips were not long—ten to fifteen minutes on the average—the longest less than twenty-five minutes.[82] Mercifully, the Italian enclave of East Boston, separated from the rest of the city by Boston harbor, was largely exempted from the decree because to desegregate certain "schools in that section of the city would require transporting between four and five thousand children either into or out of other parts of Boston, many through the tunnels with their gassy air at heavy traffic hours, for distances of up to 5.2 miles one way."[83]

But the plan was still stiff medicine and Judge Garrity, especially in planning for Phase II, attempted to enlist community support. A city-wide Coordinating Council of forty-two citizens with varying racial views was assigned to assist desegregation. School personnel were to confer with representatives from Boston area colleges and universities in an effort to make school desegregation a success.[84] But none of this brought peace to Boston.

The opening of school—September 12, 1974—saw much of Boston integrate without incident. Not so South Boston High, which was paired by court order with Roxbury. A white boycott cut opening-day attendance to less than 100 of the expected 1,500 students. Buses carrying black students were stoned leaving the school, their windows broken, children cut by shattered glass.[85] Charlestown was no better. "Niggers! Here come the little monkeys!" one nine-year-old was heard to exclaim just before his small friend pointed to a passing garbage truck, shouting, "That's another load of them."[86] An antibusing march of 5,000 through the streets of South Boston on October 4 attracted state legislators, members of the School Committee, and all but one member of the Boston City Council. "What we prayed wouldn't happen has happened," the Boston *Globe* despaired on October 9. "The city of Boston has got out of control."[87] On October 15, after a racial melee at Hyde Park High School in which a white student was stabbed, Governor Francis Sargent called out 450 National Guardsmen. On December 11, an angry white mob trapped 135 black students in South Boston High for four hours in retaliation for the stabbing of a white. Only a decoy operation by police permitted the blacks to depart. South Boston High was then closed. It reopened a month later with

400 returning students (31 of them black) under guard by 500 state and local police.[88]

Violence erupted in South Boston that year and the next, when Phase II of the school plan began. Protest was diversion for the idle, the newest game in town. "The graffiti which used to exhort Southie's athletic teams to victory over rival schools," wrote Andrew Kopkind, "now proclaim: 'FUCK NIGGERS!' and 'KEEP SOUTHIE WHITE!'"[89] "We didn't have these difficulties until busing began," lamented Marilyn Anderson of the black-oriented Roxbury Multi-Service Center. "There are a lot of people who may have been racists all along who have used busing as an opportunity to act out their own emotions and incite other people."[90] Antibusing groups certainly were more incitefully billed in Boston than anywhere else: ROAR (Restore our Alienated Rights) and in Charlestown, POWDERKEG. Boston, moreover, was home for America's foremost feminine demagogue. "The phenomenal Spirit of Reaction," wrote Kopkind, "is Louise Day Hicks, . . . who inevitably sweeps to electoral victory in South Boston and Dorchester . . . even while losing badly in city-wide *mano-a-mano* campaigns. There is a constant, deliverable anti-black vote in Boston— short of a majority—and Hicks knows all the tricks to make it her own."[91] Labeling Judge Garrity's Phase II decree "the product of a callous, despotic mind," Hicks predicted "rising tensions and chaos and disorder in the schools followed by a mass exodus from Boston."[92]

Not surprisingly in such an atmosphere, the exodus did take place. Average white loss for the six years prior to busing was 3.7 percent per year. In 1974, the first year of busing, it jumped to 16.2 percent, followed by 7.9 percent in 1975. If the 1975 rate continued, Professor Coleman noted, Boston's school population in a decade would be nearly three-quarters Hispanic and black.[93] Whites who could afford it had three exits from Boston's public schools: to the suburbs, to the strong Catholic school system (despite Cardinal Madeiros's determination not to make it an escape hatch), and to rump private schools such as South Boston Heights Academy.[94] Those who could not afford it but felt bitterly enough simply left school altogether. "There are plenty of kids still boycotting school," boasted Pat Russell, head of Charlestown's POWDERKEG in 1977. "We have kids who haven't been to school in three years."[95]

The United States Civil Rights Commission blamed Boston's woes on a lack of civic leadership: "A virtual total lack of support for court desegregation orders by public and private leaders, especially the mayor, city council members, and those in business, reinforced the opposition view that desegregation would never come to pass." Heading the opposition, of course, was the Boston School Committee, on which, as of 1976, no black had served. According to the Commission, the School Committee's recalcitrance forced Judge Garrity to involve himself in the details of school administration, to the ultimate detriment of community compliance.[96] Garrity, Anthony Lewis once noted, "even held hearings to decide, one by one, which temporary teachers could be laid off—and refused to allow most of the proposed layoffs. He has directed the city, whose finances are strained, to spend more money on a school system that many experts think wastes vast sums now."[97]

His deepening involvement notwithstanding, Garrity found himself hampered by community resistance. A skilled politician, Orval Faubus had shown, could always stop one small step short of contempt. "For my part," the chairman of the Boston School Committee stated, "I will not go any further than doing what Judge Garrity directly orders me to do. And I will not end up as a salesman for a plan which I do not believe in." It was possible, as every politician knew, to be at once law-abiding and defiant. Said Boston School Committee member John Kerrigan: "[I intend], and of course I am only one vote, to appeal every word that comes out of Garrity's mouth."[98] Even citation for contempt was a treacherous course for the judge. It risked making martyrs of the opposition and pushing the ethnic villagers into open revolt.[99]

South Boston had no patience for leadership from anyone. Outsiders of all varieties were distrusted. Police were an occupying force and met a nightly resistance of bricks, bottles, rocks, chunks of wood and paving stones, darts shot from slings, and Molotov cocktails.[100] More resented than police were the authorities behind them, the "eggheads" and "do-goods" who manipulated Southie's fate while securing their own. Appearances were not aided by Judge Garrity's residence in posh, suburban Wellesley, safely outside the Boston school district. Clarence McDonough, a tall, handsome Irishman with curly, reddish hair, was outraged. "They did it to me," he yelled. "They went and did it to me, those goddamn sons of bitches. I told you they would. I told you there'd be no running from 'em. You lead your life perfect as a pane of glass, go to church, work 40 hours a week at the same job—year in, year out—keep your complaints to yourself, and they still do it to you. . . . Someone's got to explain it to me. I'll listen to anybody, but someone's got to tell me how this Garrity guy, this big deal judge gets all this power to move people around, right the hell out of their neighborhood, while everybody else in the world comes out of it free and equal."[101]

But Garrity was not the only target. "Over and over," noted one reporter, "South Boston residents contend that the state's racial imbalance act was supported by white suburban legislators, that both Senators and the Mayor send their children to private schools, . . ."[102] "[We] are being asked to do something," protested state Senator William Bulger, "that all the rest of the world confides they won't do themselves."[103] That was not an easy claim to refute. "[T]he leading advocates of transportation for integration," Professor Nathan Glazer has written, "journalists, political figures, and judges—send their children to private schools which escape the consequences of these legal decisions. This does raise a moral question. The judges who impose such decisions, the lawyers who argue . . . for them would not themselves send their children to the schools to which, by their actions, others poorer and less mobile than they are must send their children. Those not subject to a certain condition are insisting that others submit themselves to it, which offends the basic rule of morality in both the Jewish and Christian traditions."[104]

There was, indeed, a double standard, and all South Boston sensed it. For Harvard's Phi Beta Kappa address in June of 1975, Robert Coles selected an unsettling subject—a conversation with a South Boston factory worker, Irish, and father of five: "My brother," said the worker, "says the people near Harvard, the professors and doctors and lawyers and fat-cat businessmen, their kids, a lot of them, don't go to the Cambridge public schools, they go to fancy private schools and they have nice summer homes and all the rest. Well, who has the money to afford those private schools? Not us. And if we even mention trying to form our own private schools here in South Boston, then they tell us we're trying 'to evade the federal court order' and we're 'racists.' But if rich people send their children to private school, they're not trying to 'evade' anything. . . . Oh, no. They're just trying to give their children the 'best education possible,' that's what my brother hears them say—and he's no professor, but he can listen with his ears and he can figure out what he hears."[105]

Such Irish indignation was nothing new. "The cleavage between Irish and Yankees," wrote one observer, "plagued Massachusetts life for more than a century. Up to World War I, the Boston newspapers segregated social items about Yankees and Irish Catholics in different pages. Yankees looked down on Irish as a kind of social scum. The Irish detested Harvard, because, as John Gunther observed, 'Harvard is the great rival of the archbishopric for intellectual control of the community.' "[106] Success greeted the Irish more frequently after World War II, but only selectively. For those left behind there remained those staples of Irish life in America from the beginning: ward politics and the Catholic Church. Yet busing left the local politicos blustery but helpless and much of the Roman Catholic leadership on the other side. Priests even rode school buses with black children, and though vacancies existed at the Gate of Heaven school, busing refugees were not let in.[107] To whom, in his hour of crisis, might the South Boston worker turn?

Alone he stood: beyond reach of Mayor White, the Boston *Globe*, the Harvard professor, and the Boston professional. The *Globe*, he felt, would not tell his side of the story; the Mayor did not need his vote.[108] The ethnic sensed himself expendable and out of fashion, the discard in the modern liberal hand. But he would not march gladly to the altar of sacrifice. "It's a goddamn joke," beefed Clarence McDonough, "busing my kid half way around Boston so that a bunch of politicians can end up their careers with a clear conscience. You know why they're busing? Because the kindly old Mayor of this city wants to be President, . . . so who does he pick on? The rich? He picks on the people right here, this street. What the hell does he care about us? What the hell does he care about South Boston? We don't vote for him; he ain't losing no votes by busing our kids around the city."[109] "GO HOME MAYOR BLACK," signs in Southie read.[110] Even Senator Kennedy's support for integration earned only jeers, insults, and at a speech in Quincy, Mass., a poking in the ribs with the point of a small American flag. "This is just the start of a war," declared one police officer assigned to South Boston. "These people will never give up. People outside don't understand that Southie High is to them what Harvard is to the people in Wellesley. This busing has just torn the city apart. It never used to be like this."[111] "You heard of the Hundred Years War? This will be the eternal war," swore Jimmy Kelly. "It will be passed down from father to son."[112]

Violence would in time subside, but would attitudes change? In November, 1977, Boston voters rejected the three foremost symbols of antibusing, Louise Day Hicks, John Kerrigan, and Pixie Palladino.[113] Elected to the School Committee was the first black in seventy-six years, a development likely to hasten Judge Garrity's withdrawal as overseer of the school system.[114] Yet the strongholds of resistance remained unreconciled. As one Associated Press report that November put it: "The white people of Charlestown don't hold rallies or motorcades anymore. But within their neat wooden tenements, grim resentment toward court-ordered busing still seethes."[115]

For some the Irish ethnic was the villain of the Boston piece. Like the southern "cracker," his prejudice was often violent, always up front. He caught most of the publicity and nearly all of the blame. It was convenient to think of him as the problem, but not altogether accurate. If the Irish villagers were Boston's shock troops, others rooted quietly for them to succeed. "We're not ashamed of Southie; we're grateful," a resident of more upwardly mobile Roslindale explained.[116]

Southie, indeed, was but the iceberg's tip. If the prejudice of poor whites had been the only difficulty, the race problem in America would have been solved years back. But there was more. "Do you think it is chiefly the red-neck who causes violence?" Robert Penn Warren was asked long ago. "No," he answered. "He is only the cutting edge. He, too, is a victim. Responsibility is a seamless garment. And the northern boundary of that garment is not the Ohio River."[117] A chief contribution of V. O. Key, Jr.'s classic study of southern politics was to dispel "what many top-drawer southerners firmly believe, viz., that the poor white is at the bottom of all the trouble about the Negro."[118] Blacks, twenty years after *Brown*, certainly knew better. "A lot of blacks had it figured wrong," said Carl Holman, President of the National Urban Coalition in 1974. "They thought that poor whites acted viciously and badly, but that 'quality' whites did not . That was wrong. Racism comes much more naturally, and to a much broader spectrum of whites, than we could have imagined."[119]

This is not to condone South Boston's tactics or to embrace its cause. Yet one must try to understand it. Unlettered, unmoneyed, and unheeded, the Boston ethnic counterpunched the only way he knew how: with workshop words and street-corner violence. His methods sickened, but he spoke some blunt truths.

One was that busing suffered an unpardonable, class double standard. When Vietnam was thought to be a poor man's war, student exemptions were withdrawn and a national lottery instituted. But with busing, similar steps toward equality were never taken. The rich could always buy their way off buses by attending private schools or moving to the suburbs. Poor whites griped and sometimes even sabotaged, but in the end they rode. Perhaps Boston suggests the way we handle racial problems in this country: by leaving poor blacks and working-class whites to trench warfare, while most of middle-class America remains comfortably quartered outside the battle zone.

Busing's double standard did more than disadvantage impecunious whites. Rather it risked "leaving public school systems the preserve of the disadvantaged of both races."[120] Blacks were no more enchanted than poor whites with conditions in many "integrated" public schools. Yet blacks were often the most captive of them. Private and suburban schooling were not only unaffordable, but often hostile to blacks as well.

Racial strife among the poor is to some extent inevitable, given the distribution of resources and skills. The effort to overcome discrimination in employment did not pinch primarily the middle or upper class. Rather poor black and poor white wrestled over poor jobs.[121] In housing, the most affordable homes outside the ghetto were often in white working-class neighborhoods. Thus the black's upward thrust threatened mostly those for whom better-than-black was a chief source of security and pride. The ethnics sensed, said Noel Day, an organizer of black school boycotts in Boston in the middle 1960s, "that Boston's blacks are their main competition for jobs, for decent housing, for self-respect, and in all those other races that poor and powerless people must run."[122] Like the old up-country farmer in Mississippi, Boston's ethnic resented alternately the upward mobility of the black and the downward glances of the gentry, landed or moneyed or learned as the case may be.

But what good did it do, one might ask, this exchange between Roxbury and South Boston? To think some common class interest would develop seems little more than a Fabian pipe dream. South

Boston demonstrates, if anything, the opposite: that race divides, more than class unites, the American proletariat. If the end of busing was more cosmopolitan contact, was that achieved with this forced conclave of the poor? If its purpose was better education for blacks, that surely was not to be found in the schools of South Boston. "Instead of pushing for better schools," remarked Noel Day, "black people and white people are fighting over who will sit next to whom in some of the worst schools in the nation, . . . If quality education has any meaning, a busing program would be set up to move the white kids out of South Boston, too."[123] But the Constitution spoke to race, not to class. If busing remedies were not color-blind, they at least were class-blind. Under the Supreme Court's approach, so long as black and white mingled in appropriate numbers, it mattered not who they were or what their background.

The tragedy of South Boston whites, Day believed, is that "they think they have something worth defending."[124] He was wrong, of course. South Boston did have something worth defending. Not in worldly store or conventional measures of value. But in principle: in the right to be left alone, to control one's own destiny, to live by one's own lights, not those of an unelected district judge or theorists whose notions of equality had become constitutional law. South Boston argued, in a sense, the cause of *white power*. It wanted, ironically, what black power advocates also sought: control of community schools reflecting community values, unorthodox though those values were.

One should say, finally, that South Boston acted parochially, self-interestedly, viciously, anarchically. It did not take the broad, the generous, or even the lawful view. It refused, when asked, to sacrifice itself to the settlement of America's foremost, tragic problem. But who else, asked the Irish workingman, had done so?

This leads us to one last point. Social upheaval, to be sure, is never evenhanded. It is the young men mainly who die in war. Recession takes no even bites. Every great national commitment exacts its unfair tithe. Thus, the burden of ending racial discrimination in America will never be equitably shared. Lower income whites, we have noted, bear the brunt of new black competition in housing and jobs. Racial adjustment generally is most difficult in the areas where most Negroes live—throughout most of the old Confederacy and the larger cities of the North and West. It is the duty of government, however, to perceive and to counteract these inequities, not to accentuate them. And therein lies the problem. The irony of busing is that, in the name of equal protection of the laws, fair treatment has been denied one particular region of this country and one particular economic class. The South and white workingmen in the North sensed themselves more culpable in the eyes of law than they were in fact. The Supreme Court saw guilt as selective, not universal, and chose to communicate the thesis that a condition created by all Americans might be selectively overcome. The Court swore in *Green* to eliminate state-imposed segregation "root and branch." With busing it declared an all-out war, but then decided that much of the citizenry was not obliged to participate. Not surprisingly, the necessary national commitment never developed. The chief question among whites became how to avoid the conscription of the courts. Perhaps from the very beginning the achievement of a unitary society was beyond the capacity of judges. But during the 1970s, the spirit of judicial partiality undercut not only hopes for busing but the entire moral authority of constitutional law.

9

Busing the Suburbs:
Milliken v. *Bradley*

Brown v. *Board of Education*'s twentieth birthday was marked by blacks with mixed emotions. Yes, there had been conspicuous successes. Southern schools were increasingly integrated; Negroes had become more active politically; public facilities now opened to black and white alike; more federal programs attacked black poverty and illiteracy; job opportunities and income levels, though still behind those of whites, had risen appreciably; and, most important, blacks had gained in racial pride and self-respect. Yet something lacked. Few causes had ever had more federal energy thrown behind them than racial equality, yet the job remained undone. And there was uncertainty and suspicion over what the future held. "The question," wrote Roger Wilkins in May of 1974, "is whether the momentum generated by the activities of the last 20 years . . . will almost automatically lead to racial justice in this country, as some whites seem to think, or whether, as most blacks hold, the largest and hardest job is yet to be done, and whites have quit the game before the first quarter has even ended."[1]

Indeed, the hard part did lie ahead. Metropolitan areas, where by 1970 nearly three-quarters of all blacks lived,[2] still had the most rigidly segregated school systems. And one-third of America's black population remained desperately impoverished. The legal and economic gains propelling more and more blacks into middle-class ranks were themselves a mixed blessing. "The real danger," noted black economist Robert Browne, "is that an enormous gap will develop between the blacks who have, and those who don't. Then we're on our way to having a permanent black underclass. That would be intolerable."[3]

Brown's twentieth anniversary came and went with Richard Nixon still President, and still, to blacks, distant and indifferent. His southern strategy dismissed the black vote; his domestic advisor had counseled "benign neglect" of black problems; and his lieutenants dismantled "black" federal programs only barely begun. The Departments of Justice and HEW now whistled white tunes. "By 1971," contended Gary Orfield, "it was clear that HEW had given up its mission of bringing the nation's public schools into compliance with constitutional requirements for desegregation. The ultimate sanction of fund cutoffs had been publicly abandoned and its last administrative proponent fired. The White House openly warned federal officials that they would be fired if they continued to urge busing."[4] The Justice Department, once an ally of integrationists, now "gave low priority to school cases and sometimes led the opposition to legal theories advanced by civil rights lawyers."[5] In both the Charlotte and Denver cases, the Department sided emphatically with proponents of less integration.[6] The job of urban school desegregation thus fell almost entirely on private organizations, for whom the cost, complexity, and lengthiness of litigation posed formidable barriers.

No one in 1974 quite knew how to figure the Supreme Court. For a time, the Court's zeal seemed rekindled, even as that of the executive slackened. In Charlotte and Denver, the Court rebuffed the president on busing, as it would likewise rebuff him on abortion, wiretapping, parochial school aid, and, at the end, executive privilege.[7] Yet blacks in 1974 were anxious about the Supreme Court also, and with reason. Four Nixon appointees—Burger, Blackmun, Powell, and Rehnquist—now sat on the high bench. Obviously independent of the president's political views and fortunes, they shared, to varying degrees, his judicial philosophy of strict construction and self-restraint. In areas other than school desegregation, that restraint had been evident. The Burger Court had narrowed the rights of criminal defendants,[8] rejected the pleas of indigents for constitutional rights to welfare, housing, and education,[9] and defeated black claimants in cases not involving school integration.[10] Even in school decisions, the once unanimous, dependable Supreme Court now was splitting, in one recent case five to four.[11]

Before the Court on *Brown*'s twentieth anniversary was a case of signal importance: *Milliken* v. *Bradley*.[12] The question in *Milliken* was ostensibly one of remedy: whether courts could use suburban pupils to desegregate inner city schools. Federal District Judge Stephen Roth had found the Detroit Board of Education guilty of the usual ploys to obstruct integration: optional-attendance zones, gerrymandered school boundaries, and segregative transportation and school construction policies. The state of Michigan was also found to have delayed Detroit's desegregation by its funding policies and through special legislation.[13] Judge Roth had thereupon joined fifty-three of Detroit's eighty-five outlying suburban school districts with the city in his desegregation decree and ordered a nine member panel to draft a detailed plan.[14]

The scope of Judge Roth's order was staggering enough, thought one editor, to make "all previous busing programs look like class excursions."[15] The new metropolitan school district would contain 780,000 pupils, of whom some 310,000 would be daily transported in the interests of desegregation. Busing would be "a two-way process with both black and white pupils sharing the responsibility for transportation requirements at all grade levels." Even kindergarten was to be included. At so formidable an undertaking, Judge Roth professed no great alarm. "[I]n the recent past," he noted, "more than 300,000 pupils in the tri-county area regularly rode to school on some type of bus." Busing, concluded the judge, was "a considerably safer, more reliable, healthful and efficient means of getting children to school than either car pools or walking, and this is especially true for younger children."[16] The Sixth Circuit Court of Appeals affirmed by a vote of six to three Judge Roth's findings of culpability and the need for a metropolitan desegregation plan.[17]

The effect of the suburban busing threat on Michigan was electric. In the May, 1972 Michigan Democratic primary, George Wallace swept to victory over Hubert Humphrey and George McGovern. Stephen Roth was pilloried like southern judges of old. "It has been suggested . . ." the Detroit *News* observed, "that [Roth] considered precipitate action necessary in order to get his picture on the cover of *Time* before the busing issue is settled by the Supreme Court."[18] In Congress, the traditional southern antibusing fight suddenly was headed by Michigan members. The turnabout of once liberal congressmen caused some dismay. "The congressional mood in the 1971–76 period," wrote Gary Orfield, "was reminiscent of that in southern state legislatures in the late 50s. Although most legislators knew they lacked the authority to repeal Supreme Court decisions, public pressure was so intense that legislators often cast almost unanimous ballots for patently ridiculous positions. . . . On Capitol Hill in the 1970s members of Congress found themselves debating measures to cut off the gasoline for school buses, to permit resegregation of southern schools, and to tell the Supreme Court how to handle its school cases."[19]

Michigan's conversion was not surprising. The surest way to stir passions was to prick the suburban bubble. But was there an alternative? Many saw in metropolitan desegregation the sole salvation of equal educational opportunity. In no other way, it was argued, could America's urban apartheid be overcome. No story was racially bleaker than urban school demographics. For many reasons, central city schools had become even blacker than the central city as a whole. White parents could better afford private or parochial schooling than could black ones. Many city whites, moreover, were singles or childless couples who might indulge themselves in the attractions of urban life without exposing their offspring to its vicissitudes. Out-migration statistics often reflected "the tendency of young married couples to leave the city as they expand their families."[20] Whites remaining were often elderly residents of elderly neighborhoods. The black population, on the other hand, was younger and of school age. In Detroit, for example, blacks comprised in 1970 a mere 23 percent of the city's sixty-five and over population, but 61 percent of its school age population.[21] And the latter figure crept steadily upward: 64.9 percent in 1971; 67.3 percent in 1972, and 69.8 percent in 1973.[22]

"How do you desegregate a black city, or a black school system?" Judge Roth wondered at trial.[23] To bus in Detroit only would leave many schools 75 to 90 percent black. It would have resulted, as the Court of Appeals noted, "in an all black [city] school system immediately surrounded by practically all white suburban school systems, with an overwhelmingly white majority population in the total metropolitan area."[24] The prevailing racial isolation of the metropolis would have continued as before. Including the suburbs with the city, on the other hand, promised a new school system nearly three-quarters white.[25]

The Fourteenth amendment spoke in racial terms: thus litigants and judges had to also. But the true appeal of metropolitan remedies lay more in the need for class than racial interaction. By the mid-1970s, in fact, integration had begun to assume class as well as racial overtones. Disadvantaged whites stood to benefit alongside disadvantaged blacks from having the suburbs "bused in."[26] With metropolitan busing, moreover, middle America might share in the struggle for racial justice. Tangible sacrifice would be more evenly required, not left only to whites of limited means and clout. Private schooling, of course, would remain a middle-class alternative, but it was not well established in many northern suburbs because public integration, until recently, had seemed remote. And there would be, of course, the question of how many whites would willingly pay both public school taxes and private school tuition.

To integrate only the underprivileged of each race was, as busing in Boston dramatized, to risk great social discord for small educational gain. The poor of whatever race or ethnicity often brought to school the same educational deficiencies and the same limited home backgrounds. And poor schools, integrated or not, suffered the same dim status as did all-black ones. For busing to make educational sense, it was believed, all strata of society had to be included.[27] Thus some district judges, while integrating the races in theory, sought, in fact, to mix classes. In Charlotte, for example, the school board proposed to send children from a nearby white neighborhood to black West Charlotte High School, "but the district judge refused to approve this plan. . . . The judge made it clear that he wanted socio-economic integration as well as racial integration" and thus required 600 whites from "the more affluent [and more distant] southeast portion of [the] county."[28]

The middle class brought with it prospects of better funding for inner city schools. The dilemma of urban school finance can be briefly explained. Deprived home backgrounds created educational deficiencies in minority students that were expensive to overcome. Yet urban school systems possessed paltry funds with which to do so, primarily because public health, welfare, housing, sanitation, and safety costs badly drained municipal budgets. Due to this overburden, the average city devoted about 30 percent of its budget to schools, the average suburb about half.[29] Beset also by white exodus and declining property values, urban school finance was in desperate shape.[30] The Court had not helped much either. In *San Antonio Independent School Dist.* v. *Rodriguez*,[31] the Court held states under no constitutional obligation to overcome disparities in the expenditures of school districts within their borders.

Metropolitan desegregation might alleviate this condition. Suburban property might be taxed to support all schools within the new district. Inner city schools would be fairly treated because, under Judge Roth's decree, the racial composition of schools throughout the new district would supposedly be similar. Money would flow to urban schools, because middle-class children would now be attending them. *Milliken* posed, in short, a way for the Court to soften the fiscal blow dealt the dispossessed in *Rodriguez*.

Metro busing plans, it was also argued, were more practical than intracity ones. Black neighborhoods were often closer to white neighborhoods in the suburbs than to those on the opposite end of town. In *Milliken*, for instance, seventeen of the fifty-three suburban school districts actually bordered on Detroit; the rest all lay within eight miles of the city limits. Thus Judge Roth attempted to limit student travel time to a maximum of forty minutes, one way. The metropolitan remedy might even be more economical than one limited to the city only. For an intracity plan, 900 additional buses were allegedly necessary, only 350 for a metropolitan one, presumably because of a number of underutilized buses in the suburban districts.[32] Thus Judge Roth concluded that "for all the reasons stated heretofore—including time, distance, and transportation factors—desegregation within the [metropolitan] area described is physically easier and more practicable and feasible, then desegregation efforts limited to the corporate geographic limits of the City of Detroit."[33]

Lastly, busing the suburbs might help stem the urban exodus. Judge Roth found that school desegregation limited to Detroit "would change a school system which is now Black and White to one that would be perceived as Black, thereby increasing the flight of Whites from the city and the system. . . ."[34] With metropolitan busing, however, white flight would diminish, because there would be few places to flee. Suburban and central city schools would now be equally integrated. Even the exodus to private schools might be minimized, because public schools in a metropolitan system would be predominantly white.

Metropolitan school integration, it was also hoped, would create more integrated housing, because "families with children, and everyone else, too, may use school attendance zone lines to make their housing decisions."[35] Whites departed neighborhoods upon black arrival partly from fear that schools were about to turn black. But equally integrated schools everywhere would remove that incentive to leave. In fact, wrote one supporter of the metropolitan concept, "it is hard to imagine how stable housing integration . . . could be achieved in any reasonable period of time without a framework of areawide integrated schools."[36]

Thus read the brief for busing between city and suburb. And it looked like a winner. The Supreme Court in *Green* had required desegregation plans that promise "realistically to work *now.*"[37] Busing, to "work," must include the suburbs. *Swann* called upon school authorities "to achieve the greatest possible degree of actual desegregation."[38] The suburbs alone could ensure that. Unless the Court were to backtrack, suburban busing would be judicially blessed.

But it was not. Instead, the Court "saved" the suburbs. By a vote of five to four, it ruled Judge Roth had wrongly included them with Detroit in the desegregation decree.[39] The Court thus allayed, said Professor Bell, "middle class fears that the school bus would become the Trojan Horse of their suburban Troys."[40] In some ways, the Court's opinion was more stunning than its holding. Gone was *Green's* focus on the effectiveness of school desegregation plans. The practicality and the promise of metropolitan remedies was simply brushed aside. In its stead, the Court turned to legalism. "The nature of the violation," it had noted in *Swann*, "determines the scope of the remedy."[41] Translated to Detroit, that meant an interdistrict remedy required an interdistrict violation.[42] Or, in plainer English, because the suburbs had not themselves caused Detroit's segregation, they need not be part of the cure.

Yet the Court's turn to legalism was artlessly executed. It had good reason to suspect metropolitan busing plans, but not because of the lack of an inter-district violation. As it was, the Court falsely limited the search for suburban complicity. What had to be explained in Detroit was the overconcentration of blacks in the ghetto and that of whites in the suburbs. That, Judge Roth thought, had a variety of causes: Governments "at all levels, federal, state and local, have combined, with . . . private organizations, such as loaning institutions and real estate associations and brokerage firms, to establish . . . residential segregation throughout the Detroit metropolitan area."[43] To what extent, then, had racially motivated zoning laws, location of public housing projects, racially restrictive covenants or FHA and VA mortgages created the white character of Detroit's suburban neighborhoods and the black character of core city neighborhoods?[44]

Housing policies, more than school decisions, had metropolitan consequences, because housing discrimination in one jurisdiction, by definition, requires blacks to locate in another. And the effects of past housing practice are persistent. In fact, they may strengthen rather than diminish over time, as racial concentrations intensify and the racial character of neighborhoods in the mind of the larger community becomes ever more complete. "Many suburban whites," noted Judge J. Skelly Wright, "purchased their homes when prices were significantly lower than they are currently, at a time when minorities were excluded by overt and offically sanctioned discrimination."[45] One practice, the racially restrictive covenant, contended Martin Sloane, counsel for the National Committee Against Discrimination in Housing, was "a formidable factor in developing and perpetuating the pattern of residential segregation in metropolitan areas that exists today. Moreover, in many cases, they remain on deeds, are read and taken seriously by purchasers as binding obligations."[46]

The Court in *Milliken* had professed to apply to Detroit a theory of compensatory justice. "[T]he remedy is necessarily designed," it said, "as all remedies are, to restore the victims of discriminatory conduct to the position they would have occupied in the absence of such conduct."[47] But victimization could not be understood or genuine restoration attempted without looking at housing. Yet the Court finessed the question. Because the Court of Appeals had not examined testimony as to segregated housing practices, said the Court, the Detroit case did "not present any question concerning possible state housing violations."[48] In failing to remand to district court for findings on past housing practices or even to explain their relevance, the Supreme Court failed to address the foremost cause of metropolitan segregation: precisely what *Milliken* v. *Bradley* purported to be about.

The ultimate question was why blacks should undergo the delay, effort, and expense of proving past segregative practices, in either schools or housing. Where segregation existed, residentially or educationally, was there not a presumption of prior state complicity which it, not black plaintiffs, was obliged to explain? Justice Powell had urged this presumption as to school boards:

> School board decisions obviously are not the sole cause of segregated school conditions. But if, after such detailed and complete public supervision, substantial school segregation still persists, the presumption is strong that the school board, by its acts or omissions, is in some part responsible. . . . [T]his Court is [then] justified in finding a prima facie case of a constitutional violation. The burden then must fall *on the school board* to demonstrate it is operating an integrated school system.[49] (Emphasis added).

Was not a similar presumption justified in housing? Did school or housing segregation in the American metropolis owe nothing to official action? Why did black plaintiffs bear so laborious a burden of proof? The process of proving constitutional violations in northern cities turned school desegregation into "monster" litigation, an obstacle course of trials, appeals, remands, and retrials.[50] How much of that was necessary? Had the Court's insistence in Detroit on interdistrict violations done no more than set up a fool's search for evidence of the obvious? And then, by ignoring housing, limited the search so the obvious might remain obscure?

By ignoring housing, the Supreme Court began to lift from white America responsibility for the ghetto. *Milliken* v. *Bradley* was an act of absolution. Segregated Detroit schools were not the suburbs' creation and thus not their burden. In 1968, the National Advisory Commission on Civil Disorders prefaced its history of ghetto development thusly: "What white Americans have never fully understood—but what the Negro can never forget—is that white society is deeply implicated in the ghetto. White institutions created it, white institutions maintain it, and white society condones it."[51] The impetus for progress in Civil Rights in the 1960s had been white America's recognition of its part in creating the black's degraded state. *Milliken* foretold a time of greater innocence, of freer conscience; there were limits, it said, to assigning guilt and shame.

Milliken also marked blacks' first loss in a school case since *Brown*. Its timing hurt. "Twenty years later," the NAACP's Herbert Hill said, "instead of what should have been a joyous celebration of progress, we're in the middle of the second post-Reconstruction."[52] The bugle of retreat had blown. "After 20 years of small, often difficult steps toward that great end [of equal justice under law]," regretted Justice Marshall in dissent, "the Court today takes a giant step backwards."[53]

The Court seemed to many to have left the nation helpless. *Milliken* had "perpetuated the lure of white suburban sanctuaries, beyond reach of constitutional equity," wrote the Milwaukee *Journal*. "The origins of these sanctuaries may be complex, but a society that cannot find ways to break them down, so as to fulfill the historic promise of its great Constitution, will continue to live in shame."[54] Because the Court had been the last hope for blacks, its decision rang like a final sentence. For Thurgood Marshall, more than anyone else, *Milliken* ended a dream: of one land and one people, "indivisible, with liberty and justice for all." Beaten by the present, Marshall, like Justice Harlan nearly a century ago, composed for the future: "In the short run," said he, "it may seem to be the easier course to allow our great metropolitan areas to be divided up each into two cities—one white, the other black—but it is a course, I predict, our people will ultimately regret."[55]

The majority in *Milliken* appealed to fundamental values also. The Court became the crier for the town meeting, the champion of local rights over local schools. "No single tradition in public education," wrote Chief Justice Burger for the Court, "is more deeply rooted than local control over the operation of schools; local autonomy has long been thought essential both to the maintenance of community concern and support for public schools and to the quality of the educational process."[56] A hefty footnote followed, listing the statutory powers of locally elected school boards. For twenty years, but especially since *Green*, racial integration had been a higher constitutional priority than educational democracy. Now that was reversed. And metropolitan administration seemed as impossible to the Court as local control was desirable. The Chief Justice foresaw no end to problems of governance and finance in Judge Roth's "vast new super school district."[57]

The Court's plea, not surprisingly, failed to move the dissenters. "Local control," they thought, only invited suburbia to wall itself in, not just with schools, but with zoning and land-use laws. Metropolitan areas were never meant to be balkanized in the name of local control, Justice Douglas insisted. "Metropolitan treatment of metropolitan problems is commonplace. If this were a sewage problem or a water problem, or an energy problem," rather than a race problem, the utility of metropolitan remedies would not be disputed.[58] The dissenters all thought local control little more than a pretext: local school districts were nothing more than creations of the state. Michigan extensively supervised many aspects of local education; Michigan itself had helped perpetuate segregated schools within Detroit; and, finally, Michigan could consolidate local school districts, with or without their consent.[59] And school district consolidation, far from being an administrative horror, seemed to some a routine educational advance. In 1931–32, there were some 128,000 school districts in the United States. Forty years later, in 1971–72, there were but 17,000.[60] Given the frequency of consolidation, most states had developed the administrative machinery to handle it,[61] though not necessarily on the scale Judge Roth proposed.

In its eulogy to local control, the Supreme Court really meant to say that judicial remedies were not limitless. The majority was appalled to see one single district judge operating on so grand a scale, reorganizing the nation's fifth largest metropolitan area, deciding the fate of 780,000 school children, combining fifty-four independent school systems. *Milliken* drove home the awesome new dimensions of judicial authority, from which the Burger Court majority, inclined to caution under the best of circumstances, simply shrank. The very notion of self-governance seemed inescapably affronted by Judge Roth's decree. Where, the Court must have wondered, would it end? Despite the judiciary's prodigious efforts, the horizons of racial justice had continued to recede. Was this next step of metropolitan desegregation a solution or simply another mirage to be chased at great cost?

In theory, the Detroit plan did seem plausible enough. With the suburbs included in the integration plan, there would be no sanctuary reserved for middle-class whites. Further, the impetus to white flight would be blunted in a school system nearly three-quarters white. Yet the very abstract "infallibility" of the Detroit decree engendered suspicion. *Milliken* reflected deep conservative distrust of the workability of central planning: human nature would find a way to thwart what on paper had seemed "perfect."

How the decree would be thwarted, the Court declined to guess. It knew only that predicted white enrollments were one thing; actual white attendance another. White parents, the Court also knew, would not be lining the streets of suburbia, cheering their children on into the middle of the Detroit ghetto. To avoid that ride, black schools might have to be closed, attendance lines redrawn.[62] Some whites might flee to Detroit's outer suburbs, not included in the court decree;[63] others seek private schooling; still others leave the Detroit area altogether. Whites might tolerate black students in suburban schools, but even there second-generation problems posed a danger: suspected prejudice in grades and discipline, segregated classes through tracking, leading inexorably to racial flare-ups. Maybe such fears might never materialize. But maybe, in such an unprecedented plan, they would arise in unprecedented numbers. Then to save its "sinking ship," and to shield its authority from the veto of threatening violence, the district court would be supervising metropolitan school operations for years to come.

On a broader front, suburban busing could stoke the fires of a constitutional amendment or a congressional attempt to curb the jurisdiction of federal courts in school litigation.[64] More judicial activism, the Court began to sense, might not be the end of this conundrum, if, indeed it ever is, but only the beginning of new and more portentous problems. In the words of Robert Burns:

> But, Mousie, thou art no thy lane (not alone)
> In proving foresight may be vain;
> The best laid schemes o' mice an' men
> > Gang aft agley,
> An' lea'e us nought but grief an' pain,
> > For promised joy.[65]

So activism had its pitfalls. Was the answer, then, to give up? Justice Marshall saw in *Milliken* only the Court's capitulation to an angry white mood. "Desegregation," he warned, "is not and was never expected to be an easy task." But "public opposition, no matter how strident, cannot be permitted to divert this Court from the enforcement of the constitutional principles at issue in this case. Today's holding, I fear, is more a reflection of a perceived public mood that we have gone far enough in enforcing the Constitution's guarantee of equal justice than it is the product of neutral principles of law."[66]

Suppose *Milliken* was, as Marshall contended, a judicial concession to the furor over busing. Was such a concession wrong? Unfortunately, the proper role of public temper in Supreme Court decisions has never been satisfactorily resolved. One understands, of course, that it would not do to have the Court slave to election returns or to Dr. Gallup's latest summaries. American political institutions have been designed to be removed, by stages, from popular will: the House of Representatives is the closest; next the Senate with its six year terms; next, perhaps, top executive appointees who, though not themselves elected, respond to one who is. But the Court has been chartered for the longest course. Justices are not elected, but appointed, and their appointment is for life. They serve at the pleasure of no constituency. The constitution they interpret reflects the values of the ages, not the exigencies of the moment.[67] And the public expects Supreme Court justices to be sagacious, meditative, compassionate, and visionary, or at least something unique and apart from our democratic whirlwinds.

Maybe race, above all other issues, must transcend the public mood. For one thing, the Civil War amendments commend to the Court protection of the Negro.[68] Yet the Court's refusal to rebuke popular mores of the late nineteenth century had consigned blacks to further generations of bondage and servitude. This tragic error had not been magically undone by *Brown*. On the contrary, reminders of the legacy of judicial apathy showed daily in the impoverishment and isolation of the Detroit ghetto. Surely, the justices must have feared that *Milliken* v. *Bradley* might one day be regarded as this century's *Plessy* v. *Ferguson*, an all-too-familiar story of a commitment renewed and then reneged upon. Ironically, the Court's nineteenth-century withdrawal had also occurred in the name of public peace. In enforcing segregation, said *Plessy*, the legislature "is at liberty to act with reference to the established usages, customs, and traditions of the people, and with a view to the promotion of their comfort, and the preservation of the public peace and good order."[69] Surely, the justices knew by now of segregation's fleeting, false tranquility, of injustice's uneasy calm. To buy "peace in our time," *Plessy* had shown, was to will discord to the next.

Much in recent precedent also advised against withdrawal. There was the famous nostrum of *Brown II*—"the vitality of these constitutional principles cannot be allowed to yield simply because of disagreement with them"[70]—that steeled district judges during the most difficult days of the southern struggle. There was the lesson of Little Rock: public defiance must not delay or bend the law.[71] There were *Green* and *Alexander* and *Carter* and *Swann* that marched forth in the face of determined opposition, even from the president himself.[72] For the Court to concede for a moment that public clamor might alter the judicial course was to encourage resistance ever after.

In *Milliken*, the opposition of the suburbs was the most potent and determined the Court could have faced. If so, was it not all-the-more-necessary that the justices hold fast? Here the Court's failure to act meant no action at all. Elected officials would never muster enough courage to desegregate the suburbs; only the Court could do that. The abandonment of the black by the Court meant, in *Milliken*, the loss of a last friend.

Was *Milliken* thus the unpardonable retreat? Or was withdrawal the better part of judicial wisdom? Judging had never been an impractical art; the ideal could not outpace the achievable. White fears as well as black aspirations had to be taken into account. The Court had acknowledged this in *Brown II* with its "all deliberate speed" directive. "[V]irtually every plan that will be ordered into effect by a district court [under *Brown II*]," Professor Black wrote in 1957, "will contain some substantial admixture of gradualism."[73] *Swann* likewise recognized practical limits to integration. Some small number of one-race schools was not "of itself the mark of a system which still practices segregation by law."[74] Valid objections might even be raised to bus rides which risked "either the health of the children or significantly impinge[d] on the educational process."[75]

Lower courts too had often scanned school busing plans with an eye toward white acceptance. On occasion, this meant permitting school closures in black communities lest whites refuse to attend them. Courts allowed closures only for nonracial reasons, which school officials invariably alleged to be the dilapidated condition of black schools or dangers in the communities surrounding them. In Jacksonville, Florida, the closing of five formerly black schools was permitted because "all were deteriorated; one was surrounded by a slaughter house, a polluted creek, and a city incinerator; and in three other schools the '[i]ncidences of vandalism and intrusion [were so frequent and serious] that teachers and children [were] locked in their rooms for safety.' "[76] If conditions in the schools were so deplorable, however, why had school officials waited for the onset of integration to shut them down?

On other occasions, judges condoned the busing of black students only. "In Pinellas County, Fla.," protested the NAACP, "6.4% of the white students are bused because of the desegregation order in comparison to 75.2% of the black children. . . . Seventy-five percent of the bused students in Jackson, Miss., are black."[77] Blacks were often bused at an earlier age, so that young whites might remain in their neighborhoods. In both Nashville and Charlotte, for example, plans were approved busing black students in grades one to four, whites not until grades five and six.[78]

The object of such provisions was clear: to relieve white anxiety over attending once-black schools. The dilemma is hideous: it is precisely our past oppression that creates our present aversions. And though whites had established segregation, blacks, under busing, often bore the burden of disestablishing it. It all seemed illogical and unfair. Yet the Court, for the most practical of reasons, was careful not to rule the practices unconstitutional. Though *Swann* purported to define "in more precise terms than heretofore" the duty of school boards to achieve desegregation,[79] some questions, such as one-way busing and black school closings, managed to escape definition.

Deference to white opinion, then, had been part of school desegregation law from the beginning. But was such deference justified in *Milliken?* First, one must appraise the character of white resistance. To some, that character was transparently racist. Whites accepted, even welcomed, busing for all purposes save integration. *It's Not the Distance, 'It's the Niggers,'* as the NAACP Legal Defense Fund pithily put it.[80] Antibusing atmospherics of the mid-1970s seemed no different than southern school openings of the late 1950s. "Carrying books and paper-bag lunches," *Time* magazine reported in September 1975, "some 200 inner-city black boys and girls walked quickly but quietly from five yellow school buses, past dozens of armed state and county troopers, and into Louisville's suburban Valley High School."[81] Some saw in that scene Little Rock all over: whites accepting black schoolmates only at the point of a bayonet. "The North," charged Kenneth Clark that fall, "is trying to get away with what the South tried. If the North succeeds, and I don't think that it will, it will make a mockery of our courts and laws."[82]

Suppose, however, that white resistance to busing had a more legitimate basis than had the Deep South's resistance to *Brown*. Should not courts prove more willing to accommodate it?[83] The remedial task of courts, *Swann* noted, was "to correct, by a balancing of the individual and collective interests, the condition that offends the Constitution."[84] Surely a balanced busing remedy would weigh the objections of those whites affected.

What are courts to make of the suburban student who finds in neighborhood schools a safe and healthy environment, a sense of identity and community, a decent education, and convenient home-school access? He and his parents have heard that blacker schools feature greater drug use, more physical extortion, less rigorous instruction. Consider Al and Mildred McCauley, residents of Highview, a white middle-class suburb outside Louisville. Louisville had been distinguished from *Milliken* by the Sixth Circuit Court of Appeals and in the fall of 1975 was undergoing metropolitan busing.[85] The two McCauley boys—David, fifteen, and Danny, fourteen— had to rise at 6:35 A.M. for a fifty-minute bus ride to Parkland Junior High, twenty-two miles off in Louisville's black ghetto. Mrs. McCauley visited Parkland and didn't like what she saw. "It hadn't been painted in eight years. There was no maintenance." She claimed Parkland offered inferior education, an absence of discipline. She had heard rumors of stabbings and rapes in the Parkland neighborhood. Their old neighborhood school of Fern Creek, despite a minor drug problem, suited the McCauleys just fine.[86]

It was all very well for those not affected to label the McCauleys' apprehensions baseless or blind. The McCauleys, obviously, did not wish to take that chance.[87] Were they wrong for not wanting to trade known advantages for unknown hazards in the name of a social end of unproven benefit? Suppose their neighborhood school had been but 8 percent black. That was no different from thousands of others across the country serving their communities regardless of race. Yes, Mrs. McCauley admitted, she could understand that blacks wanted better education, but "why don't they just upgrade their schools? I just can't see sending my children in there to get a lower education so that *they* can get a better one."[88] Racist? In one sense, clearly so. Yet racial attitudes were not the exclusive impetus to resistance to inter-district busing. At some point, the search for stability and community in public schooling becomes a moral quest. At some point too, in America, personal lives, especially those of the young, cease to be proper subjects for judicial experiment and sacrifice.

In 1954, the Southerner had also spoken of quality education and had railed against the dangers of integrated schools. But in *Brown*, beneath all paeans to the southern way of life, lay this nasty fact: no black could attend any white school, no matter how high his intelligence, how close his residence, how keen his desire. Segregation, over time, was ready to topple of its own immoral dead weight. But in Detroit, the suburban case was not based on values the nation as a whole had condemned as degenerate. What the Court faced in *Milliken* was a profound clash of legitimate aspirations. Judges should resolve racial conflict if one side is morally wrong and if the country can be so persuaded. In *Milliken*, the Court felt the former untrue, the latter impossible.

White resistance to busing often overshadowed the more subtle question of black attitudes. The external evidence seemed wholly contradictory. "I'm in favor of busing to achieve integration," said Mrs. Shirley Waites, a black mother in Philadelphia. "Obviously, you can't achieve it any other way. The schools work on a neighborhood system, and the neighborhoods are segregated. Separate but equal doesn't work [because] the white politicians don't care about black schools."[89] In Louisville, the Woods children were as inconvenienced by busing as any white suburbanite. Up at 5:45 A.M. for breakfast; on the bus at 6:50; at school by 7:30: it made for a very long day. But the suburban Stuart school was better than the black one left behind. Byron, thirteen, was taking a remedial mathematics course; Kenneth, twelve, an elective in chess. Busing "is the best thing that has happened since the Supreme Court ruling of 1954," said their father, Elmer Woods, a brewing company supervisor. "We're twenty years late, but it is going to better my kids."[90] Other black parents were not at all sure. "As far as I'm concerned, I've always been against busing," said Mrs. Doris Mc-Crary, a black mother in Detroit. "I have built my kids where they have confidence in themselves. If you take them out to Grosse Point where they would be looked down on, that would do something to their self-image."[91]

Two events underscored the cleavage in black views: one, the

National Black Political Convention in Gary, Indiana; the other, the much-publicized Atlanta Compromise. In Gary, over 3,000 black delegates convened on March 10–12, 1972 to shape a political agenda for black people. At the end of the convention, no more than a third were still participating, the others having stormed out in various disagreements. But the convention did oppose busing, thanks largely to CORE's executive director, Roy Innis, who insisted that black people were "tired of being guinea pigs for social engineers and New York liberals."[92] No one claimed the convention a mirror of black opinion. But the *Wall Street Journal* thanked the conventioners "for reminding everyone that the busing issue is not easily divisible along racial lines, since there are blacks and whites alike who take contrary views on what best serves the interests of their children."[93]

A year later, in Atlanta, the local NAACP approved a drastic reduction in busing (less than 3,000 pupils were to be transported) in return for more black school administrators, including a black school superintendent. The plan was agreed to, said Atlanta NAACP president Lonnie King, because 78 percent of Atlanta's school population was already black, and because white flight from the city had to be halted.[94] The district court approved the plan, noting that it satisfied "the overwhelming majority of the [black] plaintiff class."[95] But it completely failed to satisfy the national NAACP in New York, which urged busing over 18,000 pupils and now suspended its Atlanta branch for accepting so much less.[96]

The enigma of black attitudes was hardly surprising. For one thing, blacks opposing busing might not want to speak out. To do so might brand one an Uncle Tom in the black community and provide ammunition to white racists. And blacks were not eager to side publicly with Richard Nixon and against the NAACP, whatever their private feelings.

Black attitudes toward busing probably hinged, in the end, on the manner of its implementation. Blacks need not leave their own neighborhoods to be placed in a "slow learners" track, assumed academically incapable, suspended as troublemakers, in short, to be resegregated within a white school's walls.[97] The right kind of busing in the right kind of school system, on the other hand, might elicit a favorable black response. Polls, therefore, many of which showed the black community almost evenly split on busing, were frequently too general in their questioning.[98]

Genuine black opposition did, however, threaten the entire idea of forced busing. It made busing seem less a program to serve the disadvantaged than an elitist contrivance in opposition to the concensual wishes of both races. One might argue that popular attitudes—black or white—do not govern the Constitution, that black views were transitory or obscure, and that similar attitudinal "evidence" had been cited by segregationists since the beginning of time to keep blacks in their place. Still, it was awkward to support a course of action if even the supposed beneficiaries resisted it. Not surprisingly, therefore, most judges preferred to ignore the whole question.[99]

If many blacks themselves opposed busing, why not make it optional? Let blacks who would attend white schools be bused, the argument ran, and let those opposing busing remain in their neighborhoods. Even the Supreme Court endorsed optional integration in *Swann* (though not, apparently, as a substitute for compulsory busing). "An optional majority to minority transfer provision," the Court noted, "has long been recognized as a useful part of every desegregation plan. Provision for optional transfer of those in the majority racial group of a particular school to other schools where they will be in the minority is an indispensable remedy for [state-imposed segregation]. . . . In order to be effective, such a transfer arrangement must grant the transferring student free transportation and space must be made available in the school to which he desires to move."[100]

Several communities had experimented with optional black-transfer programs. Since 1966, Boston's METCO program bused city blacks to white suburban schools with some success. And in Portland, some 2,700 pupils, mainly black, had transferred by 1975 to white neighborhood schools. Because whites could remain in their own neighborhoods, optional integration would not, in the opinion of Washington *Post* columnist William Raspberry, "generate the fear-spawned opposition" that busing had.[101]

Another advocate of optional integration, Dr. James Coleman, made the most far-reaching proposal: "That each central-city child should have an entitlement from the state to attend any school in the metropolitan area . . . with per-pupil funds going with him. That's a right no black child has now," said Coleman, "and it would be extremely valuable in a place like Boston. This would entail some restrictions: The program wouldn't be subject to a local veto; whites couldn't move from black schools to white schools. . . . Also, there would have to be some kind of limit on out-of-district children, say 20 or 30 percent."[102] Coleman claimed for his proposal the best of both worlds. It would grant neighborhood schooling to whites and integrated suburban schooling to those blacks desiring it.

The Coleman proposal, while promising, was also problem-ridden. Because it restricted local vetoes and white transfers and encouraged the influx of blacks to the suburbs, many legislatures would refuse to enact it. Yet court-ordered plans of the Coleman variety involved the same interference with local control and school administration that the *Milliken* majority decried.

The real liabilities of optional integration were more basic. Optional integration would be seen by some blacks as a white escape from busing with a bone tossed back to assuage racial guilt. It would again make integration depend on black initiative and abandon in the inner city those blacks whose parents did not insist they be bused out. It probably meant that blacks would attend suburban schools in only token numbers and not represent a real presence or community force. For example, Boston's METCO program had produced in 1969 only tiny black fractions of white suburban student bodies, never more than 4 percent in any one school. And those blacks who participated were disproportionately middle class.[103] Optional integration, therefore, hardly represented thoroughgoing interaction but rather an invitation to "selected" blacks to come to school on "white" terms.

Optional programs may depend for effectiveness on the threat of more coercive alternatives. Left to themselves, they may wilt. In the end, one suspects, many localities would discover ways to discourage blacks from exercising their option to transfer. In fact, the new optional integration more than slightly resembled the old freedom of choice, though with several important differences. Freedom of choice allowed white transfers from black schools; optional integration might not. Freedom of choice expressed the rural South's aversion to neighborhood schools; optional integration indicated urban America's fondness for them. But a similarity outshone all differences. Both freedom of choice and optional integration reflected white America's preference for modest integration at most.

If optional integration promised no certain solution to racial segregation, then what did? Some believed America would achieve integrated schooling on its own, without student busing. The only durable solution to the school problem lay not in such artificial, court-imposed remedies, but in the black man's natural, inevitable rise. Courts could forego coercive plans, it was contended, because integration by the mid-1970s had become irreversible. Given time, the problem would, indeed, cure itself.

The view of school integration as an irreversible process rests on several intriguing premises. One is that racial prejudice in America is indisputably on the decline. It still exists, to be sure, but it is out of fashion. It is being driven from public life and commerce (though not so fast from locker rooms and cocktail parties). Younger generations of Americans are especially committed to its demise. All this represents not a cosmetic change, but a real revolution in American attitudes. The polls attest to it. From the early 1940s to the mid-1960s, whites who believed Negroes as intelligent and educable as whites rose from 40 to 80 percent.[104] The percentage of whites who would not be disturbed with a Negro of the same income and education on their block increased from 35 in 1942 to 84 in 1972.[105] And National Opinion Research Center surveys indicated that the proportion of whites favoring integrated schools rose from 30 percent in 1942, to 49 percent in 1956, to 64 in 1963 and 75 percent in 1970.[106] The great enactments of the 1960s (especially the Civil Rights Act of 1964) all reflected this growing white enlightenment. Even busing, moreover, appears to have left white views on other racial matters generally intact.[107]

Negro ascendency, of course, had firmer roots than in changing white opinions. Blacks themselves became more willing and better able to demand their rights. Since the Johnson presidency, a vast network of law and bureaucracy protected Civil Rights. Most important, blacks could vote. Prior to the Voting Rights Act of 1965, blacks were roughly one-tenth of the Deep South's registered voters. By 1970 they comprised approximately 30 percent of the Mississippi electorate, a quarter of that in South Carolina, a fifth in Alabama, Georgia, and Louisiana.[108] Former segregationists, Senator Strom Thurmond chief among them, ardently courted black votes. And blacks elected to office more of their own: from 100 black officials in 1964 to 4,300 fourteen years later.[109] The Voting Rights Act, observed The Urban League's Vernon Jordan, "was probably the most significant accomplishment [of the whole civil rights movement]. . . . [V]oting is power—the whites in the South knew that, and that's why they killed people who were trying to get black people registered."[110]

Legal rights and political power translated themselves into economic gains. Movement of blacks to metropolitan areas meant more diverse economic opportunity than in 1940 when one black in three worked on a farm. (Today the figure is one in fifty.)[111] "Between 1955 and 1973," noted Professor Lester Thurow, "earnings of black males rose from 56 percent to 66 percent of those of white males, and earnings of black females rose from 56 percent to 86 percent of white females."[112] But, argued Professor Nathan Glazer, "more significant than this overall trend . . . is the remarkable rise, to a position near equality with that of whites, of the income of young, unbroken black families, with heads under 35 years of age: This has taken place in the South as well as in the North."[113] The rise in income matched a rise in occupations. In 1964, 16 percent of black males were white-collar workers; by 1974, 24 percent, while the percentage of white male white-collar workers remained constant.[114] And some of this black economic progress was even thought to be recession-proof. "During the prosperous 1960s," Professor Reynolds Farley noted, "racial differences in education, occupation, and income generally declined. . . . [But] the gains of the 1960s apparently were not solely attributable to the prosperity of that decade, since racial differences in status narrowed [also] in the 1970s." Fundamental changes in American life, concluded Farley, "mean that, even during a pervasive recession, blacks did not lose the gains they previously experienced," though blacks unquestionably remained recession's chief victims.[115]

The theory of irreversible integration rests on this causal chain: black political and legal victories improve black economic status, which, in turn, improves black housing opportunities, which, in turn, changes the racial composition of many neighborhood schools. As Nathan Glazer, a chief proponent of the theory, put it: Housing "is based, in large measure, on income, occupation, and education, and if blacks approach whites in these respects, then inevitably black residential distribution will become less concentrated, and school systems based on proximity will become more integrated."[116] Blacks with higher incomes and better jobs are the ones whites will accept most readily as neighbors and classmates. Thus school integration would occur more harmoniously if it followed the natural integration of neighborhoods. Under this reasoning, of course, schools are the last, climactic step in integration, not the first foundation as the Court believed in *Brown*. But schools would be integrated nonetheless. "I do not wish to suggest," said Glazer, "that the millenium has arrived. Yet there have been remarkable changes, owing to the black struggle for equality, . . . and these changes are by now institutionalized, and continue without the need for drastic measures."[117]

The theory of irreversible integration was a comfortable one, as were all theories that suggest that difficult problems will resolve themselves. The judiciary, the federal government, the entire country could now afford to relax. Daniel Moynihan had something similar in mind when, citing census income figures, he advised President Nixon that "the Negro is making extraordinary progress" and that "the time may have come when the issue of race could benefit from a period of 'benign neglect.' "[118]

Others, however, were far less sure of integration's inevitability. The song of Ecclesiastes was also sung. The course of busing had demonstrated to many not the demise of racist attitudes but their depth. And for all the talk of new voting power, only one-half of 1 percent of the nation's elected officials in 1974 were black.[119] Economic gaps between the races remained wide; black rates of unemployment for the first half of the 1970s were twice those of whites, the same ratio as in the two previous decades. Even the rise in black income seemed illusory to some. "Black income is principally consumer income," one economist pointed out. "Most of that money goes right back into white hands for consumer goods and services."[120] Real economic control remained in lily-white hands: in industry, publishing, broadcasting, education, philanthropy, and government. "Those blacks who do penetrate to some place near the upper reaches of such institutions," argued Roger Wilkins, "lead a lonely existence, surrounded and sometimes almost suffocated, by white attitudes, values, and fantasies."[121] The day of equality, inevitable or not, was certainly eventual. "If current progress [in relative earnings of the races] were to continue," Professor Thurow believed, "black females would achieve parity with white females in about ten years, but black males would not reach parity for another 75 years."[122]

The assumption that black economic gains would lead to integrated neighborhoods and thus to integrated schools was most sharply disputed. Professors Hermalin and Farley contended in one 1973 study that blacks already possessed the economic potential "to occupy housing at all value levels in the cities and suburbs." With family income as the only criterion, they believed, 55 percent of black families would live in the suburbs of the nation's twenty-nine largest cities. Actually, only 17 percent did. Of that 17 percent, many lived in so-called "inner suburbs," mostly black and closest to the city. If economic criteria, then, "account[ed] for little of the observed concentration of blacks in central cities and their relative absence from the suburbs," what was the dominant factor? Hermalin and Farley saw the villain as a " 'web of discrimination'—the real estate practices, the mortgage lending arrangements, the climate of opinion and the like—which deter blacks from obtaining the housing for which they are economically qualified."[123]

Can such discrimination be overcome? Recent progress has not been dramatic. One study, for example, noted that whites and blacks had fewer neighbors of the other race in 1970 than in 1960.[124] Another concluded in 1975 that "the nation's neighborhoods are almost as segregated now as they were thirty years ago. If present tends persist, schools organized on a neighborhood basis will remain racially segregated indefinitely."[125]

There are several reasons why neighborhood segregation in America may not disappear soon. One involves the dynamics of neighborhood turnover. Initial black penetration of white neighborhoods is often no easy task. Even in the absence of racially restrictive covenants, selling to blacks is often thought a "dirty trick" to play on one's friends. Once initial penetration has occurred, however, the neighborhood falls into danger of turning completely black.

A simple example should illustrate. Suppose twenty white families live on an imaginary Elm Street where homes sell for an average of $75,000. Blacks too would like to live there. Suppose also that white families on Elm Street exhibit varying levels of racial tolerance. The Scotts would accept a neighborhood 50% black; the Jones 30% black; the Williams 20%; the Johnsons 10%; but the Smiths no blacks at all. Suppose another white family, the Does, moves and sells its home to blacks. This causes the Smiths to leave, perhaps with a black family moving in. The two black families on Elm Street now upset the Johnsons, who also depart. By now, prospective white buyers sense that Elm Street is turning

black and stay away. Thus the Johnsons, in moving, must sell to a
black purchaser also. Soon the Williams's level of acceptance is exceeded; then the Jones's; finally the Scotts's. This whole process
was traditionally aided by the "block buster," the eager agent in
panic turnovers. "In lieu of blunt statements that Negroes are 'taking over the neighborhood,' he makes subtle references to changing
neighborhoods, to the expansion of neighboring ghettoes, to his
personal fear of crime in the area, and to the increasing difficulty of
finding [white] purchasers for homes in the neighborhood."[126] Before long, the neighborhood is mostly black.

What happens, Professor Bruce Ackerman explains, is that
neighborhoods "lose their white families as the actions of the least
tolerant and least stable families tip, or appear about to tip, the
neighborhood to a point that is racially unacceptable to some of the
more tolerant and more stable families."[127] It is the classic case of
extreme opinions stampeding more moderate ones, and it accounts
for much of the rapid racial transition in working-and middle-class
neighborhoods today.[128] (The same phenomenon also affects
schools, though to a lesser extent. As the least tolerant whites depart urban schools for private academies or the suburbs, they pressure whites who initially wished to give integration a chance.)

There are now, of course, federal statutes that prohibit housing
discrimination, the most prominent being the 1968 Fair Housing
Act. Landmark laws on Civil Rights required, above all, emotional
momentum: from the death of John Kennedy, from the Selma
march of Martin Luther King, and, with the 1968 Act, from King's
own shooting on the balcony of a shabby Memphis motel. Passed
partly as a monument to the stricken leader, the act sweepingly forbade discrimination in the sale, rental, financing, and advertising of
housing, as well as such institutional tactics as blockbusting and
steering (i.e., realtors directing blacks into black neighborhoods and
whites into white ones).[129] Enforcement existed through administra-
trative action or through private or public civil litigation.

Yet six years after its enactment, the United States Commission
on Civil Rights concluded that the act had had "little impact on the
country's serious housing discrimination problem."[130] Subsequent
appraisals were similar.[131] There were numerous reasons for that
assessment: among them, the limits of law in reaching discriminatory behavior of individual brokers, landlords, and homeowners,
a low level of awareness among minorities of the act's remedies, in-

ordinate delay in the Department of Housing and Urban Development in processing complaints, and the split of enforcement authority between HUD and the Department of Justice.[132] The Civil Rights Commission also managed to note that "the zeal with which federal officials carried out policies of discrimination in the early days of the government's housing effort has not been matched by a similar enthusiasm in carrying out their current legal mandate of equal housing opportunity."[133]

Finally, prospects for residential integration were not brightened by the Supreme Court. The Court in the 1970s did not leap to challenge segregated neighborhoods. On the contrary, it frequently left standing the formidable barriers surrounding them. During the late 1960s, the Warren Court had hinted of a massive, impending assault on housing segregation.[134] The Burger Court made clear that any such plan had been scrapped. The housing laws challenged before that Court did not discriminate openly on the basis of race. They did, however, operate to exclude blacks from nicer neighborhoods. Early in the decade, the Court declared that decent housing was not a fundamental constitutional right,[135] which meant that laws burdening the access of indigent families to the suburbs would receive lenient judicial treatment. In 1971, the Court upheld a California constitutional requirement that "[n]o low rent housing project shall hereafter be developed [by] any state public body" without prior approval in a local referendum.[136] The decision helped cement local political control over the character of local neighborhoods, despite the fact that blacks and minorities might not influence local politics (living, as they did, *outside* the jurisdiction). In 1975, the Court held that parties challenging housing bias in federal court lacked standing to sue.[137] And in 1977, the Court gave local land use controls (e.g., minimum dollar value or lot size or street setback distance for homes in a neighborhood) a significant boost.[138] It was not sufficient merely to show that such ordinances had a racially disproportionate impact, said the Court. For such an ordinance to violate the constitution, discriminatory motive had to be proven.[139]

Residential segregation, then, was as much a stubborn fortress as the neighborhood school. It may well be, as proponents of irreversible integration contend, that black political and economic progress will change all that. But it is far from sure. The final question, however, is not when or even whether housing integration will occur. Advocates of a housing solution to school segregation, it is crucial to understand, are urging something very different from supporters of student busing. Housing is principally an individual remedy, busing a class one. Integrated schools through integrated neighborhoods will benefit those individual blacks determined and prosperous enough to escape the ghetto and buy into white areas.[140] Busing, on the other hand, seeks to aid those whom fate has left stranded. Integrated neighborhoods largely await those blacks who already have made it in other ways—in employment, for instance, or education. Busing was to provide an opportunity for those deprived in other ways to make it still. Thus housing solutions urge a racially integrated society but tolerate one segregated by class. Many demographers have noted that "economic classes are more visible among the black population now" than they were ten to fifteen years ago.[141] The housing solution accepts that development; proponents of busing would not.

Thus *Milliken* v. *Bradley* rejected what some believed to be the last hope for mass betterment of America's blacks. Instead, the Court tacitly placed faith in such lesser alternatives as optional or irreversible integration. The conventional wisdom after *Green* had been that judicial pressure gained more than it lost from white backlash. When pressure eased, momentum lagged. *Milliken* questioned all that and wondered whether the limits of white acceptance had not finally been passed. But the great gamble of the Court in *Milliken* v. *Bradley* was that black progress would continue in the absence of an activist judiciary. Perhaps, the Court believed, white attitudes had now matured, and black self-sufficiency developed, to the point that it could. It was not a novel judgment. "[T]here must be some stage," the Court had long ago remarked, "in the progress of his elevation when he [the Negro] takes the rank of a mere citizen, and ceases to be the special favorite of the laws, . . ."[142] That time, we now know, was not 1883. Was it, as *Milliken* judged, 1974?

Some lower courts still sought to implement metropolitan desegregation after *Milliken*. That case, they believed, reflected the unmanageability of large metropolitan areas such as Detroit. In middle-sized urban areas, such as Wilmington, Delaware and Louisville, Kentucky, suburban busing appeared more feasible.

Thus, the district court in the Wilmington case emphasized that there were "779,000 students in the Detroit 'desegregation area,' but there are only 87,696 in all of New Castle County."[143] In Detroit, there were some fifty-four school districts to be consolidated. In Wilmington, there were, at most, twelve[144] and in Louisville but three.[145] In Detroit, three counties were involved; in Wilmington and Louisville only one.

Not only was the organization of metropolitan government much simpler in these areas than in Detroit; more flagrant inter-district violations were found as well. School district lines—both in Wilmington and Louisville—had been disregarded, mostly prior to *Brown*, in the interests of student segregation.[146] Finally, the court in Wilmington pointed to segregated housing policies and exemption of Wilmington from a 1968 school district consolidation statute in finding that *"de jure* segregation in New Castle County was a cooperative venture involving both city and suburbs."[147] The Supreme Court declined to upset either the Wilmington or Louisville judgments.[148] In Louisville, after initial outbursts over busing caused cancellation of President Ford's visit in the fall of 1975, an uneasy racial truce settled in.[149] The Wilmington plan continued to thrash about in lower federal court and was to take effect in the fall of 1978.[150]

As the nation's first experiment in metropolitan busing, Louisville afforded little ground for optimism. In some respects, it followed the usual pattern. By the fall of the third year, antibusing demonstrations began to subside. There were fewer, calmer protesters and "unlike past years, when they were met at the school by riot-equipped police, the demonstrators found the large [Southern High School] unguarded last night, its parking lot, where buses were burned in 1975, empty."[151]

As street demonstrations began to decline, however, classroom tensions began to build. In Louisville schools, as in other communities, the second year of busing (1976–77) proved worse than the first. "Last year," noted Stuart Sampson, Louisville's director of student relations, "the kids, as racial groups, had a sort of standoffish attitude. Both groups almost went out of their way to avoid conflict by sitting apart in class and in the cafeteria and walking down different sides of the halls. Now, in a very subtle way they're trying to reestablish their racial identity in their schools. They're asking themselves, 'Whose school is this?' People are getting braver. Some of the most vocal, mouthy people, both black and white, are standing behind crowds shouting racial slurs."[152]

In the spring of 1977 racial brush fires broke out in Louisville area schools. Officials spoke of an "echo effect" where trouble at one school encouraged trouble at the next, especially within the same busing cluster.[153] Student life was on edge, susceptible to racial rumor. One rumor around Fairdale High School was that Cindy Campbell, seventeen, had been stabbed in a racial incident. "Look at me," Ms. Campbell told a reporter, pulling open her jacket. "I'm okay. I ain't bleeding." Her mother later explained that Cindy had only been involved "in a little lady-type fight, with a few blows and some hair-pulling and name-calling."[154] School officials rushed to quash minor school incidents before they could trigger serious racial disturbances. "The rumors and threats kept getting bigger and bigger every day," said Kathy Cash, seventeen, and a junior at Stuart High. "There were a lot of scared people. I was scared myself. The word was going around that kids were bringing chains, guns, knives and everything. But when the principal checked all the lockers, only a few articles that could be considered weapons were found."[155]

Louisville's troubles flashed a warning to advocates of metropolitan busing. Merging the Louisville and Jefferson County school districts created a joint system that was but 20 percent black. While such low black percentages may diminish white flight, they may also foment black discontent. Because the metropolitan school district contained relatively fewer core city schools and relatively more suburban ones, blacks had to be bused from seven to ten years, whites for no more than two.[156] That seemed unfair, especially when some whites left public schools altogether during their "busing year," only to return the next.[157] Over time, moreover, the inconvenience of forty-five minute black bus rides from inner city to outer suburbs (and back again) might begin to wear thin. The low black percentage in the metropolitan system also ensured that blacks were most often a minority of outsiders, bused in to white neighborhoods. Not surprisingly, in some Louisville schools, blacks complained of white cliquishness, of feeling left out.[158] In such an atmosphere, academic decisions, disciplinary measures, and peer comments are all the more readily seen as acts of racial prejudice.

Thus one disadvantage of a sprawling, mainly white metropolitan school system may be the gradual buildup of black opposition, the feeling that busing was not worth the hassle or cultural exile encountered in white schools. Polls in Louisville lent fragmentary support to this conclusion. A survey by the University of Louisville Urban Studies Center showed 63 percent of blacks favoring busing the first year; only 49 percent the second.[159] A Harris poll in Louisville showed black opposition to busing increasing from 35 to 40 percent between the first and second year, with white opposition holding fast at about 90 percent.[160]

Whatever the course of lower courts in Louisville and Wilmington, *Milliken* clearly symbolized for the Supreme Court a period of retrenchment. Two years after *Milliken*, the Court returned to school desegregation in *Pasadena Board of Education* v. *Spangler*.[161] There the plan approved by the district judge required that "there shall be no school in the [Pasadena] District, elementary or junior high or senior high school, with a majority of any minority students,"[162] the kind of provision guaranteed to ignite the Court's more conservative members. The judge, moreover, had interpreted this provision to require adjustments in the racial composition of schools on an annual basis. "[A]t least during my lifetime," said he, "there would be no majority of any minority in any school in Pasadena [California]."[163]

The Supreme Court emphatically rejected that view. Once desegregation was accomplished, and student assignments placed on a racially neutral basis, yearly readjustments were not required. Resegregation might even take place with impunity, held the Court, if it did so through "random" population movement and not by official blessing or design.[164] Justice Marshall, joined this time in dissent only by Justice Brennan, argued that the Pasadena system had never truly been desegregated, both because of the uncooperative attitude of Pasadena school officials and because desegregation in faculty hiring and placement had not been shown.[165]

There was much that *Pasadena* did not address. It spoke only to student reassignments, not to when busing itself might end. Yet clearly it furthered the new trend of restraint. In *Pasadena*, as in *Milliken*, an aggressive district judge had been cut down to size. Again, as in *Milliken*, the conservative face of the compromise in *Swann* emerged more and more.[166] For litigation-weary school officials, *Pasadena* was the light at tunnel's end. It hinted a long-awaited liberation from judicial supervision, a chance to make decisions on a clean racial slate. And *Pasadena* promised students quietude and stability: an end to annual judicial reshufflings.[167] But, as in *Milliken*, the price of peace might be resegregation. The Court's ruling, Justice Marshall worried, could "sign the death warrant of the Pasadena Plan and its [integrationist] objectives."[168]

The next year (1977), in *Dayton Board of Education* v. *Brinkman*, the Court's restriction of busing continued.[169] The Sixth Circuit Court of Appeals had ordered Dayton to eliminate "all vestiges of state-imposed school segregation,"[170] which the district judge reluctantly understood to require "the transportation of approximately 15,000 students on a regular and permanent basis."[171] The Supreme Court, however, held the amount of busing intended by the Sixth Circuit far exceeded what was needed to remedy any untoward behavior on the part of the Dayton School Board. Unless the district judge on remand found additional constitutional violations, busing in Dayton had to be substantially curtailed.

Dayton was a godsend to northern school districts. It meant that school boards might indulge in marginal behavior—minor indiscretions—without being subjected to city-wide busing as a result.[172] The Court's emphasis on "isolated" violations[173] ran counter to *Keyes* (Denver), which only four years earlier saw racial discrimination in one part of a school district as strong evidence of discrimination throughout the whole.[174] But that was not all. The Court's insistent citation in *Dayton* of employment and zoning cases where racial discrimination was not found[175] meant that not only had busing remedies been narrowed but that proof of constitutional violations was about to become more difficult as well.

The school cases in Detroit, Pasadena, and Dayton were, in the end, decisions of resignation. The 1960s had been, domestically, the decade of the Great Society, where all things were possible, even the exorcism of racial injustice. The Court beat a tempo of reform as well: "A broadly conceived egalitarianism," wrote Professor Bickel, "was the main theme in the music to which the Warren Court marched."[176] By the 1970s, whether as a result of disillusionment over Vietnam and Watergate or a cyclical shift away from idealism, Americans seemed gripped by a sense of limitation and by an uncertainty of purpose as well. The school cases of the mid-1970s mirrored accurately this national mood. They reflected a sense of what was not possible rather than what was. To integrate schools in the absence of integrated neighborhoods began to seem a desperately difficult task.

The Court also accepted the immobility of history: that centuries of racial injustice could not be wiped clean in one forward judicial thrust. America could not achieve a classless society or an unimpoverished one. "The poor always ye have with you," it was said in St. John,[177] though in America the poor, by dint of historical discrimination, happened to be disproportionately black. Yet so long as opportunity was not purposely denied on account of race, the Court's constitutional scruples would be satisfied.

Racial separation, as well as class stratification, was, the Court now believed, unavoidable. A racially imbalanced school system "without more, of course, does not offend the Constitution."[178] Separation, as well as integration, was the American way. Every ethnic group tended to be separate to some extent. Yet statistical balance had not been sought for "the Irish, the Jews, the Italians, and other ethnic groups,"[179] though only, perhaps, because past discrimination against them was not so oppressive, so enduring, so unique. For whatever reason, the fear of the Kerner Commission in 1968—that we are becoming two societies, "a white society principally located in suburbs, . . . and a Negro society largely concentrated within central cities"[180]—now was something constitutional law stood powerless to prevent.

It can be argued that the promise of law had been broken, that *Brown* had been betrayed, that the Negro had been abandoned, that racism had been indulged, and that by 1977, the Compromise of 1877 had been all but re-enacted. But rebuttals can be offered also: that the Constitution cannot reform private behavior; that the judiciary alone cannot swim against democratic tides; and that a mass reshaping of society had never before been asked of courts, either in this century or the preceding. It is always, at bottom, the classic divide: the liberal believing that stateways might forever change folkways, the conservative that human nature will, in the end, confound all attempts to improve it. Each view, it now seems, has its season. And the race problem in America will be resolved only many annums hence.

A September morning, 1978. Robin Smith waited with her children at the bus stop. The judge had ordered busing some four years back now. Robin was not happy, but, again, her worst fears had not come to pass.

Busing, that most frenzied issue, had continued to lose heat. True, antibusing referenda would pass by large margins in Massachusetts and Washington state. And true, several cities—Seattle, Wilmington, and most notably Los Angeles—would bus in 1978 for the first time. But Wilmington and Seattle were relatively quiet. Only in Los Angeles, where 62,000 fourth- to eighth-graders were assigned bus rides up to two hours, was there really great stir.[181] It was all a far cry from earlier years when Boston's schools were alternately closed or under military guard, when George Wallace swept the Michigan Democratic primary, when Congress talked of little else.

What had apparently emerged was a busing cycle, a more or less predictable pattern of behavior from cities under court order to integrate. The first year was often the blustery one, full of massive rallies, newly-sprung parents' groups, letters, petitions, political rhetoric, sporadic violence, and school boycotts. The second year witnessed much of the same, sometimes in diminished intensity. During the third year, though racial tensions often continued in classrooms, the issue began to drop from public sight.

Calm is often more difficult to interpret than protest. Supporters of busing, most notably the United States Commission on Civil Rights, contended that once the air cleared and adult demagogues left children alone, things would work out fine. The absence of public pyrotechnics signaled the venture's success.

That view, however, was always oversimplified. Public acceptance was not to be confused with public fatigue. Many parents submitted to the inevitable. The rhetoric of politicians, when not followed by action, came to appear hollow and clichéd. The media became bored and moved to other topics. And many made their private peace with busing, either by leaving cities for the suburbs or placing their children in private schools. Ironically, the Court, which endorsed busing in 1971, also facilitated escape from it by later shielding most suburban schools from central city busing plans.

Busing's effect on cities had varied dramatically. Charlotte and Tampa had been relatively more hopeful cases, Boston and Memphis discouraging. Busing had harmed Richmond's public school system beyond the point of easy repair. In Norfolk, Virginia, the school administration, in the face of budget shortages, still pushed curriculum diversity: courses for the collegebound as well as the potential dropout. Such diversity was expensive but essential for the racially mixed school to remain a viable enterprise.[182]

So people finally adjust and make do. But the ultimate question is how a policy so consistently opposed by great majorities of Americans, including many blacks, ever came to be the law. The answer lies partly in the unevenness of the litigation process, in the staggered sequence by which lawsuits are pursued and resolved. Thus, busing struck Richmond and Charlotte very early in the decade; Boston and Louisville in the middle, and Los Angeles and Wilmington only of late. Cities were often isolated in opposition; a concerted national fury never entirely took hold. As a result, busing continued. Robin Smith, waving goodbye, was compelled to make the best of it.

PART IV
Bakke

10

The Argument

At first glance Allan Bakke seemed to be just another ordinary citizen whom landmark litigation was about to cast up from obscurity. The fortuity of other Supreme Court decisions had earlier taken Linda Brown, Clarence Earl Gideon, and Danny Escobedo and made them household names for a spell. Now the Court would do so for Allan Bakke. But, in fact, in at least one significant aspect Bakke was different.

For years the focus of the Constitution had been the underside of American life. The Court had reached into shabby schools and mean alleys to succor the lowly, the despised, the dispossessed. One recalls Linda Brown, daughter of a welder on the Rock Island Railroad, standing plain-dressed before the drab edifice that was the segregated Monroe School in Topeka. Or Clarence Earl Gideon, the drunken woebegone from the Florida panhandle whose dogged requests for a lawyer became one of the most significant criminal cases of our century. The Constitution, it was thought, might help those who could not help themselves.[1] But Allan Bakke did not exactly fit the mold.

He had blue eyes, blond hair, and Norwegian ancestry, and stood just under six feet tall. Above all, Bakke was a structured, shaped-up person. He struck Dr. Theodore West of the Davis Medical School as "pleasant, mature . . . tall and strong and Teutonic in appearance . . . , a believer in personal health and fitness; he is careful about his diet and vices, runs every day and is generally interested in improving his actuarial statistics."[2] But another admissions officer thought him "humorless" and "zealous," like a "character out of a Bergman film."[3]

Bakke was never especially wealthy or advantaged. His was a storybook life of middle-class virtue. His father was a mailman, his mother a teacher. Bakke himself attended the University of Minnesota, majored in mechanical engineering, and earned just under a straight A average. To help finance his education, he joined the Naval Reserve Officers Training Corp., then fought after graduation as a Marine captain in Vietnam. Upon returning to the States in 1967, he earned a masters degree at Stanford, and signed on as an aerospace engineer at a NASA research center near Palo Alto, California. "I don't know anyone brighter or more capable," his boss, David Engelbert, once said. Family man and father of three, comfortably salaried and housed, Bakke appeared well-set.[4]

But Bakke really wanted to become a doctor. So compelling was the urge, he wrote, that while employed as an engineer, "I undertook a near full-time course load of medical prerequisites—biology and chemistry. To make up class and commuting hours, I worked early mornings and also evenings at my job."[5] Bakke later worked off hours as a hospital emergency room volunteer. He took "tough assignments, often working late with battered victims of car accidents or fights."[6] In 1973, at thirty-three, he applied to a dozen medical schools. Every one turned him down.[7]

Bakke was most incensed at being twice rejected by the University of California at Davis. Davis, he learned, had a special admissions program which reserved 16 of 100 places in its entering class for minority students, principally blacks, Chicanos, and Asian-Americans.[8] Not only were Bakke's objective qualifications (undergraduate grades and Medical College Admissions Test scores) higher by far[9] than those admitted under the special program; he also had laudatory letters of recommendation, proven motivation, and an engineering background that several doctors believed would assist him in his medical career.[10] In a letter to Dr. George Lowrey, chairman of the Davis admissions committee, Bakke vented his frustrations. "I am convinced," said he, "that a significant fraction [of medical school applicants] is judged by a separate criteria. I am referring to quotas, open or covert, for racial minorities. I realize that the rationale for these quotas is that they attempt to atone for past racial discrimination, but insisting on a new racial bias in favor of minorities is not a just situation."[11]

The rest of the story is better known. Following his second rejection, Bakke brought suit in California court, claiming the University's racial preferences excluded him from medical school, in violation of state and federal law. The trial court ruled against the University but denied Bakke admission because he failed to establish that the special program had caused his rejection.[12] On appeal, the California Supreme Court, historically a progressive tribunal, ruled for Bakke and ordered him admitted to the medical school.[13] The University appealed, and on February 22, 1977, the Supreme Court decided to hear the *Bakke* case.[14] Bakke's admission was stayed pending Supreme Court review.

Thus, Allan Bakke, constructive, capable, driven, resentful, marched into history. If "one man is carrying the ball for all white males," wrote one reporter, "they could not have picked a more representative specimen."[15] Silent majority symbol, great white hope, avenging angel of the middle classes, heroic in his very ordinariness, Bakke rode the riptides to the Second Reconstruction. The message was as appealing as it was oversimplified: Down with special preference, up with fair play.

Like most vivid symbols, Bakke was divisive. Or perhaps it is fairer to say the program he challenged was. There was no agreement even on its proper name. Proponents called it affirmative action; opponents, reverse discrimination. "Benign discrimination" seemed a compromise of sorts, analogous to the pithy paradox "deliberate speed." "Benevolent cruelty," suggested one wag.[16] However labeled, the policy of special minority admissions standards was a two-edged sword. Benignly intentioned, perhaps, but "certainly not benign with respect to nonminority students who are displaced by it."[17] The Court was being asked to regulate racial access to a scarce American resource—the elite professions—and all the status, financial earnings and satisfactions that would follow.

I

Affirmative action promised to restore to the Supreme Court a sense of control over integration that had slipped badly during busing. From 1968 to 1970 the exercise of judicial will had borne remarkable results. The rural South was brought to heel. Then suddenly, with busing, the Court seemed all but impotent. After *Swann*, cities erupted in open revolt. Whites fled, leaving some school systems more segregated than before. Unintended, unpredictable, and unpleasant consequences often ensued. Events seemed in the saddle, the Court on the sidelines.

With affirmative action, however, the Court might yet regain the tiller hand. True, many of the old jurisprudential problems remained. How would theories of compensatory justice, so prevalent in busing, apply to affirmative action? How did the model of violation-remedy, central to court-ordered transportation, apply to voluntary initiatives such as affirmative action plans? Though such issues were difficult, at least the Court would now be working on a more manageable scale. The Justices would be reviewing the plan of a single institution rather than one for an entire metropolitan area. And the arena now was higher education, where, hopefully, reasoned discourse was more valued and racial fever ran less high. Here, as in *Brown*, the illusion of simple choices reemerged. In *Brown* the Court had simply to uphold or strike down segregation statutes. In *Bakke* it had simply to permit or prohibit race in graduate admissions. The prospects of a problem of finite proportions and the simple clash of basic principles drew scholars, newsmen, and armchair experts the country over to Bakke's case.

Never had an issue been so exhaustively debated. *Bakke* was certainly not the Court's first look at the problem. An earlier case had involved Marco DeFunis, a young man quite as determined as Bakke. DeFunis, wrote one faculty member, is "the planner. He sets his goal and steadily works toward it, come hell or high water. I admire him in his persistence, but there seems to be the slight tendency of not caring upon whom he might step in the process."[18] Like Bakke, DeFunis helped finance his college education, in his case as a book store clerk and laborer for the Seattle Park Department. He finished the University of Washington with a strong 3.62 grade average out of a possible 4, including, to the astonishment of one judge, nine Straight-A hours of Latin.[19] But the Law Boards proved a problem. De Funis took them three times before achieving the respectable score of 668.[20] He was accepted by several law schools: the University of Oregon, Idaho, Williamette, and Gonzaga. But because he lived and wished to practice in Seattle, DeFunis sought to attend the University of Washington. Like Bakke, he applied twice and was twice rejected.[21]

Washington's selection process decidedly favored minority applicants. The most important factor in admission was the candidate's Predicted First Year Average (PFYA), a formular combination of the applicant's average LSAT score and his last two years of undergraduate grades. Candidates with PFYAs above 77 were nearly always accepted; those below 74.5 presumptively rejected. DeFunis's 76.23 placed him in a middle group, a borderline case.

For blacks, Chicanos, American Indians, or Filipinos, however, the admissions process worked quite differently. They were reviewed under a separate procedure and not compared competitively with white applicants. Less weight was given the PFYA; the "entire" record was scrutinizd "to identify, within the minority category, those persons who had the highest probability of succeeding in law school."[22] Of thirty-seven minority students accepted at Washington for the fall of 1971, thirty-six had PFYAs below DeFunis. Thirty fell below 74.5 and, had they been white or a nonfavored minority, would almost certainly have been rejected.[23]

An angry DeFunis thus brought suit in state court. That in itself was unusual. Since *Brown*, the federal courts had been hearing claims of racial bias, but with too much of a minority tilt to suit DeFunis. DeFunis won at trial and was admitted to Washington pursuant to the trial court's decree. On appeal, the Washington Supreme Court reversed and upheld the law school's affirmative action plan.[24] The Supreme Court then granted certiorari, thus setting the stage for a glorious anticlimax. For by virtue of a stay of the Washington Supreme Court judgment issued by Justice Douglas, DeFunis had already registered for his last term in law school by the time the U.S. Supreme Court came to hear his case. Because it was conceded he would graduate regardless of the outcome, a Supreme Court majority declared the question before it moot.[25]

Four Justices dissented, urging that the constitutionality of the special admissions program ought to be resolved at once. Unforeseen circumstances—"illness, economic necessity, even academic failure"—might yet prevent DeFunis's graduation and resubject him to Washington's admissions procedure. The case, moreover, had been fully argued and was ripe for decision. "The constitutional issues which are avoided today," wrote Justice Brennan, "concern vast numbers of people, organizations, and colleges and universities, as evidenced by the filing of twenty-six *amicus curiae* briefs. Few constitutional questions in recent history have stirred as much debate, and they will not disappear."[26]

Justice Douglas alone reached the merits and concluded that even "benign" racial preferences were unconstitutional. "Whatever his race," wrote Douglas, "[DeFunis] had a constitutional right to have his application considered on its individual merits in a racially neutral manner." A law school committee might select a "black applicant who pulled himself out of the ghetto into a junior college" over "the son of a rich alumnus who achieved better grades at Harvard" but *only* if the black's upward mobility demonstrated that, "as an individual," he possessed greater potential for the practice of law.[27] Such words were noteworthy, coming from so committed a champion of minority rights. Douglas's whole opinion—in many ways his adieu—was a celebration of individualism, a Thoreauvian remonstrance against the powerful homogenizing forces of American life. The Law School Admission Test, in particular, provoked his displeasure. "The more profoundly gifted the candidate is," he wrote, "the more his resentment will rise against the mental strait jacket into which the testers would force his mind."[28] America had many peoples, many cultures. "The Indian who walks to the beat of Chief Seattle of the Muckleshoot Tribe in Washington has a different culture from examiners at law schools. . . . Insofar as LSAT's reflect the dimensions and orientation of the Organization Man they do a disservice to minorities." Douglas's solution, too radical for most: "A new trial to consider *inter alia*, whether the established LSAT's should be eliminated so far as racial minorities are concerned."[29]

The Court's majority had ducked a tough issue and left the country on tenterhooks. "[A] Court famed for raising landmarks has a way of sometimes raising sand dunes instead," wrote James J. Kilpatrick after the *DeFunis* nondecision.[30] In *Brown*, postponement gave the impression of thoroughness and served the cause of unanimity. But in *DeFunis* there seemed little left to reargue, and unanimity was out of reach. Knowing the issue was bound to resurface, why had the Court delayed? Others supported the Court's cautious course. "[S]ome public questions," argued Washington attorney Nathan Lewin, "are not decided better simply because they are decided sooner, and the important issue presented by *DeFunis* is probably among them." For Lewin, decision was a no-win proposition. "Had DeFunis won, all efforts to escalate opportunities for the education and employment of minorities would have been jeopardized. Had the University of Washington prevailed, there would have been little reason for sober judgment or restraint in the formulation of future affirmative-action programs." Indecision, on the other hand, still left the political branches some room "to weigh the interests of those currently displaced along with those historically deprived."[31]

DeFunis, then, was scarcely more than warm-up for the main event. The Court's evasion prolonged anxiety and raised the emotional stakes. And *Bakke* itself would add to the bitterness. A leader of the National Conference of Black Lawyers accused a Davis admissions official of "virtually inviting" Bakke to sue.[32] "Many members of California's minority community," wrote San Francisco law professor Charles Lawrence, "believe that the university set the case up to rid itself of a program it never wanted." Lawrence himself thought the university's trial performance was at best "lackadaisical." It had unpardonably conceded that Bakke was better qualified than minority applicants who were accepted, had failed to develop the real purposes of affirmative action programs, and had neglected even to mention "the dean's special admissions program, under which white children of politically well-connected university supporters or substantial financial contributors have been admitted in spite of being less qualified than other applicants, including Bakke."[33]

So weak, in fact, did the case appear that many prominent Civil Rights lawyers urged the university not to appeal to the Supreme Court.[34] Far more than an inept trial performance flawed the university's case. Founded only in 1968, the Davis medical school had no apparent history of discrimination for which its affirmative action program could be offered as a remedy. Davis's two-track admissions policy and the reservation of sixteen places for minority applicants had all the earmarks of an outright quota, likely to offend the Court and stir intense public backlash. Bakke, moreover, was a model plaintiff whose objective qualifications far outshone those of minority matriculants.[35] To let the California ruling stand was itself a setback to the cause of Civil Rights. But many in the movement feared a Supreme Court decision in Bakke's favor would have devastating, incalculable consequences.

The university, resenting insinuations of halfheartedness, appealed anyway. "If [*Bakke*] is an example of someone trying to lose a case," said university counsel Donald Reidhaar, "I don't know how the hell you go about winning one."[36] For its final effort, the university did retain top talent. Paul Mishkin, a respected scholar on the Berkeley law faculty, directed preparation of the brief, and Archibald Cox, Harvard law professor and former Watergate special prosecutor, was to present the oral argument.

Theirs were but two of many voices the Supreme Court was to hear. At every step of *Bakke's* journey from the Yolo County Courthouse to the nation's high tribunal, the clamor grew. Two thousand gathered in San Francisco's Civic Center Plaza to protest the pro-Bakke ruling of the California Supreme Court.[37] At the United States Supreme Court, fifty-eight briefs were filed, easily the record for a single case.[38] The Court seemed less a judicial sanctum than a tug-of-war among contesting lobbyists. For *Bakke* climaxed a trend toward "public litigation." Supporting the university were, among others, the American Bar Association, the Association of American Medical Colleges, the NAACP Legal Defense and Educational Fund, the American Civil Liberties Union, the Americans for Democratic Action, the National Council of Churches, the National Education Association, the prestigious private universities of Columbia, Harvard, Stanford, and Pennsylvania, and the United Auto Workers—an obligatory roll call, in short, for America's liberal elite.

The Carter administration, shifting under pressure,[39] also argued that "a state university admissions program may take race into account to remedy the effects of societal discrimination."[40] That, lamented columnist George Will, was "the most ominous document concerning race to issue from the federal government in this century."[41] Briefs supporting Bakke were much less numerous; the most articulate came from Jewish groups, principally the Anti-Defamation League of B'nai B'rith and the American Jewish Committee, and Congress. Hardly noticed in the heavy volume of submissions was a brief in Bakke's behalf by one Marco DeFunis, now a Seattle lawyer, for the Young Americans for Freedom.

In a sense, each side in *Bakke* found itself embarrassingly situated. Conservatives, who by nature counseled judicial restraint, now sought the Court's intervention.[42] Liberals, who long before *Brown* had urged judicial activism with regard to education,[43] now implored the Court to stay its hand. Advocates of black advancement ironically invoked *San Antonio Indep. School Dist.* v. *Rodriguez*, the foremost decision of judicial forebearance.[44] "Universities," noted one brief, "need some elbowroom in which to experiment in their quest for solutions. . . . This case would seem to be particularly appropriate for the exercise of judicial restraint. The policy questions are difficult, and conscientious educators are dealing with them to the best of their abilities, undoubtedly making mistakes, but learning as they do. . . ."[45] All this, of course, made good tactical sense. "The Burger Court," Professor Howard noted, "has shown a tendency not to want to second-guess those who set educational policy."[46] But in the upside down world of "reverse discrimination," past assumptions often failed to operate.

"*Bakke,*" wrote one commentator, "is a great case, regardless of what the Supreme Court of the United States does with it, because it is one of the very few (again, *very few*) cases in constitutional law in which powerful political and social and historical currents congeal at a central point, upon a thin but adequate factual base."[47] Questions loomed large. Might a public institution undertake to overcome not its own but all America's racist past? Was America now and henceforward a color-blind society? Or might race yet be used to parcel out professional power and prestige? Would minorities ever take their fair place in the American sun? If so, who must stand aside? That was *Bakke*'s magnetism; it would show, above all, how America saw itself. Issues were starkly joined; great principles clashed mortally in the night.

Oral argument at the Supreme Court often spoils the occasion. Because litigants, not the Court, generally choose their attorneys, magnificent chances have been squandered. Yet the argument in *Bakke* might have been worse. Archibald Cox, wrote *Newsweek*, "was at his donnish best, fielding questions with confidence, sometimes lecturing the Justices as if they were his Harvard law school students."[48] Like all accomplished advocates, Cox grasped the jugular: "For generations, racial discrimination in the U.S. isolated certain minorities [and] condemned them to inferior education. . . . There is no racially blind method of selection which will enroll today more than a trickle of minority students in the nation's colleges and professions."[49] Justice Blackmun wondered if minority admissions were comparable to athletic scholarships since "most institutions seek athletic prowess." "Well," replied Cox, "I come from Harvard, sir. . . ." and the courtroom erupted in relieved laughter.[50]

Cox's opponent, Reynold Colvin, was less winning. "You have devoted 20 minutes to belaboring the facts, if I may say so," Justice

Powell noted quietly. "I would like help, I really would, on the constitutional issues." No member of the *Brown* Court still sat; the last, William O. Douglas, had retired only months before. History's chief figure was Thurgood Marshall, an advocate in *Brown*, in *Bakke* a judge. "You are talking about your client's [Bakke's] rights," said Marshall to Colvin. "Don't these underprivileged people have some rights?"

> Colvin: They certainly have the right to. . . .
> Marshall: To eat cake.
> Colvin: They have the right to compete. The right to equal competition.[51]

For two hours the justices listened and questioned, then retired for months to ponder their special problem.

II

Bakke, some believed, had "an importance not exceeded by any single case from the past, not [even] the *Brown* case of 1954. . . ."[52] Yet in telltale ways, the issue of affirmative action has been inflated. It is difficult to view special admissions programs as gestures of white magnanimity. Many of these programs were enacted late in the 1960s to appease student militants. Nor was affirmative action really a traumatic course for universities to pursue.[53] Those who approved such programs did not jeopardize their *own* educational or career opportunities; nor were they acountable to constituent displeasure at election time.[54] Instead, "A and B [regents and faculties] got together to decide what C [Bakke] should do for X [favored minorities]."[55]

Even so, the quantum of white sacrifice was typically quite small. Sixteen of one-hundred places was not a lot, especially when California's population was more than one quarter minority.[56] Whites would "continue to fill the lion's share of spaces in medical schools."[57] Even to view blacks as the chief cause of Bakke's exclusion was to miss the point. The most dangerous rivals of white men "are not specifically admitted black or Hispanic males, but women of all races," wrote McGeorge Bundy. "Since 1968 the number of women entering medical schools has risen from 8 percent to 25 percent of the total. A parallel increase has occurred in law schools. No constitutional issue is raised by this dramatic change, which is probably not at an end; the women admitted have had generally competitive records on the conventional measures. But their new presence is certainly a large part of the social reality which can create, at least temporarily, a sense of some frustration among ambitious white males."[58]

Black benefits from programs like Davis's should likewise not be oversold. Busing was at least an instrument of mass racial uplift, affirmative action a limited remedy available only to the members of a small black elite within reach of college or graduate education. For most American blacks, *Milliken* v. *Bradley*,[59] more than *Bakke*, was the important case. The illusion of *Bakke* was that affirmative action in higher education represented a practical solution to the de facto exclusion of blacks from proper representation in the society. "[A]s an instrument to raise a whole community out of isolation and poverty," wrote the *New Republic*, "the quota system is unlikely to work. Quotas will guarantee mobility only to a small percentage of the members of disadvantaged groups, many of whom could make it on their own. It is unlikely to improve the lot of black or Hispanic-Americans generally. That would require a more far-reaching and radical strategy. . . ."[60]

To compare *Bakke* to *Brown* in importance is likewise to overstate. *Brown* pitted those demanding equal rights for the Negro against those who would oppress and degrade him. The difference in purposes could not have been more clear. But by the time of *Bakke*, debate on means overshadowed any remaining disagreement on ends. "This controversy," Professor Cohen has written, "is not between good guys and bad guys, but between very sophisticated parties who differ about what, in the effort to achieve a very pressing and very difficult end, we may rightly use as means."[61] Even opponents of affirmative action, noted Professor Etzioni, "include many who *favor* greater efforts on behalf of equality for women and minorities, but by other means."[62] The California Supreme Court, in ruling for Bakke, took pains to suggest other ways—however disputable their efficacy—by which integration of minorities into higher education could be achieved.[63] Even the American public, overwhelmingly opposed to "preferential treatment" through affirmative action, favored other publicly financed means of bettering minority status.[64] Thus beneath the great debate in *Bakke* lay a less publicized consensus. *Bakke* was not only a symbol of how far toward racial justice we still have to go, but of how very far since *Brown* we had come.

It is important, then, to keep *Bakke* in perspective. *Bakke* involved
not a promised land for blacks, nor a racial renaissance for whites,
nor even a racial controversy on the same fundamental order as
Brown. It is important for different reasons. For *Bakke* posed the
arch conflict between equality and meritocracy. Meritocrats believed, with the California Supreme Court, that upholding racial
preferences would sacrifice "principle for the sake of dubious expediency and would represent a retreat in the struggle to assure that
each man and woman shall be judged on the basis of individual
merit alone. . . ."[65] The fact that the threat to meritocracy came
appealingly garbed in the cause of racial justice made it only more
suspect.

Brown had not involved any such conflict. Segregated schools
were not only separate and unequal; they were also unmeritocratic.
Brown promised equality through opportunity. Henceforward
blacks would be judged on ability, not race. In *Brown*, for a fleeting
moment, equality and meritocracy seemed one. By tapping both
strains, *Brown* won the nation's heart.

Soon this uneasy truce began to fray. The nation discovered that
merely removing barriers of racial inequality did not produce the
competitive ideal. Formal equality for the present could not undo
the genuine inequalities of the past. Thus egalitarians demanded
the incorporation by judicial edict of color-conscious constitutional
principles—busing being one—to overcome the legacy of racism
and to place the runners of life on the same starting line. And meritocrats mounted their counter-assault. Rapid assimilation of blacks,
they feared, meant a rapid dilution of academic standards. Quality,
not equality, became their watchword. Tracking was installed to
preserve meritocracy in newly-desegregated schools. Superior private and suburban systems became much sought after. Busing,
many worried, only diverted "attention and resources from the
foremost goal of any school system: the best quality education for
all pupils."[66]

All meritocrats, of course, were not of one mind. Some saw in
meritocracy the formula for national success in a dangerously competitive world. Their message was that of William Graham Sumner, as updated by Ayn Rand. Education, advised one business
president, should encourage the gifted "to grow faster and grow
taller than their associates. They are outstanding individuals and
should be recognized and treated as such. In many instances we

tend to force them to grow at the same pace as the slowest member of the group with which they are associated. . . . We need these high performers to carry the ball for all of us. Instead of criticizing and being jealous of these outstanding few, we Americans should be eternally grateful for the contributions they have made and the leadership they have given."[67]

But the greatest defenders of meritocracy laid claim to egalitarian values. Merit itself, they believed, was the great guarantor of equal opportunity. Thomas Jefferson, founder of the University of Virginia, once heralded "a natural aristocracy among men" based on "virtue and talents" that might save America from the "artificial aristocracy, founded on wealth and birth."[68] An allegiance to a similar creed governed Felix Frankfurter, once a professor of law at Harvard. "What mattered," he said, "was excellence in your profession, to which your father or your face was equally irrelevant."[69] The decline of merit meant the rise of prejudice and favor, whether on wealth, race, parentage, or creed. Given that society's rewards would always be unequally apportioned, what fairer way to do so than through merit? The lesson for *Bakke* was plain. "In a society in which men and women expect to succeed by hard work and to better themselves by making themselves better," wrote Professor Bickel, "it is no trivial moral wrong to proceed systematically to defeat this expectation . . . [T]o reject an applicant who meets established, realistic, and unchanged qualifications in favor of a less qualified candidate is morally wrong, and in the aggregate, practically disastrous."[70]

To introduce racial preference to higher education was to assault the citadel of meritocracy itself. Higher education was not universal education; there were no compulsory attendance laws. By purpose and tradition, universities were elite, the best of them golden gateways to the elitism beyond their walls. The badges of higher education—Phi Beta Kappa, summa cum laude, Law Review—not only boasted inequality but equated merit with grades, those ultimate objectifications of talent and desire. As such, higher education reflected, in its own way, the values prized by free enterprise society.

Advocates of affirmative action, then, attacked an ideal embedded deep in western culture. And the attack took place on several different levels. First, some argued, universities were never quite the meritocracies they pretended to be. Admissions policy had always had its less noble side. "Throughout American higher edu-

cation," noted Professor O'Neil, "alumni, friends, and trustees
. . . legislators and other political officials have not only sought
special consideration for the admission of their own children, but
have often interceded on behalf of others to whom they owed or on
whom they wished to confer a favor. Institutions . . . have typically found room for such applicants."[71] Nor had merit itself ever
been defined solely as a matter of objective intellect. Military veterans and musicians, athletes and Alaskans attended distinguished
universities despite undistinguished test scores, all because their
presence served important social or educational needs. Why were
minority admissions any different? [72]

The university, others insisted, had a grander mission than meritocracy. Affirmative action first arrived on most campuses around
1970,[73] a time of tumult in higher education. It was the era of cause
commitment: an attempt, so its adherents said, at human oneness—
between rich and poor, black and white, university idealist and
oppressed Vietnamese. Institutions were judged by their relevance,
by the fervor of their moral commitment and by their part in social
protest and upheaval. So it was that President Charles Odegaard,
later a defendant in *DeFunis*, recognized "that some more positive
contribution had to be made to the resolution of this [racial] problem in American life, and something had to be done by the University of Washington."[74] Merit would be bent to accommodate the
needs of social justice; as an absolute principle its days seemed
numbered. Until, that is, DeFunis and Bakke brought suit.

So *Bakke* was a struggle for the soul of higher education, with
race regrettably as the focal point. But beyond that, did *Bakke* communicate a culture "in the grip of merit madness," blind to the "in-
nate unfairness" of a principle that rewards "intelligence, imagination, education, and a variety of other factors that are either genetic
or instilled by environment at a very early age?"[75] Was Bakke himself a symbol of what Charles Reich once called the Consciousness
II man, who "measures himself and his achievements by the tests,
examinations, grades, and other formal hurdles of life? He becomes
a projectile, ready to be set in motion by outside energies . . . he
often seems to keep pushing beyond rational limits; the exterior
goals consume the inner ones," until life becomes chiefly "a fiercely
competitive struggle for success."[76] *Bakke:* the parochial and proto-
typical American case. How much did it matter in the stampede for
admission whether Bakke or his black adversaries won? Might one

serve humankind only as a doctor? Was life lost to those whom
Davis rejected? What myopia had hold of us? Were we not meant
for larger things? In the words of the poet of India, Rabindranath
Tagore:

> Thou hast made me endless, such is thy pleasure. This frail vessel
> thou emptiest again and again, and fillest it ever with fresh life.
> This little flute of a reed thou hast carried over hills and dales,
> and hast breathed through it melodies eternally new.
> At the immortal touch of thy hands my little heart loses its limits
> in joy and gives birth to utterance ineffable.
> Thy infinite gifts come to me only on these very small hands of
> mine. Ages pass, and still thou pourest, and still there is room to
> fill.[77]

III

The Supreme Court in *Bakke* would decide whether future generations of minorities were to have meaningful access to the learned
professions. Disallowance of affirmative action, the University
warned in its brief, would leave the professions white enclaves.[78]
Integrating the professions remained the foremost justification for
special admissions programs. Many concluded with the Carnegie
Commission on Higher Education that "[t]he greatest single handicap" minorities face "is their underrepresentation in the professions
of the nation."[79]

The fact of underrepresentation was not disputed. Blacks by
1970 comprised nearly 12 percent of the population of the United
States, only 2.2 percent of the doctors and 2.8 percent of the medical students.[80] The picture in law was fully as grim. By 1970, only
3,845 of 355,242 American attorneys were black, little more than
1 percent.[81] For Chicanos and American Indians the figures were
even worse. In California, for example, there was one Chicano lawyer per 9,482 Chicano residents, while the ratio of lawyers to the
general population was 1 to 530.[82] And there was scarcely an
American Indian attorney to be found in the country.[83] By the
time of *Bakke*, moreover, affirmative action programs had only
begun to work significant change.

Granted that minority lawyers and doctors were few. Was increasing their number the proper business of the state? Many
argued that the "proportionate society" was neither wise nor workable. Distinctive ethnic histories and preferences, contended

Nathan Glazer, accounted for many of "the 'unrepresentative' work distributions we see." Tradition made it "easier for the Irish to become policemen, the Italians fruit dealers, Jews businessmen, and so on."[84] It was wrong for the state either to maintain such patterns through discrimination or to purposely break them down. An even stronger defender of disproportion was Professor Thomas Sowell: "One fourth of the professional hockey players in the United States come from one state [Minnesota]; more than a quarter of all American Nobel prize winners are Jewish; more than half of all professional basketball stars are black." Ethnic aptitudes simply differed. "Some groups," Sowell concluded, "that have been tremendously successful in some activities have been utter failures in other activities requiring no more talent. Even such an economically successful urban group as American Jews had an unbroken string of financial disasters in farming, while immigrants from a peasant background succeeded, even though peasant immigrants could not begin to match the Jews' performance in an urban setting."[85] To each its own, ran the theme, never mind the statistics.

Once government started down the road of occupational proportionality, where would it stop? Proposals for racial proportionality "in schools of dentistry, education, architecture, and other service professions are regularly advanced and in many cases adopted, each resting on the same premise" as that of the Davis Medical School, one pro-Bakke brief contended.[86] If more black lawyers and doctors are important to society, are not black teachers, economists, and engineers also? Proportionality would not only extend to other professions. "If valid [as to race], it would be equally applicable to ethnic, religious and sexual groups."[87] Demands "for appropriate numerical representation by various ethnic groups—Italian-Americans . . . Catholic Americans—have already been heard."[88] Might lack of proportionality come to imply a lack of legitimacy as well? "It has been suggested, for example," said Professor Cohen, "that a legislature or a jury that does not manifest proportionality of race (or sex, or age) is without legitimate authority."[89] Just how far, the Court in *Bakke* had to wonder, would sanctioning racial preferences carry the nation? "The proponents of proportional representation," wrote Professor Posner, "do not as yet urge adoption of the standard of perfect equality, but there seems to be no logical stopping point short of it within the structure of their argument. . . . [G]overnmental intervention in the labor markets (and in the educational process insofar as it affects occupational choice and success) will have to continue forever if proportional equality in the desirable occupations is to be secured."[90]

The parade of horribles is an old technique in law. One reasonable step cannot be taken, it is argued, because a hundred less reasonable ones must then ensue. (The National Rifle Association skillfully employs the technique to defeat registration of handguns.) Thus, we are warned, if any racial perference is upheld in *Bakke*, "perfect proportionality" is nigh to hand. The fear in this instance is not to be taken lightly: every imaginable minority may press supine bureaucrats for favored treatment for itself.

But neither should the fear be swallowed whole. Proportionality has long been known to politics. Governors have used appointments to appeal to various geographic, ethnic, and racial groupings within their own constituencies. Shortly before *Bakke*, President Carter pledged to use 152 new federal judgships to increase significantly female and minority representation on the bench.[91] That was hardly shocking news. Even on the Supreme Court, there was, by tradition, a Jewish seat, for President Nixon a southern seat, and for President Johnson (and probably his successors) a black seat too.[92] There is talk now of a female seat as well. Yet the Supreme Court has not become a body of perfect or even proximate proportionality, with a revolving ethnic seat, for example, or a majority of women. Why, indeed, are there now two Minnesotans and no Californians?[93] Politicians have long sensed that principles of merit and representativeness must manage to coexist. In a pluralistic society, there seems no other way.

In one sense, of course, comparisons between higher education and appointive offices are inapt. Higher education might better be compared to the civil service, with its tests and greater immunity from politics. But even in higher education, notions of diversity, representativeness, and even politics have played their part in admissions. Such notions have existed without suffocating the commitment to merit. Is not the plausible forecast always for adjustment and accommodation of competing principles, not for the perfectly proportionate society? And is not the intense public commitment to merit ultimately an important counterweight to bureaucratic tendencies to proportion?[94]

Views down the road of proportionality have tended to divert attention from the immediate issue in *Bakke* and *DeFunis:* the integration of minorities into medicine and law. For blacks, under-representation in the legal profession has had the most devastating consequences. Obviously, lawyers in America possess uncommon influence, prestige, and wealth. They become legislators more frequently than members of any other calling, and only a handful of nonlawyers have ever become judges. And the legal profession until recently neglected the needs of minorities and the poor.[95] But the need for blacks in the profession is even more deep rooted than recitation of such failings could ever imply. The law and lawyers have made special victims of blacks in ways that other professions cannot match. This abuse can best be illustrated in the system of criminal justice that, as applied to whites, has been our proud boast.

To many, criminal justice hypocritically called a black person "to answer for his or her supposed 'crimes against society,' in a society that has never been called to answer for its crimes [against blacks]."[96] Historically, once again, the greatest abuses occurred in the South. Indeed, the skeletons of southern criminal justice fairly rattled in the Court's own closet. There was *Brown* v. *Mississippi*, the first confession case during the depths of the Depression, a case in which the presiding deputy conceded that one of the defendants had been whipped, but "not too much for a negro; not as much as I would have done if it were left to me."[97] And *Chambers* v. *Florida* in 1940, the "sunrise confession" case, where "ignorant young colored tenant farmers" were "grilled" in a Florida jail from 3:30 one Saturday afternoon until early Sunday morning when they "broke."[98] Most notorious, of course, were the Scottsboro boys, nine black teenagers charged with gang-raping two white women of uncertain reputation on an Alabama freight train. The Supreme Court found proceedings in their first (and later second) trial unacceptable. "The defendants, young, ignorant, illiterate, surrounded by hostile sentiment, hauled back and forth under guard of soldiers, charged with an atrocious crime regarded with especial horror in the community where they were to be tried, were thus put in peril. . . ." Under circumstances as these, where death was the penalty, the Court had held the defendants entitled to appointed counsel.[99]

There was a time when few American political institutions were regarded more suspiciously than the southern process of criminal justice, from start to finish. The "living law of Alabama today," wrote Eugene Rostow in 1965, is "the law at the end of the policeman's stick. . . ."[100] The southern sheriff was a figure of fabled meanness. "Why," asked one critic, "does the 'necessary force' employed by an Alabama sheriff in subduing two unruly prisoners leave the white with a headache and the Negro with a brain concussion?"[101] The police force in the rural South was often poorly educated and all white; the few Negro policemen were generally permitted to arrest only members of their own race. Once the Negro was arrested, he was "kept in a segregated cell. On the way to the courtroom he passes drinking fountains labelled 'white' and 'colored.' In the courtroom his Negro relatives and friends sit separately from whites. . . . The laws have been enacted by politicians elected by whites. In the words of one Alabama lawyer, only the electric chair is desegregated."[102]

Trial itself was frightening and isolating. Often the local judge was a pillar of white society, perhaps elected where only whites could vote. Jurors were white too, as were the lists of registered voters, property owners, and Rotary Club members from which they were drawn.[103] For a black defendant to object to this was the surest way to offend jury, judge, and prosecutor, all at once, and objections were rare. There were few black attorneys to represent black defendants; nor was a black clientele the road most white lawyers followed to community esteem.[104] It hardly mattered anyway. Few blacks could afford a lawyer, and as late as 1963, there was no right to appointed counsel, even in serious, but noncapital, felony offenses.[105] Finally, the often illiterate, stammering black witness was not taken seriously in court.

Sentencing in southern courtrooms was also defined by race:that of the suspect and that of the victim. Where black abused black, leniency and tolerance often prevailed, because the "Negroes are primitive and emotional, like children or animals, with little sense of right and wrong."[106] Much the same condescension explained lax treatment for white crime against blacks. But childlike references vanished in a hurry where blacks victimized whites; for that Negroes would assume full adult responsibility.[107] Rape, of course, was the ultimate treason. One Florida study showed that from 1960 to 1964, less than 5 per cent of intraracial rapists received the death sentence, while 54 percent of black men convicted of raping white women were sentenced to die.[108]

Such horror tales of southern justice may seem quite unfair to conscientious judges and lawyers throughout the region, but they illustrate black subjugation as does nothing else. "You the lawyer I spoke with yesterday on the phone?" his Honor from Oktibbeha County, Mississippi was quoted as saying. "I'm glad to see you're white. I done called your boy's name at ten o'clock and he weren't here so we forfeited the bail, found him guilty, fined him $200 and we was just fixing to get out a warrant for him. Ain't that Charley [the lawyer's black client] out there?"[109] Such instances reflected the larger, sadder truth: that "the racially exclusionary system of southern justice, its white juries and white lawyers, judges, sheriffs and deputies, police and clerks, stenographers and segregated facilities [was] the sophisticated and effective guarantor of the southern way of life."[110]

Inevitably, the problem turned north. The signal issues there were relations between blacks and the police, especially in the great urban interiors. "There are few things under heaven more unnerving than the silent accumulating contempt and hatred of a people," wrote James Baldwin in 1962. "[The policeman] moves through Harlem, therefore, like an occupying soldier in a bitterly hostile country; which is precisely what, and where he is, and is the reason he walks in twos and threes."[111] Most volatile of all police procedures was the "stop and frisk." To police and a city's beleaguered small businessmen, it was an invaluable tool of preventive law enforcement. To blacks, it was debasement, often in public for all to see: "One and all were searched. And thoroughly! Empty all pockets of wallets, address books, pocketbooks. You leaned against the wall while sheriff's deputies ran their fat little fingers up and down your pants legs, up around your armpits, in and around the ole crotch."[112]

It probably took the Black Panthers, a nationalist cult afire with hatred of "the oppressor," to turn public attention to criminal justice outside the South. The criminal trials of the Panthers in 1970–71 reminded some of the old South and the Scottsboro boys, with judge, jury, and counsel in a charade to legitimate predestined results. Yale Reverend William Sloane Coffin pronounced it legally right but morally wrong to bring the Panthers to trial.[113] President Kingman Brewster kept peace on campus through war with alumni by doubting openly, at the time of Bobby Seale's trial in New Haven, whether a black revolutionary could ever get a "fair trial anywhere in the United States."[114]

But the problem was more subtle and less dramatic than the

plight of the Panthers. American criminal justice is ultimately, and to some extent unavoidably, discretionary.[115] Police exercise discretion in deciding to arrest or search; magistrates in setting bail and issuing warrants; prosecutors in pressing or dropping charges; juries in finding facts; judges in sentencing; wardens in awarding inmate privileges and "good" time; parole boards in granting parole. But in every discretionary joint of the system, racial bias might set in. Snap judgments by overworked bureaucrats in the criminal justice mills of the nation's large cities may be racist judgments as well. Police especially, blacks felt, lacked respect for black persons and homes. In one important case in the mid-sixties, Baltimore police made 300 "turn ups" of mostly black homes to locate a murder suspect, an unimaginable happening in white parts of town.[116] Where white attitudes did not degrade the black, the system's structure often did. Bail, for example, was routinely set in the United States according to the nature of the alleged offense. Blacks, often poor, had most trouble meeting it. Yet bailed defendants fared substantially better at sentencing than those in pretrial detention.[117] In sum, the black outlook toward criminal justice—North and South—was one of alienation and disillusionment. "Daily," complained one prominent black lawyer, "in courts throughout the country, black and poor defendants suffer the humiliations of a legal system which refuses to accord them full recognition of their dignity as human beings."[118]

There are, of course, ways to improve the situation short of affirmative action in law schools. One can appoint more black policemen, clerks of the court, and sergeants at arms. One can insist that jury selection be racially fair. And the Supreme Court, notably the Warren Court, strove to correct the major black grievances. Its most enduring contribution was *Gideon* v. *Wainwright*,[119] which accorded indigent felony defendants the right to counsel at trial. The black at last was guaranteed one friend in court, of questionable vigor and competence perhaps, but at least better versed in law than an illiterate tenant farmer. And the guarantee of counsel did not stop at trial. Gradually, it extended to first appeals, to station house interrogations, to police lineups, to sentencing and preliminary hearings, even to juvenile court and to misdemeanor proceedings where imprisonment was imposed.[120]

The Warren Court likewise challenged the second great failing of criminal justice in the eyes of the black: that of discretionary, racially intuited justice. To the extent it could, the Court laid down bright rules that would limit the policeman's authority and whim. Standards for search warrants were stiffened and clarified;[121] police were instructed to get them more often before attempting to search.[122] Officers were to read suspects their rights before questioning began; a suspect's request for counsel or silence was to be honored and respected. The link between *Miranda* v. *Arizona*[123] and black grievance was not difficult to discern. *Miranda* was, in effect, the Supreme Court's cry of police brutality, a spasm of judicial indignation at the world James Baldwin saw.

One senses, however, the inadequacies of such efforts in the absence of black lawyers. Is it really enough for whites to proclaim law fair to blacks? Or must blacks themselves participate throughout the system? Distrust of law runs so deep in the black experience. Granted the problem yields no single, quick solution, how yet do we proceed? Proponents of affirmative action were not, as some suggest,[124] urging black lawyers for black clients or black juries and judges for black accused. Rather, they believed the whole persistent imagery of white law and black subject somehow had to be changed. "[T]he shortage of minority attorneys—and, consequently, minority prosecutors, judges and public officials— constitutes an undeniably compelling state interest," concluded the Washington Supreme Court in *DeFunis*. "If minorities are to live within the rule of law, they must enjoy equal representation within our legal system."[125] To believe an integrated bar would make a difference is perhaps all wishful thinking. Yet understanding is not exactly aided by comparing the number of blacks in law school to the numbers of Italians in fruit markets, or whites in the NBA.

IV

Past mistreatment of blacks at the hands of law is but one current in a very large stream. Yet it helps to illustrate that the most powerful impulse behind affirmative action was one of compensation for historical abuse. For many, affirmative action was, purely and simply, compensatory justice. It served both to redeem the sins of whites and hasten true equality for blacks. As past discrimination had been color-conscious, so must the corrective be. The legacy of generations could not now be erased by treatment that was merely evenhanded. For supporters of affirmative action, American history hung like a pall. "[T]here can be no blinking the enormous and unique set of handicaps which our whole history, right up to the present, has imposed on those who are not white," wrote McGeorge Bundy. "The burden of centuries has not been lifted in the short and stressful decades since *Brown*."[126]

Compensatory, color-conscious remedies had been utilized before *Bakke*. Busing for racial balance was the most obvious example. "Just as the race of students must be considered in determining whether a constitutional violation has occurred," the Court said in one busing case, "so also must race be considered in formulating a remedy."[127] Busing, however, had generally been court-controlled. As a race-conscious remedy, it had been judicially dispensed only to a particular school district to redress its own past discrimination.[128] Affirmative action in higher education, on the other hand, was neither court-controlled nor court-compelled. Rather, institutions had *voluntarily* undertaken to redress past racial wrongs. Should such voluntary efforts be unlimited in scope? Was Davis, in other words, to be allowed to compensate, not for its own racial history, but for the sins of society at large?[129]

What made *Bakke* so difficult was the absence of any prior discrimination on the part of the Davis Medical School for which affirmative action might compensate. Thus confusion developed over just what the Davis program was meant to redress. Innumerable rationales were offered the Court. The NAACP Legal Defense Fund argued that Davis's plan was needed to overcome past and present discrimination in California public schools.[130] But that suggested oddly that only blacks whose prior schooling had been intentionally segregated were eligible for special admissions. Perhaps, then, the Davis program might help remedy the effects of past discrimination in medical education; as late as 1948, twenty-six of the country's seventy-seven medical schools openly practiced racial segregation.[131] Or perhaps to redress past segregation in the whole system of health care, where until recently black doctors were frequently excluded from staffs of white hospitals, and black patients, if admitted, were often placed in segregated wards and rooms."[132]

But past medical history does not altogether justify affirmative action for other professions or for undergraduate schools. Thus the university's supporters really sought a more expansive view. "[T]he effect of our nation's sad legacy of racial discrimination runs deep and wide," Justice Matthew Tobriner wrote, "and is in no sense limited to those schools, or to those states, which practiced de jure segregation."[133] If racism was to be cured, all America had to help do so, not just states and institutions with histories of unclean hands. There were in 1970 more California blacks born in the South than in California.[134] These black families carried west not the spirit of self-reliance but the handicap of generations of segregated life. Should not California attempt to overcome what another region's ancient custom had imposed?[135] The absence of minorities from higher education reflected the entire black tradition of state-imposed impotence, not any single strand or part. Blacks of meager income, ramshackle homes, and marginal jobs not surprisingly exhibited "a measure of fear and a sense of remoteness or irrelevance about college."[136] Could not Davis do its own small bit to correct that?

Sketched in sweeping terms, this theory of compensatory justice seems almost irresistible. But was it really? Was even the most accurate portrait of the past a desirable diagnosis upon which to base a prescription for the present? Two wrongs, it is ever argued, do not make a right. "Generalized historical assertion about conditions somewhere in the United States some time in the past," wrote Professors Bickel and Kurland, "is not the premise of the remedial cases decided by this Court, nor should it be. If such a predicate were allowed to replace careful, specific findings of discrimination as the necessary condition for maintaining reverse discrimination, such state racial preferences would be constitutionally sanctioned in a wide range of circumstances that would denigrate if not destroy the concept of racial equality specified in the Equal Protection Clause."[137] Compensatory justice, they feared, augured racial injustice for future generations whose skins happened to be white.

Whom we compensate through affirmative action is altogether as important as for what we compensate. Although Davis admissions policy benefited blacks, Chicanos, Asian Americans, and American Indians, that this particular combination ought properly to make up the beneficiary group is by no means self-evident. Justice Rehnquist once remarked, in debating which groups merited the Supreme Court's special protection, that "it would hardly take extraordinary ingenuity for a lawyer to find . . . [deserving] minorities at every turn in the road."[138] So too the potential beneficiaries of affirmative action form an endless line.

Much depends, of course, on one's criteria for inclusion. Groups victimized by past discrimination present, at first blush, the strongest claim. Yet what of those past victims who are now academically successful: women, Jews, Japanese and Chinese Americans? The tendency is to say that those who have overcome past prejudice on their own need no preferential program to help them,[139] although wide-ranging discrimination against these groups still persists and the prevalence of racial, sexual, and religious stereotypes still prevents many of them from realizing their full potential. What of those ethnics—Irish, Italian, and Polish Americans— who have suffered past public discrimination,[140] the effects of which cannot be said to have totally vanished. Many Irish have achieved middle-class status; others in their ethnic ghettos are less fortunate. Are such ethnic Americans to be "in" or "out" when it comes to affirmative action? The problem is that within every exploited group, victimization has been uneven. Why, for instance, is the middle-class black still entitled to compensatory treatment? The Davis program, its opponents charged, "makes no distinction between the minority applicant whose lowered scores can be attributed to obstacles arising from economic or educational disadvantages due to race discrimination and those who have attended the finest prep schools and colleges."[141]

If the middle-class black was favored by the Davis program, why was the poor white not? Why, indeed, wasn't present disadvantage, not past discrimination, the relevant focus? The trial judge found that though some whites had applied to Davis for special consideration, none had been granted it.[142] Yet "many whites suffer economic and cultural deprivation; many are blighted by poverty; many attend inadequate schools; and many must work while in school to support themselves and their families."[143] A case in point was Rita Clancy, the Russian-born daughter of parents who had survived concentration camps. On her arrival in the United States at age 14, Ms. Clancy spoke only Russian and Hungarian. Shortly after immigration, her father was incapacitated by brain surgery, and the family went on welfare. But Ms. Clancy worked her way through school and graduated at 22 an A- psychobiology major at UCLA. Though disadvantaged, Ms. Clancy also happened to be white and thus ineligible for the Davis program. She was placed on the waiting list, brought suit against Davis for racial discrimination, and was finally admitted to the medical school by a federal judge.[144]

Such anomalies are not easily explained. Preferment of middle-class blacks to the detriment of disadvantaged whites might be justified if special admissions were a matter of racial reparations. Reparationists tend to see history as a ledger of cumulating racial and national debts. Whites, under their theory, bear a special obligation toward blacks and American Indians, as Germans might toward European Jews, an obligation that survives both "the death of oppressors and direct victims. . . ."[145] Reparations are due blacks because past racial atrocities were unique in severity. True, white immigrants also suffered discrimination, yet they came to America voluntarily, not in chains. No identifiable group of whites suffered "injustice as extreme as that imposed on blacks under the American version of slavery"[146] and the postemancipation generations of segregation. Because the whole black race—not just its "disadvantaged" or "poor" or "culturally deprived" members[147]—suffered past debasement, reparations are due the *entire* race also, even its more fortunate members. And because race prejudice is still more virulent than ethnic prejudice and its effects have proved less eradicable, a black-only preference remains defensible. For the moment, argues Professor Graham Hughes, a leading proponent of reparations, "the mere fact of a person's being black in the United States is sufficient reason for providing compensatory techniques, even though that person may appear fortunate enough in his personal background."[148]

As the impetus to a practicable policy, however, reparations creates problems, not least of which is that it stands virtually no chance of attaining consensual public acceptance of its validity. The day of slaves and slave owners and even of segregation statutes must seem ever more distant to each new body of applicants to law and medical schools. At some point, history begins to lose its persuasiveness. It will be hard, moreover, to induce whites to right wrongs they personally did not commit, simply because they are members of the malefactor race. And while one may argue that race prejudice is special, a Jew or an Irishman, conscious of the abuse to which his own forebears were subjected, may argue back. There are certain aspects of preference, moreover, that the theory of reparations fails to justify. Why, opponents ask, are recently immigrated Hispanics from Mexico, Jamaica, and Cuba, uninjured by past discrimination at the hands of this country, nonetheless favored in special admissions programs?[149]

There is no combination of beneficiaries or set of criteria that will be entirely satisfactory, politically or intellectually.[150] But should all these tough questions at the margins derail programs whose central thrust is sound? If the interest behind affirmative action is sufficiently compelling—such as, for example, neutralizing our especially shameful legacy of racism—then should public bodies enjoy wide latitude in choosing means?[151]

Once we decide that some compensatory process is justifiable, the next question is how much compensation is defensible. Some schools adopted only a general racial preference; others, like Davis, set a numerical goal or quota. If the latter is chosen, how many places should be reserved? How Davis decided on 16 of 100 minority seats remains a mystery.[152] Probably the faculty picked a number that was more than token, less than inundating. One might, of course, "assess how grievously each group has suffered from discrimination, and allocate" accordingly,[153] but that involves impossible calculations. In *DeFunis*, the University of Washington law school sought a 20 percent minority enrollment, roughly the combined percentage of its four favored minorities in the national population as a whole.[154] But population percentages have many perspectives. In 1972, each minority student caucus at Berkeley used that population formula most favorable to itself. Blacks looked to national population figures; Chicanos to California ones; Asian Americans to population in the San Francisco Bay area. Together, they demanded about half the places in the entering law school class.[155]

The final question is how long do we compensate. In *Bakke*, the Court was assured that affirmative action was only temporary. "Color-conscious special-admissions programs are not viewed as a permanent fixture of the admissions landscape," the university maintained. "The underlying philosophy of programs like the one at Davis is that they will eliminate the need for themselves and then disappear."[156] In another brief, the Court was informed how "in 1975 the law school of the University of California at Berkeley eliminated Japanese-American participation in its special admissions program and reduced participation of Chinese-Americans in light of the success of these groups in gaining admission through the regular admissions process."[157] In time, when blacks had "overcome the handicaps of previous generations of prejudice," special treatment would end for them too.[158]

That hopeful a scenario is, alas, not inevitable. Rather than disappear, might racial preference not take root and spread? Pressure to relax standards would exist everywhere. If minorities were admitted specially, might some not have to be graded more leniently[159] or favored on bar exams[160] to avoid embarrassing results? And what benefit, once conferred, is ever lightly withdrawn? Racial preference, some worried, would be the price forever paid for campus peace.[161] When in 1975, observed Nathan Glazer, "many private colleges and universities tried to cut back on special aid for racially defined groups . . . black students occupied school buildings and demanded that the privileges given on the basis of race be retained."[162] Preference, concluded the brief of the American Jewish Committee, "is likely to be interminable, particularly when it is caught up in campus, community, and political pressures. There is no cut-off principle."[163]

Should blacks come to fare well in regular admissions, these fears will probably pass. The real fear is one that is never expressed. Our dark unspoken dread—what makes affirmative action so remorseless an issue—is that after generations of compensatory treatment, racial gaps may yet remain. That while individual blacks will continue to distinguish themselves in all walks of life, the mass of Negroes still will not compare on whatever is used to measure professional aptitude at the time. Our stated credo is that "all races can compete fairly at all professional levels."[164] Our lurking fear is that they cannot. What happens then? Does the temporary become permanent? In this scenario, as years pass, compensatory justice shades almost imperceptibly into preferential treatment.

Thankfully, that is not a question we have to face now, and may be one we will never have to face. The most thoughtful proponents of affirmative action have never defined their set of proposals as a quick fix. "For only about ten years out of two centuries as a nation has there been a serious nationwide attempt to make room in the higher reaches of the world for those who have been held back for so long. . . ." wrote McGeorge Bundy. "Some of those who defend affirmative action sometimes speak of it as if it could be a relatively short matter. If we measure in generations, they may be right. It seems fair to hope that we can have made decisive progress by the time the children of today's children are of college age. But that single generation takes us well beyond the year 2000. For the rest of the working lives of those who are now concerned with these matters, persistence will be the name of the game."[165]

V

"The overriding purpose of affirmative action," Professors Karst and Horowitz believed, "is not to remedy yesterday's discrimination, but to serve today's social needs."[166] Racial history all too often aroused white guilt or black indignation, two painful sentiments. Thus utilitarian supports for affirmative action emerged, which emphasized not past wrongs but present benefits. The integration of minorities into the learned professions was, of course, the transcendent benefit. But other advantages were routinely advanced. First, affirmative action would serve to enrich and diversify higher education. Secondly, it would help meet the acute needs of minorities for medical and legal service. Last, it would provide more professional role models for black youths to emulate.

These rationales came under heavy fire. Each, we shall see, rested on unprovable assumptions. But opponents of affirmative action especially distrusted any contemporary approach. History, as used by the Supreme Court, placed powerful limitations on the use of racial preference. Race-conscious steps could be taken only to compensate for past discrimination on the part of a particular institution or school district.[167] Utilitarians, however, justified "benign" discrimination not as a finite matter of remedy but because it struck educational policy makers as a good idea.

"Where are the black students? Where are the black students?" President Charles Odegaard wondered, watching the long white columns at the University of Washington's commencement exercises in 1963.[168] How curious that universities, preparing students for life in a plural society, had such lopsidedly Anglo student bodies. Something had to be done. Affirmative action sought to broaden the base of higher education, to grant "intellectual house room to a broad spectrum of diverse cultural insights," thereby overcoming the "white myopia among students and faculty in many academic disciplines."[169]

Aspiring to diversity, of course, has its special hazards, as does any treatment of individuals as members of groups (whether racial, ethnic, geographical, or occupational). Diverse student bodies were doubtless more representative (at least of what admissions officers felt was worth representing). Whether they were more motivated or intelligent was something else again. Nevertheless, diversity was widely acclaimed. "Fifteen or twenty years ago, . . ." in the admissions policy of Harvard College, "diversity meant students from

California, New York, and Massachusetts; city dwellers and farm boys; violinists, painters and football players; biologists, historians and classicists; potential stockbrokers, academics and politicians." Affirmative action was an overdue update of that time-honored concept. "A farm boy from Idaho can bring something to Harvard College that a Bostonian cannot offer. Similarly, a black student can usually bring something that a white person cannot offer."[170]

Diversity, it was argued in *Bakke*, was badly needed in medical education. Blacks would give white medical students "an enhanced awareness of the medical concerns of minorities" and the challenges of delivering health care to minority communities.[171] Whites would be encouraged to regard blacks as professional peers, not invariably as nurses, orderlies, or members of the maintenance crew. Above all, diversity would assist interracial communication. "Many white students . . . ," Professor Sandalow has noted, "need to learn to be able to disagree with blacks candidly and without embarrassment."[172] Communication would enable future white physicians to better understand their black patients and to "build bonds to minority physicians for future consultation and referral."[173] And diversity aided faculty as much as students. "It has been the experience of many university teachers," noted one brief supporting the university, "that the insights provided by the participation of minority students enrich the curriculum, broaden the teachers' scholarly interests, and protect them from insensitivity to minority perspectives. Teachers have come to count on the participation of those students."[174] Like so much in affirmative action, such arguments were a reverse twist. The assumption had always been that integration was mainly intended to benefit blacks. Now, the university emphasized to the Court in *Bakke*, the chief beneficiaries of a racially diverse student body might be white.[175]

To work, diversity required more than token numbers. A critical mass of black students was necessary to dispel feelings of isolation and uptightness. A few blacks, moreover, could no more communicate the "black experience" to whites than a Montanan or two could convey "big sky" country to City University of New York. And it was blacks only—not poor people generally—who were said to be necessary: "The minority experience is distinct from the experience of poverty. Growing up black—even middle-class black—involves a whole range of different encounters, perceptions, and reactions."[176] Affirmative action, by admitting minorities in

meaningful numbers, alone made possible this effective interchange.[177]

But was interracial interchange a realistic goal of minority-
favored admissions programs. The first years of affirmative action
sometimes drove the races farther apart. Minorities demanded their
own "dormitory wings, black studies or La Raza programs, soul
food in the cafeteria" and other symbols of separateness.[178] Affirmative action, with its numerical double standards, might undercut
communication by making whites feel superior and blacks self-
conscious. Interaction was discouraged in subtler ways as well.
Blacks resisted being subjects for white racial curiosity. One black
law student felt that "the real test of a white law student's friendship . . . is indicated by the types of subjects on which he solicits
the ideas of the black. If the source of all his questions is ultimately
a hunger for ideas on racial matters . . . it is a fair assumption that
the white student sees no further into the black student than his
skin and may have little respect for his intellect or his ideas of what
the law is all about."[179]

Problems in communication also affected the classroom. One
recent study of classroom dynamics indicated that women in male-
taught classes were more silent than in those taught by women.[180]
Would blacks be reluctant to participate in white-taught classes
too? In law school, however, blacks could not sit quiet. And speaking carried racial weight. "The silence, the heavy sense of expectation, fell on all of the blacks in a classroom whenever one of us was
called upon for an answer. We waited, with the class, for the chosen man to justify the right of all of us to be there."[181] But did not
the excruciating awkwardness of such moments argue for more
racial contact, not less, if the races were ever to learn to feel at ease?

Racial diversity, then, was one chief goal of affirmative action.
Another was bringing professionals into minority communities.
Substantial numbers of black medical and law students, it was
hoped, would devote their careers to serving their race.

The need for better black health care has been poignantly documented. There was, to begin with, a shortage of black doctors: 1
black physician per 2,779 blacks as opposed to 1 white doctor per
599 whites. In the deep South, the shortage was most severe, some
states having only one black physician per 15,000 to 20,000 black
residents.[182] The growth of specialization in American medicine
and loss of general practitioners hit black communities especially

hard, noted the NAACP Legal Defense Fund. "[A]s those physicians who offer the point of entry into the health system and continuing contact with it, primary care doctors dispense preventative and ambulatory care, and can best ameliorate the needs of underserved, low-income minorities."[183]

Statistics tell a distressing story. Blacks in 1970 had a life expectancy of 64.6 years; whites of 71.7. Black infant mortality was almost twice that of whites; maternal mortality three times as high.[184] "Blacks," noted one authority, "visit doctors less frequently than whites and when they go to the hospital they are more likely than whites to need a longer stay, which reflects the fact that they have been medically neglected."[185] Blacks suffered more from serious diseases. Tuberculosis was ten times more prevalent among blacks than whites; diabetes and hypertension three times more so. Communicable diseases, such as whooping cough, meningitis, and diphtheria still ran high, because many black children had not been immunized.[186] Unsanitary shelter, malnutrition, and other incidents of poverty probably contributed more to black illness than shortages of black physicians. Yet more doctors (and nurses and family health workers) in black communities could hardly fail to help.

But would they come? White doctors certainly had not. While white physicians frequently treated black patients in a clinic or hospital, they were reluctant to establish family practice in a black neighborhood. Primary care practice in the ghetto generally meant less status, more patients, longer hours, less pay.[187] Negative attitudes toward indigent patients also kept whites away, beliefs that dissolute lifestyles, for example, caused much disease among the poor.[188]

Were blacks more likely than whites to return to ghetto practice? Some observers thought not. Blacks, like whites, would find money, lifestyle, and status the lures of practice location. Was not medicine often an escape for blacks, the road to "upward mobility, away from poverty and continued association with the community from which they came"?[189] In the rural South, where physician shortages were most acute, illiberal racial attitudes might keep black doctors away. Lastly, medical education itself might entice even well-intentioned blacks away from ghetto practice. "The whole focus of more than 20,000 full-time medical school faculty and an equal number of part-time faculty," complained one critic, "is to address the abstruse and arcane subjects and knowledge that affect [only a] tiny part of a doctor's responsibility."[190]

One must not be too cynical. Racial allegiance still matters. Black elites, out of loyalty or guilt, cannot forget the less fortunate of their race. A common history of repression may remain a great unifying bond. Since 1740 when a black named Simon "pretended to be a great doctor among his people,"[191] most black physicians have served black patients. One 1972 survey of 200 black doctors and dentists in New York, for example, found less than 5 percent with a predominantly white practice.[192] Recently at Davis Medical School, four minority students established a weight-reduction clinic in Del Paso Heights, a Sacramento area with many black residents.[193] And black doctors may continue serving black communities, whether out of idealism or by default. Even those who would not could still help by alerting local medical associations, hospitals, and health boards to minority medical needs.

To some, this line of thought was abhorrent. "The purpose of the University of Washington," wrote Justice Douglas in *DeFunis*, "cannot be to produce black lawyers for blacks, Polish lawyers for Poles, Jewish lawyers for Jews, and Irish lawyers for Irish. It should be to produce good lawyers for Americans. . . ."[194] On the one hand, we are told affirmative action will promote diversity in higher education. Then, on the other, that professional practice will be organized along intraracial lines. Should not professional as well as classroom life prize interracial contact? A more talented white doctor will serve blacks far better than a less talented black one, and vice versa.[195] Moreover, argues Professor Cohen, "to expect that black professionals will practice only in the black community, or Mexican-Americans only in the Mexican-American community, is quite wrong. The parochialism inherent in that expectation exerts heavy and unfair pressure upon minority professionals."[196] Worse yet, it acted to absolve white professionals from servicing black needs. "It is true that black physicians are providing much of the health care for the black ghetto," noted one commentator, "but the health of ghetto residents is everyone's responsibility."[197]

These comments, while valid, still belie the special role of the minority professional. Professional service, Justice Douglas's aphorism notwithstanding, is, in part, intraracial. Many blacks, it has been noted, have their own health culture. They attach great importance to good or bad luck, wait until the point of crisis before seeking attention, and often prefer home remedies to hospitalization.[198] A black physician might encourage trust in more modern medical methods. Such physician-patient empathy is not to be disparaged. The need for Spanish-speaking doctors for Spanish-speaking communities may be greater still, as well as for American Indian physicians who know the tribal tongue.

For lawyers the story is much the same. Black lawyers might better locate, interview, and examine black witnesses and communicate with black clients. "Certain tasks," explains Professor O'Neil, "can be best performed by one who knows the terrain."[199] Kent Greenawalt, a Civil Rights lawyer in Mississippi in 1965, admitted having "difficulty trying to talk to the grandmother of a boy who had been released from reform school; when I tried to outline what she might do to help him from going back to reform school, her distrust of me as a stranger who had no idea what her life was like was evident. . . . [A] black lawyer from Mississippi would surely have managed better than I did. . . . [M]erely to have been from Mississippi would not have been enough, because the black grandmother would probably not have trusted a local white lawyer any more than she trusted me."[200]

More important than lawyer-client rapport was pursuit of litigation in which the black community has a special interest. The director of the southern regional office of the ACLU once observed that black lawyers had successfully challenged discriminatory practices that whites would not risk raising or even had failed to detect.[201]

None of this implies that service to minorities can only be delivered by minority professionals. Quite the contrary. There is much professional schools can do to alert all students to the problems of the underprivileged of each race. They can offer more courses in public health and epidemiology, devise outreach programs to serve disadvantaged areas, offer special consideration in admissions to whoever makes a commitment to spend time among the medically deprived.[202] Such initiatives, while useful, do not come close to guaranteeing depressed communities adequate service. At most, they would supplement, not substitute for, a growing cadre of minority professionals.

A final argument for affirmative action involves the creation of black role models. Role modeling, unlike service to minority communities, was a job only black professionals could do. White lawyers could do little to convince ghetto youth that America was a land of equal racial opportunity. Black professionals, on the other hand, would stimulate aspirations of black children and demonstrate that in America "there are ways of 'making it' without resort to violence."[203]

There is value, of course, in whatever will broaden the horizons of black youth. The travails of teenage blacks—drug dependency, high unemployment, run-ins with the law, dropouts from school—are all well known. The future held scant sense of possibility. "The Negro boys," wrote one observer in 1971, "have little if anything to say about the future. Generally, their alternatives were to work in a factory or perhaps join the armed forces. . . . However, just as likely were the possibilities of unemployment and a bad marriage. The sensed absence of choice, of 'potentials' and 'challenges' was more than obvious."[204] To escape, many young black males adopted as role models romance figures such as Ray Charles, perhaps, or Mohammed Ali.[205] But theirs were largely mythic worlds of limited access. The learned professions, as the saying goes, had broad shoulders.

Professional role modeling, however, raises serious questions. For blacks to be good role models, they had to be effective. But Professor Graglia worried that dual standards in affirmative action programs would "in the long-run reinforce stereotypes of [minority] incompetence. It will soon come to be believed that to get a *real* lawyer he had better be very white."[206] That fear, however, can be exaggerated. Black lawyers after graduation would earn divergent reputations, just as white ones have. And there are enough walking examples of white incompetence to dispel any notion that one race has a monopoly.

The more troubling problem is how to make black professionals realistic to ghetto youths who need them most. The most fertile source of role models—television advertising and professional dramas such as Perry Mason, Marcus Welby or Lou Grant—may be pure fantasy, whatever the race of the lead roles. Faith in role models merely as "black faces to behold" seems misplaced. Effective role playing probably requires personal contact, and all the adult advice and encouragement that goes with it. Yet the daily regimen of middle-class blacks may soon be as removed from the ghetto as that of middle-class whites. The chief beneficiaries of black role models may, therefore, be their own middle class offspring.

Utilitarian arguments have their value. Yet to support affirmative action in terms of educational diversity, service to minority communities, or role models for black youth is intellectually a dangerous game. For what the utilitarians borrowed were the old tools of southern racism, though for a worthier cause. Utilitarians, like the South before *Brown*, indulged fatuously overbroad racial assumptions. For purposes of special admissions eligibility, *all* blacks were presumed "diverse" or likely to return to serve minority communities, or to set future examples for minority youth. In real life, of course, these assumptions are quite errant. Many blacks may not be "diverse" at all, but share "the same tastes, manners, experiences, aptitudes, and aspirations as the whites with whom one might compare them."[207] Many are less interested in helping downtrodden members of their race than in achieving heightened status for themselves. Yet affirmative action was prepared to overlook these and other individual differences in favor of using the common trait of blackness. To some, this was a frightening step. If blackness were a permissible proxy for diversity of viewpoint and missionary service to the poor, might it not again be allowed to represent, as it had in the law of the pre–*Brown* South, less flattering characteristics as well?[208] With affirmative action, race threatened once again to overshadow individuality, to become the most important trait in evaluation of the human persona.

That, however, does not conclude the matter. May we not, in the name of noble ends, take chances with means, even means that are avowedly racialistic? Affirmative action not only announced the compelling goal of ending racial separation in American life. Supporters insisted, quite vehemently, that racial means were the sole effective way of doing so. "If a college or university truly seeks a substantial increase from a particular minority or disadvantaged group," noted one, "it must choose them directly and explicitly. . . . [T]here is no effective substitute for the explicit use of race as a preferential criterion for most colleges and universities."[209]

The most mentioned alternative to affirmative action was an admissions preference based upon economic disadvantage.[210] This alternative, though untested, was roundly condemned. Nothing, said supporters of the university, could be worse. Such a program would further stretch scarce scholarship funds and disqualify by definition many of the ablest minority students, those from middle-class backgrounds.[211] While a high percentage of blacks were doubtless disadvantaged, almost two-thirds of the nation's poor were white.[212] And because low income whites outscored low income blacks, "adoption of a truly racially 'neutral' disadvantaged approach would do little more than substitute less-affluent whites for more-affluent whites."[213] The Educational Testing Service predicted that if racial preferences in law school admissions were eliminated, the percentage of blacks in first year classes would plummet from the current 5.3 percent to between 1 and 2 percent.[214]

The effect of this argument was to present the Court with a doomsday choice. America's most urgent task, it seemed, could be accomplished only in the most abhorrent possible way.

VI

Just how abhorrent is impossible to convey. Many thought that the battle for color blindness had already been won. That never again after *Brown* could the state group citizens according to race. Thus *Brown* was regarded not as a victory for blacks alone, but as a universal human triumph against discrimination.

If that was ever *Brown*'s import, it was short-lived. Or at least that view of *Brown* was said in *Bakke* to be shortsighted. The state might yet consider citizens by race, so long as its intent, as in affirmative action, was "not to separate the races, but to bring them together."[215] Racial admissions could be permitted to benefit the minority race but not, as in *Brown*, to stigmatize it.[216] The white majority, it was now being said, could constitutionally be trusted "to discriminate against itself."[217] Indeed, whites were proper subjects for discrimination because, unlike blacks, they had not been historically disadvantaged and always controlled their "own political destiny."[218] Yet all such arguments for affirmative action suffered the same infirmities. They bisected a pluralist society into crude black and white camps.[219] And they failed to acknowledge that racial means are treacherous—however, by whomever, and for whatever ends they are used.

What is a constitution but a withdrawal of means from the hand of the state? Our Constitution is, after all, a disabling document. As against government, the most wretched have their rights. Government must not, in pursuit of its purposes, silence dissent, abridge the franchise, search without cause, extort confessions, dispense with juries or until recently, infringe the joint powers of Congress and the states.[220] Declaring war, maintaining order, promoting all the state deems just and wise must yield in the end to the integrity of means, "the supremacy of the procedural principle."[221] For "the highest morality," Professor Bickel maintained to the end, "almost always is the morality of process."[222]

And not without reason. Must not our public allegiance run foremost to means? The commitment to process alone allows us to negotiate differences of substance. The spirit of fair play, as embodied in process, alone lets losers abide adverse results. Process alone gives democracy its identity, distinct and apart from the omnipotent state. And what, other than process, ensures liberty in the end?

The point must not be pressed too far. We may debate what process, in given instances, is constitutionally required.[223] And the "procedural principle," as Chief Justice Marshall recognized, at some point threatens not just inconvenience but paralysis.[224] Still society "cannot sustain the continuous assault of moral imperatives"[225] in the noble name of which means of unquestioned value are ignored. Like old-fashioned chastity, process must remain inviolate. Every person disregarding it gives every other a greater claim to do so. For private citizens to ignore democratic modes of behavior—as many Vietnam protesters did—is at least punishable. For government to do so, as happened during Vietnam and Watergate, draws into question the very character of the republic. And for the Court—the acknowledged guardian of process—to sanction suspect means is, to say the least, a weighty blow.

Ought not race to be among those means absolutely disallowed? Why is not color blindness the sole permissible principle of process? It had been the ideal of racial reform since Justice Harlan dissented in *Plessy* v. *Ferguson*: "Our Constitution is color-blind, and neither knows nor tolerates classes among citizens. . . . The law regards man as man, and takes no account of his surroundings or of his color when his civil rights as guaranteed by the supreme law of the land are involved." Then in words the Court in *Bakke* could not fail to heed: "It is, therefore, to be regretted that this high tribunal, the final expositor of the fundamental law of the land, has reached the conclusion that it is competent for a State to regulate the enjoyment by citizens of their civil rights solely upon the basis of race."[226]

Surely Justice Harlan meant to give voice to not only the needs of a downtrodden race but basic notions of western justice. Nothing seems more unfair than to measure man by his race—a characteristic he can neither change or control. Race runs "contrary to the basic concept of our system that legal burdens should bear some relationship to individual responsibility or wrongdoing."[227] And skin color seems irrelevant not just to the practice of law or medicine but to any fair appraisal of personal worth. Even were it proven that whites generally made better lawyers than blacks—or vice versa—it would not matter. For men stand before the law as individuals, not as representatives of racial groups.

As a matter of pure theory, radical classifications are not unique. Consider, for example, the selective service regulation exempting from conscription persons over seven feet in height. Like race, this regulation turns on an uncontrollable characteristic. And even were it proven that very tall people generally make very poor soldiers, there would inevitably be individual exceptions to the generalization. But the convenience to government of broadly classifying citizens would permit this statute to stand.

Why, then, is race so different? Precisely because it is, above all, a historical concept. The most odious passions in all of modern history have been those based upon race. Because race is so fixed, so visible, so divisive, so insinuated into human self-esteem, it has been seized upon to assert superiority in unconscionable ways. The history of slavery and segregation needs no retelling now. But Jim Crow was not the worst example. The atrocities of the Third Reich were more racial than religious. "The Jew," Adolf Hitler wrote in *Mein Kampf*, "has always been a people with definite racial characteristics and never a religion; only in order to get ahead he early sought for a means which could distract unpleasant attention from his person. And what would have been more expedient and at the same time more innocent than the 'embezzled' concept of a religious community?"[228] The laws of Nazi Germany reflected this racist outlook. A Jew was defined as anyone with a Jewish ancestor; a Christian who had converted from Judaism was, because of parentage, still a Jew.[229] Sadly, the American record of tolerance on this score is not unblemished. WASP elites, whether in law firms, country clubs, or colleges, took offense at a large Jewish presence.

Thus American universities "set the style in excluding or restricting Jewish students" through quotas or "the *'numerus clausus'* " as it came to be known.[230]

Was it not lacking in sensitivity for schools to serve up so pungent an historical reminder? True, the historical examples involved minorities abused by majorities, while affirmative action was supposedly the reverse. And, true, the old quotas were directed against Jews in particular while Davis limited prospects for the white race at large. Yet such claims may be more a salve for those who formulate the quotas than for those who are excluded by them. Many ethnic and religious minorities know only that once again there is a quota and that once again *they* are on the adverse end. "The lesson of the great decisions of the Supreme Court," wrote Professor Bickel, "and the lesson of contemporary history have been the same for at least a generation: discrimination on the basis of race is illegal, immoral, unconstitutional, inherently wrong, and destructive of democratic society. Now this is to be unlearned and we are told that this is not a matter of fundamental principle but only a matter of whose ox is gored."[231]

The attack on affirmative action was more than theoretical and historical. Practical difficulties were also cited. There are always those, for example, who will use deception to obtain a government benefit. Thus the customary reliance of special admissions on self-classification by the applicant may not always suffice. Already, in the realm of employment, racial redefinition was beginning to occur. In San Francisco, the *Village Voice* noted that "53 police officers calling themselves American Indians were summoned before the Equal Opportunity Commission and asked to prove their claim. All 53 were reclassified as white."[232] The *New Republic* observed that in Massachusetts "the Division of Personnel ruled, apparently on the basis of a 'visual inspection,' that a police officer who claimed to be black actually was white."[233] Affirmative action may thus draw government into the dirty business of racial labeling, recalling Homer Plessy's expulsion from the white railroad car for being one-eighth black. Today's definitional difficulties are more likely to involve Chicanos or American Indians, whose physical appearance is less distinctive than blacks. What of the applicant with only one Chicano grandparent? How much Mexican or Indian or Filipino blood will suffice for special treatment?[234]

Maybe such difficulties will be marginal. In the vast majority of cases, the racial identity of the applicant may be clear. And classification problems of one sort or another will inhere in any admissions plan to assist the disadvantaged. A more serious criticism of affirmative action is the change it threatens in our political life. "American politics," George Will once predicted, "will be permanently poisoned. Politics will be an endless struggle for preference, a scramble to determine which minorities will receive what slice of educational and employment opportunities."[235]

The result will pit monorities against each other. At whose expense, it is asked, will affirmative action in higher education occur? "Jewish groups," Nathan Lewin observed, "representing a community that had suffered discrimination and found a refuge in certain professions and in the universities, complained—with substantial justification—that an excessive share of the costs of repair comes out of the Jewish community."[236] Professor Sandalow guessed that "the primary burden of existing racial and ethnic preferences falls not upon Jews, but upon the white working class whose children find it more difficult to obtain financial aid because of the preferences given to minority groups."[237] On this question, appearances are as important as reality. Many groups may perceive themselves first in line for sacrifice and react accordingly. And all sorts of individuals will, rightly or wrongly, blame their unhappy fates on blacks. This reservoir of embitterment we hardly need: yet special admissions threatens to make of racial "resentment a plausible, even justifiable emotion."[238]

Perhaps, as the First Circuit Court of Appeals reminds, "our society cannot be completely colorblind in the short term if we are to have a colorblind society in the long run."[239] Yet in the name of such hopeful speculation, do we adopt programs that divide and polarize? Schisms elsewhere flash warnings here: Canada with its French minority; Great Britain with its Welsh and Scottish separatists; Belgium with its Flemings and French; the Soviet Union where the majority of inhabitants are not of Russian stock.[240] How sad if our quest for an integrated society were to diminish our sense of nationhood and mock that motto on the back, of all things, the Lincoln penny, "*E pluribus unum.*" It is one thing for groups to nurture their own ethnic and racial identity, quite another for government to allocate upon it. "If one examines the countries in which nepotism in the allotment of civil-service jobs prevails, . . ." contends Professor Etzioni, "not only is each clan or party entitled to x jobs for its members, but constant feuds rage among *sub*clans and factions within the parties over *sub*allotments. It would be sad and ironic if, having surmounted the truly virulent race and ethnic prejudices of earlier eras in order to forge a common American identity, the U.S. would be tribalized by efforts to eradicate what remains of past discrimination."[241]

The tensions of affirmative action collide, finally, in the Fourteenth amendment. The "one pervading purpose" of the amendment, the Court wrote so very long ago, was "the freedom of the slave race, the security and firm establishment of that freedom, and the protection of the newly-made freeman and citizen from the oppressions of those who had formerly exercised unlimited dominion over him."[242] Yet the language of the amendment's first great section spoke not of "the slave race" but supremely of the individual: no *person*, it insists, shall be denied due process or the equal protection of the laws. The tension between group claims and individual rights is not, at this stage of history, readily resolved. Opponents warn that affirmative action foreshadows the era of the " 'group think'," where man's race would eclipse his individuality and where each "would regard himself as a representative of the group from whose quota he comes; and individual aspiration would be limited by the proportionate size of the group to which the individual belongs. . . . [Such a society] would be something quite different from the America we have known."[243] But would it really? America has been "group thinking" for several centuries now, and the ultimate irony of our history is that it can be invoked in quite paradoxical ways. History teaches, we have noted, the prodigious dangers of encouraging racial patterns of thought. Yet it asks us something else besides: whether a constitution, after generations of endorsing color-consciousness, can abruptly demand that the world be color-blind.

There is one final point to make about color-conscious means. Racial preference, in the selective and competitive environment of higher education, insults blacks in a way that busing never did. Unfortunately, the best intentioned arguments for affirmative action are some of the most condescending as well.

It is argued, for example, that special admissions students are all "fully qualified,"[244] which sidesteps the question of who is most qualified, surely a germane inquiry in the allocation of the limited

number of places in graduate schools. It is said that objective criteria—such as grades and test scores—do not "accurately predict"
minority performance,[245] but it is never quite said what does. The
value of quantitative data in admissions has been questioned,[246] but
what nonquantitative systems would be better or fairer has not
been deeply pursued.[247] The godfather of this whole line of argument is that law and medical school admissions tests are themselves
culturally biased: that "many Eskimos, American Indians, Filipinos, Chicanos, Asian Indians, Burmese, and Africans come from
such disparate backgrounds that a test sensitively tuned for most
applicants would be wide of the mark for many minorities."[248]

Cultural bias, like other phrases of fashion, is "a sort of verbal
butterfly net for a lot of loose-flying concepts."[249] One has to ask
what precisely the accusation really means. Is it more than an understandable reaction of frustration to low minority test scores?
The Law School Admission Test (LSAT), to begin with, does not
purport to predict ultimate success as a lawyer but rather the skills
necessary to success in the first year of law school. At that, in the
aggregate, it does pretty well.[250] Similarly, as between black and
white, it has been shown to be an equally accurate predictor.[251]
Though its predictive value is racially neutral, the test may still be
culturally slanted because it emphasizes skills or trades on assumptions with which middle-class whites are more conversant than
disadvantaged blacks. But where, one wonders, does that logic
end? If the LSAT is culturally biased, then are not law school
tests, bar examinations, the practice of law, and, for that matter,
life? American law will profit from minority perspectives. And yet
one ought to recognize that the legal culture of any country will
embody majoritarian conventions and beliefs.

One can react to the reality of a majority white culture and low
minority test scores in several ways. One is to demand a morato-
rium on standardized tests, as the Association of Black Psychologists did.[252] Or suggest separate tests for separate minorities.[253] Or
follow the lead of most affirmative action programs and deempha-
size minority scores. Yet discrediting the test may be, as one commentator put it, "equivalent to breaking a thermometer because it
registers a body temperature of 101°."[254] A better approach is to
accept the test scores as the bad news they are and try to address
the problems that contributed to them. William Raspberry's reaction to low black performance on a Florida high school achievement

test is relevant here. The test, he thought, exposed the whole "ineffectiveness of the public schools in educating—acculturating—so many of our children. The answer lies not in throwing out the tests, . . . [but] in doing what is necessary, at whatever exertion and expense, to see to it that the children acquire the skills that are the admission tickets to full participation in American society."[255]

The furor over cultural bias and the imperfections of quantitative data has a yet more poignant side. Such arguments are often raised by those who feel compelled to excuse minority performance and to explain all black difficulties in terms of the continuing presence of white racism. As the cruder forms of racism have gradually receded in this country, Civil Rights leaders have felt a need to maintain its existence. Under their theory, racism never disappears but only reincarnates itself in even subtler and more sophisticated guises, cultural biases on standardized tests being one such guise. While there is truth in this view, the costs of maintaining it are very high. Complaints of "cultural bias" probably strike most white Americans as ill-concealed cover-ups for minority shortcomings.[256] And "cultural bias" may demoralize blacks who think the game so rigged toward white society that it is not worth bothering to play. Finally, it may encourage blacks who do play to interpret every personal setback as the product of subtle racism in grades and tests.

We ought never to forget that the debate on race and education in the years since *Brown* has been roughest of all on black pride. Every white initiative aimed at integration has demeaned and patronized in its own unwitting way. Integration itself was a way to improve blacks through contact with whites; busing came to involve a black chase and white escape; affirmative action alleged a need for favored treatment and a double standard. Race-conscious means, we have discovered, carry their own special capability to insult. Not surprisingly, the proudest blacks have protested, if not to the idea of integration, then at least to the way whites were pressing it. The Black Power movement of the late 1960s urged separate culture, institutions, appearance, and pride. Black objections to affirmative action were different. Rather than exulting black separateness, they sought white acceptance, not as blacks, but as individuals. "As an American I have a right to equal citizenship," insisted attorney Thomas Curtis. "I cannot conceive of anything more, and I will not settle for anything less. . . . Rather than even a pious pretense of equal citizenship, the current official government doc-

trine seems to be that we black people, and some other selected minority groups, are by definition inferior, and therefore must be permanently monitored and controlled—by quotas and racial
balancing acts, by racial apportionment and reverse discrimination."[257]

Blacks succeeding without a racial preference were, because of
their skin color, assumed to have benefited from one. The presumption of second-ratedness galled Professor Thomas Sowell:
"What all the arguments and campaigns for quotas are really saying, loud and clear, is that *black people just don't have it*, and that they
will have to be *given* something. . . . [Competent blacks] will be
completely undermined, as black becomes synonymous—in the
minds of black and white alike—with incompetence, and black
achievement becomes synonymous with charity or payoffs."[258]

It will be said that these black voices are a minority, though a minority often vocalizes what a majority fears may be true. It will be
said that those blacks who dislike special treatment can refuse it, a
point that ignores the nature of temptation and the capacity of
"charity" to make one grateful and resentful at the same time. It will
be said that those are the voices of middle-class blacks and that life
looks different to blacks from below. A lot will be said, in fact, to
escape this paradox: 'to integrate you, we must segregate you, to
make you equal we must treat you unequally. Though only, of
course, for the time being.'

11

The Decision

Thrust and parry, charge and counter-charge, a duel of minds and morals dominated the long year before *Bakke*. Yet no decisive advantage was ever won. Perhaps there has never been a case before the Supreme Court with opposing arguments of more equal legitimacy. The Court's own task in *Bakke* was to avoid a conclusive outcome. It must not, in this most divisive of cases, hoist the arms of a victorious contestant. Meg Greenfield of the Washington *Post* prayed the Supreme Court "will find a way to blur the edges of the controversy and reaffirm the important values raised by both sides. You say that is fudging the issue? Fine. It ought to be fudged."[1]

The Court did just that. If *Brown* was a great moral blow, *Bakke* was a brokered judgment. The Supreme Court offered "a Solomonic compromise,"[2] in which "the nine justices spoke in many voices, a chorus of competing viewpoints adding up to a well-modulated counterpoint."[3] The Court struck down the Davis program with its "specified number of [minority] seats"[4] but upheld the use of race or ethnicity as "a 'plus' in a particular applicant's file" so long as "it does not insulate the individual from comparison with all other candidates for the available seats."[5] QUOTAS: NO / RACE: YES capsuled the cover of *Time* magazine. Because Bakke's exclusion was to all appearances the result of Davis's unlawful program, the Court ordered his admission.[6] "Mr. Bakke won, but so did the general principle of affirmative action," wrote Anthony Lewis. "That was the comforting paradox communicated to the world."[7]

The Court in *Bakke* tried to keep faith with *Brown*. To the university, *Brown* stood for minority educational opportunity, "but implementation of the commitment expressed in *Brown* has taken years and is even today not complete."[8] To others, *Brown* stood for the ideal of color blindness: "It must be the exclusion on racial grounds which offends the Constitution, and not the particular skin color of the person excluded."[9] *Bakke* stood for both, perhaps, or for neither. It attempted, at least, to bridge the unbridgeable: the disparate legacies of *Brown*.

Many were left vaguely uneasy, few bitterly displeased. Most disconsolate was Thurgood Marshall, who found it "more than a little ironic that after several hundred years of class-based discrimination against Negroes, the Court is unwilling to hold that a class-based remedy for that discrimination is permissible."[10] Other black leaders were more sanguine. Benjamin Hooks, executive director of the NAACP, termed *Bakke* "a mixed bag, both a victory and a defeat." Vernon Jordan of the National Urban League, while deploring the loss of Davis-style admissions, felt the Court's judgment "should constitute a green light to go forward with acceptable affirmative-action programs."[11] All sides combed the 154 pages of opinions for language they liked.[12] For the Court, once again, political diplomacy prevailed; its decision "gave almost everyone—Bakke, the government, civil rights groups, and most universities—a victory, if a small one."[13]

Bakke himself had spent the week avoiding reporters, even to the point of covering his face with a newspaper. "Hi, I heard the news," his secretary beamed the morning of the decision. Bakke smiled, nodded slightly, then ducked into his office.[14] The Court, for all of its power, could not make men whole. For Bakke at age thirty-eight, the dream came true, but five years late. The dream had also come dear. For the sake of medicine, Bakke had forsaken anonymity. "People aren't going to forget what he represents," said one second year student at Davis. "He will never not be Allan Bakke," Dr. Morton Levitt, the medical school's associate dean, remarked.[15]

To say that the Court as a whole "fudged" in *Bakke* is really misleading. Eight justices took polar positions. Four—Stevens, Stewart, Rehnquist, and Chief Justice Burger—argued that the Davis program violated Title VI of the 1964 Civil Rights Act by excluding Bakke because of his race.[16] There is, of course, that venerable bromide of restraint that statutory grounds of decision are to be preferred to constitutional ones.[17] Its application to *Bakke*, however, was questionable. The parties had argued and the courts below had ruled on constitutional grounds alone. Thus the Court had to request supplemental briefing on the statutory issue, i.e. it stretched for restraint. Though the language of Title VI when read literally did cover Bakke's case,[18] how could a Congress preoccupied with the evils of segregation have addressed the much later issue of minority preferences as well?[19] To hold for Bakke on Title VI was to postpone the constitutional issue in a case where the Court's constitutional competence was clear, and on an issue that, after *DeFunnis*, had suffered more than its share of postponements already. It was also to throw the onus of decision on Congress—an evasive course of action for the Court of last resort. Finally, and by all odds most important, to discover in Title VI requirements of color blindness risked re-estranging minorities and rolling back much of the long progress since *Brown*.

The statutory foursome lent *Bakke* itself an air of impermanence. Since a majority of the Court held Title VI did permit race to be considered in admissions, the statutory foursome may face the constitutional issue in some later case. Their views on this question are by no means certain. It is not impossible that one or more of the four will one day join with the justices advocating affirmative action to uphold sweeping and far-reaching programs.

The justices most supportive of affirmative action also numbered four—Brennan, White, Marshall, and Blackmun. Together they found that Title VI permitted the adoption of race-conscious means to overcome past societal discrimination.[20] The Constitution was no less generous. Racial remedies were quite permissible where, as in medicine, "minority underrepresentation is substantial and chronic" and where there was reason to believe past societal discrimination was the cause.[21] These justices thus adopted the broadest and most permissive view of compensatory justice. A particular entity, such as Davis, itself free of past discrimination, might repent the sins of society at large.[22] Their formulation was as timeless as it was universal. Davis might consider, as part of the basis for its program, the experience of "slavery, [where] penal sanctions were imposed upon anyone attempting to educate Negroes."[23] When the age of compensation might end was likewise left open. The choice of means was left also to Davis's discretion. Inclusion of academically successful Asian Americans in its program went unquestioned. As long as Davis's purpose was benign and its program nonstigmatic, the reservation of "a predetermined number of places" for minority applicants was quite acceptable.[24]

The most heartfelt pleas for affirmative action came individually, from Justices Marshall and Blackmun. "The experience of Negroes in America has been different in kind, not just in degree, from that of other ethnic groups," Marshall declared. "It is not merely the history of slavery alone but also that a whole people were marked as inferior by the law. And that mark has endured. The dream of America as the great melting pot has not been realized for the Negro; because of his skin color he never even made it into the pot."[25] Justice Blackmun was scarcely less moving. "I yield to no one," he confessed, "in my earnest hope that the time will come when an 'affirmative action' program is unnecessary and is, in truth, only a relic of the past. . . . [But] in order to get beyond racism, we must first take account of race. There is no other way."[26] Such sentiments, unfortunately, framed but half the picture. The factional hostilities aroused by admission by the numbers, the stereotypes encouraged, the caprice, insult and treacherousness of sorting by race all appeared to have left little mark. Such dangers were paid lip service,[27] and little more.

Thus *Bakke*'s noted compromise was largely the making of the Court's "ninth man." Between the statutory foursome of Burger, Stevens, Stewart, and Rehnquist, and the permissive foursome of Brennan, White, Marshall, and Blackmun was Justice Powell. "Powell took his position at the outset and never got anyone to go along with him," one Court insider was quoted as saying.[28] Because the swing judgment was Powell's alone, the Court may yet shift from him.

To some, Powell's vote came as a surprise. An irony of *Bakke*, wrote Washington attorney and Civil Rights activist Joseph Rauh, was that "affirmative action was saved by a conservative Southern justice."[29] Yet the result was typical of Powell the diplomat, Powell the balancer, Powell the quiet man of the middle way.[30] Law, he believed, had to serve the cause of social stability. Instinctively he dreaded chaos and upheaval; the 1960s had been a most unnerving decade. Back then he had denounced civil disobedience as "a heresy which could weaken the foundations of our system of government,"[31] part of "the disquieting trend—so evident in our country—toward organized lawlessness and even rebellion."[32] Yet rebellion was never just something to stamp out by fiat and force; the causes of unrest, he recognized, "involve[d] complex and deepseated social and economic problems."[33]

Bakke, too, was a rebellious case, menacing to social peace, the most volatile case of Powell's time on the Court. A compromise would have to be struck. Affirmative action plans were now the status quo; Powell did not wish to upend them. But he distrusted quotas, "those direct and provocative approaches which stir so much envy and distemper in the society."[34] The solution was typically Powellian: a sober opinion with words precise but pale; a narrow result that allowed the employment and sex discrimination cases to continue their own separate channels;[35] and, above all, a compromise that majorities of both races might abide.

Since Powell's was the swing vote in *Bakke*, his opinion was naturally the most scrutinized. What did it mean for the future of affirmative action? Powell certainly disapproved Davis's program not only because it reserved "a fixed number of [minority] places"[36] but because it insulated minorities "from comparison with all other candidates" for the reserved spots.[37] But a program "where race or ethnic background is simply one element—to be weighed fairly against other elements—in the selection process" would meet Powell's approval.[38] What, one wondered, was the difference? The admissions process at Harvard College, which Powell acclaimed as a model because of its "flexible" use of race,[39] produced much the same minority enrollments as those at Davis: 8.1 percent black, 4.6 percent Hispanic, 5.7 percent Asian American, and 0.4 percent American Indian for the freshman class of 1978. Nor was it clear that these percentages varied much from year to year.[40]

Citation of Harvard was an important cue. Simply by hearing *DeFunis* and *Bakke*, the Court had thrown affirmative action into limbo. Powell meant to remove the cloud, dispel the doubt, in short, to legitimate.[41] His tone, in fact, was more permissive than not. It will be "the very rare affirmative action program that is disqualified under the *Bakke* standards," the *New Republic* predicted.[42] Educators guessed that 90 percent of existing admissions programs—all but the crasser varieties—would satisfy Justice Powell.

"It's music to our ears," said John Harding, counsel to Columbia University. "Now we can continue to do what we are already doing."[43]

By approving a plethora of factors in admissions decisions—"exceptional personal talents, unique work or service experience, leadership potential, maturity, demonstrated compassion, a history of overcoming disadvantage, ability to communicate with the poor, or other qualifications"[44]—Powell enthroned the discretion and biases of admissions deans everywhere. "Institutionally and practically," noted Norman Dorsen of the ACLU, "it is the school admissions officers and administrators who will be crucial in determining what the impact of the *Bakke* decision will be."[45] Powell had sanctioned not only taking race into account but a subjective approach to admissions as well. Intellectual aptitude, he implied, need not be the only ticket to academic life. Character, personality, motivation— that cluster of attributes known as the "intangibles"—might count as well. Whether subjective systems would actually produce exceptional people or simply reward the well-connected remained an open question.

Powell's approach and that of the four justices to his left differed markedly. Powell rejected unbounded notions of compensatory justice as a basis for affirmative action plans. That, said he, only created "a privilege that all institutions throughout the Nation could grant at their pleasure to whatever groups are perceived as victims of societal discrimination."[46] What justified the "flexible" use of race and, indeed, subjective admissions generally was educational diversity. Indeed, noted Powell, "it is not too much to say that 'the nation's future depends upon leaders trained through wide exposure' to the ideas and mores of students as diverse as this Nation of many peoples."[47] Diversity, he even felt, was of constitutional origin: the First amendment and its promise of broad traffic in ideas.[48]

Invocation of diversity was Powell's master stroke. It was also his healing gesture. Diversity was the most acceptable public rationale for affirmative action, because it has been, historically, clearly related to a university's function. It was the most traditional justification, because the most analogous to geographical preference. Diversity, to be real, implied more than token minority numbers. But it supposed also that minority students had something genuine to contribute to higher education; they had not been let in simply

to avenge ancestral sins. Diversity, as such, was a narrower rationale than compensatory justice; it applied obviously to education,
not so clearly to employment. And it skirted the sticky questions of
compensatory justice: whom do we compensate, how much, and
for how long. For the need for diversity will continue forever, as
long as race matters to men. But diversity, though color-conscious,
was also color-blind. Working class whites might one day be seen
as capable of bringing more diversity to middle-class havens of
higher education than well-off blacks.[49] All, in fact, can be diverse,
because all are different: the Alaskan or Greek American, the oboist
or naturalist, all, said Powell, who "exhibit qualities more likely to
promote beneficial educational pluralism."[50]

Powell was predictably criticized by both sides for doing nothing
more than chasing "reverse racism" underground. Opponents of special admissions complained that universities "will be able to continue almost all their current efforts to help minorities, especially if
they're willing to engage in a bit of dissembling to satisfy Justice
Powell, the swing vote."[51] Allan Bakke at least knew what was up.
The Harvard model was more subtle than Davis's and thus more
sinister. Applicants—black and white—might distrust all the more
what they could not see. Diversity itself was idiosyncratic, depen-
dent on the eye of the beholding institution. The four justices supporting the Davis program were as reluctant as opponents to embrace covertness as a constitutional goal. "[T]here is no basis for
preferring a particular preference program," they argued, "simply
because . . . it proceeds in a manner that is not immediately apparent to the public."[52]

Yet to call Powell's approach dissembling is not quite fair.[53] The
great pretense would have been to insist upon color blindness but
then allow some proxy characteristic—disadvantage, cultural bias—
to subtly substitute for race in admissions decisions. Powell did not
do that. He said, quite openly, that race *qua* race could be used.
Perhaps charges of dissembling and concealment are the inevitable
cost of any approach that bans prior numerical reliance. If so, it is a
cost to bear. Preset numbers stain any affirmative action plan,
whether they be goals, targets, quotas, guideposts or other labels
Powell might decide to dismiss as "semantic distinction[s]."[54]
Numbers divide; numbers demean; numbers dehumanize by subor-
dinating personhood to race. Numbers recall most vividly historical
villainy and abuse. Numbers create the incentives to divvy up the

admissions pie. The value of Justice Powell's approach depends largely on avoiding prefixed numbers based on ethnicity or race.

That will not be easy. Numbers attract, because they assure minimum minority representation. But *Bakke*, of course, made the numbers game more dangerous to play. After *Bakke*, numerical guideposts are likely to be so subtle, so tacit, so internalized and unwritten as to defy judicial discernment. And the line between prior numerical reliance and the "individualized, case by case" review urged by Justice Powell[55] is so fine as to make future litigation a certainty. Powell himself would give admissions officers the benefit of good faith.[56] But at what point do unvarying percentages of annual minority enrollments create the presumption of a de facto quota? What of numerical objectives much more flexible than that of Davis? What of the admissions officer who feels true educational diversity requires a student body roughly 10 to 15 percent black? Or one who, after surveying low minority enrollment percentages for the past several years, announces openly a need to "improve?" What of an otherwise objective admissions system that, to ensure racial diversity, adds 12 percent to minority test scores? Would courts proscribe such mechanical use of race? Borderline cases are legion. The volume of subsequent litigation might force a closer relationship between courts and university admissions than Justice Powell himself would prefer.

Bakke, for all Justice Powell's distaste for numbers, contained a large loophole that may yet make racial percentages commonplace. Numerical preference for blacks, Justice Powell conceded, might be necessary in the event of "judicial, legislative, or administrative findings of constitutional or statutory violations."[57] Proof of past discrimination against minorities, in other words, might justify remedial quotas; "the legal rights of the victim must be vindicated."[58] Because Davis Medical School began only in 1968, it had little chance to engage in such past practices. But how many institutional histories were as spotless?

This exception, so Powell thought, was necessary to explain those busing and employment precedents in which racial percentages formed part of the remedy.[59] But it threatened to swallow the rule and to reduce *Bakke* to insignificance. A scenario similar to busing might emerge, whereby racial quotas could yet be achieved through ingenious incursions into institutional pasts. What kind of prior discrimination on the part of a university justified preferential

numbers now? De jure segregation in 1954? Past admissions preferences for sons of alumni, wealthy donors, influential legislators
from which whites but not blacks stood to benefit? Past recruitment
efforts at white, but not black schools? Past discrimination in fra-
ternities or extracurriculars? A past absence of black faculty, cur-
ricular neglect of black history and culture, all of which made black
students reluctant to apply? Or any past admissions policy, in violation of federal statute, with a "disparate and unjustified racial impact?"[60] How far into the past must we peer? Who may determine
historical wrongdoing? A university clearly could not. "Its broad
mission," noted Powell, "is education, not the formulation of any
legislative policy or the adjudication of particular claims of illegal-
ity."[61] But a court, a legislature, or a legislatively authorized administrative body[62] could. All this suggested to Davis's supporters
on the Court how the Powell approach might yet be undercut.
Violations necessary to justify numerical minority preferences
might even be collusively rigged.[63]

Answers to such questions will determine how significant a legal
milestone *Bakke* really is. "The very fact that [*Bakke*] is somewhat
fuzzy," noted Professor Freund, "leaves room for development, and
on the whole that's a good thing."[64] Congress and the Department
of Health, Education, and Welfare were virtually invited by the
Court to share in this development, both in defining violations[65]
and shaping affirmative action plans.[66] How much *Bakke* itself
would influence the future remained to be seen. Contemporaries
knew *Brown* to be a landmark case. "But none," noted Professor
Kurland, "could really say in 1954 just how important it was to
be."[67] So it was in 1978. *Bakke*, as *Brown* had been, was only a
beginning. Where, one has to wonder, will it end?

Epilogue

As a boy, I liked to visit courthouses. I would sit against some tree on courthouse greens in rural Virginia, watching and observing by the hour. Exactly why I did this, I don't rightly know. Perhaps, in their slow stir lay the most pleasant somnolent sensations. Sometimes a few sparrows pecked about; the sun-bleached bulletins seemed immune to all sense of urgency or time. On the front lawn stood the statue of the valiant Confederate infantryman or a cannon, long mute. On a nearby bench, a few farmers might spit tobacco or swap pleasantries on the trip to town. The courthouse brought together community life: the judge was there and the county clerk and the treasurer, sheriff, and state's attorney. I was so young— and my sense of things so settled—I scarcely noticed they were always white. Watching, I must have felt a peace of mind and setting many Americans had long forgotten or professed not to care for. Yet the quiet of those courthouse greens was also the quiet of eternal custom, the sum of unspoken racial understandings that life's lots had been irrevocably cast.

Brown disturbed the calm of the courthouse. Along with better roads, television, new political trends, and population growth. And, of course, I was growing older. Those quiet little places no longer seemed the same. But things were changing for the better too. Before *Brown*, there was but one possible verdict on race relations in the South. *Brown*, of course, had not set race relations right. The new order never follows neatly the destruction of the old. But at least now the hopeful case can be plausibly advanced. Before *Brown* there was no hope, only the still courthouse air.

The effort to change the world of the courthouse later spilled over to more dubious initiatives, the two most notable being busing and racial numbers in affirmative action plans. On busing the evidence is not all in, nor is it all on one side. But what there is suggests that only in the most select circumstances can busing be expected to succeed. Both busing and affirmative action goals suffered practical drawbacks. More important, each clashed with legitimate competing ideals: the desire for neighborhood schools and color-blind admissions. Against such opposing values, the drive for racial equality began to stall. The single-mindedness of national purpose gave way to a decade of accommodation and compromise. First the Court in *Milliken* v. *Bradley* served notice that the aspirations of the majority counted constitutionally too. Then, in *Bakke*, that competing moral claims must be brokered and negotiated.

The long voyage from *Brown* to *Bakke* has been one from optimism and confidence to confusion and doubt. School integration has entered a period of seeming contradiction: productive in one setting, disappointing somewhere else. Harmony in one school, tension in another. White flight in one city, stability elsewhere. Black academic progress here, but not there. To generalize nationwide now seems foolish. Rather, one must work to understand the particulars that explain diverse results.

From *Brown* to *Bakke* has been a maturing journey also. Findings in the education cases laid bare the depth of American prejudice and made clear the true dimensions of our difficulties. We now seem to be many sad and wise days away from those happy forecasts of playground bliss. What we better understand is our own lack of understanding. School integration has taught us at home what Vietnam did abroad: how much eludes the American capacity to reshape. That is hardly surprising. Public education represented so many different things to many different people. To some, schools were symbols of democracy, equal opportunity, upward mobility for the dispossessed. To others they were places for promoting intellectual excellence. To still others, places for class compatibility and social exclusion. Many regarded public schools as they did housing, as extensions of advantage and choice in their own private lives. When these conflicting preconceptions of public education combined with the emotions of race, a monstrous problem confronted the courts. Why were quick results ever expected? Was school integration thought somehow to be less complex a problem or one more manageable than others in this vexing age? Was the specter of prejudice, so prominent in our history, one that anyone would have thought capable of vanishing before Supreme Court decree?

Yet white racism is receding, at least in its coarser forms. This is true of public attitudes as well as under the law. Talk of absolute segregation has given way to talk of tolerance levels and tipping points. And each of these changes is progress of a sort. Life for the small but growing black professional class has been greatly enriched. It may even be, as William Julius Wilson thinks, that "class has become more important than race in determining black life-chances."[1] But one should not speak too soon. Race has been too much a part of our past not to be part of our foreseeable future. Solutions that make race immaterial or minorities equal or understanding total are not now in sight. A quarter century after *Brown*, American life has become a bit fairer, black opportunities slightly greater, black contributions somewhat more significant. If talk of racial millennia now seems foolhardy, chances for further gradual improvements in black status seem bright.

Yet the nature of racial progress, at least in education, affords little reason to boast. Those making the decisions on school integration were too often not those whose lives were affected by these decisions. Genuine self-sacrifice has been rare; white magnanimity something of a myth. In the early days after *Brown*, the nation told the South what to do for the Negro. This same eagerness to watch others pay the price of progress continued into the 1970s. Many of the most forceful advocates of forced busing held their own children back. Integration itself often left the suburbs and the affluent relatively untouched. And those who devised generous affirmative action goals were not those who bore their real costs. Nowhere was the nature of racial reform better illustrated than with the courts. Judges could spearhead school integration, because they would not risk re-election. Direct personal accountability and sacrifice could, once again, be escaped.

In the end, however, the school cases sharpen one's sense of the Supreme Court as a pragmatic institution. For only five years during the past quarter century (1968–73), did the Court demand substantial integration. More often it pleaded, mediated, mollified, or even withdrew. In almost all the landmark school cases, white racial sensibilities weighed heavily. In *Brown* and *Swann* they influenced the tone of the Court's opinion; in *Brown II*, *Milliken*, and *Bakke* the actual result.

The decisions involved the extent to which rule by law can alter popular racial beliefs. They ranged from *Plessy* (law cannot change popular attitudes), to *Brown I* (it can and will), to *Brown II* (but it must bear them in mind), to *Green* and *Swann* (but not forever), to *Milliken* (but, after all, law cannot function in the teeth of intense popular dissent). The Court's perambulations on this score are understandable. Its central dilemma is that of an institution protecting minority rights in a nation of majority rule. Its members feel not just their special obligation to protect minorities but the lurking inconsistencies of judicial activism with democratic notions of self-governance. Due to this tension, the Supreme Court's decisions on race and education may never steer any clear course.

These final observations have stressed complexity and confusion, gradualism and pragmatism, contradiction and compromise. Such notes will certainly strike some as indifferent or dour. Yet they are not so intended. The goal of racial justice remains luminous as ever. Better lives for blacks—and, indeed, for all oppressed peoples—remains a grand and worthy end. Yet the clash of moral forces before the Court has shifted since *Brown*. Justice was no longer the monopoly of any outlook or race in the education cases of the 1970s. Progress had to be sought in ways majorities of both races might perceive as fair. The limits as well as the potential of law had to be explored. The old courthouse had come to signify both the real progress of blacks in America and that stubborn sediment in human habit and behavior of which all racial reform, sooner or later, would have to take account.

Notes

Introduction

1. Brown v. Board of Educ., 347 U.S. 483 (1954).
2. Note the per curiam orders following *Brown*, which found segregation unconstitutional in public facilities other than schools, e.g., Mayor of Baltimore v. Dawson, 350 U.S. 877 (1955) (beaches); Gayle v. Browder, 352 U.S. 903 (1956) (buses); Holmes v. City of Atlanta, 350 U.S. 879 (1955) (golf courses); New Orleans City Park Imp. Ass'n. v. Detiege, 358 U.S. 54 (1958) (parks). Segregation in courtrooms and in prisons was subsequently invalidated. Johnson v. Virginia, 373 U.S. 61 (1963); Lee v. Washington, 390 U.S. 333 (1968).
3. See, e.g., the Court's reversal of the convictions of the early sit-in demonstrators, Peterson v. Greenville, 373 U.S. 244 (1963); Lombard v. Louisiana, 373 U.S. 267 (1963); and Bell v. Maryland, 378 U.S. 226 (1964).
4. See Swann v. Charlotte-Mecklenburg Board of Educ., 402 U.S. 1 (1971), a rebuff to President Nixon's southern strategy.
5. Milliken v. Bradley, 418 U.S. 717 (1974), limiting the availability of metropolitan relief for central city school segregation.
6. E.g., Civil Rights Cases, 109 U.S. 3 (1883).
7. E.g., Lochner v. New York, 198 U.S. 45 (1905).
8. E.g., Carter v. Carter Coal Co., 298 U.S. 238 (1936).
9. This time Justice Sutherland spoke in dissent. Home Building and Loan Assoc. v. Blaisdell, 290 U.S. 398, 471, 483 (1934).
10. H. Abraham, *Justices and Presidents* 53–54 (1974).
11. R. Kluger, *Simple Justice* 643 (1976).
12. Oct. 13, 1968, at 56. The author, Lewis M. Steel, was a white lawyer for the NAACP. The article led to his abrupt dismissal from the NAACP legal staff, "which thereupon resigned en masse." A. Paul, ed., *Black Americans and the Supreme Court Since Emancipation, Betrayal or Protection?* 7 (1972).

13. King, "The Time for Freedom has Come," *New York Times Magazine*, Sept. 10, 1961, at 25.
14. Gayle v. Browder, 352 U.S. 903 (1956).
15. A. Lewis, *Portrait of a Decade: The Second American Revolution* 84 (1964).
16. *New York Times*, Aug. 29, 1963.
17. Brown v. Board of Educ., 347 U.S. 483, 494 (1954).
18. Missouri ex rel. Gaines v. Canada, 305 U.S. 337 (1938); Sweatt v. Painter, 339 U.S. 629 (1950); McLaurin v. Oklahoma State Regents, 339 U.S. 637 (1950).
19. Rostow, "The Negro In Our Law," 9 *Utah L. Rev.* 841, 847 (1965).
20. For Theodore Roosevelt, see C. Woodward, *Origins of the New South* 465–67 (1951); for Wilson, R. Baker, *Woodrow Wilson: Life and Letters*, vol. 4, 220–25 (1968); and for Franklin Roosevelt, the telling anecdote in R. Kluger, *supra* n. 11, at 166–67. The Eisenhower and Nixon compromises will be discussed in succeeding chapters.
21. G. Myrdal, *An American Dilemma: The Negro Problem and Modern Democracy* 26 (1944).

Chapter 1

1. Bickel, "The Original Understanding and the Segregation Decision," 69 *Harv. L. Rev.* 1, 64 (1955).
2. See section 2 of the Thirteenth amendment, section 2 of the Fifteenth, and the similarly worded provision in section 5 of the Fourteenth.
3. DeLeon, "The New South: What It is Doing and What It Wants," *Putnam's* magazine, 15 (April 1870) at 458, as quoted in P. Gaston, *The New South Creed* 15 (1970).
4. P. Gaston, *The New South Creed* 3 (1970).
5. See K. Stampp, *The Era of Reconstruction: 1865–1877* 89–108 (1966).
6. *Ibid.* at 105 and 12.
7. Amendment XIII to the United States Constitution (1865).
8. Amendment XV to the United States Constitution (1870); Civil Rights Act of 1870, 16 Stat. L. 140.
9. Civil Rights Act of 1866, 14 Stat. L. 27; Civil Rights Act of 1870, 16 Stat. L. 140.
10. Civil Rights Act of 1870, *supra*; Civil Rights Act of 1871, 17 Stat. L. 13.
11. Civil Rights Act of 1875, 18 Stat. L. 335.
12. Amendment XIV to the United States Constitution (1868). A summary of the Civil Rights Acts and the judicial counter assault may be found in Gressman, "The Unhappy History of Civil Rights Legislation," 50 *Mich. L. Rev.* 1323 (1952).
13. Strauder v. West Virginia, 100 U.S. 303 (1879). Examples of favorable decisions not involving juries include, Railroad Company v. Brown, 84 U.S. 445 (1873); Ex parte Yarbrough, 110 U.S. 651 (1883); United States v. Waddell, 112 U.S. 76 (1884).
14. Virginia v. Rives, 100 U.S. 313 (1879). A fuller treatment of the obstacles posed by the jury cases to black defendants may be found in L. Miller, *The Petitioners: The Story of the Supreme Court of the United States and the Negro* 118–35 (1966).
15. Note the use of the jury cases, especially Strauder v. West Virginia, *supra*, in footnote 5 of the *Brown* opinion.
16. 100 U.S. at 306.
17. 16 Wall. 36, 71 (1873).
18. Brown v. Board of Educ., 347 U.S. 483, 490 n.5 (1954). See also Black, "The Unfinished Business of the Warren Court," 46 *Wash. L. Rev.* 3, 25 (1970); idem, "The Lawfulness of the Segregation Decisions," 69 *Yale L. J.* 421, 421–22 (1960).
19. E.g., Weber v. Aetna Casualty & Surety Co., 406 U.S. 164, 178 (1972) (Rehnquist, J., dissenting); Sugarman v. Dougall, 413 U.S. 634, 649–50 (1973) (Rehnquist, J., dissenting).
20. The Court, said Field, had made of the clause "a vain and idle enactment, which ac-

complished nothing, and most unnecessarily excited Congress and the people on its passage." 16 Wall. 36, 96 (1873).

21. Ibid. at 79–80. See also Gressman, *supra* n.12, at 1338.

22. See Kurland, "The Privileges or Immunities Clause: 'Its Hour Come Round at Last'?" 1972 *Wash. U. L.Q.* 405.

23. E.g., United States v. Cruikshank, 92 U.S. 542 (1875), where a Negro's right to assemble was held not to be a privilege or immunity of national citizenship, if the assembly did not grow out of the Negro's relationship to the federal government.

24. 109 U.S. 3 (1883).

25. C. Woodward, *Origins of the New South* 57 (1951).

26. Ibid.

27. Charleston *News and Courier*, May 12, 1877, as quoted in G. Tindall, *South Carolina Negroes, 1877–1900* 237 (1952).

28. Edgefield *Advertiser*, June 2, 1876, as quoted in G. Tindall, *supra* n.27, at 237.

29. See notes 8 and 10 *supra*.

30. United States v. Cruikshank, 92 U.S. 542 (1875); United States v. Harris, 106 U.S. 629 (1882). *Cruikshank* concerned section 6 of the Civil Rights Act of 1870, while *Harris* involved a criminal provision of the Civil Rights Act of 1875 prohibiting conspiracies to deprive any person "of the equal protection of the laws or of equal privileges or immunities under the laws."

31. L. Miller, *supra* n.14, at 136.

32. Civil Rights Cases, 109 U.S. 3 (1883).

33. The Court likewise rejected an argument under the Thirteenth amendment that discrimination by private persons amounted to an incident of slavery.

34. Strauder v. West Virginia, 100 U.S. 303, 306 (1879).

35. Slaughterhouse Cases, 16 Wall. 36 (1873).

36. 109 U.S. at 25.

37. See G. White, *The American Judicial Tradition* 129 (1976).

38. M. Harlan, *Some Memories of a Long Life, 1854–1911* 100–102 (1915), as quoted in Westin, "John Marshall Harlan and the Constitutional Rights of Negroes: The Transformation of a Southerner," 66 *Yale L.J.* 637, 678 (1957).

39. The Court began in the 1940s to adopt a broader concept of state action. Smith v. Allwright, 321 U.S. 649 (1944); Marsh v. Alabama, 326 U.S. 501 (1946); Shelley v. Kraemer, 334 U.S. 1 (1948).

40. Garner v. Louisiana, 368 U.S. 157, 183–85 (1961) (Douglas, J., concurring); Lombard v. Louisiana, 373 U.S. 267, 281–83 (1963) (Douglas, J., concurring). Although the Civil Rights Cases involved an act of Congress, Harlan's comments on the public nature and function of the facilities suggests that he might find, as did Douglas, that section 1 of the Fourteenth amendment alone proscribed discrimination.

41. 109 U.S. at 61–62.

42. 163 U.S. 537 (1896).

43. Westin, *supra* n.38, at 675–76.

44. C. Woodward, *supra* n. 25, at 212.

45. T. Dixon, *The Leopard's Spots* 244 (1902).

46. A. Barth, *Prophets with Honor* 26–27 (1975).

47. 163 U.S. at 559.

48. R. Harris, *The Quest for Equality* 98 (1960). See also Oberst, "The Strange Career of *Plessy* v. *Ferguson*," 15 *Ariz. L. Rev.* 389, 408 (1973).

49. 163 U.S. at 550.

50. Ibid. at 551.

51. Ibid.

52. The quotation was that of Senator James O. Eastland of Mississippi in response to the

Brown decision. Green, "The Children of the South: School Desegregation and its Significance," 4 *Law and Educ.* 18 (1975).

53. See e.g., *The Southern Manifesto*, signed by 19 southern Senators and 82 Congressmen as an expression of opposition to the *Brown* decision. U.S. *Congressional Record*, 84th Congress, 2nd Session, March 12, 1956, at 4460.

54. See Williams v. Mississippi, 170 U.S. 213 (1898); Cumming v. Richmond County Bd. of Educ., 175 U.S. 528 (1899).

55. See generally Tucker, "Reflections on Virginia's Reaction to *Brown*," 4 *J. Law and Educ.* 36 (1975).

56. A. Kirwan, *Revolt of the Rednecks: Mississippi Politics, 1876–1925* 162 (1951). The words used in the text are those of Mr. Kirwan, paraphrasing Mr. Vardaman.

57. G. Myrdal, *An American Dilemma* 339 (1944).

58. See R. Kluger, *Simple Justice* 345 (1976).

59. Brief for Plaintiff in Error, p. 8, Plessy v. Ferguson, 163 U.S. 537 (1896), as quoted in Fairman, "Foreword: The Attack on the Segregation Cases," 70 *Harv. L. Rev.* 83, 88 (1956).

60. C. Warren, *The Supreme Court in United States History*, vol. 3, 330 (1922).

61. A complete account is C. Woodward, *Reunion and Reaction* (1951).

62. White, "The Supreme Court's Public and the Public's Supreme Court," 52 *Va. Q. Rev.* 370, 371 (1976).

63. *Nation*, 24, April 5, 1877, at 202, as quoted in C. Woodward, *supra* n.61, at 214.

64. New York *Tribune*, April 7, 1877, as quoted in C. Woodward, *supra* n.61, at 214.

65. Civil Rights Cases, 109 U.S. 3, 25 (1883).

66. P. Magrath, *Morrison R. Waite: The Triumph of Character* 149 (1963).

67. E.g., Yick Wo v. Hopkins, 118 U.S. 356 (1886).

68. C. Woodward, *The Strange Career of Jim Crow* 71–72 (1974).

69. Ibid. at 33–35. Note, however, that this view has been criticized as overly optimistic. E.g., Potter, "C. Vann Woodward," in M. Cunliffe and R. Winks, eds., *Pastmasters* 395–405 (1969).

70. C. Woodward, *supra* n. 68, at 69–71.

71. United States v. Cruikshank, 92 U.S. 542 (1875); United States v. Harris, 106 U.S. 629 (1882).

72. Strauder v. West Virginia, 100 U.S. 303 (1879).

73. See especially Lochner v. New York, 198 U.S. 45 (1905); Coppage v. Kansas, 236 U.S. 1 (1915). For related discussions under the due process clause of the Fifth amendment, see Adair v. United States, 208 U.S. 161 (1908); Adkins v. Children's Hospital, 261 U.S. 525 (1923).

74. Slaughterhouse Cases, 16 Wall. 36 (1873).

75. On some idle law problems of the Warren Court see A. Bickel, *The Supreme Court and the Idea of Progress* 91–95 (1970).

76. The turnaround case is thought to be Missouri ex rel. Gaines v. Canada, 305 U.S. 337 (1938). See also Sipuel v. Oklahoma, 332 U.S. 631 (1948); Sweatt v. Painter, 339 U.S. 629 (1950); McLaurin v. Oklahoma State Regents, 339 U.S. 637 (1950). (McLaurin was seeking a doctorate in education, not a law degree.)

77. Serious review of the white primary began with Nixon v. Herndon, 273 U.S. 536 (1927). See also Nixon v. Condon, 286 U.S. 73 (1932); United States v. Classic, 313 U.S. 299 (1941); Smith v. Allright, 321 U.S. 649 (1944); Terry v. Adams, 345 U.S. 461 (1953). But cf. Grovey v. Townsend, 295 U.S. 45 (1935).

78. Shelley v. Kraemer, 334 U.S. 1 (1948).

79. 347 U.S. at 490 n.5.

80. E. Warren, *The Memoirs of Earl Warren* 291 (1977). This assessment of Eisenhower is not Warren's alone. See A. Bickel, *The Least Dangerous Branch* 265–66 (1962).

81. A. Bickel, *supra* n.75, at 6.

82. Memorandum on *Brown* of Justice Robert H. Jackson, February 15, 1954, as quoted in R. Kluger, *supra* n.58, at 689.

83. See especially Sweatt v. Painter, 339 U.S. 629 (1950); McLaurin v. Oklahoma State Regents, 339 U.S. 637 (1950).

84. Belton v. Gebhart, 87 A.2d 862 (1952); *affirmed* by Del. Supreme Ct. 91 A.2d 137 (1952).

85. R. Kluger, *supra* n.58, at 520, 522–24, 535–36.

86. Brown v. Board of Educ., 349 U.S. 294, 301 (1955).

Chapter 2

1. *Time*, Dec. 21, 1953, at 18 as quoted in W. Harbaugh, *Lawyer's Lawyer: The Life of John W. Davis* 514 (1973).

2. L. Friedman, ed., *Argument: The Oral Argument before the Supreme Court in Brown v. Board of Education of Topeka, 1952–55* 215–16 (1969).

3. W. Harbaugh, *supra* n. 1, at 518.

4. This story is poignantly told in R. Kluger, *Simple Justice* (1976).

5. Chief Justice Warren was puzzled that black lawyers, speaking from a background of oppression, made the more legalistic, less emotional argument. E. Warren, *The Memoirs of Earl Warren* 287 (1977).

6. See Barnes, "Study Cites Loss of 30,000 Black School Jobs," Washington *Post*, May 19, 1972; Watson, "School Integration: Its Meaning, Costs, and Future," 4 *J. of Law and Educ.* 15 (1975).

7. Browne, "The Case for Two Americas—One Black, One White," *New York Times Magazine*, Aug. 11, 1968, at 13.

8. See McLaurin v. Oklahoma State Regents, 339 U.S. 637 (1950). For an account of the resistance to James Meredith's entry into the University of Mississippi see J. Silver, *Mississippi: The Closed Society* (1964).

9. Carter, "The Warren Court and Desegregation," 67 *Mich. L. Rev.* 237, 247 (1968).

10. 384 U.S. 436 (1966).

11. 377 U.S. 533 (1964).

12. "To separate them [Negroes] from others of similar age and qualifications solely because of their race generates a feeling of inferiority as to their status in the community that may affect their hearts and minds in a way unlikely ever to be undone." 347 U.S. at 494.

13. R. Kluger, *supra* n.4, at 686. But the memorandum in which Frankfurter expressed these views suggested a more extensive opinion than Warren eventually wrote.

14. Cahn, "Jurisprudence," 30 *N.Y.U.L. Rev.* 150, 152 (1955).

15. G. Dunne, *Hugo Black and the Judicial Revolution* 27 (1977). See also D. Meador, *Mr. Justice Black and his Books* 14 (1974).

16. J. Simon, *In his own Image: The Supreme Court in Richard Nixon's America* 55–56 (1973).

17. As quoted in H. Abraham, *Freedom and the Court* 372 n.90 (3rd ed., 1977).

18. E.g., Chambers v. Florida, 309 U.S. 227 (1940).

19. Kluger was describing the Court in December of 1952, under Chief Justice Fred Vinson. When Warren replaced Vinson, in 1953, the Court's other personnel remained unchanged. R. Kluger, *supra* n. 4, at 585.

20. Bickel, "The Original Understanding and the Segregation Decision," 69 *Harv. L. Rev.* 1, 2 (1955).

21. See generally I. Newby, *Challenge to the Court: Social Scientists and the Defense of Segregation 1954–1966* (1969).

22. K. B. Clark, Effect of Prejudice and Discrimination on Personality Development (Mid-century White House Conference on Children and Youth, 1950).

23. I am oversimplifying here the tests and procedures Professor Clark utilized in preparation for Briggs v. Elliott, 98 F. Supp. 529 (E.D.S.C. 1951), the school segregation case from Clarendon County, South Carolina. A fuller explanation may be found in Cahn, "Jurisprudence," 30 *N.Y.U.L. Rev.* 150, 161–63 (1955).

24. See Cahn, *supra* n. 14, at 163–64.

25. Van den Haag, "Social Science Testimony in the Desegregation Cases—A Reply to Professor Kenneth Clark," 6 *Vill. L. Rev.* 69 (1960). The article replied to is Clark, "The Desegregation Cases: Criticism of the Social Scientist's Role" 5 *Vill. L. Rev.* 224 (1960).

26. Cahn, *supra* n. 14, at 159–61. See also Cahn, "Jurisprudence," 31 *N.Y.U.L. Rev.* 182 (1956).

27. Brown, "Supreme Court Cannot Bestow White Man's Inheritance on Another Race," 17 *Ala. Lawyer* 438, 441 (1956).

28. As quoted in Byrnes, "The Supreme Court must be Curbed," *U.S. News & World Report*, May 18, 1956, at 53.

29. Ibid. at 53–54.

30. Cook and Potter, "The School Segregation Cases: Opposing the Opinion of the Supreme Court," 42, *A.B.A.J.* 313, 316 (1956).

31. Rushton, "Why Southerners Think As They Do," 17 *Ala. Lawyer* 339, 342 (1956).

32. Wechsler, "Toward Neutral Principles of Constitutional Law," 73 *Harv. L. Rev.* 1, 34 (1959).

33. Ibid. at 31–34.

34. For an article conceding serious deficiencies in *Brown* and attempting a substitute, see Pollak, "Racial Discrimination and Judicial Integrity: A Reply to Professor Wechsler," 108 *U. Pa. L. Rev.* 1, 24–34 (1959). Articles questioning the need for neutral principles at all are Mueller and Schwartz, "The Principle of Neutral Principles," 7 *UCLA L. Rev.* 571 (1960); Miller and Howell, "The Myth of Neutrality in Constitutional Adjudication," 27 *U. Chi. L. Rev.* 661 (1960).

35. 347 U.S. at 493–95.

36. Beiser, "Review of *Simple Justice*, R. Kluger," 89 *Harv. L. Rev.* 1945, 1950–51 (1976).

37. Bender, "The Techniques of Subtle Erosion," *Harper's* magazine, Dec. 1972, at 26.

38. Ibid.

39. Black, "The Lawfulness of the Segregation Decisions," 69 *Yale L.J.* 421, 424 (1960).

40. W. Workman, *The Case for the South* 165 (1960).

41. Ibid.

42. Ervin, "The Case for Segregation," *Look* magazine, April 3, 1956, at 32.

43. See generally J. Silver, *Mississippi: The Closed Society* (1964).

44. Cahn, *supra* n. 14, at 158.

45. G. Myrdal, *An American Dilemma* 38 (1944).

46. Hamilton v. Alabama, 376 U.S. 650 (1964).

47. Black, *supra* n. 39, at 426.

48. Henkin, "Some Reflections on Current Constitutional Controversy," 109 *U. Pa. L. Rev.* 637, 655 (1961).

49. See, e.g., Hart, "The Supreme Court 1958 Term, Foreword: The Time Chart of the Justices," 73 *Harv. L. Rev.* 84, 99 (1959).

50. The phrase is Professor Bickel's. *supra* n. 20, at 2.

51. Roe, "Review of *Simple Justice*, R. Kluger," 64 *Cal. L. Rev.* 1291, 1297 (1976).

52. V. Lasky, *It Didn't Start with Watergate* (1977).

Chapter 3

1. Plessy v. Ferguson, 163 U.S. 537 (1896).

2. 347 U.S. 483, 493 (1954).

3. McCullom v. Bd. of Educ., 333 U.S. 203, 231 (1948) (concurring opinion).

4. Ashmore, "The Desegregation Decision: Ten Years After," *Saturday Review*, May 16, 1964, at 90.

5. L. Friedman, ed., *Argument: The Oral Argument Before The Supreme Court in Brown v. Board of Education of Topeka, 1952–55* 239 (1969).

6. Phillips, "What Happens When Segregation Ends," *New York Times Magazine*, May 30, 1954, at 7.

7. Anderson, "The South Learns Its Hardest Lessons," *New York Times Magazine*, Sept. 11, 1960, at 27.

8. A. Bickel, *The Supreme Court and the Idea of Progress* 121 (1970).

9. As quoted in Kamisar, "The School Desegregation Cases in Retrospect," in L. Friedman, ed., *supra* n. 5, at xxii.

10. R. Kluger, *Simple Justice* 714 (1976).

11. G. Myrdal, *An American Dilemma* 103 (1944).

12. Rushton, "Why Southerners Think As They Do," 17 *Ala. Lawyer* 339, 343 (1956).

13. McDonald, "The Song Has Ended But the Melody Lingers On," 4 *J. Law & Educ.* 29, 30 (1975). See also Caldwell v. Craighead, 432 F.2d 213 (CA6 1970); Melton v. Young, 465 F.2d 1332 (CA6 1972).

14. Cox, "Desegregation," Richmond *Times-Dispatch*, July 9, 1978.

15. See Havighurst, Smith, and Wilder, "A Profile of the Large-City High School," *National Association of Secondary School Principals Bulletin*, Jan. 1971, at 76.

16. See Southern Regional Council and the Robert F. Kennedy Memorial, *The Student Pushout: Victim of Continued Resistance to Desegregation* 6 (1974); Wilkinson, "*Goss* v. *Lopez*: The Supreme Court As School Superintendent," 1975 *Sup. Ct. Rev.* 25, 31–32; Yudof, "Suspension and Expulsion of Black Students from the Public Schools: Academic Capital Punishment and the Constitution," 39 *Law and Contemp. Prob.* 374, 378–79, 383 (1975).

17. Nemy, "Violence in Schools Now Seen as Norm Across the Nation," *New York Times*, June 14, 1975; Barnes, "Violence Soars in U.S. Schools," *Washington Post*, April 10, 1975; U.S. Congress, Senate, Judiciary Committee, Subcomm. to Investigate Juvenile Delinquency, *Our Nation's Schools—A Report Card: 'A' in School Violence and Vandalism*, 94th Cong., 1st sess., 29 (1975).

18. See, e.g., Sinclair, "Desegregation's Quiet Success," *Washington Post*, June 17, 1978. The article describes schools in Tampa, Florida.

19. W. Morris, *Yazoo: Integration in a Deep Southern Town* 27 (1971).

20. Jencks, "Busing—The Supreme Court Goes North," *New York Times Magazine*, Nov. 19, 1972, at 120.

21. "College enrollments tripled for blacks in the last 15 years, a harbinger of economic progress. . . . In 1976, among young people, 18 to 24, 23 percent of all blacks were enrolled in colleges and universities, compared with 27 percent of all whites, though black students were enrolled more often in vocational-technical programs." Greider, "After Dr. King: Strong Currents of Social Change," *Washington Post*, April 2, 1978.

22. A review of the conflicting evidence on this question may be found in Weinberg, "The Relationship between School Desegregation and Academic Achievement: A Review of the Research," 39 *Law and Contemp. Prob.* 241, 268–70 (1975).

23. Jencks, "Private Schools for Black Children," *New York Times Magazine*, Nov. 3, 1968, at 30.

24. See C. Jencks, *Inequality* (1972).

25. Jencks, *supra* n.20, at 132.

26. Feinberg, "Florida Tests Literacy: 37% of Juniors Fail," *Washngton Post*, April 2, 1978.

27. Ibid.

28. See C. Woodward, *The Strange Career of Jim Crow* 219 (1974).

29. Keyes v. Denver School District, 413 U.S. 189, 218 (1973) (Powell, J., concurring in part and dissenting in part).

30. Bell, "Waiting on the Promise of Brown," 39 *Law and Contemp. Prob.* 341, 345–46 (1975).

31. Bell, "Foreword," 3 *Black Law Journal* 105 (1973).

32. As quoted in Bell, *supra* n.30, at 357 n. 74.

33. 347 U.S. at 493.

34. Weinberger, "Some Thoughts on the Twentieth Anniversary of *Brown* v. *Board of Education,*" 4 *J. Law and Educ.* 33 (1975).

35. Clark, "The Social Scientists, The Brown Decision, and Contemporary Confusion," in L. Friedman, ed., *supra* n.5, at xxxi, xlvi (1969).

36. B. Rustin, *Down the Line* 154 (1971).

37. Pointing to black separatists, white segregationists were able to claim integration unpopular with both races.

38. W. Grier and P. Cobbs, *Black Rage* 212 (1968). See also S. Carmichael and C. Hamilton, *Black Power: The Politics of Liberation in America* (1967).

39. See generally, Hamilton, "The Nationalist vs. The Integrationist," *New York Times Magazine,* Oct. 1, 1972, at 36.

40. Browne, "The Case for Two Americas—One Black, One White," *New York Times Magazine,* Aug. 11, 1968, at 50.

41. Ibid. at 51.

42. Bell, *supra* n.30, at 357–58, 373.

43. Gellhorn, "A Decade of Desegregation—Retrospect and Prospect," 9 *Utah L. Rev.* 3, 7 (1964).

44. Mayor of Baltimore v. Dawson, 350 U.S. 877 (1955) (beaches); Gayle v. Browder, 352 U.S. 903 (1956) (buses); Holmes v. City of Atlanta, 350 U.S. 879 (1955) (golf courses); New Orleans. City Park Imp. Ass'n v. Detiege, 358 U.S. 54 (1958) (parks); Johnson v. Virginia, 373 U.S. 61 (1963) (courtrooms); Lee v. Washington, 390 U.S. 333 (1968) (prisons).

45. The two enactments are the Civil Rights Act of 1964, 78 Stat. 241 (1964) and the Voting Rights Act of 1965, 79 Stat. 437 (1965). A general overview of the struggle for Negro suffrage before the Voting Rights Act of 1965 is P. Lewinson, *Race, Class, and Party: A History of Negro Suffrage and White Politics in the South* (1963).

46. Maynard, "The *Brown* Decision: 20 Years Later," Washington *Post,* May 12, 1974.

47. That Kansas was involved and was, in fact, the lead case was for many Kansans a matter of no little embarrassment. See Wilson, "*Brown* v. *Board of Education* Revisited," 12 *Kan. L. Rev.* 507, 508 (1964).

48. 347 U.S. 497 (1954).

49. Swann v. Charlotte-Mecklenburg Bd. of Educ., 402 U.S. 1, 6 (1971).

50. C. Rowan, *Go South to Sorrow* 15 (1957).

51. Popham, "The Southern Negro: Change and Paradox," *New York Times Magazine,* Dec. 1, 1957, at 133. Mr. Popham was the *Times's* southern correspondent.

52. As quoted in J. Martin, *The Deep South Says Never* 22–23 (1957). See generally N. McMillen, *The Citizens' Council, Organized Resistance to the Second Reconstruction, 1954–1964* (1971).

53. As quoted in C. Rowan, *supra* n.50, at 7. Mr. Rowan, a native southerner, was working at the time for the Minneapolis *Tribune.*

54. J. Kilpatrick, *The Southern Case for School Segregation* (1962); W. Workman, *The Case for The South* (1960).

55. Woodward, "What Happened to the Civil Rights Movement?" *Harper's* magazine, Jan. 1967, at 29. Professor Woodward, it must be added, did not succumb to the notion of a historical replay. Indeed, he found that "the differences [between the First and Second Reconstructions] are more impressive than the similarities." Ibid. at 30.

56. See Sutherland, "The American Judiciary and Racial Desegregation," 20 *Mod. L. Rev.* 201, 208 (1957).

57. Fleming, "Brown and the Three R's: Race, Residence, and Resegregation," 4 *J. Law and Educ.* 8 (1975).

58. Six Pulitzer prizes in the decade after *Brown* went to southern editors who advanced unpopular views about race and education. The recipients were Buford Boone of the Tuscaloosa *News* (Ala.) (1957); Harry Ashmore of the Arkansas *Gazette* (1958); Ralph McGill of the Atlanta *Constitution* (1959); Lenoir Chambers of the Norfolk *Virginian-Pilot* (1960); Ira Harkey of the Pascagoula *Chronicle* (Miss.) (1963); Mrs. Hazel Brannon Smith of the Lexington *Advertiser* (Miss.) (1964). See generally R. Sarratt, *The Ordeal of Desegregation* 247–63 (1966).

59. A. Bickel, *The Least Dangerous Branch* 267 (1962).

60. W. Cash, *The Mind of the South* vii (1941).

61. H. Zinn, *The Southern Mystique* 6 (1964).

62. W. Faulkner, *Light in August* (1932).

63. J. Dollard, *Caste and Class in a Southern Town* (1937).

64. G. Myrdal, *An American Dilemma: The Negro Problem and Modern Democracy* (1944).

65. See Black, "The Lawfulness of the Segregation Decisions," 69 *Yale L. J.* 421, 424 (1960).

66. V. Key, *Southern Politics* 675 (1949).

67. C. Woodward, "The Search for Southern Identity," 34 *Va. Q. Rev.* 321, 324–25 (1958).

68. See, e.g., Swann v. Charlotte-Mecklenburg Bd. of Educ., 402 U.S. 1 (1971).

69. Dykeman and Stokely, " 'The South' and the North," *New York Times Magazine*, April 17, 1960, at 8.

70. Powledge, " 'Mason Dixon Line' in Queens," *New York Times Magazine*, May 10, 1964, at 12.

71. Lewis, "Since the Supreme Court Spoke," *New York Times Magazine*, May 10, 1964, at 93.

72. Pollak, "Ten Years after the Decision," 24 *Fed. Bar J.* 123, 129 (1964).

73. The Negro population of New York city, for example, increased two-and one-half times between 1940 and 1960. See generally, J. Franklin, *From Slavery to Freedom* 636, 640 (1967).

74. K. and A. Taeuber, *Negroes in Cities* 14 (1965). The urban migration was to southern cities also.

75. Ibid. at 11–14.

76. Coles, "When the Southern Negro Moves North," *New York Times Magazine*, Sept. 17, 1967, at 26.

77. See N. Peirce, *The Border South States* 126 (1975). North Carolina was one of the foremost southern contributors to the urban north. Peirce notes that "there are 126,000 North Carolina-born blacks in New York, 57,000 in New Jersey, 46,000 in Pennsylvania, and 47,000 in Washington, D.C.—a full 6 percent of the capital city's population." Ibid.

78. The two quotations are from Coles, *supra* n.76, at 98 and 27.

79. Fishman, "Bridging the Prejudice Gap," *New York Times Magazine*, Oct. 23, 1966, at 114.

80. Dykeman and Stokely, *supra* n.69, at 8.

81. A demographic study of the South at mid-century is J. Maclachlan and J. Floyd, *This Changing South* (1956).

82. See generally the description in W. Morris, *North Toward Home* (1967).

83. G. Myrdal, *An American Dilemma* 652 (1944), suggesting that the Negro servant possessed an intimate knowledge of the white's private world, but not vice versa.

84. Dykeman and Stokely, *supra* n.69, at 84.

85. See D. McKay, *Housing and Race in Industrial Society* 45 (1977).

86. Ibid. at 50–57.

87. M. Danielson, *The Politics of Exclusion* 84 (1976).
88. Coles, *supra* n.76, at 27.
89. M. Harrington, *The Other America* 3 (1962).
90. Black, "The Unfinished Business of the Warren Court," 46 *Wash. L. Rev.* 3, 21 (1970).
91. W. Morris, *supra* n.19, at 167–68.

Chapter 4

1. See, e.g., Rogers v. Paul, 382 U.S. 198 (1965); Bradley v. School Board, 382 U.S. 103 (1965); Calhoun v. Latimer, 377 U.S. 263 (1964); Griffin v. Prince Edward County School Board, 377 U.S. 218 (1964); Goss v. Knoxville Bd. of Educ., 373 U.S. 683 (1963); McNeese v. Board of Educ., 373 U.S. 668 (1963); Bush v. Orleans Parish School Bd., 364 U.S. 500 (1960); Cooper v. Aaron, 358 U.S. 1 (1958); Florida ex rel. Hawkins v. Board of Control, 350 U.S. 413 (1956).
2. 347 U.S. at 495–96.
3. L. Friedman, ed., *Argument: The Oral Argument before the Supreme Court in Brown v. Board of Education of Topeka, 1952–55* 409 (1969).
4. Ibid. at 432.
5. Ibid., at 428.
6. Brown v. Board of Educ., 349 U.S. 294 (1955).
7. Ibid. at 301.
8. Ibid. at 300–301.
9. Take, for example, a southern county with two elementary schools. Half the elementary students in the county might attend school A, the other half school B. If school A (the formerly all-white school) were bigger and better than school B (the formerly all-black one), then two-thirds of the children might go to A, just so long as neighborhood and not race was the basis of attendance. Or the schools might be paired, with school A serving grades one through three, B grades four through six. In fact, the sudden presence of white students in formerly all-black B might be just the incentive needed by the school board for capital improvements.
10. Green v. County School Bd., 391 U.S. 430, 442 n.6 (1968).
11. See, e.g., Cleveland Bd. of Educ. v. LaFleur, 414 U.S. 632, 646–47 (1974); Frontiero v. Richardson, 411 U.S. 677, 690–91 (1973); Reed v. Reed, 404 U.S. 71, 76 (1971). But see Mathews v. Lucas, 427 U.S. 495, 509–10 (1976).
12. 349 U.S. at 300.
13. *Southern School News,* June 8, 1955, at 8.
14. Ibid.
15. 349 U.S. at 298, 299, 300.
16. R. Sarratt, *The Ordeal of Desegregation* 200 (1966).
17. 349 U.S. at 300.
18. B. Muse, *Ten Years of Prelude* 228 (1964).
19. Note, "The Courts, HEW, and Southern School Desegregation," 77 *Yale L.J.* 321, 322 (1967).
20. Watson v. City of Memphis, 373 U.S. 526, 530 (1963) (segregation in municipal recreation facilities).
21. Griffin v. County School Bd., 377 U.S.218, 229 (1964).
22. Black, "The Unfinished Business of the Warren Court," 46 *Wash. L. Rev.* 3, 22 (1970).
23. Carter, "The Warren Court and Desegregation," 67 *Mich. L. Rev.* 237, 246 (1968).
24. L. Miller, *The Petitioners* 351, 356 (1966).
25. Black, *supra* n.22, at 22.

26. That course actually was considered by the Court in *Brown II*. See R. Kluger, *Simple Justice* 738–39 (1976).

27. See Northcross v. Memphis Bd. of Educ., 397 U.S. 323 (1970); Carter v. West Feliciana Parish School Bd., 396 U.S. 290 (1970); Alexander v. Holmes County Bd. of Educ., 396 U.S. 19 (1969); Green v. County School Bd., 391 U.S. 430 (1968).

28. Black, *supra* n.22, at 22.

29. Ibid.

30. Clark, "The Social Scientists, the Brown Decision, and Contemporary Confusion," in L. Friedman, ed., *supra* n.3, at xxxi, xxxiii.

31. See A. Paul, ed., *Black Americans and the Supreme Court since Emancipation* 7 (1972).

32. Steel, "Nine Men in Black Who Think White," *New York Times Magazine*, Oct. 13, 1968, at 112–15.

33. R. Warren, *Segregation* 65 (1956).

34. A. Bickel, *The Least Dangerous Branch* 248 (1962).

35. *Look* magazine, April 3, 1956, at 24.

36. B. Muse, *supra* n.18, at 31, 33.

37. U.S. Dep't of Commerce, Bureau of the Census, *Historical Statistics of the United States* 24–37 (1975) (1950 figures).

38. The regions of heaviest black population were usually, though not always, on the banks of the Mississippi River or along the Atlantic coast. The black belts of Alabama and Georgia are exceptions and run through the middle of those states.

39. J. Wilkinson, *Harry Byrd and the Changing Face of Virginia Politics, 1945–1966* 9–22 (1968).

40. McCauley, "Be It Enacted," in D. Shoemaker, ed., *With All Deliberate Speed*, 130, 134 (1957). The author also notes that the black belts send the same representatives to the legislatures over greater numbers of years than do other sections. This gives the black belts added influence in terms of prestige, committee and leadership appointments, and greater parliamentary experience. To some extent the same may be true of rural constituencies generally and not only black belts. Ibid. at 135.

41. McCauley found, however, that "Virginia, North Carolina, and South Carolina Black Belts are not greatly over-represented in their lower chambers." Ibid. at 135.

42. "The impressive—and unfortunate—political victory of the large slaveholders came in their success, despite their small numbers, in carrying their state for [civil] war." V. Key, *Southern Politics* 6 (1949).

43. Ibid., at 5.

44. See generally P. Lewinson, *Race, Class and Party* 79–97 (1963).

45. Attwood, "Fear Underlies the Conflict," *Look* magazine, April 3, 1956, at 26.

46. Richmond *Times-Dispatch*, Sept. 5, 1956.

47. See A. Heard, *A Two-Party South?* 215 (1952).

48. N. Bartley, *The Rise of Massive Resistance* 142–43 (1969).

49. Ashmore, "The Southern Style," *Saturday Review*, May 23, 1959, at 16, 46.

50. S. Lubell, *Revolt of the Moderates* 197 (1956), *as quoted in* N. Bartley, *supra* n.48, at 190.

51. Richmond *Times-Dispatch*, July 28, 1956.

52. *Reporter*, Jan. 24, 1957, *as quoted in* B. Muse, *supra* n.18, at 83. In this particular instance, Negroes were successful in organizing a counter-boycott.

53. J. Peltason, *Fifty-Eight Lonely Men* 60 (1961).

54. N. Bartley, *supra* n.48, at 192.

55. Ibid. at 193.

56. H. Carter, *The South Strikes Back* 18 (1959).

57. B. Muse, *supra* n.18, at 171.

58. Ibid. at 161. Hodding Carter was the editor of the Greenville, Mississippi *Delta Democrat-Times*, a winner of the Pulitzer prize, and one of the few balanced observers of the

deep southern scene in the years after *Brown*. He had been branded a liar by a lopsided vote in the Mississippi House of Representatives for an unflattering article on the Citizen's Council movement in the state. His observations in 1959 captured well the difficulties in the Deep South:

> Certainly in much of the South today it is far more difficult and much less fruitful for whites and Negroes to meet openly than it was five years ago. The only common denominator of most white and Negro leaders today is mistrust. . . . Any clergyman, any editor, any professor in a state-supported institution who gets out of step—and a considerable number nevertheless do—can testify to the social and political and economic pressures that follow. . . . Anti-Semitism, in a region where its expression has historically been slight, is being fanned through the identification of Jewish organizations and individuals with the Negroes' drive for civil rights.

Carter, "Problem and Prospect," *Saturday Review*, May 23, 1959, at 14.
59. Ashmore, *supra* n.49, at 16.
60. Ibid. at 46.
61. Rowan, "The Travesty of Integration," *Saturday Evening Post*, Jan. 19, 1963, at 6.
62. C. Woodward, *The Strange Career of Jim Crow* 139 (2nd ed., 1966).
63. N. Bartley, *supra* n.48, at 62.
64. For the possible varying interpretations of the Government's brief, see R. Kluger, *supra* n.26, at 726–27; F. Wilhoit, *The Politics of Massive Resistance* 143 (1973). Kluger generally views the brief as a middle position between the southern states and Negro plaintiffs, Wilhoit as only a slightly toned down version of the southern position. In fact, the government's brief resembled the southern position more in critical points of substance than in style.
65. Pub. L. No. 85–315, 71 Stat. L. 634 (1957). The act's chief accomplishment was to establish a nonpartisan Civil Rights commission to gather evidence on voting violations. As two observers note: "The law enacted by the 85th Congress on September 9, 1957, was the first civil rights bill since 1875. . . . It was not a far-reaching measure in substance, but it was a clear indication that the legislative branch was at last undertaking responsibilities that had previously been left to the executive and the judiciary." A. Blaustein and R. Zangrando, eds., *Civil Rights and the American Negro* 471 (1968).
66. A. Bickel, *supra* n.34, at 252.
67. The best account of the Compromise of 1877 is C. Woodward, *Reunion and Reaction* (1951).
68. A. Bickel, *supra* n.34, at 250.
69. Woodward, "The Search for Southern Identity," 34 *Va. Q. Rev.* 321, 333 (1958).

Chapter 5

1. 391 U.S. 430 (1968).
2. See generally McKay, " 'With All Deliberate Speed:' A Study of School Desegregation," 31 *N.Y.U. L. Rev.* 991 (1956) and " 'With All Deliberate Speed:' Legislative Reaction and Judicial Development 1956–1957," 43 *Va. L. Rev.* 1205 (1957).
3. N. Bartley, *The Rise of Massive Resistance* 144 (1969).
4. Lee v. Washington, 390 U.S. 333 (1968) (prisons); Johnson v. Virginia, 373 U.S. 61 (1963) (courtrooms); New Orleans City Park Improvement Ass'n v. Detiege, 358 U.S. 54 (1958) (parks); Gayle v. Browder, 352 U.S. 903 (1956) (buses); Holmes v. City of Atlanta, 350 U.S. 879 (1955) (golf courses); Mayor of Baltimore v. Dawson, 350 U.S. 877 (1955) (beaches).
5. E.g., Burton v. Wilmington Parking Auth., 365 U.S. 715 (1961).

6. NAACP v. Alabama, 357 U.S. 449, 462 (1958). See Bates v. City of Little Rock, 361 U.S. 516 (1960). See also NAACP v. Button, 371 U.S. 415 (1963) (rejection of Virginia's attempts to restrict the NAACP under its power to regulate the legal profession).

7. E.g., Lombard v. Louisiana, 373 U.S. 267 (1963); Peterson v. City of Greenville, 373 U.S. 244 (1963).

8. E.g., Cox v. Louisiana, 379 U.S. 559 (1965); Cox v. Louisiana, 379 U.S. 536 (1965); Edwards v. South Carolina, 372 U.S. 229 (1963). See Kalven, "The Concept of the Public Forum: Cox v. Louisiana," 1965 *Sup. Ct. Rev.* 1, and Howard, "Mr. Justice Black: The Negro Protest Movement and the Rule of Law," 53 *Va. L. Rev.* 1030 (1967).

9. Loving v. Virginia, 388 U.S. 1 (1967).

10. S. Wasby, A. D'Amato, and R. Metrailer, *Desegregation From Brown to Alexander* 149 (1977).

11. See generally ibid. at 162–73.

12. E.g., Cooper v. Aaron, 358 U.S. 1 (1958).

13. E.g., Griffin v. County School Bd., 377 U.S. 218 (1964).

14. E.g., Goss v. Bd. of Educ., 373 U.S. 683 (1963).

15. The figures are those for the year 1960. Circuits other than the Fourth and Fifth dealt on the edges of the school desegregation problem. Arkansas was in the Eighth Circuit, Tennessee and Kentucky in the Sixth, and Delaware in the Third.

16. See J. Peltason, *Fifty-Eight Lonely Men: Southern Federal Judges and School Desegregation* 114 (1961).

17. F. Wilhoit, *The Politics of Massive Resistance* 183 (1973). See J. Peltason, *supra* n.16, at 221.

18. J. Peltason, *supra* n.16, at 118–19.

19. R. Sarratt, *The Ordeal of Desegregation* 203 (1966).

20. Brown v. Board of Educ., 349 U.S. 294, 300 (1955).

21. R. Sarratt, *supra* n.19, at 201–2.

22. H. Abraham, *Justices and Presidents* 34–35 (1974).

23. E.g., Rice v. Elmore, 165 F.2d 387 (CA4 1947).

24. Briggs v. Elliott, 132 F. Supp. 776, 777 (E.D.S.C. 1955).

25. Bickel, "The Decade of School Desegregation: Progress and Prospects," 64 *Col. L. Rev.* 193, 205 (1964).

26. Meador, "The Constitution And the Assignment of Pupils to Public Schools," 45 *Va. L. Rev.* 517, 524 (1959).

27. See B. Muse, *Virginia's Massive Resistance* 28–34 (1961). See also R. Gates, *The Making of Massive Resistance: Virginia's Politics of Public School Desegregation, 1954–1956* 167–90 (1962).

28. J. Ely, *The Crisis of Conservative Virginia* 45 (1976).

29. B. Muse, *supra* n.27, at 29.

30. Ibid. at 111–12. A three-judge district court noted that "the plight of the school children and the teaching personnel who would have been at the six schools has been adequately described as 'tragic.' Children who would be in their last year of high school are at a loss as to what to do, and those who had planned to attend college are completely frustrated." James v. Almond, 170 F. Supp. 331, 336 (E.D. Va. 1959).

31. B. Muse, *supra* n.27, at 86–94, 106–10.

32. James v. Almond, 170 F. Supp. 331, 337 (E.D. Va. 1959).

33. For a careful evaluation of the pupil-placement statutes, see McKay, " 'With All Deliberate Speed:' Legislative Reaction and Judicial Development 1956–1957," *supra* n.2, at 1214–21.

34. Meador, *supra* n.26, at 527.

35. N.C. Gen. Stat. §§ 115–77 (1955). See generally Note, "State Efforts to Circumvent Desegregation: Private Schools, Pupil Placement, and Geographic Segregation," 54 *NW. U. L. Rev.* 354, 363–65 (1959).

36. Note, "The Federal Courts and Integration of Southern Schools: Troubled Status of the Pupil Placement Acts," 62 *Col. L. Rev.* 1448, 1453 (1962) (footnotes omitted).

37. Adkins v. Newport News School Bd., 148 F. Supp. 430 (E.D. Va. 1957), *aff'd*, 246 F.2d 325 (CA4 1957), *cert. denied*, 355 U.S. 855 (1957); Bush v. Orleans Parish School Bd., 138 F. Supp. 337 (E.D. La. 1956), *aff'd*, 242 F.2d 156 (CA5 1957), *cert. denied*, 354 U.S. 921 (1957).

38. 238 F.2d 724 (1956), *cert. denied*, 353 U.S. 910 (1957).

39. Ibid. at 728.

40. 353 U.S. 910 (1957).

41. B. Muse, *Ten Years of Prelude* 113 (1964); N. Peirce, *The Border South States* 141 (1975).

42. Dykeman and Stokely, "Integration: Third and Critical Phase," *New York Times Magazine*, Nov. 27, 1960, at 24.

43. Gellhorn, "A Decade of Desegregation—Retrospect and Prospect," 9 *Utah L. Rev.* 3, 6 (1964).

44. King, "The Case Against 'Tokenism,' " *New York Times Magazine*, August 5, 1962, at 11.

45. Carter, "The Warren Court and Desegregation," 67 *Mich. L. Rev.* 237, 244 (1968). See also Covington v. Edwards, 264 F.2d 780 (CA4 1959), *cert. denied*, 361 U.S. 840 (1959); Hood v. Bd. of Trustees, 232 F.2d 626 (CA4 1956), *cert. denied*, 352 U.S. 870 (1956); Shuttlesworth v. Birmingham Bd. of Educ., 162 F. Supp. 372 (N.D. Ala. 1958), *aff'd*, 358 U.S. 101 (1958).

46. See Kelley v. Bd. of Educ., 270 F.2d 209 (CA6 1959), *cert. denied*, 361 U.S. 924 (1959); Slade v. Bd. of Educ., 252 F.2d 291 (CA4 1958), *cert. denied*, 357 U.S. 906 (1958); Carter, *supra* n.45, at 244. The Court also denied certiorari of courts of appeals' rulings that disapproved grade-by-grade desegregation. See, e.g., Evans v. Ennis, 281 F.2d 385 (CA3 1960), *cert. denied*, 364 U.S. 933 (1961).

47. Gellhorn, *supra* n.43, at 6.

48. Carter, "Desegregation Does Not Mean Integration," *New York Times Magazine*, Feb. 11, 1962, at 21.

49. B. Muse, *supra* n.27, at 114–15.

50. King, *supra* n.44, at 11.

51. See Griffin v. County School Bd., 377 U.S. 218 (1964) (Prince Edward); Cooper v. Aaron, 358 U.S. 1 (1958) (Little Rock). Justice Frankfurter's concurrence in *Cooper*, 358 U.S. at 20, was a personal elaboration of the views held by the majority. Justices Clark and Harlan disagreed in *Griffin* with the part of the Court's holding that federal courts might be empowered to reopen public schools in Prince Edward County, 377 U.S. at 234, but, probably because of the tradition of unanimity in school desegregation cases, declined to elaborate.

52. Yates, "Arkansas: independent and Unpredictable," in W. Havard, ed., *The Changing Politics of the South* 233, 264 (1972).

53. Ibid. at 265.

54. R. Sherrill, *Gothic Politics in the Deep South* 83 (1968).

55. Yates, *supra* n.52, at 271.

56. A. Lewis, *Portrait of a Decade: The Second American Revolution* 47 (1964).

57. N. Peirce, *The Deep South States* 132 (1974).

58. R. Sherrill, *supra* n.54, at 89.

59. V. Key, *Southern Politics* 8–9 (1949).

60. J. Wilkinson, *Harry Byrd and the Changing Face of Virginia Politics, 1945–1966* 153–54 (1968).

61. A. Lewis, *supra* n.56, at 47.

62. Quoted in N. Peirce, *supra* n.41, at 132.

63. Cooper v. Aaron, 358 U.S. 1, 11 (1958) (quoting Aaron v. Cooper, 156 F. Supp. 220, 225 (E.D. Ark. 1957)).

64. U.S. Commission on Civil Rights, *Fulfilling the Letter and Spirit of the Law: Desegregation of the Nation's Public Schools* 1 (1976).

65. A. Lewis, *supra* n.56, at 51.

66. "Eisenhower Address on Little Rock Crisis," *New York Times*, Sept. 25, 1957.

67. B. Muse, *supra* n.41, at 140–41.

68. Samuels, "Little Rock: More Tension Than Ever," *New York Times Magazine*, March 23, 1958, at 88–89.

69. Cooper v. Aaron, 163 F. Supp. 13, 20–26, *rev'd*, 358 U.S. 1 (1958).

70. 257 F.2d 33 (CA8 1958), *aff'd*, 358 U.S. 1 (1958).

71. Cooper v. Aaron, 358 U.S. 1, 12, 15 (1958).

72. See Miscellaneous Order No. 1, 358 U.S. 27 (1958).

73. 358 U.S. 1 (1958); see E. Warren, *The Memoirs of Earl Warren* 298 (1977).

74. 358 U.S. at 18. See also United States v. Nixon, 418 U.S. 683, 703 (1974).

75. 358 U.S. at 16.

76. Ibid. at 22.

77. See Gunther, "The Subtle Vices of the "Passive Virtues"—A Comment on Principle and Expediency in Judicial Review," 64 *Col. L. Rev.* 1, 25 n.155 (1964).

78. 358 U.S. at 18.

79. Bickel, *supra* n.25, at 200–201. See also A. Bickel, *The Least Dangerous Branch* 254–72 (1962).

80. Goss v. Bd. of Educ., 373 U.S. 683 (1963).

81. See G. White, *The American Judicial Tradition* 325–31 (1976).

82. See R. Kluger, *Simple Justice* 598–602 (1975).

83. 338 U.S. 25 (1949).

84. 328 U.S. 549 (1946).

85. See A. Cox, *The Warren Court* 5 (1968).

86. See, e.g., Baker v. Carr, 369 U.S. 186 (1962), and Mapp v. Ohio, 367 U.S. 643 (1961), both of which found Frankfurter in dissent.

87. See also Youngstown Sheet and Tube Co. v. United States, 343 U.S. 579 (1952) and Harbaugh, "The Steel Seizure Reconsidered," 87 *Yale L.J.* 1272 (1978).

88. Aaron v. McKinley, 173 F. Supp. 944 (E.D. Ark. 1959) (per curiam).

89. See Yates, *supra* n.52, at 272–77.

90. N. Peirce, *supra* n.41, at 133.

91. See Green v. Roanoke School Bd., 304 F.2d 118 (CA4 1962) (discussed in Bickel, *supra* n.25, at 206–9).

92. 373 U.S. 683 (1963).

93. Goss v. Bd. of Educ., 301 F.2d 164 (CA6 1962), *rev'd*, 373 U.S. 683 (1963). See also Maxwell v. County Bd. of Educ., 301 F.2d 828 (CA6 1962).

94. 373 U.S. 668 (1963).

95. 42 U.S.C. § 1983 (1970).

96. See generally "Developments in the Law: Section 1983 and Federalism," 90 *Harv. L. Rev.* 1133, 1264–74 (1977).

97. Indeed, only Justice Harlan's dissent in *McNeese* even mentions the pupil-placement rulings, 373 U.S. at 676–77.

98. 382 U.S. 103 (1965) (per curiam).

99. Racial allocation of teachers has been doubly condemned as denying equal protection both to black teachers and to black schoolchildren, whose educational experience is thereby impaired. See Lieberman, "Teachers and the Fourteenth Amendment—The Role of Faculty in the Desegregation Process," 46 *N.C. L. Rev.* 313, 320–40 (1968).

100. Coles, "How Do The Teachers Feel?" *Saturday Review*, May 16, 1964, at 72.

101. Ibid. at 89.

102. Nicholson, "From Hattiesburg, Mississippi," F. Levinsohn and B. Wright, eds., in *School Desegregation: Shadow and Substance* 187, 187–88 (1976).

103. In fact, in 1972 in five southern states, "4,207 Black educators were dismissed, demoted, assigned out of field or unsatisfactorily placed." Watson, "School Integration: Its Meaning, Costs and Future," 4 *J.L. & Educ.* 15 (1975).

104. See United States v. Jefferson County School Bd., 372 F.2d 836, 853–54 (CA5 1966).

105. 382 U.S. at 105.

106. Rogers v. Paul, 382 U.S. 198, 200 (1965).

107. For an evaluation of various remedies for racial allocation of teachers, see Lieberman, *supra* n.99, at 350–59.

108. Goodman, "Public Schools Died Here," *Saturday Evening Post*, April 29, 1961, at 32, 86.

109. P. Rouse, *Below the James Lies Dixie-Smithfield and Southside Virginia* (1968).

110. Sullivan, "Making History in Prince Edward County," *Saturday Review*, Oct. 17, 1964, at 59.

111. Davis v. County School Bd., 347 U.S. 483 (1954).

112. Allen v. Prince Edward County School Bd., 266 F.2d 507 (CA4 1959). The Fourth Circuit directed the school board to desegregate the white high school in the fall of 1959 and to make plans for elementary school desegregation. Ibid. at 511.

113. Goodman, *supra* n.108, at 87.

114. B. Smith, *They Closed Their Schools* 168 (1965). This book presents the most comprehensive view of the Prince Edward school closings.

115. Ibid. at 166.

116. Ibid. at 167–68. See also Goodman, *supra* n.108, at 32.

117. Goodman, *supra* n.108, at 85.

118. Griffin v. County School Bd., 377 U.S. 218, 223–24 (1964).

119. Ibid. at 223.

120. Goodman, *supra* n.108, at 86.

121. Ibid. at 32.

122. See C. Brauer, *John F. Kennedy and the Second Reconstruction* 95 (1977); Sullivan, *supra* n.110, at 59.

123. Sullivan, *supra* n.110, at 60.

124. Ibid., at 71.

125. 377 U.S. 218 (1964).

126. Ibid. at 230–32.

127. The injunction was appropriate, at least where public schools remained closed. Ibid. at 233.

128. Ibid. at 234.

129. That remedy, of course, would have led the Court to define what level of involvement between government and "private" schools was necessary for the Fourteenth amendment to apply. See Burton v. Wilmington Parking Auth., 365 U.S. 715 (1961).

130. Kurland, "Foreword to The Supreme Court: 1963 Term," 78 *Harv. L. Rev.* 143, 158 (1964).

131. See Green v. County School Bd., 391 U.S. 430 (1968).

132. See Swann v. Charlotte-Mecklenburg Bd. of Educ., 402 U.S. 1 (1971).

133. Eisman, "U.S. Courts Now Society's Lightning Rods," Richmond *Times-Dispatch*, July 17, 1977.

134. 373 U.S. at 689.

135. 377 U.S. at 229, 234.

136. 382 U.S. at 105.

137. 377 U.S. 533 (1964). The standard of compliance in *Reynolds* was one of equal population for state legislative districts, subsequently refined in Gaffney v. Cummings, 412 U.S. 735 (1973); Mahan v. Howell, 410 U.S. 315 (1973); Abate v. Mundt, 403 U.S. 182 (1971).

138. 384 U.S. 436 (1966). In *Miranda*, of course, giving the warnings specified by the Court constituted compliance.

139. As to *Miranda*, see, e.g., Michigan v. Moseley, 423 U.S. 96 (1975) and Harris v. New York, 401 U.S. 222 (1971).

140. See n.175 *infra*.

141. Gellhorn, *supra* n.43, at 6.

142. Ashmore, "The Desegregation Decision: Ten Years After," *Saturday Review*, May 16, 1964, at 68.

143. Ibid. at 69.

144. A. Blaustein and R. Zangrando, eds., *Civil Rights and the American Negro* 524 (1968).

145. Pub. L. 88–352, 78 Stat. 241 (1964).

146. Ibid. at tit. II, § 201(a), 42 U.S.C. § 2000a(a).

147. Ibid. at tit. II, § 201(b), 42 U.S.C. § 2000a(b).

148. Ibid. at tit. IV, § 407(a) (2), 42 U.S.C. § 2000c-6(a).

149. Note, "The Courts, HEW, and Southern School Desegregation," 77 *Yale L.J.* 321, 334 (1967).

150. Fiss, "The Fate of An Idea Whose Time Has Come: Antidiscrimination Law in the Second Decade after Brown v. Board of Education," 41 *U. Chi. L. Rev.* 742, 754 (1974).

151. U.S. Office of Education, HEW, *General Statement of Policies under Title VI of the Civil Rights Act of 1964 Respecting Desegregation of Elementary and Secondary Schools* (1965). See generally Dunn, "Title VI, The Guidelines and School Desegregation in the South," 53 *Va. L. Rev.* 42, 44 (1967).

152. U.S. Office of Education, HEW, *Revised Statement of Policies for School Desegregation Plans under Title VI of the Civil Rights Act of 1964* (1966). See generally Dunn, *supra* n.151.

153. Roberts, "Pupil Placement Law Faces Stiff Test," *New York Times*, April 10, 1966.

154. U.S. Office of Education, *supra* n.152, § 181.54, as quoted in Dunn, *supra* n.151, at 62–63.

155. 110 Cong. Rec. 14,439, 14,434 (1964), as quoted in Note, *supra* n.149, at 360 n.137.

156. As quoted in G. Orfield, *The Reconstruction of Southern Education* 229 (1969).

157. Roberts, *supra* n.153.

158. *New York Times*, April 12, 1966.

159. *New York Times*, May 23, 1966.

160. Howe, "The Time is Now," *Saturday Review*, July 16, 1966, at 57.

161. Ibid. at 57–58.

162. See, e.g., United States v. Jefferson County Bd. of Educ., 372 F.2d 836 (CA5 1966); Lee v. Macon County Bd. of Educ., 267 F. Supp. 458 (M.D. Ala. 1967), *aff'd sub nom.* Wallace v. United States, 389 U.S. 215 (1967); Fiss, *supra* n.150 at 755.

163. United States v. Jefferson County Bd. of Educ., 373 F.2d 836, 847 (CA5 1966) (italics in original).

164. Civil Rights Act of 1964, Tit. VI, § 602, 42 U.S.C. § 2000-1.

165. Ibid.

166. Ibid.

167. Fiss, *supra* n.150, at 758.

168. 20 U.S.C. § 821.

169. U.S. Bureau of the Census, *Statistical Abstract of the United States*, 1969, at 115. The figures given are revenue sources for the year 1966.

170. Note, *supra* n.149, at 329–30.

171. United States v. Jefferson County Bd. of Educ., 380 F.2d 385, 390 (CA5 1967) (per curiam). *Accord*, United States v. Jefferson County Bd. of Educ., 372 F.2d 836, 847 (CA5 1966); Singleton v. Jackson Mun. School Dist., 348 F.2d 729, 731 (CA5 1965).

172. See generally Note, *supra* n.149, at 356–65.

173. United States v. Jefferson County Bd. of Educ., 372 F.2d 836, 855, 858.

174. See Note, *supra* n.149, at 335–36.
175. Dunn, *supra* n.151, at 43 n.8. These are HEW's Office of Education figures. Other estimates are slightly lower. Most statistics did not count as "desegregated" a school where a handful of whites (less than 5 percent) attended predominantly black institutions.
176. 391 U.S. 430 (1968).
177. Singleton v. Jackson Mun. School Dist., 355 F.2d 865, 871 (CA5 1966), *after remand from* 348 F.2d 729 (CA5 1965). (The 1966 case is known as *Singleton II;* the 1965 case as *Singleton I*).
178. Kemp v. Beasley, 352 F.2d 14, 21 (CA8 1965).
179. Bradley v. Richmond School Bd., 345 F.2d 310 (CA4 1965).
180. Ibid. at 323 (Sobeloff & Bell, JJ., concurring and dissenting).
181. See HEW School Desegregation Guidelines, 45 CFR § 181.54 (1966), quoted in Dunn, *supra* n.151, at 62 n.111.
182. Dunn, *supra* n.151, at 70.
183. 268 U.S. 510 (1925).
184. Ibid. at 535. See also Meyer v. Nebraska, 262 U.S. 390 (1923). The Court in *Pierce* upheld the parent's right against state legislative interference. Advocates of freedom of choice asserted the parent's right against judicial interference. The principle, however, is the same in both cases.
185. Carter, *supra* n.48, at 72.
186. United States v. Jefferson County Bd. of Educ., 372 F.2d 836, 890 (CA5 1966).
187. Student Nonviolent Coordinating Committee, *Special Report* 24–26 (Sept. 30, 1965), as quoted in G. Orfield, *supra* n.156, at 128.
188. Carter, "School Integration Is Still On the Agenda," *Saturday Review*, Oct. 21, 1967, at 70, 85.
189. Ibid. at 85. See also United States v. Jefferson County Bd. of Educ., 372 F.2d 836, 891 (CA5 1966).
190. See U.S. Commission on Civil Rights, *Southern School Desegregation, 1966–1967* 88 (1967).
191. 391 U.S. 430 (1968).
192. Wisdom, "Random Remarks on the Role of Social Sciences in the Judicial Decision-Making Process in School Desegregation Cases," 39 *Law & Contemp. Probs.* 134, 147 (1975).
193. 348 F.2d 729 (CA5 1965).
194. 355 F.2d 865 (CA5 1966).
195. 372 F.2d 836 (CA5 1966). In a fourth opinion, United States v. Jefferson County Bd. of Educ. (*Jefferson II*), 380 F.2d 385 (CA5 1967) (per curiam) (en banc), the Fifth Circuit adopted Judge Wisdom's basic approach in *Jefferson I*.
196. The other three being Swann v. Charlotte-Mecklenburg Bd. of Educ. 402 U.S. 1 (1971); Brown v. Board of Educ., 347 U.S. 483 (1954); Green v. County School Bd., 391 U.S. 430 (1968). Read, "Judicial Evolution of the Law of School Integration Since Brown v. Board of Education," 39 *Law & Contemp. Probs.* 7, 20, 23 (1975).
197. Singleton v. Jackson Mun. School Dist., 348 F.2d at 729.
198. United States v. Jefferson County Bd. of Educ., 372 F.2d at 849 (quoting a statement made by Senator Everett Dirksen shortly before passage of the 1964 Civil Rights Act).
199. Ibid. at 896.
200. United States v. Jefferson County Bd. of Educ., 372 F.2d at 847. See also United States v. Jefferson County Bd. of Educ., 380 F.2d 385, 390 (CA5 1967) (per curiam) (en banc).
201. See notes section 4.
202. "The question to be resolved in each case is: How far have formerly de jure segregated

schools progressed in performing their affirmative constitutional duty to furnish equal educational opportunities to all public school children?" United States v. Jefferson County Bd. of Educ., 372 F.2d at 896.

203. Ibid. at 869 (Emphasis in original).
204. Ibid. at 866.
205. 132 F. Supp. 776, 777 (E.D.S.C. 1955).
206. See Carson v. Warlick, 238 F.2d 724, 729 (CA4 1956).
207. United States v. Jefferson County Bd. of Educ., 372 F.2d at 866.
208. "All persons born or naturalized in the United States and subject to the jurisdiction thereof, are citizens of the United States and of the States wherein they reside."
209. See generally United States v. Jefferson County Bd. of Educ., 372 F.2d at 866, 873.
210. United States v. Jefferson County Bd. of Educ., 372 F.2d at 846 n.5; Singleton v. Jackson Mun. School Dist., 355 F.2d at 869–70; Singleton v. Jackson Mun. School Dist., 347 F.2d at 730 n.5.
211. As was done in Green v. County School Bd., 391 U.S. 430 (1968). Note also the discussion of *Briggs* in Keyes v. Denver School Dist., 413 U.S. 189, 200–1 n.11 (1973).
212. United States v. Jefferson County Bd. of Educ., 372 F.2d at 897–900.
213. 349 U.S. at 299.
214. United States v. Jefferson County Bd. of Educ., 372 F.2d at 847–48.
215. See e.g., Morgan v. Kerrigan, 401 F. Supp. 216 (D. Mass. 1975); Keyes v. Denver School District, 380 F. Supp. 673 (D. Col. 1974); Swann v. Charlotte-Mecklenburg Bd. of Educ., 311 F. Supp. 265 (W.D.N.C. 1970).
216. E.g., Brunson v. Clarendon School Dist., 429 F.2d 820 (CA4 1970).
217. See, e.g., George v. O'Kelly, 448 F.2d 148, 150 (CA5 1971); United States v. Texas, 447 F.2d 441, 443, 448 (CA5 1971); Plaquemines Parish School Bd. v. United States, 415 F.2d 817, 831 (CA5 1969); Stell v. Bd. of Pub. Educ., 387 F.2d 486, 492, 496–97 (CA5 1967). See also Morgan v. Kerrigan, 401 F. Supp. 216, 235 (D. Mass. 1975); Hart v. Community School Bd., 383 F. Supp. 699, 757 (E.D.N.Y. 1974). *Jefferson* was not the first case to order a remedial program. See Miller v. School Dist., 256 F. Supp. 370, 377 (D.S.C. 1966).
218. See, e.g., United States v. Missouri, 523 F.2d 885, 887 (CA8 1975); Moore v. Tangipahoa Parish School Bd., 304 F. Supp. 244, 253 (E.D. La. 1969); Smith v. Saint Tammany Parish School Bd., 302 F. Supp. 106, 110 (E.D. La. 1969).
219. See, e.g., Lemon v. Bossier Parish School Bd., 444 F.2d 1400, 1401 (CA5 1971); Singleton v. Jackson Mun. School Dist., 419 F.2d 1211, 1219 (CA5 1969) (*Singleton III*). The ability of district judges to order remedial and support programs was affirmed in Milliken v. Bradley, 433 U.S. 267 (1977) (*Bradley II*).
220. Monroe v. Bd. of Comm'rs of Jackson, 391 U.S. 450 (1968); Raney v. Bd. of Educ., 391 U.S. 443 (1968); Green v. County School Bd., 391 U.S. 430 (1968).
221. See Green v. County School Bd., 391 U.S. 430, 441 (1968).
222. As quoted in S. Wasby, *supra* n.10, at 382, 384–85.
223. Ibid. at 392–93.
224. 391 U.S. 430 (1968).
225. Ibid. at 437–38.
226. 349 U.S. at 300.
227. 132 F. Supp. 776, 777 (E.D.S.C. 1955).
228. 391 U.S. 439.
229. See Fiss, *supra* n.150, at 763.
230. See United States v. Jefferson County Bd. of Educ., 372 F.2d 836, 876 (CA5 1966).
231. 391 U.S. at 442 n.6.
232. Ibid.
233. 395 U.S. 225 (1969) *aff g* 289 F. Supp. 647 (1968).

234. Ibid. at 235 (citation omitted).

235. 289 F. Supp. 647, 652–56 (1968).

236. See L. Panetta and P. Gall, *Bring Us Together* 251–57 (1971).

237. R. Murphy and H. Gulliver, *The Southern Strategy* 58 (1971). See Read, *supra* n.196, at 30–31 n.101.

238. R. Murphy and H. Gulliver, *supra* n.237, at 58.

239. See Alexander v. Holmes County Bd. of Educ., 396 U.S. 1218 (1969) (Black, Circuit Justice).

240. Greenberg, "Revolt at Justice," *U. Chi. Magazine*, March-April 1970, at 24; G. Orfield, *Must We Bus?* 325–27 (1978).

241. R. Murphy and H. Gulliver, *supra* n.237, at 58.

242. Orfield, *supra* n.240, at 327; Read, *supra* n.196, at 30–31 n.101.

243. 396 U.S. 19 (1969) (per curiam).

244. Ibid. at 20.

245. Read, *supra* n.196, at 31.

246. Singleton v. Jackson Mun. School Dist., 419 F.2d 1211, 1217 (CA5 1969), *rev'd sub nom.* Carter v. West Feliciana Parish School Bd., 396 U.S. 290 (1970) (per curiam).

247. 396 U.S. 290 (1970) (per curiam). See also Northcross v. Bd. of Educ., 397 U.S. 232 (1970); Dowell v. Bd. of Educ., 396 U.S. 269 (1960) (opinions rejecting further delay in desegregation suits).

248. Read, *supra* n.196, at 31.

249. 396 U.S. at 294 (Memorandum of Burger, C.J., and Stewart, J., dissenting).

250. Read, *supra* n.196, at 32 n.108.

251. See 118 Cong. Rec. 564 (Jan. 20, 1972) (remarks of Sen. Stennis).

252. Munford, "White Flight from Desegregation in Mississippi," *Integrated Education*, May-June 1973, at 20.

253. Ibid. at 12.

254. Munford's thesis is that the black percentage of the *general population* of a school district is the single greatest influence on white flight. His conclusion disagrees "with the two most common theories of white flight from *school desegregation:* the 'tipping' theory which says whites shun desegregated schools according to the percentage of blacks in the schools and the 'leadership' theory which places major responsibility for determining white resistance on the stance taken by community leaders." Ibid. at 12–13. See also H. Blalock, *Toward a Theory of Minority Group Relations* 145 (1967); V. Key, *Southern Politics* 5 (1949).

255. McIlwain, "On The Overturning of Two School Buses in Lamar, S.C.," *Esquire*, Jan. 1971, at 98.

256. Stanley v. Darlington County School Dist., 424 F.2d 195, 196 (CA4 1970).

257. Ibid. at 198 (on petition for rehearing in a companion case to *Stanley*, Whittenberg v. Greenville School District).

258. McIlwain, *supra* n.255, at 99, 162–63.

259. Ibid. at 102–03.

260. Louisville *Courier-Journal*, Mar. 6, 1970.

261. Cincinnati *Enquirer*, Mar. 6, 1970.

262. J. Buncher, ed., *The School Busing Controversy: 1970–1975* 209 (1975).

263. 407 U.S. 451 (1972).

264. Ibid. at 466. See also United States v. Scotland Neck Bd. of Educ., 407 U.S. 484 (1972).

264. 407 U.S. at 464.

266. See, with respect to the relative condition of city and county schools, ibid. at 475–76 (Burger, C. J., dissenting).

267. Such is the case with white flight. Ibid. at 474–76 (Burger, C.J., dissenting). See L.

Graglia, *Disaster by Decree: The Supreme Court Decisions on Race and the Schools* 148–49 (1976).

268. 407 U.S. at 474, 472, 477–82.
269. Dayton Bd. of Educ. v. Brinkman, 433 U.S. 406 (1977); Pasadena Bd. of Educ. v. Spangler, 427 U.S. 424 (1976); Milliken v. Bradley, 418 U.S. 717 (1974) (Detroit); Keyes v. Denver School Dist., 413 U.S. 189 (1973).
270. Indeed, Swann v. Charlotte-Mecklenburg Bd. of Educ., 402 U.S. 1 (1971), operates as a bridge between them, a "southern urban" case.
271. Milliken v. Bradley, 418 U.S. 717 (1974).
272. See Keyes v. Denver School Dist., 413 U.S. 189, 200 (1973).
273. See, e.g., Dayton Bd. of Educ. v. Brinkman, 433 U.S. 406 (1977); Keyes v. Denver School Dist., 413 U.S. 189, 202 (1973); United States v. Omaha School Dist., 521 F.2d 530, 537 (CA8 1975); Morgan v. Kerrigan, 509 F.2d 580 (CA1 1974).
274. Morgan v. Hennigan, 379 F. Supp. 410, 460 (D. Mass 1974).
275. See Swann v. Charlotte-Mecklenburg Bd. of Educ., 402 U.S. 1 (1971), whose remedial requirements also governed northern urban school systems found guilty of past intentional segregative acts. See also Keyes v. Denver School Dist., 413 U.S. 189, 213 (1973).
276. Brest, "Foreword to The Supreme Court, 1975 Term," 90 *Harv. L. Rev.* 1, 33 (1976).
277. 402 U.S. 1 (1971).

Chapter 6

1. Cottle, "Bus Start," *New York Times Magazine*, March 9, 1975, at 18.
2. C. Jencks, *Inequality* 106 (1972).
3. Swann v. Charlotte-Mecklenburg Bd. of Educ., 402 U.S. 1, 13 (1971).
4. 402 U.S. 1. *Swann* was argued in 1970, delivered in 1971.
5. Mills, "Busing: Who's Being Taken for a Ride," in N. Mills, ed., *The Great School Busing Controversy*, 3, 4 (1973).
6. Ibid.
7. 402 U.S. at 29.
8. Mills, *supra* n.5, at 9.
9. Everson v. Board of Educ., 330 U.S. 1, 7 (1947).
10. See North Carolina Bd. of Educ. v. Swann, 402 U.S. 43 (1971).
11. Barrows, "School Busing: Charlotte, N.C.," *Atlantic Monthly*, Nov. 1972, at 18.
12. Mondale, "Busing in Perspective," *New Republic*, Mar. 4, 1972, at 18.
13. See generally Glazer, "Is Busing Necessary?" *Commentary*, Mar. 1972, at 39.
14. J. Doherty, *Race and Education in Richmond* 44 (1972).
15. Mills, *supra* n.5, at 13.
16. Goodman, "Busing for Integration is Working Well in Central 7 School District—Knock Wood," *New York Times Magazine*, April 9, 1972, at 31.
17. As quoted in Mills, *supra* n.5, at ix.
18. Read, "Judicial Evolution of the Law of School Integration Since *Brown* v. *Board of Education*," 39 *Law & Contemp. Probs.* 7, 33 (1975).
19. Editorials, Charlotte *News*, Sept. 5, 1970 and Jan. 10, 1970.
20. Editorial, Richmond *Times-Dispatch*, July 30, 1970.
21. Barrows, *supra* n.11, at 19.
22. L. Graglia, *Disaster by Decree: The Supreme Court Decisions on Race and the Schools* 105 (1976).
23. Swann v. Charlotte-Mecklenburg Bd. of Educ., 300 F. Supp. 1358, 1360 (W.D.N.C. 1969).
24. See 402 U.S. at 9.

25. See L. Graglia, *supra* n.22, at 110 for a critique of these fingers and how they were deduced.
26. Ayres, "Cross-Town Busing, Begun in '71, Is Working Well In Charlotte," *New York Times*, July 17, 1975; Barrows, *supra* n.11, at 17–20.
27. Barrows, *supra* n.11, at 19–20.
28. Editorial, Charlotte *News*, Aug. 29, 1970, quoting an earlier editorial in the Greensboro *Daily News*.
29. 402 U.S. at 13–14.
30. Ibid. at 16.
31. See generally J. Franklin, *From Slavery to Freedom: A History of Negro Americans* (3rd ed., 1967); L. Bennett, *Before the Mayflower: A History of Black America* (4th ed., 1969).
32. G. Myrdal, *An American Dilemma: The Negro Problem and Modern Democracy* 77 (1944).
33. K. Taeuber and A. Taeuber, *Negroes in Cities* 2 (1965). Though the Taeuber study appeared in 1965, the picture has not changed much in the 1970s. See Farley, "Residential Segregation and Its Implications for School Integration," 39 *Law & Contemp. Probs.* 164, 167 (1975).
34. Milliken v. Bradley, 418 U.S. 717, 756 n.2 (1974) (Stewart, J., concurring).
35. K. Taeuber and A. Taeuber, *supra* n.33, at 94.
36. Farley, "Population Trends and School Segregation in the Detroit Metropolitan Area," 21 *Wayne L. Rev.* 867, 882 (1975).
37. Farley, *supra* n.33, at 167.
38. G. Orfield, *Must We Bus?* 91 (1978).
39. Farley, *supra* n.36, at 884–85.
40. Taeuber, "Demographic Perspectives on Housing and School Segregation," 21 *Wayne L. Rev.* 833, 838 (1975) citing Pettigrew, "Attitudes on Race and Housing: A Social Psychological View," in A. Hawley and V. Rock, eds., *Segregation in Residential Areas* 21 (1973). See also Farley, *supra* n.36, at 888 and Campbell and Schuman, "Racial Attitudes in Fifteen Cities," for the Institute for Social Research, Ann Arbor, Mich., 15–16 (1968).
41. M. Ovington, *The Walls Came Tumbling Down* 115 (1970). See also A. Spear, *Black Chicago: The Making of a Negro Ghetto 1880–1920* (1967).
42. As quoted in A. Waskow, *From Race Riot to Sit-In, 1919 and the 1960s* 54–55 (1966).
43. Ibid. at 55.
44. Buchanan v. Warley, 245 U.S. 60 (1917).
45. U.S. Commission on Civil Rights, *Statement on Metropolitan School Desergregation* 22 (1977).
46. Federal Housing Administration, *Underwriting Manual* ¶ 935 (1936) as quoted in Chandler, "Fair Housing Laws: A Critique," 24 *Hast. L. Rev.* 159, 161 (1973). See also R. Helper, *Racial Policies and Practices of Real Estate Brokers* 202 (1969).
47. Grier, "The Negro Ghettos and Federal Housing Policy," 32 *J. Law & Contemp. Probs.* 550, 554 (1967); Chandler, *supra* n.46, at 161.
48. As quoted in N. Straus, *Two Thirds of a Nation* 221 (1952).
49. As quoted in U.S. Commission on Civil Rights, *Twenty Years After Brown: Equal Opportunity in Housing* 4 (1975). See generally R. Helper, *supra* n.46.
50. M. Danielson, *The Politics of Exclusion* 1 (1976).
51. Shelly v. Kraemer, 334 U.S. 1 (1948).
52. U.S. Commission on Civil Rights, *supra* n.49, at 3.
53. See Hills v. Gautreaux, 425 U.S. 284 (1976); M. Danielson, *supra* n.50, at 78–106.
54. W. Taylor, *Hanging Together: Equality in an Urban Nation* 92 (1971).
55. See Hills v. Gautreaux, 425 U.S. at 303; Crow v. Brown, 457 F.2d 788 (CA5 1972).
56. U.S. Commission on Civil Rights, *supra* n.45, at 28.
57. As to schools, see Keyes v. Denver School District, 413 U.S. 189, 208 (1973). As to housing, see Village of Arlington Heights v. Metrop. Housing Devel. Corp., 429

U.S. 252 (1977). *Arlington Heights* involved a zoning ordinance; presumably the same standard of discriminatory intent would apply to suburban vetoes of public housing projects. A further question in housing discrimination is whether the presence of racially restrictive covenants during a community's formative years would automatically suffice to establish a constitutional violation, much as the presence of a school segregation statute at the time of the first *Brown* decision.

58. Indeed, the Court has hinted as much, Hills v. Gautreaux, 425 U.S. 284 (1976).
59. 402 U.S. at 23.
60. See Keyes v. Denver School Dist., 413 U.S. 189, 222–23 (1973) (Powell, J., concurring in part and dissenting in part).
61. Milliken v. Bradley, 418 U.S. 717, 728 n.7 (1974).
62. Swann v. Charlotte-Mecklenburg Bd. of Educ., 243 F. Supp. 667 (W.D.N.C. 1965), *aff'd*, 369 F.2d 29 (CA4 1966).
63. 402 U.S. at 5–7.
64. Ibid. at 12.
65. Ibid. at 21. Likewise condemned was the closing of schools "which appeared likely to become racially mixed through changes in neighborhood school patterns." Ibid.
66. Davis, "Foreword," in A Rubinstein, ed., *Schools Against Children: The Case for Community Control* 17, 19 (1971).
67. Levin, "Introduction" and "Summary of Conference Discussion," in Levin, ed., *Community Control of Schools* 5 and 281 (1970). See also G. LaNoue and B. Smith, *The Politics of School Decentralization* (1973).
68. 402 U.S. at 21.
69. As to faculty desegregation, the Court reaffirmed United States v. Montgomery County Board of Education, 395 U.S. 225 (1969), which upheld a district court order setting "an initial ratio for the whole [Montgomery] system of at least two Negro teachers out of each 12 in any given school." 402 U.S. at 19. The Court also approved " 'pairing,' 'clustering' or 'grouping' of schools," a step that itself necessitates student busing. 402 U.S. at 27.
70. Editorial, Charlotte *News*, Sept. 5, 1970.
71. Totenberg, "Behind the Marble, Beneath the Robes," *New York Times Magazine*, Mar. 16, 1975, at 63–64.
72. 402 U.S. at 25–30. See also Davis v. Bd. of Commissioners, 402 U.S. 33 (1971) and North Carolina Bd. of Educ. v. Swann, 402 U.S. 43 (1971).
73. Editorial, Los Angeles *Times*, April 22, 1971.
74. Editorial, Richmond *Times-Dispatch*, April 25, 1971.
75. 402 U.S. at 24–32.
76. Editorial, Richmond *Times-Dispatch*, April 25, 1971.
77. "The Supreme Court, 1970 Term," 85 *Harv. L. Rev.* 3, 42 (1971).
78. See chapter nine.
79. See Winston-Salem/Forsyth County Bd. of Educ. v. Scott, 404 U.S. 1221 (1971) (Mr. Chief Justice Burger, Circuit Justice). The chief justice denied for various procedural reasons the school board's request.
80. 404 U.S. at 1227–31.
81. Editorial, Louisville *Courier-Journal*, Sept. 2, 1971.
82. *New York Times*, Sept. 1, 1971, as cited in L. Graglia, *supra* n.22, at 140. Court officials "had no comment on whether Chief Justice Burger had requested the unusual mailing." Ibid.
83. L. Graglia, *supra* n.22, at 140. In a like vein, the chief justice was also credited with gratuitous remarks on the ability of Congress to curb judicial power to order busing as a school desegregation remedy. See Volpe v. D.C. Federation of Civic Assns. 405 U.S. 1030 (1972) and L. Graglia, *supra* n.22, at 141.

84. Northcross v. Memphis Bd. of Educ., 466 F.2d 890, 894 (CA6 1972).
85. Northcross v. Memphis Bd. of Educ., 489 F.2d 15, 16 (CA6 1973).
86. Thompson v. Newport News School Bd., 465 F.2d 83, 87 (CA4 1972).
87. Flax v. Potts, 464 F.2d 865, 866 (CA5 1972).
88. As quoted in Keyes v. Denver School Dist., 413 U.S. 189, 237–38, n.17 (1973) (Powell, J., concurring in part and dissenting in part).
89. Northcross v. Memphis Bd. of Educ., 489 F.2d 15, 16–17 (CA6 1973).
90. Flax v. Potts, 464 F.2d 865, 869 (CA5 1972).
91. As quoted in Thompson v. Newport News School Bd., 465 F.2d 83, 86 (CA4 1972). Judge Hoffman's view was finally *affirmed* in Thompson v. Newport News School Bd., 498 F.2d 195 (CA4 1974).
92. C. Silberman, *Crisis in Black and White* 298 (1964); J. Porter, *Black Child, White Child* 214 (1971).
93. Finger, "Why Busing Plans Work," in F. Levinsohn and B. Wright, eds., *School Desegregation: Shadow and Substance* 58, 64 (1976).
94. Holland, "The Year of the Bus," *National Review*, May 4, 1971, at 475.
95. See generally V. Dabney, *Richmond* (1976).
96. Doherty, *supra* n.14, at 103–4.
97. As quoted in Editorial, Washington *Post*, Aug. 4, 1970.
98. Bradley v. Richmond School Bd., 338 F. Supp. 67 (W.D. Va. 1972).
99. Bradley v. Richmond School Bd., 462 F.2d 1058, 1060 (CA4 1972). The Fourth Circuit held that school boundaries had not been established to promote segregation, that each of the three systems in the metropolitan area was unitary, and that no two of the systems had conspired between themselves "for the purpose of keeping one unit relatively white by confining blacks to another." Ibid. at 1064–65. The opinion thus foreshadowed to a significant degree the Supreme Court ruling in Milliken v. Bradley, 418 U.S. 717 (1974). See chapter nine.
100. Richmond School Bd. v. Virginia Bd. of Educ., 412 U.S. 92 (1973). A detailed account of the Richmond litigation is Leedes and O'Fallon, "*School Desegregation in Richmond: A Case History*," 10 *Rich. L. Rev.* 1 (1975).
101. See Report of the Richmond Resources Committee of the Central Richmond Association 1, 13 (Aug. 1, 1977). The report indicated the belief that court-ordered busing was the chief cause of the decline. Ibid. at 13–14; Edwards, "New Officials Shun Richmond Schools," Washington *Post*, Dec. 10, 1977, estimated Richmond's white public school enrollment to be about 10 percent.
102. Cox, "Desegregation," Richmond *Times-Dispatch*, July 9, 1978; Editorial, Richmond *Times-Dispatch*, Feb. 3, 1977.
103. Miller, "4 Schools Here Reverse Trends," Richmond *Times-Dispatch*, Sept. 16, 1977, and Campbell, "Parents Back Hunter's K-5 School Plan," Richmond *Times-Dispatch*, Feb. 1, 1978.
104. Cox, *supra* n.102.
105. Ibid.
106. Ibid.
107. Ibid.
108. Editorial, Washington *Post*, Aug. 4, 1970.
109. Havard, "The South: A Shifting Perspective," in W. Havard, ed., *The Changing Politics of the South* 3, 17 (1972).
110. Ibid.
111. J. Bass and W. Devries, *The Transformation of Southern Politics* (1976).
112. See E. Black, *Southern Governors and Civil Rights* 330 (1976); J. Bass and W. Devries *supra* n.111, at 41–42; W. Havard, *supra* n.109, at 18–23.
113. Editorial, Washington *Post*, Mar. 27, 1978.

114. Holton, *Inaugural Address*, Va. S. Doc. no. 3, at 5 (1970).

115. *Time* magazine, Sept. 14, 1970, at 39; *New York Times*, Sept. 1, 1970.

116. Washington *Post*, Sept. 1, 1970.

117. Rich, "Decency and Loyalty: Linwood Holton Learns the President's Views," *Washington Monthly*, April 1973, at 48; *Time* magazine, Nov. 15, 1971, at 59.

118. Editorial, Richmond *Afro-American*, Jan. 16, 1971.

119. Dewar, "Holton's Achievement: Building Bridges Between Va. People," Washington *Post*, Jan. 2, 1974.

120. Editorial, Richmond *Times-Dispatch*, Oct. 24, 1971.

121. Personal Interview, Oct. 6, 1977.

122. U.S. Congress, House, Subcomm. no. 5 of the Comm. on the Judiciary, *School Busing: Hearings on Proposed Amendments to the Constitution and Legislation Relating to Transportation and Assignment of Public School Pupils*, 92d Cong., 2d sess., 1292, 1691 (1972) (statement of Arthur Lynch).

123. *New York Times*, April 21, 1971.

124. Editorial, Charlotte *Observer*, April 21, 1971.

125. 402 U.S. at 7–11.

126. Editorial, Charlotte *News*, June 28, 1969.

127. See ibid.

128. Such is the general thesis of the U.S. Commission on Civil Rights.

129. See the discussion on the Boston School Committee in chapter eight.

130. Editorial, Charlotte *News*, June 19, 1971.

131. Barrows, *supra* n.11, at 18.

132. U.S. Commission on Civil Rights, *Five Communities, Their Search for Equal Education* 37 (1972).

133. *School Busing Hearings, supra* n.122, at 1309.

134. See Swann v. Charlotte-Mecklenburg Bd. of Educ., 334 F. Supp. 623, 625 (W.D.N.C. 1971) and Swann v. Charlotte-Mecklenburg Bd. of Educ., 362 F. Supp. 1223, 1230, 1237 (W.D.N.C. 1973).

135. *School Busing Hearings, supra* n.122, at 1297.

136. U.S. Commission on Civil Rights, *supra* n.132, at 35.

137. Barrows, *supra* n.11, at 20.

138. Ayres, *supra* n.26.

139. Ibid.

140. Barrows, *supra* n.11, at 20.

141. Charlotte *Observer*, April 22, 1971.

142. Gaillard and Paddock, "Charlotte's Busing Breakthrough," *Progressive*, Oct. 1975, at 37.

143. Swann v. Charlotte-Mecklenburg Bd. of Educ., 379 F. Supp. 1102, 1103 (W.D.N.C. 1974).

144. 67 F.R.D. 648, 649 (W.D.N.C. 1975); Ayres, *supra* n.26.

145. 402 U.S. at 9.

146. Ayres, *supra* n.26.

147. Finger, *supra* n.93, at 60.

148. Of course, attending suburban schools requires a change of residence while private school attendance may not. In this respect, private schooling is a more feasible escape from busing than movement to the suburbs.

149. Swann v. Charlotte-Mecklenburg Bd. of Educ., 402 U.S. 1, 30 (1971); Mills, *supra* n.5, at 11.

150. Finger, *supra* n.93, at 61; U.S. Commission on Civil Rights, *supra* n.132, at 36.

151. Barrows, *supra* n.11, at 19.

152. Ibid. at 22.

Chapter 7

1. See Alexander v. Holmes County Bd. of Educ., 396 U.S. 19 (1969).
2. See generally chapter five.
3. 391 U.S. 430 (1968).
4. See also United States v. Montgomery County Bd. of Educ., 395 U.S. 225 (1969).
5. For two contrary tales of such Warren Court decisions see A. Cox, *The Warren Court* (1968) and P. Kurland, *Politics, the Constitution, and the Warren Court* (1970).
6. Note, for example, the justices' disagreements in Adderley v. Florida, 385 U.S. 39 (1966) (civil rights protest) and Swain v. Alabama, 380 U.S. 202 (1965) (juries). In these two cases, the black point of view did not prevail.
7. Farrell, "School Integration Resisted in Cities of North," *New York Times*, May 13, 1974.
8. See 402 U.S. at 4.
9. U.S., Congress, Senate, Committee of the Judiciary, *Nominations of William H. Rehnquist and Lewis F. Powell, Jr.*, 92d Cong., 1st sess. (1971) (statement of Sen. William B. Spong, D-Va.).
10. Editorial, Norfolk *Virginian-Pilot*, Oct. 23, 1971.
11. See Powell, "The President's Annual Address: The State of The Legal Profession," 51 *A.B.A.J.* 821, 827 (1965); "Respect for Law and Due Process—The Foundation of a Free Society," 18 *U. Fla. L. Rev.* 1, 4 (1965); "A Lawyer Looks at Civil Disobedience," 23 *Wash. & Lee L. Rev.* 205, 210 (1966).
12. Powell, "A Lawyer Looks at Civil Disobedience," 23 *Wash. & Lee L. Rev.* 205, 206–7 (1966).
13. See Bradley v. Richmond School Bd., 317 F.2d 429, 431–32 (CA4 1963).
14. A feeder system is one in which black elementary student bodies are routinely assigned or "fed" to black junior highs, which in turn, feed into black high schools.
15. 317 F.2d at 438.
16. *Confirmation Hearings, supra* n.9, at 393.
17. Ibid., at 380. For an overview of Justice Powell's philosophy at the time of his elevation to the Supreme Court, see Howard, "Mr. Justice Powell and the Emerging Nixon Majority," 70 *Mich. L. Rev.* 445 (1972).
18. Keyes v. Denver School District, 413 U.S. 189, 238 (1973) (Powell, J. concurring in part and dissenting in part).
19. Wright v. City of Emporia, 407 U.S. 451 (1972).
20. See also J. Wilkinson, *Serving Justice: A Supreme Court Clerk's View* 76 (1974).
21. 413 U.S. at 253.
22. In his *Keyes* opinion, for example, Powell would have required the drawing of neighborhood attendance zones, construction of new schools, assignment of faculty, and transfer of students in such a way as to maximize integration. 413 U.S. at 240–41.
23. Ibid. at 250.
24. 402 U.S. at 26.
25. 413 U.S. at 242.
26. Ibid. at 248.
27. NAACP Legal Defense and Educational Fund, "It's Not the Distance, It's the 'Niggers,' " in N. Mills, ed., *The Great School Bus Controversy* 322, 337 (1973).
28. See L. Graglia, *Disaster by Decree: The Supreme Court Decisions on Race and the Schools* 110 (1976).
29. J. Bolner and R. Shanley, *Busing: The Political and Judicial Process* 243 (1974).
30. U.S., Congress, House, Subcomm. No. 5, Comm. on the Judiciary, *School Busing: Hearings on Proposed Amendments to the Constitution and Legislation Relating to Transportation and Assignment of Public School Pupils* 92d Cong., 2d Sess., 1311 (1972) (statement of Julia Maulden).

31. As quoted in Mondale, "School Busing in Perspective" *New Republic*, Mar. 4, 1972, at 18.
32. 20 U.S.C. §§ 1228 and 1652 (a) and Public Law 94-94, 89 Stat. 468, § 315(b). The Sixth Circuit held attacks on these federal funding prohibitions to present no case or controversy because there was no other federal statutory authorization for a community's student transportation costs. Carroll v. Jefferson County Bd. of Educ., 561 F.2d 1, 4 (CA6 1977), *cert. den.* 98 S. Ct. 1449 (1978).
33. NAACP Legal Defense and Educational Fund, *supra* n.27, at 336.
34. *School Busing Hearings, supra* n.30, at 1296 (statement of William Poe).
35. Carroll v. Department of Health, Education, and Welfare, 410 F. Supp. 234 (W.D.Ky. 1976).
36. Brewer v. Norfolk School Bd., 456 F.2d 943, 946–47 (CA4 1972).
37. Mondale, *supra* n.31, at 18–19.
38. Ibid. at 19.
39. *School Busing Hearings, supra* n.30, at 1297 (statement of William Poe).
40. Ibid., at 1295.
41. See Finger, "Why Busing Plans Work," in F. Levinsohn and B. Wright, eds., *School Desegregation: Shadow and Substance* 60 (1976).
42. *Swann* noted that in the event of "default by the school authorities of their obligation to proffer acceptable remedies, a district court has broad power to fashion a remedy that will assure a unitary school system." 402 U.S. at 16.
43. See *School Busing Hearings, supra* n.30, at 1298 (statement of William Poe).
44. Annual revision of bus routes and inclusion of suburban school districts in desegregation decrees were curtailed, though not eliminated, by Supreme Court rulings in Pasadena Bd. of Ed. v. Spangler, 427 U.S. 424 (1976) and Milliken V. Bradley, 418 U.S. 717 (1974).
45. For example, scores on college board examinations fell. See Harnischfeger and Wiley, "Achievement Test Score Decline: Do We need to Worry?" *Central Midwestern Regional Educational Lab.*, Dec. 1975; Boyd and Sciolino, "The Decline in SAT Scores," *Newsweek*, Mar. 8, 1976, at 58.
46. Keyes v. Denver School District, 413 U.S. 189, 250 (1973) (Powell, J. concurring in part and dissenting in part).
47. Middleton, "Desegregation of Schools: Mood and Pace Changing," Washington *Star*, July 31, 1977.
48. Kohl, in "Busing: A Symposium," *Ramparts*, Dec.-Jan. 1974–75, at 38.
49. 402 U.S. at 30.
50. R. Coles, *The South Goes North*, vol. 3 of *Children of Crisis* 101 (1972).
51. Nordheimer, "Richmond's Black Pupils Want Whites to Feel at Home," *New York Times*, Sept. 1, 1970.
52. Fiss, "Racial Imbalance in Schools: The Constitutional Concepts," 78 *Harv. L. Rev.* 564, 566 (1965).
53. Pierce v. Society of Sisters, 268 U.S 510 (1925).
54. San Antonio Ind. School Dist. v. Rodriguez, 411 U.S. 1 (1973).
55. See chapter five.
56. Fiss, *supra* n.52, at 567.
57. Coles, "When Northern Schools Desegregate," *Integrated Education*, Feb.–Mar. 1966, at 11.
58. Cottle, "Bus Start," *New York Times Magazine*, Mar. 9, 1975, at 20.
59. Prayer Breakfast Speech to American Bar Association, August 13, 1972, pp. 2–3. Excerpts from the speech were reported in *U.S. News & World Report*, Aug. 28, 1972.
60. 413 U.S. at 246.
61. 402 U.S. at 28.

62. It is possible, of course, for neighborhood friends to attend different schools under neighborhood zoning, if attendance lines run between their homes. But busing makes dispersal much more likely.

63. See Cunningham v. Jefferson County Bd. of Educ., 541 F.2d 538, 540 (CA6 1976).

64. Haycraft v. Jefferson County Bd. of Educ., 560 F.2d 755 (CA6 1977).

65. The reshuffling was permitted under Pasadena Bd. of Educ. v. Spangler, 427 U.S. 424 (1976) because it was judged to be "precompliance." 560 F.2d at 756.

66. The busing burden between blacks and whites in the Louisville area could not be evenly distributed, because the combined school system was but 20 percent black. Thus, blacks would necessarily be bused more years than whites.

67. Staff report, "The Shawnee cluster: Why did it get hot?" Louisville *Courier-Journal*, Mar. 4, 1977.

68. The quotations in this paragraph are from Aprile, Howington, and Simmons, "School Violence: Who Knows Why?" Louisville *Courier-Journal*, Mar. 8, 1977.

69. Rides of forty to fifty minutes one-way were not uncommon in the Louisville plan. See *Time* magazine, Sept. 22, 1975, at 12.

70. See generally Havighurst, "Educational Policy for the Large Cities" 24 *Social Problems* 271 (1976); U.S. Dept. of Health, Education and Welfare, *Equality of Educational Opportunity* (1966) (the first Coleman Report).

71. 413 U.S. at 250.

72. The tipping point for schools is often thought to be 30 percent black. See R. Crain and C. Rossell, *Evaluating School Desegregation Plans Statistically* 18 (1973). The tipping point in housing is a subject of considerable debate but is generally thought to be lower than that for schools. K Taeuber and A. Taeuber, *Negroes in Cities* 100 (1965).

73. For a discussion of this same phenomen in housing turnover, see chapter nine.

74. See, for example, the discussion of Charlotte in chapter six.

75. Farrell, *supra* n.7.

76. Ayres, "Desegregation of Southern Schools Since '54 Produces Confusing Patterns of Impressive Gains, Bitter Setbacks," *New York Times*, May 13, 1974.

77. J. Coleman, S. Kelly, and J. Moore, *Trends in School Segregation 1968–73* (1975).

78. U.S. Dept. of Health, Education, and Welfare, *Equality of Educational Opportunity* (1966).

79. See Coleman, "Integration, Yes: Busing, No," *New York Times Magazine*, Aug. 24, 1975, at 10.

80. See Coleman, "Liberty and Equality in School Desegregation," *Social Policy*, Jan./Feb. 1976, at 10–11.

81. Coleman, "A Reply to Green and Pettigrew," *Phi Delta Kappan*, Mar. 1976, at 454–55.

82. Coleman, *supra* n.79, at 46.

83. Coleman, *supra* n.81, at 455.

84. As quoted in Pettigrew and Green, "School Desegregation in Large Cities: A Critique of the Coleman 'White Flight' Thesis," *Harv. Educ. Rev.* 1, 44 (1976).

85. Coleman, *supra* n.79, at 11.

86. Coleman, "Courts Scored As Going Too Far in School Integration," Los Angeles *Times*, May 29, 1975.

87. As quoted in Pettigrew and Green, *supra* n.84, at 11.

88. When the media at first gave only scant attention to Coleman's views, Pettigrew and Green observed, Coleman began granting personal interviews. These interviews "met three of the mass media's major criteria as to what constitutes big news. They appeared to represent (1) a 'surprising' reversal of position (2) by a publicly known authority (3) in a direction that fitted snugly the prevailing national mood of retrenchment. Almost at once, newspapers throughout the country ran 'Coleman' stories, and conservative editorialists had a field day. Rarely, if ever, had a sociologist's opinions been so sought after

by the media. Earlier reluctant to deal with the media, Coleman granted dozens of separate interviews, many of them by telephone. In late June, *Newsweek* even sent two reporters to talk with Coleman at his remote vacation home in West Virginia." Ibid. at 10.

89. Ibid. at 52–53.

90. Ibid. at 4–5.

91. Rossell, "School Desegregation and White Flight" 90 *Pol Sci. Quarterly* 675, 676 (1975–76). See also Farley, "Racial Integration in the Public Schools, 1967 to 1972: Assessing the Effects of Governmental Policies," *Sociological Focus*, vol. 8, no. 1, 1975, at 3.

92. Orfield, "Is Coleman Right?" *Social Policy*, Jan./Feb. 1976, and 25; Rossell, *supra* n. 91, at 688.

93. For example, Coleman contended he had not included more northern cities because few northern cities had undergone extensive desegregation from 1968 to 1973, the years of his study. He claimed that his sample was representative and consisted of the twenty largest school districts classified by the U.S. Office of Education as central city school districts, excluding Washington, D.C., which had a 97 percent black population. And he refused to accept Pettigrew's contention that Atlanta and Memphis were atypical districts. A fuller version of Coleman's reply to his critics may be found in the articles cited *supra*, notes 79–81.

94. Brunson v. Clarendon School Dist., 429 F.2d 820 (CA4 1970).

95. Ibid. at 820–23 (Craven, J., concurring and dissenting). Judge Craven later retracted his position in Bradley v. Richmond School Bd., 462 F.2d 1058, 1063–64 n.5 (CA4 1972).

96. Ibid., at 823–27 (Sobeloff J., concurring).

97. For a hopeful story, see Greider, "Mayor Restores Detroit's Faith," Washington *Post*, June 25, 1978.

98. See R. Kluger, *Simple Justice* 85 (1975).

99. Armor, "The Evidence on Busing," *Public Interest*, Summer 1972, at 91.

100. G. Allport, *The Nature of Prejudice* (1954).

101. Armor, *supra* n.99, at 99.

102. Ibid. at 100.

103. Ibid. at 101. Armor did find that the one positive effect of busing was "the 'channeling' effect whereby black students who attend white middle-class schools tend to get into higher quality colleges. . . ." Ibid. at 114.

104. Ibid., at 101, 103, and 111.

105. Ibid. at 111 and 115–16.

106. See, e.g., Northcross v. Memphis Bd. of Educ., 466 F.2d 890, 903 (CA6 1972) (Weick, J., dissenting).

107. Pettigrew, Useem, Normand and Smith, "Busing: A Review of 'The Evidence,' " *Public Interest*, Winter 1973, at 88.

109. N. St. John, *School Desegregation Outcomes for Children* 119 and 88 (1975).

110. 347 U.S. at 494.

111. St. John, *supra* n. 109, at 92–93.

112. Ibid. at ix-x.

113. Hawley and Rist, "On the Future Implementation of School Desegregation: Some Conisderations," 39 *Law and Contemp. Probs.* 412–13 (1975).

114. In the same questioning vein, See H. Gerard and N. Miller, *School Desegregation* (1975).

115. See, e.g., McPartland, "The Relative Influence of School and of Classroom Desegregation on the Academic Achievement of Ninth Grade Negro Students," *J. Social Issues*, vol. 25, no.3, 1969, at 93.

116. See generally for a discussion of the most favorable conditions for school integration, N. St. John, *supra* n.109, at 87–117; Hawley and Rist, *supra* n.113; Weinberg, *"The Relationship Between School Desegregation and Academic Achievement: A Review of the Re-*

search," 39 *Law and Contemp. Probs.* 241, 269 (1975); Pettigrew et al., *supra* n.107, at 91–92; Crain, "Why Academic Research Research Fails to Be Useful," in F. Levinsohn and B. Wright, eds., *School Desegregation: Shadow and Substance* 31 (1976).

117. N. St. John, *supra* n.109, at 39.
118. Middleton, "Does Integration Help Kids to Learn?," Washington *Star*, Aug. 1, 1977.
119. Middleton, "Desegregation: Tolerance Replacing School Violence," Washington *Star*, Aug. 2, 1977.
120. Aronson, with Blaney, Sikes, Stephan, and Snapp, "Busing and Racial Tension: The Jigsaw Route to Learning and Liking," *Psychology Today*, Feb. 1975, at 47.
121. Ibid., at 49.
122. One suspects, for example, that the approach would prove less successful with older children.
123. Wisdom, "Random Remarks on the Role of Social Sciences in the Judicial Decision-Making Process in School Desegregation Cases," 39 *Law and Contemp. Prob.* 134, 135 (1975). Wisdom's remark pertained specifically to Milliken v. Bradley, 418 U.S. 717 (1974), the Detroit school case in which the Court reversed a lower court plan ordering metropolitan school desegregation.
124. See, in addition to discussions of certain of these cities elsewhere in this book, N. Glazer, *Affirmative Discrimination* 121–22 (1975).
125. N.St. John, *supra* n.109, at xii.
126. Green v. County School Board, 391 U.S. 430, 439 (1968).
127. Milliken v. Bradley, 433 U.S. 267, 279 (1977).
128. Ibid. at 276.
129. Ibid. at 287–88.
130. Outside the context of a desegregation decree, the Court has been careful to protect the academic autonomy of educational institutions. See Board of Curators of the Univ. of Missouri v. Horowitz, 98 S. Ct. 948 (1978).
131. It is likely that they could. See the discussion of lower court cases so doing (433 U.S. at 285–86) and the comment in Justice Marshall's concurring opinion (433 U.S. at 292).

Chapter 8

1. As quoted in J. Buncher, ed., *Facts on File: The School Busing Controversy: 1970–75* 99 (1975).
2. Ibid.
3. Editorial, Detroit *Free Press*, Feb. 11, 1970.
4. Editorial, *New York Times*, April 22, 1971.
5. 402 U.S. at 5–6 and 13.
6. See Bell v. School City of Gary, Ind., 213 F. Supp. 819, 822 (N.D. Ind. 1963). Burns Indiana Statutes Annotated, 1948 Replacement, Section 28–5104.
7. Goodman, "De Facto School Segregation: A Constitutional and Empirical Analysis," 60 *Calif. L. Rev.* 275, 297 (1972). Professor Goodman continues: "True, the earlier the policy of segregation was abandoned the less danger there is that it continues to operate covertly, is significantly responsible for present day patterns of residential segregation, or has contributed materially to present community attitudes toward Negro schools. But there is no reason to suppose that 1954 is a universally appropriate dividing line between de jure segregation that may safely be assumed to have spent itself and that which may not. For many remedial purposes, adoption of an arbitrary but easily administrable cut-off point might not be objectionable. But in a situation such as school desegregation, where both the rights asserted and the remedial burdens imposed are of such magnitude, and where the resulting sectional discrimination is passionately resented, it is surely questionable whether such arbitrariness is either politically or morally acceptable." Ibid.

8. As cited in Keyes v. Denver School District, 413 U.S. 189, 218 n.3 (1973) (Powell, J., concurring in part and dissenting in part).

9. Ayres, "Desegregation of Southern Schools Since '54 Produces Confusing Patterns of Impressive Gains, Bitter Setbacks," *New York Times*, May 13, 1974.

10. See Keyes v. Denver School District, 413 U.S. 189, 218 n.4 (1973) (Powell, J., concurring in part and dissenting in part).

11. Taeuber, "Residential Segregation," *Scientific American*, Aug. 1965, at 14.

12. See chapter six.

13. Bickel, "Untangling the Busing Snarl," *New Republic*, Sept. 23, 1972, at 23.

14. See, e.g., Bell v. School City of Gary, Ind., 324 F.2d 209 (CA7 1963), *cert. denied*, 377 U.S. 924 (1964); Downs v. Kansas City Bd. of Educ., 336 F.2d 988 (CA10 1964), *cert. denied*, 380 U.S. 914 (1965); Deal v. Cincinnati Bd. of Educ., 369 F.2d 55 (CA6 1966), *cert. denied*, 389 U.S. 847 (1967).

15. Editorial, Los Angeles *Times*, April 22, 1971.

16. Jencks, "Busing—The Supreme Court Goes North," *New York Times Magazine*, Nov. 19, 1972, at 41.

17. See Sterba, "Denver School Busing Succeeds; Social Mixture Called a Factor," *New York Times*, Oct. 26, 1974; Keyes v. Denver School District, 413 U.S. 189, 191 and 195 (1973).

18. Jones v. Newlon, 81 Colo. 25, 253 P. 386 cited by the Supreme Court in Keyes v. Denver School District, 413 U.S. 189, 191 (1973).

19. N. Peirce, *The Mountain States of America* 38–39 (1972); L. Graglia, *Disaster by Decree, The Supreme Court Decisions on Race and the Schools* 161 (1976).

20. L. Graglia, *supra* n.19, at 161–62; Keyes v. Denver School District, 413 U.S. 189, 192–205 (1973) and the dissenting opinion of Justice Rehnquist at 258–61.

21. U.S. Commission on Civil Rights, *Fulfilling the Letter and Spirit of the Law: Desegregation of The Nation's Public Schools* 41 (1976).

22. Keyes v. Denver School District, 413 U.S. 189, 192 (1973); N. Peirce, *supra* n.19, at 39. Professor Graglia argues that rescission of the desegregation resolutions most influenced the district judge's finding of de jure segregation in Denver and that, in essence, Denver was the victim of its own good intentions. See L. Graglia, *supra* n.19, at 165–73.

23. 413 U.S. at 201–2, and 205.

24. Ibid. at 199 n.10.

25. Ibid. at 192, 199–203; Keyes v. Denver School District, 313 F. Supp. 61 (D. Colo. 1970); Civil Rights Commission, *supra* n.21, at 41.

26. 413 U.S. at 203.

27. Ibid. at 208.

28. Ibid. at 213; Keyes v. Denver School District, 368 F. Supp. 207 (D. Colo. 1973).

29. 413 U.S. at 200.

30. Oliver v. Kalamazoo Bd. of Educ., 368 F. Supp. 143, 152 (W.D. Mich. 1973).

31. See Morgan v. Hennigan, 379 F. Supp. 410 (D. Mass. 1974).

32. See chapter six.

33. See Keyes v. Denver School District, 413 U.S. 189, 224 (1973) (Powell, J., concurring in part and dissenting in part).

34. Ibid. at 233.

35. See L. Graglia, *supra* n.19, at 170–71.

36. Lembke, "Denver Busing Case May Set U.S. Pattern," Los Angeles *Times*, Mar. 24, 1974.

37. G. Orfield, *Must We Bus?* 27 (1978).

38. Higgins v. Grand Rapids Bd. of Educ., 395 F. Supp. 444 (W.D. Mich. 1973).

39. Oliver v. Kalamazoo Bd. of Educ., 368 F. Supp. 143 (W.D. Mich. 1973).

40. 508 F.2d 779 (CA6 1974) (Grand Rapids); 508 F.2d 178 (CA6 1974) (Kalamazoo).

41. Marshall, "The Standard of Intent: Two Recent Michigan Cases," 4 *J. Law & Educ.* 227, 233 (1975).

42. Orfield, *supra* n.37, at 24.

43. Sterba, *supra* n.17.

44. Civil Rights Commission, *supra* n.21, at 44–48.

45. Keyes v. Denver School District, 380 F. Supp. 673, 686–87 (D. Colo. 1974).

46. Finger, "Why Busing Plans Work," in F. Levinsohn and B. Wright, eds., *School Desegregation: Shadow and Substance* 62 (1976).

47. Keyes v. Denver School District, 521 F.2d 465, 477–79 (CA10 1975). The "part-time pairing plan," held the court, "would leave most participating minority schools intensely segregated during periods of instruction in basic subjects." Part-time pairing, in essence, was unconstitutional because it meant only part-time desegregation. Ibid. at 479. See also Arvizu v. Waco Ind. Sch. Dist., 495 F.2d 499, 503 (CA5 1974).

48. Finger, *supra* n.46, at 62.

49. 521 F.2d at 479 n.12. Minority elementary students were bused long distances for six years to white neighborhoods. But, noted the Court of Appeals, "nearly all of the elementary students who are to be bused long-distance to the southern portion of the district will attend neighborhood high schools and junior high schools; likewise, elementary school pupils in the extreme southeast and southwest portions of the city will ultimately be bused to junior high schools in the central and northeastern portions of the city." Ibid. at 479.

50. Associated Press, Austin, Texas *American-Statesman*, Dec. 19, 1974, as quoted in L. Graglia, *supra* n.19, at 201–2.

51. Lembke, *supra* n.36.

52. N. Peirce, *supra* n.19, at 40.

53. Associated Press, *supra* n.50.

54. See generally Kifner, "North's Schools Face a Long, Hot Autumn," *New York Times*, Aug. 24, 1975, and Wooten, "The Focus on Busing Is Now in the North," *New York Times*, June 6, 1976.

55. J. Buncher, *supra* n.1, at 222, 228, and 231.

56. U.S. Commission on Civil Rights, *Twenty Years after Brown* 54 (1974).

57. As quoted in Farrell, "School Integration Resisted in Cities of North," *New York Times*, May 13, 1974.

58. Kifner, *supra* n.54.

59. See Morgan v. Kerrigan, 401 F. Supp. 216, 223 (D. Mass. 1975).

60. Mass. Gen. L. c. 71 §§ 37C and 37D.

61. Editorial, Dallas *Times Herald*, Sept. 15, 1974.

62. U.S. Commission on Civil Rights, *supra* n.21, at 27.

63. Day, "A Symposium on Busing," *Ramparts* magazine, Jan. 1975, at 41.

64. Morgan v. Hennigan, 379 F. Supp. 410, 422 (D. Mass. 1974).

65. Associated Press, "Blacks Still Stay Out of Charlestown," Norfolk *Virginian-Pilot*, Nov. 20, 1977.

66. 379 F. Supp. at 422.

67. Day, *supra* n.63.

68. See Morgan v. Kerrigan, 401 F. Supp. 216, 223 (D. Mass. 1975).

69. Kifner, "On Paper, The Boston School Plan Functions," *New York Times*, Feb. 8, 1976.

70. Ford, "Busing In Boston," *Commonweal*, Oct. 10, 1975, at 459 and 457.

71. C. Woodward, *The Strange Career of Jim Crow* 19 (3rd ed., 1974).

72. Ford, *supra* n.70, at 456; Associated Press, *supra* n.65. See also J. Hillson, *The Battle of Boston* 145–60 (1977).

73. See generally, N. Glazer, *Affirmative Discrimination* 186–94 (1975).

74. Ford, *supra* n.70, at 459.

75. Woodward, "What Happened to the Civil Rights Movement?" *Harper's* magazine, Jan. 1967, at 36.
76. Morgan v. Hennigan, 379 F. Supp. 410, 482 (D. Mass. 1974).
77. Ibid. at 481.
78. Morgan v. Kerrigan, 401 F. Supp. 216, 223 (D. Mass. 1975).
79. 379 F. Supp. at 480 n.50.
80. Judge Garrity's findings on Boston's history of segregation were affirmed in Morgan v. Kerrigan, 509 F.2d 580 (CA1 1974), *cert. denied*, 421 U.S. 963 (1975).
81. 401 F. Supp. at 239.
82. 401 F. Supp. at 239; Associated Press, "U.S. Judge Orders Busing of 21,000 in Boston Schools, *New York Times*, May 11, 1975.
83. 401 F. Supp. at 238.
84. Ibid. at 248–49; Morgan v. Kerrigan, 530 F.2d 401, 407 (CA1 1976); Civil Rights Commission, *supra* n.21, at 35–36; Willie, "Racial Balance or Quality Education," in Levinsohn and Wright, eds., *supra* n.46.
85. J. Buncher, *supra* n.1, at 247; 401 F. Supp. at 225.
86. Ford, *supra* n.70, at 457.
87. Editorial, Boston *Globe*, Oct. 9, 1974.
88. J. Buncher, *supra* n.1, at 248, 251, and 257; 401 F. Supp. at 225.
89. Kopkind, "Busing Into Southie," *Ramparts* magazine, Jan. 1975, at 34.
90. Associated Press, *supra* n.65.
91. Kopkind, *supra* n.89, at 35.
92. As quoted by Associated Press, n.82.
93. Coleman, "A Reply to Green and Pettigrew," *Phi Delta Kappan*, Mar. 1976, at 455.
94. Kifner, *supra* n.69.
95. Associated Press, *supra* n.65.
96. Civil Rights Commission, *supra* n.21, at 38–39.
97. Lewis, "The Boston Schools: II," *New York Times*, May 24, 1976.
98. Civil Rights Commission, *supra* n.21, at 31.
99. See Morgan v. Kerrigan, 530 F.2d 401, 406 n.5 (CA1 1976).
100. Kifner, "Tale of 2 Cities—Boston by Day, and Night," *New York Times*, Sept. 12, 1975.
101. Cottle, "Bus Start," *New York Times Magazine*, Mar. 9, 1975, at 16–17.
102. Kifner, "South Boston, a 'Town' of Irishmen, Feels as if It's a Persecuted Belfast," *New York Times*, Sept. 23, 1974.
103. Ibid.
104. N. Glazer, *supra* n.73, at 105.
105. Coles, Harvard Phi Beta Kappa Address, June 1975, as quoted in Ford, *supra* n.70 at 459.
106. N. Peirce, *The Megastates of America* 134 (1972).
107. Kifner, *supra* n.102.
108. Ibid.
109. Cottle, *supra* n.101, at 17. See also A. Lupo, *Liberty's Chosen Home* 174–83 (1977).
110. Kifner, *supra* n.102.
111. Kifner, *supra* n.100.
112. Kifner, *supra* n.102.
113. Hicks and Kerrigan were defeated for reelection to the City Council; Palladino to the School Committee. Hicks and Palladino were narrowly beaten; Kerrigan soundly. The vote of Hicks in antibusing strongholds remained high. See Healy, "Boston Message: Never Say Never," Boston *Globe*, Nov. 9, 1977.
114. Cowen, "O'Bryant Wins A Spot," Boston *Globe*, Nov. 9, 1977.
115. Associated Press, *supra* n.65.

116. Kopkind, *supra* n.89, at 34.
117. See R. Warren, *Segregation* 64 (1956). Mr. Warren asked that question of himself.
118. V. Key, *Southern Politics* 9 (1949).
119. As quoted in Wilkins, "The Sound of One Hand Clapping," *New York Times Magazine*, May 12, 1974, at 44.
120. Keyes v. Denver School District, 413 U.S. at 250 (Powell, J., concurring in part and dissenting in part).
121. See Franks v. Bowman Trans. Co., 424 U.S. 747 (1976), and International Brotherhood of Teamsters v. United States, 431 U.S. 324 (1977), where the Court addressed the issue of retroactive seniority as a remedy for past employment discrimination.
122. Day, *supra* n.63, at 42.
123. Ibid.
124. Ibid.

Chapter 9

1. Wilkins, "The Sound of One Hand Clapping," *New York Times Magazine*, May 12, 1974, at 43.
2. U.S. Bureau of the Census, *Statistical Abstract of the United States, 1974* 17 (1975).
3. As quoted in Wilkins, *supra* n.1, at 43.
4. G. Orfield, *Must We Bus?* 291 (1978).
5. Ibid. at 333.
6. See Wooten, "The Focus on Busing Is Now in the North," *New York Times*, June 6, 1976.
7. See, e.g., Roe v. Wade, 410 U.S. 113 (1973) (abortion); United States v. United States District Court, 407 U.S. 297 (1972) (wiretapping); Committee for Public Educ. v. Nyquist, 413 U.S. 756 (1973) (parochial school aid); United States v. Nixon, 418 U.S. 683 (1974) (executive privilege).
8. E.g., Harris v. New York, 401 U.S. 222 (1971); Kirby v. Illinois, 406 U.S. 682 (1972); Adams v. Williams, 407 U.S. 143 (1972); United States v. Dionisio, 410 U.S. 1 (1973).
9. Dandridge v. Williams, 397 U.S. 471 (1970) (welfare); Lindsey v. Normet, 405 U.S. 56 (1972) (housing); San Antonio Ind. School Dist. v. Rodriguez, 411 U.S. 1 (1973) (education).
10. Palmer v. Thompson, 403 U.S. 217 (1971); Moose Lodge v. Irvis, 407 U.S. 163 (1972).
11. Wright v. City Council of Emporia, 407 U.S. 451 (1972).
12. 418 U.S. 717 (1974).
13. Bradley v. Milliken, 338 F. Supp. 582 (E.D. Mich. 1971).
14. Bradley v. Milliken, 345 F. Supp. 914 (E.D. Mich. 1972).
15. Editorial, Dallas *Morning News*, June 22, 1972.
16. 345 F. Supp. at 919, 929, and 926.
17. Bradley v. Milliken, 484 F.2d 215 (CA6 1973).
18. Editorial, Detroit *News*, June 16, 1972.
19. G. Orfield, *supra* n.4, at 248.
20. Farley, "Population Trends and School Segregation in the Detroit Metropolitan Area," 21 *Wayne L. Rev.* 867, 869 (1975). In the quoted passage, Mr. Farley spoke specifically of Detroit.
21. Ibid. at 870.
22. See Milliken v. Bradley, 418 U.S. at 765 n.1 (White, J., dissenting).
23. As quoted in 418 U.S. at 728–29 n.8.
24. 484 F.2d 215, 245 (1973).
25. See L. Graglia, *Disaster by Decree: The Supreme Court Decisions on Race and the Schools* 218 (1976).

26. If a school located in a depressed inner-city neighborhood were 85 percent black–15 percent white, for example, disadvantaged whites at the school stood to benefit from busing, since the buses would be carrying in suburban whites from higher socioeconomic levels. On the other hand, disadvantaged whites would probably not be bused out to suburban schools since that would only accentuate the racial imbalance already existing in the suburbs. The constitutional necessity to focus on race, not background, in desegregation may thus create genuine unfairness.

27. See F. Mosteller and D. Moynihan, eds., *On Equality of Educational Opportunity* 22–24 (1972); U.S. Dept. of Health, Education and Welfare, *Equality of Educational Opportunity* (1966) (the first Coleman Report).

28. U.S. Congress, Senate, Comm. on the Judiciary, Subcomm. on Constitutional Rights, *Busing of Schoolchildren: Hearings*, 93rd Cong., 2nd sess. (1974) at 96 (statement of William Poe, school board chairman).

29. J. Berke and J. Callahan, *Inequities in School Finance* (1971), reprinted in Senate Select Committee on Equal Educational Opportunity, 92nd Cong., 2d sess., *Report on Issues in School Finance* 129, 142 (Comm. Print 1972); Glickstein and Want, "Inequality in School Financing: The Role of the Law," 25 *Stan. L. Rev.* 335, 338 (1973), as cited in Milliken v. Bradley, 418 U.S. 717, 760–61, notes 11 and 12 (1974) (Douglas, J., dissenting).

30. See McBee, " 'Dennis the Menace' Shakes Up Cleveland," Washington *Post*, Jan. 29, 1978, for story of Cleveland.

31. 411 U.S. 1 (1973).

32. Milliken v. Bradley, 418 U.S. 717, 813–14 (1974) (Marshall, J., dissenting). See also ibid. and 766–67 (White, J., dissenting).

33. 345 F. Supp. 914, 930.

34. As quoted in Bradley v. Milliken, 484 F.2d at 244.

35. Taeuber, "Demographic Perspectives on Housing and School Segregation," 21 *Wayne L. Rev.* 833, 843 (1975).

36. Orfield, "Is Coleman Right?" *Social Policy*, Jan.-Feb. 1976, at 24, 27.

37. 391 U.S. at 439.

38. 402 U.S. at 26.

39. Milliken v. Bradley, 418 U.S. 717 (1974). Chief Justice Burger wrote the opinion for the Court, in which Justices Stewart, Blackmun, Powell, and Rehnquist joined. Justices Douglas, Brennan, White, and Marshall dissented. Douglas, White, and Marshall each filed a dissenting opinion.

40. Bell, "Running and Busing in Twentieth-Century America," 4 *J. Law and Educ.* 214 (1975).

41. 402 U.S. at 16.

42. 418 U.S. at 745.

43. 338 F. Supp. at 587. See chapter six.

44. Judge Roth had briefly concluded that the state was in part responsible for segregated housing patterns:

> "It is no answer to say that restricted practices grew gradually (as the black population in the area increased between 1920 and 1970), or that since 1948 racial restrictions on the ownership of real property have been removed. The policies pursued by both government and private persons and agencies have a continuing and present effect upon the complexion of the community—as we know, the choice of a residence is a relatively infrequent affair. For many years FHA and VA openly advised and advocated the maintenance of 'harmonious' neighborhoods, i.e., racially and economically harmonious. The conditions created continue." 338 F. Supp. at 587.

45. Wright, "Are the Courts Abandoning the Cities?" 4 *J. Law & Educ.* 218, 221 (1975).

46. Sloane, *"Milliken v. Bradley* in Perspective," 4 *J. Law & Educ.* 209, 212 (1975).

47. 418 U.S. at 746.

48. Ibid. at 728 n.7. See also 756 n.2 (Stewart, J., concurring).
49. Keyes v. Denver School District, 413 U.S. 189, 227–28 (1973) (Powell, J., concurring in part and dissenting in part).
50. Typically a school desegregation opinion begins: "This is one more (and hopefully the final) episode in the Denver school desegregation case." Keyes v. Denver School District, 380 F. Supp. 673, 674 (D. Colo. 1974).
51. National Advisory Commission on Civil Disorders, *Report* 1 (1968).
52. As quoted in Farrell, "School Integration Resisted in Cities of North," *New York Times*, May 13, 1974. Mr. Hill's statement actually was made two months before *Milliken* was announced, and thus understated.
53. 418 U.S. at 782.
54. Editorial, Milwaukee *Journal*, July 27, 1974.
55. 418 U.S. at 814–15.
56. Ibid. at 741–42.
57. Ibid. at 743.
58. Ibid. at 758 (Douglas, J., dissenting).
59. See ibid. at 758–59 (Douglas, J., dissenting); pp. 770–73 (White, J., dissenting); pp. 786, 790–98 (Marshall, J., dissenting).
60. U.S. Commission on Civil Rights, *Statement on Metropolitan School Desegregation* 44–45, 66–67 n.8 (1977).
61. See ibid. at 45–48.
62. The temptation to do this would be especially strong if suburban interests gained control of the reorganized school board.
63. Only fifty-three of the eighty-five outlying suburban districts were included in the decree. Those not included were, however, the most thinly populated and most distant from Detroit. 345 F. Supp. at 925–28.
64. On the difficult question of congressional authority to limit the remedial powers of federal courts in school desegregation suits, see Note, "The Nixon Busing Bills and Congressional Power," 81 *Yale L.J.* 1542 (1972). A brief summary of antibusing legislation in the Congress is in G. Gunther, *Constitutional Law: Cases and Materials* 730–32 (9th ed., 1975).
65. Burns, "To A Mouse, On Turning Her Up In Her Nest With the Plow" (1785).
66. 418 U.S. at 814 (Marshall, J., dissenting).
67. This is not, of course, to say that the Constitution is changeless or unadaptable. See, e.g., Trop v. Dulles, 356 U.S. 86 (1958).
68. It is not entrusted to the Court alone. The last section of each amendment implies some congressional responsibility also.
69. 163 U.S. 537, 550 (1896).
70. 349 U.S. 294, 300 (1955).
71. Cooper v. Aaron, 358 U.S. 1 (1958).
72. Alexander v. Holmes County Bd. of Educ., 396 U.S. 19 (1969); Carter v. West Feliciana Parish School Bd., 396 U.S. 290 (1970).
73. C. Black, *The Occasions of Justice* 144 (1963). See chapter five.
74. 402 U.S. at 26.
75. Ibid. at 30–31.
76. Mims v. Duval County School Bd., 447 F.2d 1330, 1332–33 (CA5 1971), as discussed in Levin and Moise, "School Desegregation Litigation in the Seventies and the Use of Social Science Evidence," 39 *J. Law & Contemp. Probs.* 50, 90 (1975). Several of the Jacksonville schools had reopened by 1975. Ibid. at 90 n.239. In their article, Levin and Moise proceed to point out that the Fifth Circuit increasingly resisted the closing of black schools and raised the burden on school boards to prove the closings genuinely nonracial. See United States v. Texas Educ. Agency, 467 F.2d 848, 871–72

(CA5 1972) and Arvizu v. Waco Ind. School Dist., 495 F.2d 499, 505–6 (CA5 1974).

77. NAACP Legal Defense and Educational Fund, "It's Not the Distance, 'It's the Niggers,' " in N. Mills, ed., *The Great School Bus Controversy* 330 (1973). See also the discussion in Levin and Moise, *supra* n.76, at 88–90.

78. As to Nashville, see Kelley v. Metropolitan County Bd. of Educ., 463 F.2d 732 (CA6 1972), *cert. den.* 409 U.S. 1001 (1972). As to Charlotte, see chapter six.

79. 402 U.S. at 6.

80. See *supra* n.77.

81. "The Busing Dilemma," *Time*, April 22, 1975, at 7.

82. Ibid. at 8.

83. Even racist opposition, because of its concentration and intensity, altered the pace of desegregation in *Brown II*, though not, of course, the principle that state-imposed segregation was unconstitutional. Hostile reaction has not infrequently been permitted by the Court to circumscribe the exercise of other constitutional rights, even one as precious as free expression. See Chaplinsky v. New Hampshire, 315 U.S. 568 (1942) and Feiner v. New York, 340 U.S. 315 (1951). But the Court has been reluctant to allow it to silence Civil Rights demonstrations. See e.g., Edwards v. South Carolina, 372 U.S. 229 (1963) and Howard, "Mr. Justice Black: The Negro Protest Movement And the Rule of Law," 53 *Va. L. Rev.* 1030 (1967).

84. 402 U.S. at 16.

85. Newburg Area Council v. Jefferson County Bd. of Educ., 510 F.2d 1358 (CA6 1974), *cert. den.* 421 U.S. 931 (1975).

86. "The Busing Dilemma," *supra* n.81, at 12.

87. The McCauleys joined a boycott of Louisville schools, which, in time, fizzled. Ibid.

88. Ibid.

89. Farrell, *supra* n.52.

90. "The Busing Dilemma," *supra* n.81, at 12.

91. Farrell, *supra* n.52.

92. As quoted in Editorial, *Wall Street Journal*, Mar. 11, 1972.

93. Ibid.

94. See J. Buncher, ed., *Facts on File: The School Busing Controversy: 1970–75* 231 (1975).

95. Calhoun v. Cook, 362 F. Supp. 1249, 1252 (N.D. Ga. 1973).

96. See J. Buncher, *supra* n.94, at 231.

97. These are sometimes referred to as "second generation" racial problems. See NAACP Legal Defense Fund, Division of Legal Information and Community Service, *Report on Black Student "Push-Outs"—A National Phenomenon* 1–2 (1972).

98. For a general discussion of polls and busing, see J. Bolner and R. Shanley, *Busing: The Political and Judicial Process* 237–44 (1974).

99. Levin and Moise, *supra* n.76, at 91.

100. 402 U.S. at 26–27.

101. "The Busing Dilemma," *supra* n.81, at 15.

102. Coleman, "Integration Yes, Busing No," *New York Times Magazine*, Aug. 24, 1975, at 48. See also Coleman, *"Liberty and Equality in School Desegregation,"* Social Policy, Jan.–Feb. 1976, at 13.

103. Pettigrew, Useem, Normand, and Smith, "Busing: A Review of the Evidence," 30 *Public Interest* 88–89 (1973).

104. Hyman and Sheatsley, "Attitudes Toward Desegregation," *Scientific American*, July 1964, at 20, as cited in Farley, "Trends in Racial Inequalities: Have the Gains of the 1960s Disappeared in the 1970s?" 42 *Am. Soc. Rev.* 189–90 (1977).

105. National Opinion Research Center, National Data Programs for the Social Sciences, General Social Survey, questions 39 and 46 (1972), as cited in Farley, *supra* n.104, at 190.

106. Greeley and Sheatsley, "Attitudes Toward Integration," *Scientific American*, Dec. 1971, at 14, as cited in Hermalin and Farley, "The Potential for Residential Integration in Cities and Suburbs: Implications for the Busing Controversy," 38 *Am. Soc. Rev.* 595, 596 (1973).

107. See Hermalin and Farley, *supra* n.106, at 596.

108. E. Black, *Southern Governors and Civil Rights* 330 (1976).

109. Greider, "After Dr. King: Strong Currents of Social Change," Washington *Post*, April 2, 1978.

110. As quoted in Wilkins, *supra* n.1, at 44 and 46.

111. U.S. Bureau of the Census, 1943b: Table 62; 1975a: Tables 48 and 49, as cited in Farley, *supra* n.104, at 189.

112. Thurow, "The Economic Progress of Minority Groups," *Challenge*, Mar.–April 1976, at 21.

113. Glazer, "Alternatives to Busing," *Wall Street Journal*, Feb. 17, 1976.

114. Ibid. Greider, *supra* n.109, puts the current figure at 20 percent.

115. Farley, *supra* n.104, at 206.

116. Glazer, *supra* n.113.

117. Ibid.

118. As quoted in Wilkins, *supra* n.1, at 48.

119. Ibid. at 50.

120. Ibid.

121. Ibid.

122. Thurow, *supra* n.112, at 22.

123. Hermalin and Farley, *supra* n.106, at 602, 605, 608 and 609. Personal preferences of blacks also failed to explain residential separation because, the authors contended, opinion polls all showed blacks preferring integrated neighborhoods. Ibid. at 608.

124. deLeeuw, Schnare and Struyk, "Housing," in W. Gorham and N. Glazer, eds., *Predicament* 145–55 (1976), as cited in G. Orfield, *supra* n.4, at 87.

125. Farley, "Residential Segregation and its Implications for School Integration," 39 *Law & Contemp. Probs.* 164, 167 (1975). William Greider noted in 1978 that "most census experts think the integration of all-white neighborhoods has been slight, bordering on nonexistent. One indicator to the contrary is a national poll by the National Opinion Research Center, which asked white citizens if there are any blacks living in their neighborhoods. In 1972, 30 percent said yes. Five years later, 41 percent answered yes." Greider, *supra* n.109.

126. Note, "Blockbusting," 59 *Georgetown L.J.* 170, 171 (1970).

127. Ackerman, "Integration for Subsidized Housing and the Question of Racial Occupancy Controls," 26 *Stan. L. Rev.* 245, 253 (1974). The Ackerman article discusses the tipping phenomenon on pp. 251–60. See also T. Schilling, *The Strategy of Conflict* 90–91 (1963), and Schelling, "On the Ecology of Micromotives," *Public Interest*, Fall 1971, at 61, 79–82, where the idea originated.

128. The phenomenon may be more prevalent in low income than high income white neighborhoods. In the latter, residents feel more confident that expense will limit black intrusion. Ackerman, *supra* n.127, at 255.

129. Title VIII is the operative section. 42 U.S.C. §§ 3601–19, 3631 (1970).

130. U.S. Commission on Civil Rights, *The Federal Civil Rights Enforcement Effort*, vol. 2 *Fair Housing* 328 (1974). The assessment had not changed by 1977. See United States Commission on Civil Rights, *supra* n.60, at 63.

131. See Greider, *supra* n.109.

132. For example, "if HUD conciliation efforts fail and if the complainant does not initiate an enforcement suit, HUD must defer the matter to DOJ. However, the DOJ is involved only in 'pattern or practice' litigation and thus, is not likely to pursue the HUD

complaint which usually involves a single discriminatory incident." See Spencer, "Enforcement of Federal Fair Housing Law" 9 Urban Lawyer 514, 534 (1977).

133. United States Commission on Civil Rights, *Understanding Fair Housing* 6 (1973).

134. See Reitman v. Mulkey, 387 U.S. 369 (1967); Jones v. Alfred Mayer Co., 392 U.S. 409 (1968); Hunter v. Erickson, 393 U.S. 385 (1969).

135. Lindsey v. Normet, 405 U.S. 56 (1972).

136. James v. Valtierra, 402 U.S. 137, 139 (1971).

137. Warth v. Seldin, 422 U.S. 490 (1975).

138. Village of Arlington Heights v. Metropolitan Development Corporation, 429 U.S. 252 (1977). For the reaffirmation of local zoning power in a nonracial case, see Village of Belle Terre v. Boraas, 416 U.S. 1 (1974).

139. For a ruling similar to Arlington Heights in the context of employment testing, see Washington v. Davis, 426 U.S. 229 (1976). One Court decision might, however, operate to reduce residential segregation. In Hills v. Gautreaux, the Court permitted a metropolitan housing remedy for discriminatory site selection and tenant assignment policies pursued by the Chicago Housing Authority with the knowing assistance of HUD. 425 U.S. 284 (1976). Future public housing construction need not be confined to the city limits of Chicago, held the Court. The relevant housing market was generally understood to be metropolitan in scope, and, in contrast to Milliken v. Bradley, metropolitan relief "would not consolidate or in any way restructure local governmental units." 425 U.S. at 305–6. In fact, as the Court acknowledged tacitly, the considerable prerogatives retained by suburbs under most federal housing statutes more than protected them against any influx of low income residents. 425 U.S. at 304–5.

140. This assumes, of course, that government will not vigorously push the location of low income housing in the suburbs.

141. Featherman and Hauser, "Changes in the Socioeconomic Stratification of the Races, 1962–73," 82 *Am. J. of Soc.* 621, 647 (1976).

142. Civil Rights Cases, 109 U.S. 3, 25 (1883).

143. Evans v. Buchanan, 393 F. Supp. 428, 446 (D. Del. 1975). In this instance, there was a three-judge district court.

144. Ibid.

145. Newburg Area Council v. Jefferson County Bd. of Educ., 510 F.2d 1358, 1360 (CA6 1974).

146. Evans v. Buchanan, 393 F. Supp. at 433–34; Newburg Area Council v. Jefferson County Bd. of Educ., 510 F.2d at 1360–61.

147. 393 F. Supp. at 437.

148. In Wilmington, the Supreme Court summarily *affirmed* on direct appeal the three-judge district court, 423 U.S. 963 (1975). In Louisville, *certiorari* from the Sixth Circuit was *denied*, 421 U.S. 931 (1974).

149. See Delaney, "Louisville, A Place Where Busing Seems to Work," *New York Times*, June 6, 1976.

150. Wilmington *News Journal*, Nov. 10, 1977.

151. "Calm Prevails During Three Busing Protests," Louisville *Courier-Journal*, Aug. 28, 1977.

152. Stahl, "Students' Identity Search, Frustration Blamed In Fights," Louisville *Courier-Journal*, Mar. 2, 1977.

153. Aprile, Howington, and Simmons, *"School Violence: Who Knows Why?"* Louisville *Courier-Journal*, Mar. 8, 1977. A busing cluster involves one or more once black schools that are grouped with one or more once white schools in a student exchange for purposes of desegregation.

154. Staff report, "The Shawnee Cluster: Why Did It Get 'Hot'?" Louisville *Courier-Journal*, Mar. 4, 1977.

155. Ibid.

156. Cunningham v. Jefferson County Bd. of Educ., 541 F.2d 538, 540 (CA6 1976); "Who's Going Where?" Special Section of Louisville *Courier-Journal*, June 18, 1976.

157. See Nichols, "Gordon Says Pupils Evading Busing To Avoid 'Reckoning'" Louisville *Courier-Journal*, Oct. 15, 1977.

158. "The Shawnee Cluster: Why Did It Get 'Hot'?" *supra* n.154.

159. Shafer, "Polling the County: Fewer Blacks, 49%, Now Support School Busing," Louisville *Courier-Journal*, April 20, 1977. The latest survey was taken in late February of 1977.

160. "Poll Says Busing Is Still Top Concern, But Fewer Think It's Biggest Problem," Louisville *Courier-Journal*, Oct. 4, 1977. The poll indicated that though the percentage of whites opposing busing increased slightly, the intensity of opposition may have slightly declined.

161. 427 U.S. 424 (1976).

162. Ibid. at 428.

163. Ibid. at 433.

164. Ibid. at 435–36.

165. Ibid. at 441–43.

166. The Court in *Pasadena* (427 U.S. at 436) quoted as follows from *Swann:* "Neither school authorities nor district courts are constitutionally required to make year-by-year adjustments of the racial composition of student bodies once the affirmative duty to desegregate has been accomplished and racial discrimination through official action is eliminated from the system." 402 U.S. at 31–32.

167. The *Pasadena* opinion, however, did not end annual reassignments in the 'pre-unitary' period. See Haycroft v. Jefferson County Bd. of Educ., 560 F.2d 755 (CA6 1977).

168. 427 U.S. at 444, quoting the district court at 375 F. Supp. 1309.

169. 433 U.S. 406 (1977).

170. See ibid. at 417.

171. Ibid. at 418.

172. For example, the rescission of 'remedial' measures of one Dayton School Board by its successor was thought by the Court to be immaterial, so long as the first board was under no constitutional duty to undertake them. See 433 U.S. at 414.

173. Ibid. at 413. See also Milliken v. Bradley, 418 U.S. at 749–50.

174. See Keyes v. Denver School District, 413 U.S. 189, 207 (1973).

175. Washington v. Davis, 426 U.S. 229 (1976), for example, was cited four separate times by the Court, and Village of Arlington Heights v. Metropolitan Devel. Corp., 429 U.S. 252 (1977) twice.

176. A. Bickel, *The Supreme Court and the Idea of Progress* 103 (1970).

177. The Gospel According to St. John, ch. 12, v. 8.

178. Dayton Bd. of Educ. v. Brinkman, 433 U.S. at 417.

179. Glazer, *supra* n.113.

180. National Advisory Commission on Civil Disorders, *Report* 407 (1968).

181. "Back to School Blues," *Time* magazine, Sept. 18, 1978, at 75; Editorial, Richmond *Times-Dispatch*, Nov. 12, 1978.

182. Cox, "Desegregation," Richmond *Times-Dispatch*, July 9, 1978.

Chapter 10

1. This constitutional view was celebrated most eloquently in R. Kluger, *Simple Justice* (1976) and A. Lewis, *Gideon's Trumpet* (1964).

2. Lindsey, "White/Caucasian—and Rejected," *New York Times Magazine*, April 3, 1977, at 43.

3. Arons, "Friends of the Court . . . and the Man Who Started It All," *Saturday Review*, Oct. 15, 1977 at 12.

4. "Bakke Wins, Quotas Lose," *Time* magazine, July 10, 1978, at 15; "Dr. Bakke," *Newsweek*, July 10, 1978, at 24.

5. Letter to admissions committee at University of California at Davis, as quoted in Brief for Respondent, Univ. of Cal. v. Bakke, p. 4 (1977).

6. Lindsey, *supra* n. 2, at 43.

7. "What Rights for Whites?" *Time* magazine, Oct. 24, 1977, at 95.

8. In 1973 and 1974, the entering classes for which Bakke applied, 12 blacks, 15 Chicanos, and 4 Asian Americans were admitted under the special program. Brief for Petitioner, Univ. of Cal. v. Bakke, p. 3.

9. See the table in footnote 7 of Justice Powell's opinion in Univ. of Cal. v. Bakke.

10. Bakke v. Univ. of Cal., 553 P.2d 1152, 1158–59 (Cal. 1976); Brief for Respondent, p. 4 n.3.

11. Lindsey, *supra* n.2, at 44.

12. See Bakke v. Univ. of Cal., 553 P.2d at 1156.

13. Bakke v. Univ. of Calif., 132 Cal. Rptr. 680, 553 P.2d 1152 (1976).

14. 429 U.S. 1090 (1977).

15. Lindsey, *supra* n.2, at 42.

16. Kilpatrick, "The DeFunis Syndrome," *Nation's Business*, June 1974, at 13.

17. DeFunis v. Odegaard, 507 P.2d 1168, 1182 (Wash. 1973).

18. Ibid at 1194 (Hale, C.J., dissenting).

19. Ibid. at 1190 and 1194 (Hale, C.J., dissenting).

20. His first two scores were 512 and 566. Ibid. at 1173.

21. Ibid. at 1181 n.11 (majority opinion) and 1190 (Hale, C.J., dissenting).

22. Ibid. at 1176.

23. DeFunis v. Odegaard, 416 U.S. 312, 324 (1974) (Douglas, J., dissenting). Justice Douglas also noted that forty-eight nonminority applicants were admitted with PFYA's below DeFunis. Ibid.

24. DeFunis v. Odegaard, 507 P.2d 1169, 82 Wash. 2d 11 (1973).

25. DeFunis also "did not cast his suit as a class action, and the only remedy he requested was an injunction commanding his admission to the Law School." DeFunis v. Odegaard, 416 U.S. 312, 317 (1974).

26. Ibid. at 348 and 350 (Brennan, J., dissenting). Justice Brennan's opinion was joined by Justices Douglas, White, and Marshall.

27. Ibid. at 337 and 331 (Douglas, J., dissenting).

28. Ibid. at 328, quoting B. Hoffmann, *The Tyranny of Testing* 91–92 (1962).

29. Ibid. at 334–36. The criteria on which Justice Douglas would judge candidates for admission to law school are set forth on pp. 340–41. See generally Hechinger, "Justice Douglas's Dissent in the DeFunis Case," *Saturday Review*, July 27, 1974, at 51.

30. Kilpatrick, *supra* n.16, at 13.

31. Lewin, "Which Man's Burden?" *New Republic*, May 4, 1974, at 8–9.

32. "The Furor Over 'Reverse Discrimination,' " *Newsweek*, Sept. 26, 1977, at 54.

33. Lawrence, "The Bakke Case: Are Racial Quotas Defensible?" *Saturday Review*, Oct. 15, 1977, at 14. See also *Time* magazine, *supra* n.7, at 97; *Newsweek*, *supra* n.32, at 54.

34. *Time* magazine, *supra* n.7, at 97; *Newsweek*, *supra* n. 32, at 54.

35. Bakke v. Univ. of Cal., 553 P.2d at 1158–59.

36. *Newsweek*, *supra* n.32, at 54–55.

37. Arons, *supra* n.3, at 12.

38. Weaver, "Justice Dept. Brief 1 of 58 in Bakke Case," *New York Times*, Sept. 20, 1977.

"The previous highs are believed to include the 1950 case of the 'Hollywood 10' in which motion picture writers and directors had refused to answer Congressional questions about alleged Communist activity and were sentenced to prison terms for contempt. Forty such briefs were submitted in that case."

39. *Newsweek, supra* n.32, at 53.
40. Brief for the United States As Amicus Curiae, p. 23.
41. Will, "Cultivating 'Race-Consciousness,' " *Washington Post*, Sept. 25, 1977.
42. See, e.g., Brief of Anti-Defamation League of B'nai B'rith et al. as Amici Curiae, whose chief author was Professor Philip B. Kurland.
43. See, e.g., Sweatt v. Painter, 339 U.S. 629 (1950).
44. See, e.g., Brief for Petitioner (University of California), p. 38; Brief of Columbia University, Harvard University, Stanford University, and the University of Pennsylvania as Amici Curiae, p. 30–31.
45. Brief of Columbia University et al., p. 30–31.
46. Howard, "The High Court's Road in the Bakke Case," *Washington Post*, Oct. 9, 1977. Professor Terrance Sandalow has staked a middle ground in the deference dispute. "Decisions to employ racial and ethnic preferences," he notes, "have either been made by faculties or by the governing bodies of the institutions." Because these bodies are "less representative of the public and lacking direct political responsibility," courts ought to be "a good deal less confident about the propriety of those policies than would be justified if they had been adopted by a legislature." He ultimately concludes, by a hair, that the university's power should be sustained. If it is not, courts should "consign ultimate authority for these choices to the legislature, where in a democracy it rightly belongs." Sandalow, "Racial Preferences in Higher Education: Political Responsibility and the Judicial Role," 42 *U. Chi. L. Rev.* 653, 695, 699, 702–3 (1975).
47. Harvey, "Some Different Thoughts Abiut Bakke," *National Review*, Feb. 3, 1978, at 151.
48. "Bakke Battle," *Newsweek*, Oct. 24, 1977, at 45.
49. *Time* magazine, *supra* n.7, at 97.
50. *Newsweek, supra* n.48, at 45.
51. *Time* magazine, *supra* n.7, at 95–96.
52. Bundy, "The Issue Before the Court: Who Gets Ahead in America?" *Atlantic*, Nov. 1977, at 42.
53. This is not to say it was a costless one. Affirmative action, properly implemented, may involve expensive remedial programs, scholarship funds, and recruiting efforts.
54. For the dangers of unaccountability in faculty decision-making, see Sandalow, *supra* n.46, at 696.
55. Harvey, *supra* n.47, at 151.
56. See Bakke v. Univ. of Cal., 553 P.2d at 1189 n.16 (Tobriner, J., dissenting).
57. Brief for Petitioner, Univ. of Cal. v. Bakke, p. 54.
58. Bundy, *supra* n.52, at 49–50.
59. 418 U.S. 717 (1974). See chapter nine.
60. "Disadvantaged Groups, Individual Rights," *New Republic*, Oct. 15, 1977, at 6.
61. Cohen, "Race and the Constitution," *Nation*, Feb. 8, 1975, at 137.
62. Etzioni, "Making Up For Past Injustices: How Bakke Could Backfire," *Psychology Today*, Aug. 1977, at 18.
63. See 553 P.2d at 1165–67.
64. Gallup Poll, "Ability, Not Preference, Favored in Admissions," *Washington Post*, Nov. 20, 1977.
65. 553 P.2d at 1171.
66. Keyes v. Denver School Dist., 413 U.S. 189, 242 (1973) (Powell, J., concurring in part and dissenting in part).
67. Wilson, "Americans Must Discriminate: Positive Discrimination," *Vital Speeches*, Sept.

1972, at 59. Mr. Wilson was President and Chief Executive Officer of Collins Radio Company.

68. J. Foley, ed., *1 The Jeffersonian Cyclopedia* 48 (1967).

69. As quoted in Meserve, "The Quality of Intellectual Competition," 25 *J. of Legal Educ.* 378, 383 (1973).

70. As quoted in Bundy, *supra* n.52, at 44.

71. O'Neil, "Racial Preference and Higher Education: the Larger Context," 60 *Va. L. Rev.* 925, 926 (1974).

72. Brief for Petitioner, Univ. of Cal. v. Bakke, pp. 53–54.

73. See Bakke v. Univ. of Cal., 553 P.2d at 1173 (Tobriner, J., dissenting).

74. DeFunis v. Odegaard, 507 P.2d at 1175.

75. Kinsley, "The Conspiracy of Merit," *New Republic*, Oct. 15, 1977, at 22–23.

76. C. Reich, *The Greening of America* 73, 75 (1970).

77. R. Tagore, *Collected Plays and Poems* 1 (1966).

78. Brief for Petitioner, Univ. of Cal. v. Bakke, p. 13. See also Lewis, "A White Enclave?" *New York Times*, Feb. 17, 1977.

79. The Carnegie Commission on Higher Education, *A Chance to Learn* 12–13 (1970) as quoted in Brief for Petitioner, Univ. of Cal. v. Bakke, p. 13.

80. See Alevy v. Downstate Medical Center, 39 N.Y.2d 326, 330; 348 N.E.2d 537, 541 (1976).

81. Brief for California Law Deans As Amici Curiae, Univ. of Cal. v. Bakke, p. 13. See generally Gellhorn, "The Law School and the Negro," 1968 *Duke L.J.* 1069, 1073.

82. Reynoso et al., "La Raza, The Law and the Law Schools," 1970 *U. Tol. L. Rev.* 809, 816.

83. Brief of a Group of Law School Deans as Amici Curiae, DeFunis v. Odegaard, p. 14 n.10.

84. N. Glazer, *Affirmative Discrimination* 203 (1975).

85. Sowell, "A Black Conservative Dissents," *New York Times Magazine*, Aug. 8, 1976, at 43.

86. Brief of American Jewish Committee et al. as Amici Curiae, Univ. of Cal. v. Bakke, p. 34–35.

87. Ibid.

88. Cohen, *supra* n.61, at 142.

89. Ibid.

90. Posner, "The DeFunis Case and the Constitutionality of Preferential Treatment of Racial Minorities," 1974 *Sup. Ct. Rev.* 1, 18.

91. Broder, "Legal Profession in U.S. Denounced by President," Washington *Post*, May 5, 1978.

92. For a look at the complex process of Supreme Court appointment, see H. Abraham, *Justices and Presidents: A Political History of Appointments to the Supreme Court* (1974).

93. The two Minnesotans are Chief Justice Warren Burger and Justice Harry Blackmun. Some count Burger as a Virginian, in which case there are two of those (Burger and Powell).

    To reach 'meaningful' representativeness or proportionality, the Court's membership might have to be enlarged, a thought that failed in 1937.

94. George Gallup remarked in 1977 after his inquiry on special admissions and employment programs: "Rarely has public opinion, particularly on such a controversial issue, been as united as it is over this question." As quoted in Lipset and Schneider, "An Emerging National Consensus," *New Republic*, Oct. 15, 1977, at 9.

    One might, however, feel more confident in the force of public opinion if a legislature or some elected body, rather than a faculty or executive agency, were primarily responsible for the affirmative action proposal. See generally Sandalow, *supra* n.46, at 693–703.

95. See J. Auerbach, *Unequal Justice* 263–306 (1976).

96. Burns, "Foreword," in S. Blackburn, ed., *White Justice: Black Experience in America's Courtrooms* xiv (1971).

97. 297 U.S. 278, 284 (1936).

98. 309 U.S. 227, 231–34 (1940).

99. Powell v. Alabama, 287 U.S. 45, 57–58 (1932). The Court's decision, of course, meant only that the Scottsboro boys were entitled to a retrial, the first of four. See Morris v. Alabama, 294 U.S. 587 (1935) on the second Scottsboro appeal. The best book on the subject is D. Carter, *Scottsboro: A Tragedy of the American South* (1969).

100. Rostow, "The Negro in Our Law," 9 *Utah L. Rev.* 841, 844 (1965).

101. Sitton, "When a Southern Negro Goes to Court," *New York Times Magazine*, Jan. 7, 1962, at 10.

102. A. Lester, *Justice in the American South* 11 (1964).

103. Morgan, "Segregated Justice," in L. Friedman, ed., *Southern Justice* 155, 160 (1965). See also Broeder, "The Negro in Court," 1965 *Duke L.J.* 19. If Negroes were on the jury panel, they could still be struck through peremptory challenge, see Swain v. Alabama, 380 U.S. 202 (1965).

104. See generally, Galphin, "When a Negro is on Trial in the South," *New York Times Magazine*, Dec. 15, 1963, at 17.

105. See Gideon v. Wainwright, 372 U.S. 335 (1963).

106. As quoted in A. Lester, *supra* n.102, at 12.

107. See generally Green, "Inter and Intraracial Crime Relative to Sentencing," in C. Reasons and J. Kuykendall, eds., *Race, Crime, and Justice* 284 (1972).

108. Burns, "Can a Black Man Get a Fair Trial in This Country?" *New York Times Magazine*, July 12, 1970, at 44.

109. Gutman, "Oktibbeha County, Mississippi," in L. Friedman, ed., *supra* n.103, at 80, 82.

110. Morgan, *supra* n.103, at 157.

111. J. Baldwin, *Nobody Knows My Name* 66 (1962).

112. G. Moore, *A Special Rage* 148 (1971).

113. D. Freed, *Agony in New Haven* 74 (1973).

114. Garry, "Introduction," in E. Keating, *Free Huey!* xi (1971).

115. See generally K. Davis, *Discretionary Justice* (1969).

116. Lankford v. Gelston, 364 F.2d 197 (CA4 1966).

117. See generally D. Freed and P. Wald, *Bail in the United States* (1964).

118. Burns, *supra* n.108, at 38.

119. 372 U.S. 335 (1963).

120. See Douglas v. California, 372 U.S. 353 (1963) (first appeal); Miranda v. Arizona, 384 U.S. 436 (1966) (station-house interrogation); United States v. Wade, 388 U.S. 218 (1967) (lineups); Mempa v. Rhay, 389 U.S. 128 (1967) (sentencing deferred subject to probation); Coleman v. Alabama, 399 U.S. 1 (1970) (preliminary hearing); In Re Gault, 387 U.S. 1 (1967) (juvenile proceedings); Argersinger v. Hamlin, 407 U.S. 25 (1972) (misdemeanors); Gagnon v. Scarpelli, 411 U.S. 778 (1973) (afforded to qualified right to counsel on revocation of probation or parole).

121. Aguilar v. Texas, 378 U.S. 108 (1964); Spinelli v. United States, 393 U.S. 410 (1969).

122. E.g., Chimel v. California, 395 U.S. 752 (1969).

123. 384 U.S. 436 (1966). *Miranda* and many of the Warren Court opinions in the three preceding footnotes have, of course, been severely limited by the Burger Court.

124. See DeFunis v. Odegaard, 416 U.S. at 342 (Douglas, J., dissenting).

125. 507 P.2d at 1184.

126. Bundy, *supra* n.52, at 42–43.

127. North Carolina Bd. of Educ. v. Swann, 402 U.S. 43, 45 (1971). The forerunner of racially explicit remedies was United States v. Montgomery Bd. of Educ., 395 U.S. 225 (1969).

128. See Milliken v. Bradley, 418 U.S. 717 (1974).

129. Some cases prior to *Bakke* implied a difference in color-conscious judicial remedies and voluntary ones. See especially Swann v. Charlotte-Mecklenburg Bd. of Educ., 402 U.S. 1, 16 (1971) and United Jewish Organizations of Williamsburgh Inc. v. Carey, 430 U.S. 144 (1977).

130. Brief of NAACP Legal Defense Fund as Amicus Curiae, Univ. of Cal. v. Bakke, p. 57 and Appendix B.

131. D. Reitzes, *Negroes and Medicine* 8 (1958).

132. Brief of NAACP Legal Defense Fund, pp. 7a and 9a.

133. Bakke v. Univ. of Cal., 553 P.2d at 1180 (Tobriner, J., dissenting).

134. See Brief of Petitioner, Univ. of Cal. v. Bakke, p. 19, citing 1970 census figures.

135. Not that California was itself blameless. See Brief of the NAACP Legal Defense Fund, Appendix B.

136. O'Neil, "Preferential Admissions: Equalizing the Access of Minority Groups to Higher Education," 80 *Yale L.J.* 699, 730 (1971).

137. Brief of the Anti-Defamation League of B'nai B'rith as Amicus Curiae, DeFunis v. Odegaard, pp. 22–23.

138. Sugarman v. Dougall, 413 U.S. 634, 657 (1973) (Rehnquist, J., dissenting).

139. See Brief of Law School Deans as Amici Curiae, DeFunis v. Odegaard, p. 8 n.5 and Brief of Columbia Univ. et al. as Amici Curiae, Univ. of Cal. v. Bakke, p. 33.

140. See generally J. Higham, *Strangers in the Land; Patterns of American Nativism, 1860–1925* (1955) and O. Handlin, *Boston's Immigrants* (1968).

141. Brief of American Jewish Committee et al. as Amici Curiae, Univ. of Cal. v. Bakke, p. 36–37 and 51 n.26.

142. See Bakke v. Univ. of Cal., 553 P.2d at 1159.

143. Brief of American Jewish Committee et al. as Amici Curiae, Univ. of Cal. v. Bakke, p. 51.

144. "The Other Bakke," *Newsweek*, Oct. 24, 1977, at 46.

145. Greenawalt, "Judicial Scrutiny of 'Benign' Racial Preference in Law School Admissions," 75 *Col. L. Rev.* 559, 582 (1975). Professor Greenawalt, it should be added, is not himself a wholehearted reparationist. He notes only that "a decision justified on that basis would not be evidently unsound." Ibid. at 583.

146. Ibid. at 582.

147. Brief of National Council of Jewish Women et al. as Amici Curiae, DeFunis v. Odegaard, p. 59.

148. Hughes, "Reparations for Blacks," 43 *N.Y.U.L. Rev.* 1063, 1073 (1968).

149. Brief of American Jewish Committee et al. as Amici Curiae, Univ. of Cal. v. Bakke, p. 42; N. Glazer, *supra* n.84, at 198.

150. Professor O'Neil has suggested multiple criteria for inclusion in affirmative action programs. Minorities should be included "who not only have been underrepresented, but who have disproportionately been (a) victims of overt racial discrimination; (b) socioeconomically disadvantaged; (c) unfairly appraised by standardized tests; and who are (d) graduates of over-crowded, run-down and badly-staffed high schools." O'Neil, *supra* n.136, at 750. Such criteria, however, remain vague in formulation, debatable in application, and suspiciously *post-hoc*.

151. For discussion of over- and underinclusive classifications, see Tussman and tenBroek, "The Equal Protection of the Laws," 37 *Cal. L. Rev.* 341 (1949). For the varying degrees of scrutiny applied to legislative classifications, see Gunther, "The Supreme Court, 1971 Term—Foreword: In Search of Evolving Doctrine on a Changing Court: A Model for a Newer Equal Protection," 86 *Harv. L. Rev.* 1 (1972).

152. Proportionality was apparently not the basis since 25 percent of California's total population was minority. See Brief of Petitioner, Univ. of Cal. v. Bakke, p. 47.

153. See DeFunis v. Odegaard, 416 U.S. at 339 (Douglas, J., dissenting). Justice Douglas was not advocating any such course but only illustrating the dangers of allocation in racially based admission policies.

154. Posner, *supra* n.90, at 8 n.18.

155. See Howard, *supra* n.46.

156. Brief of Petitioner, Univ. of Cal. v. Bakke, p. 42–43.

157. Brief of Columbia Univ. et al. as Amici Curiae, Univ. of Cal. v. Bakke, p. 33.

158. Ibid. See also Associated Gen. Contractors of Mass. Inc. v. Altshuler, 490 F.2d 9, 16 (CA1 1973).

159. See Haskell, "Legal Education on the Academic Plantation," 60 *A.B.A.J.* 203 (1974); Cohen, *supra* n.61, at 145.

160. Posner, *supra* n.90, at 26–27.

161. *New Republic*, *supra* n. 60, at 7.

162. N. Glazer, *supra* n.84, at 199.

163. Brief of American Jewish Committee et al. as Amici Curiae, Univ. of Cal. v. Bakke, p. 69.

164. DeFunis v. Odegaard, 416 U.S. at 343 (Douglas, J., dissenting).

165. Bundy, *supra* n.52, at 53–54.

166. Karst and Horowitz, "Affirmative Action and Equal Protection," 60 *Va. L. Rev.* 955, 964 (1974).

167. Milliken v. Bradley, 418 U.S. 717 (1974).

168. Brief of Respondents, DeFunis v. Odegaard, p. 17; Brief of National Council of Jewish Women et al. as Amici Curiae, DeFunis v. Odegaard, p. 48.

169. Brief of Columbia University et al. as Amici Curiae, Univ. of Cal. v. Bakke, p. 3.

170. Harvard College Admissions Program, Appendix to Brief of Columbia University et al. as Amici Curiae, Univ. of Cal. v. Bakke, p. 2.

171. Brief of Petitioner, Univ. of Cal. v. Bakke, p. 33.

172. Sandalow, *supra* n.46, at 686. Professor Sandalow's comment was made in the context of law schools, but obviously the need for honest disagreement obtains in medical schools as well.

173. Brief of Petitioner, Univ. of Cal. v. Bakke, p. 33.

174. Brief of Columbia Univ. et al. as Amici Curiae, Univ. of Cal. v. Bakke, p. 13.

175. "White physicians graduating from Davis during the life of the challenged program will possess greater skills and be better doctors than would be possible without the program." Brief of Petitioners, Univ. of Cal. v. Bakke, p. 33.

176. Brief of Columbia Univ. et al. as Amici Curiae, Univ. of Cal. v. Bakke, p. 17.

177. O'Neil, *supra* n.136, at 766; Harvard College Admissions Program, *supra* n.170, at 3.

178. O'Neil, *supra* n.136, at 766.

179. McPherson, "The Black Law Student: A Problem of Fidelities," *Atlantic*, April 1970, at 97.

180. Karp and Yodels, "The College Classroom: Some Observations on the Meanings of Student Participation," 60 *Sociol. & Soc. Res.* 421, 425 (1976).

181. McPherson, *supra* n.179, at 99.

182. Brief of the NAACP Legal Defense and Educational Fund as Amicus Curiae, Univ. of Cal. v. Bakke, p. 64; Thompson, "Curbing the Black Physician Manpower Shortage," 49 *J. Med. Educ.* 944, 945–46 (1974).

183. Brief of the NAACP Legal Defense and Educational Fund as Amicus Curiae, Univ. of Cal. v. Bakke, p. 62.

184. U.S. Bureau of the Census, *Current Population Reports: The Social and Economic Status of the Black Population in the* U.S., Tables 82 and 84 (1974); Gayles, "Health Brutality and the Black Life Cycle," *Black Scholar*, May 1974, at 5.

185. M. Seham, *Blacks and American Medical Care* 9 (1973) as quoted in Brief for Petitioner, Univ. of Cal. v. Bakke, p. 24.
186. See Brief of NAACP Legal Defense and Educational Fund, Appendix C p. 32a, and Brief for Petitioner, Univ. of Cal. v. Bakke, p. 24.
187. Sidel, "Can More Physicians Be Attracted to Ghetto Practice?" in J. Norman, ed., *Medicine in the Ghetto* 172–73 (1969). Brief of NAACP Legal Defense Fund as Amicus Curiae, Univ. of Cal. v. Bakke, p. 65.
188. See Sidel, *supra* n.187, at 175.
189. C. Odegaard, *Minorities in Medicine: From Receptive Passivity to Positive Action, 1966–76* 151 (1977) as quoted in Brief of American Jewish Committee et al. as Amicus Curiae, Univ. of Cal. v. Bakke, p. 27.
190. Silver, "Beyond the Bakke Case," Washington *Post*, Sept. 18, 1977.
191. Johnson, "History of the Education of Negro Physicians," 42 *J. Med. Educ.* 439 (1967).
192. Brief of NAACP Legal Defense and Educational Fund as Amicus Curiae, Univ. of Cal. v. Bakke, p. 63.
193. Cannon and Kotkin, "Most of the Minority Students Competed Successfully in School," Washington *Post*, Oct. 2, 1977.
194. 416 U.S. at 342 (dissenting opinion).
195. See Greenawalt, *supra* n.145, at 589.
196. Cohen, *supra* n.61, at 142.
197. Haynes, "Problems Facing the Negro in Medicine Today," 209 *J. Am. Med. Assoc.* 1067, 1068 (1969).
198. See M. Seham, *supra* n.185, at 23.
199. O'Neil, *supra* n.136, at 728.
200. Greenawalt, *supra* n.145, at 588–89 n.143.
201. O'Neil, *supra* n.71, at 944.
202. Brief of Anti-Defamation League of B'nai B'rith et al., p. 21 and Brief of American Jewish Committee et al., p. 57 (both Amici briefs for respondent Bakke). See also Bakke v. Univ. of Cal., 553 P.2d at 1167.
203. O'Neil, *supra* n.71, at 944.
204. S. Hauser, *Black and White Identity Formation: Studies in the Psychosocial Development of Lower Class Adolescent Boys* 59–60 (1971).
205. Ibid. at 110. Blacks seem significantly more likely than whites to select glamor figures as role models and black males much more likely than black females to do so. See Oberle, "Role Models of Black and White Rural Youth at Two Stages of Adolescence," 42 *J. Negro Ed.* 234 (1974).
206. Graglia, "Special Admission of the 'Culturally Deprived' to Law School," 119 *U. Pa. L. Rev.* 351, 355–56 (1970).
207. Posner, *supra* n.90, at 8.
208. Ibid. at 11–12. Legislation, of course, enacts over- and underinclusive classifications all the time. Were it not so, government would be driven mad by particularized determinations. The objection is only to race as a means of promoting administrative convenience.
209. O'Neil, *supra* n.136, at 746–47.
210. See, e.g., Bakke v. Univ. of Cal., 553 P.2d at 1166; Brief of Anti-Defamation League of B'nai B'rith et al. as Amici Curiae, Univ. of Cal. v. Bakke, p. 22–23. The California Supreme Court also suggested aggressive recruiting programs and an increase in medical school enrollment as less drastic means of achieving the University's goals. (553 P.2d at 1166). The effectiveness of such steps has been sharply challenged. See, e.g., Brief of Columbia Univ. et al. as Amici Curiae, Univ. of Cal. v. Bakke, p. 19–24.

211. Sandalow, *supra* n.46, at 691.
212. Brief of Cal. Law Deans as Amici Curiae, Univ. of Cal. v. Bakke, p. 28–29.
213. Brief of Petitioner, Univ. of Cal. v. Bakke, p. 38.
214. See Howard, *supra* n.46.
215. DeFunis v. Odegaard, 507 P.2d at 1179.
216. Bakke v. Univ. of Cal., 553 P.2d at 1175 (Tobriner, J., dissenting).
217. Ely, "The Constitutionality of Reverse Racial Discrimination," 41 *U. Chi. L. Rev.* 723, 727 (1974). Of course, when faculties promulgate affirmative action programs, it is doubtful how much self-discrimination is at issue. See Greenawalt, *supra* n.145, at 573.
218. Brief for Petitioner, Univ. of Cal. v. Bakke, p. 73.
219. See Lavinsky, "DeFunis v. Odegaard: The 'Non-Decision' with a Message," 75 *Col. L. Rev.* 520, 527 (1975).
220. Even this latter prohibition is being renewed. See e.g., National League of Cities v. Usery, 426 U.S. 833 (1976).
221. Cohen, *supra* n.61, at 140.
222. A. Bickel, *The Morality of Consent* 123 (1975).
223. E.g., Chimel v. California, 395 U.S. 752 (1969); Goss v. Lopez, 419 U.S. 565 (1975).
224. McCulloch v. Maryland, 4 Wheat. 316 (1819).
225. A. Bickel, *supra* n.222, at 120.
226. 163 U.S. 537, 559 (1896) (Harlan, J., dissenting).
227. Weber v. Aetna Casualty & Surety Co., 406 U.S. 164, 175 (1972).
228. A. Hitler, *Mein Kampf* 306 (Houghton Mifflin, 1943). The translator was Ralph Manheim.
229. Posner, *supra* n.90, at 23 n. 41.
230. Brief of Anti-Defamation League of B'nai B'rith et al. as Amici Curiae, Univ. of Cal. v. Bakke, p. 5 and the sources footnoted on that page.
231. A. Bickel, *supra* n.222, at 133.
232. *Village Voice*, Aug. 8, 1977, as quoted in *New Republic*, *supra* n.60, at 7.
233. *New Republic*, *supra* n.60, at 7.
234. See Posner, *supra* n.90, at 12–13.
235. Will, *supra* n.41.
236. Lewin, *supra* n.31, at 9. For the view that "the danger [of Anti-Semitism] is independent of a decision to extend preferences to Blacks," see Ely, *supra* n.217, at 738.
237. Sandalow, *supra* n.46, at 694 n.124.
238. *New Republic*, *supra* n.60, at 7.
239. Assoc. Gen. Contractors of Mass. v. Altshuler, 490 F.2d 9, 16 (CA1 1973).
240. I would not press the parallel between such countries and the United States too closely. The cited countries experience linguistic differences and/or geographical concentrations of minorities that do not characterize most racial and ethnic minorities in this country.
241. Etzioni, *supra* n.62, at 18.
242. Slaughter-House Cases, 16 Wall. 36, 71 (1873).
243. Brief of The American Jewish Congress as Amicus Curiae, DeFunis v. Odegaard, p. 10, 15, 14.
244. Brief of Petitioner, Univ. of Cal. v. Bakke, p. 45. In support of this contention, it is noted that the level of competition among minority applicants for admission is itself high. See Bakke v. Univ. of Cal., 553 P.2d at 1185 (Tobriner, J., dissenting).
245. Univ. of Cal. v. Bakke, 553 P.2d at 1186 (Tobriner, J., dissenting); Brief of National Council of Jewish Women et al. as Amici Curiae, DeFunis v. Odegaard, p. 63.
246. See, e.g., Brief of A Group of Law School Deans as Amici Curiae, DeFunis v. Odegaard, p. 6–7.
247. The dangers of favoritism in subjective admissions systems led two commentators to suggest procedural checks on administrative descretion. Gellhorn and Hornby, "Consti-

tutional Limitations on Admissions Procedures and Standards—Beyond Affirmative Action," 60 *Va. L. Rev.* 975 (1974).

248. DeFunis v. Odegaard, 416 U.S. at 334 (Douglas, J., dissenting).
249. Ringle, "Overcoming Cultural Bias," Washington *Post*, Mar. 19, 1978.
250. Consalus, "The Law School Admission Test and the Minority Student," 1970 *U. Tol. L. Rev.* 501.
251. Linn, "Test Bias and the Prediction of Grades in Law School," and Powers, "Comparing Prediction of Law School Performance for Black, Chicano, and White Law Students," in *Reports of LSAC Sponsored Research*, vol. 3, 1975–1977 at 1 and 721. See also Consalus, *supra* n.253, at 501.
252. Ringle, *supra* n.252.
253. DeFunis v. Odegaard, 416 U.S. at 336 (Douglas, J., dissenting). Justice Douglas suggested the idea not as a constitutional requirement but as "a possibility."
254. A. Anastasi, *Psychological Testing* 60 (1976).
255. Raspberry, "A Problem of Schools, not 'Cultural Bias'," Washington *Post*, April 7, 1978.
256. Two students of public opinion on the race issue note that "most whites accept the reality of at least some racial discrimination, but see black problems as stemming essentially from the moral failings of individuals. This attitude is at the core of most whites' ambiguous feelings about race." Lipset and Schneider, *supra* n.94, at 8.
257. Curtis, "A Demand for Racial Neutrality," Washington *Post*, May 27, 1978.
258. T. Sowell, *Black Education, Myths and Tragedies* 292 (1972).

Chapter 11

1. Greenfield, "How to Resolve the Bakke Case," Washington *Post*, Oct. 19, 1977.
2. "Bakke Wins, Quotas Lose," *Time* magazine, July 10, 1978, at 8.
3. Greider, "An Hour of History, Without the Thunderclap," Washington *Post*, June 29, 1978.
4. Slip opinion, Univ. of Cal. v. Bakke, (Powell, J., announcing the judgment of the Court), p. 45.
5. Ibid. at 48.
6. Davis conceded it could not prove that its unlawful program was not responsible for Bakke's exclusion. Ibid. at 51.
7. Lewis, "Bakke May Change a Lot While Changing No Law," *New York Times*, July 2, 1978.
8. Brief of Petitioner, Univ. of Cal. v. Bakke, p. 17.
9. Brief of the Anti-Defamation League of B'nai B'rith et al., Univ. of Cal. v. Bakke, p. 9 quoting A. Bickel, *The Morality of Consent* 132–33 (1975).
10. Slip opinion, Univ. of Cal. v. Bakke, (opinion of Marshall, J.), p. 14.
11. *Time* magazine, *supra* n. 2, at 15.
12. See especially Greenhouse, "Bell Hails Decision, Calls Ruling a 'Great Gain'—Plaintiff is 'Pleased' and Others Express Relief," *New York Times*, June 29, 1978.
13. Peterson, "Bakke Decision May Change Very Little," Washington *Post*, June 29, 1978.
14. "Dr. Bakke?" *Newsweek*, July 10, 1978, at 24.
15. Ibid.
16. Justice Stevens, who wrote the opinion for the four, declared that only Bakke's admission was at issue and "that the question whether race can ever be used as a factor in an admissions decision is not an issue in this case, and that discussion of this issue is inappropriate." Slip opinion, Univ. of Cal. v. Bakke, (Stevens, J., concurring in the judgment in part and dissenting in part), p. 4.
17. Ashwander v. TVA, 297 U.S. 288, 346–48 (Brandeis, J., concurring).

18. Section 601 of the 1964 Civil Rights Act reads:

> No person in the United States shall, on the ground of race, color, or national or-
> igin, be excluded from participation in, be denied the benefits of, or be subjected to
> discrimination under any program or activity receiving Federal financial assistance.

19. See Slip opinion, Univ. of Cal. v. Bakke, (Powell, J., announcing the judgment of the Court), p. 16.

20. Slip opinion, Univ. of Cal. v. Bakke, (Opinion of Brennan, White, Marshall, and Black-mun, JJ., concurring in the judgment in part and dissenting), p. 24, 31.

21. Ibid. at 38.

22. Ibid. at 41.

23. Ibid. at 47.

24. Ibid. at 54.

25. Slip opinion, p. 14.

26. Slip opinion, pp. 1 and 5.

27. Slip opinion, Univ. of Cal. v. Bakke, (Opinion of Brennan, White, Marshall, and Black-mun, J.J., concurring in the judgment in part and dissenting), pp. 34–38.

28. "The Landmark Bakke Ruling," *Newsweek*, July 10, 1978, at 25.

29. Rauh, "Marshall's Views in Bakke Case May Yet Become Law of the Land," *Atlanta Journal*, July 2, 1978.

30. See generally Gunther, "In Search of Judicial Quality on a Changing Court: The Case of Justice Powell," 24 *Stan. L. Rev.* 1001 (1972) and J. Wilkinson, *Serving Justice* 69–123 (1974).

31. Powell, "A Lawyer Looks At Civil Disobedience," 23 *Wash. & Lee L. Rev.* 205 (1966).

32. Powell, "Civil Disobedience: Prelude to Revolution?" 40 *N.Y. St. B.J.* 172 (1968).

33. Powell, *supra* n.31, at 228.

34. The words are not Justice Powell's. See Greider, "After Bakke, Blacks Need Funds, Not Good Intentions," Washington *Post*, July 2, 1978.

35. Slip opinion, pp. 32–34.

36. Ibid. at 46.

37. Ibid. at 48.

38. Ibid. at 49.

39. Ibid. at 48.

40. The figures for the fall of 1977 were 8.2 percent black, 3.9 percent Hispanic, 4.4 percent Asian American, and 0.5 percent American Indian. See Borger, "Why Harvard Was Cited in Bakke Case," Washington *Star*, July 5, 1978.

41. On the Court's legitimizing function, see A. Bickel, *The Least Dangerous Branch* (1962).

42. "The Court's Affirmative Action," *New Republic*, July 8 & 15, 1978, at 5.

43. Fiske, "Educators Welcome Bakke Ruling As Signal to Retain Current Policy," *New York Times*, July 29, 1978; Peterson, *supra* n.13.

44. Slip opinion, pp. 48 and 49.

45. *Time* magazine, *supra* n.2, at 15.

46. Slip opinion, p. 41.

47. Ibid. at 44 quoting Keyishan v. Board of Regents, 385 U.S. 589, 603 (1967).

48. Slip opinion, p. 44.

49. As one Harvard admissions officer noted, "If you have a disadvantaged white student you are fighting for, you might argue there are different kinds of diversity." Borger, *supra* n.40.

50. Slip opinion, p. 48.

51. *New Republic*, *supra* n.42, at 5.

52. Slip opinion, Univ. of Cal. v. Bakke, (Opinion of Brennan, et al.), p. 55.

53. The greatest danger of dissembling inheres in racial discrimination *against* minorities,

where the Court scrutinizes facially neutral enactments for hidden racial intent. See Arlington Heights v. Metrop. Housing Devel. Corp., 429 U.S. 252 (1977); Washington v. Davis, 426 U.S. 299 (1976). After *Bakke*, of course, racial 'intent' is permissible in benign admissions programs.

54. Whether Davis's special admissions program was to be labeled a "goal" or "quota" seemed to Powell a "semantic distinction . . . beside the point." Slip Opinion, p. 19. Whether Justice Powell would tolerate numerical reservations more flexible than Davis's is uncertain but doubtful.

55. Slip opinion, p. 50, n.53.

56. Ibid. at 49.

57. Ibid. at 38.

58. Ibid.

59. See ibid. at 31–33.

60. See Slip opinion, Univ. of Cal. v. Bakke, (Opinion of Brennan et al.), p. 43 n.42.

61. Slip opinion, p. 40.

62. Note especially Justice Powell's discussion of Lau v. Nichols, 414 U.S. 563 (1974) and United Jewish Organizations v. Carey, 430 U.S. 144 (1977). Slip opinion, pp. 34–36.

63. Why could not the University of California Board of Regents, vested by the state with "plenary legislative and administrative power" over Davis, simply pass some regulation prohibiting the use of admissions criteria with disparate racial impact and then declare Davis to have violated it, especially in the first two years of its existence before special admissions took effect. See slip opinion, Univ. of Cal. v. Bakke, (Opinion of Brennan et al.), p. 43 n.42.

64. *Time* magazine, *supra* n.2, at 9.

65. Note again Justice Powell's discussion of Lau v. Nichols, 414 U.S. 563 (1974). Slip opinion, pp. 34–36.

66. The plans would be both remedial and otherwise. If Congress or HEW has authority under *Bakke* to define violations, it possesses some authority to devise numerical remedies. Even apart from remedies, four of the five justices reaching the constitutional question in *Bakke* found few limits on Congress's power to implement affirmative action programs.

67. Kurland, "Questions Answered on Bakke Remain For the Future to Decide," *Atlanta Journal*, July 2, 1978.

Epilogue

1. W. Wilson, *The Declining Significance of Race* 144 (1978).

Index